M000296907

Blanchot

Maurice Blanchot (born 1907) is the author of a significant body of narrative fiction and countless critical essays on both literary and philosophical texts, as well as a substantial amount of political journalism. Straddling the divide between the literary and the philosophical, Blanchot is arguably one of the most challenging and influential figures in twentieth-century writing, whose work has exerted a decisive impact on thinkers as varied as Foucault, Derrida, Deleuze, Bataille, Klossowski, Levinas, Lacoue-Labarthe, Lyotard, Nancy, Barthes, and Kristeva, as well as on some of the most important contemporary writers in Europe and the United States.

Though his main works are now widely available in translation, Blanchot remains relatively unknown in the English-speaking world. *Blanchot: Extreme Contemporary* is the first book to address the entirety of Blanchot's work in one volume. It examines in detail the literary and philosophical dialogue pursued by Blanchot with Bataille, Heidegger, Levinas, Derrida, Lacoue-Labarthe, and Nancy, as well as Höderlin, Duras, Kafka, Rilke, and Beckett, and shows how for Blanchot literature is inseparable from the radical ethical and ontological questions it asks of philosophy in general. It puts forward a persuasive case for Blanchot's achievement as one of the most compelling writers of fiction of the postmodern age. It also throws new light on Blanchot's controversial political activities before and after the Second World War. This book also contains the most comprehensive bibliography of Blanchot's extensive writings to appear in any language for the last twenty years.

Blanchot: Extreme Contemporary will be essential reading for students of continental philosophy and poststructuralism, literature and French studies.

Leslie Hill is Reader in French Studies at the University of Warwick, and the author of *Beckett's Fiction: In Different Words* and *Marguerite Duras: Apocalyptic Desires*.

Warwick Studies in European Philosophy

Edited by Andrew Benjamin
Professor of Philosophy, University of Warwick

This series presents the best and most original work being done within the European philosophical tradition. The books included in the series seek not merely to reflect what is taking place within European philosophy, rather they will contribute to the growth and development of that plural tradition. Work written in the English language as well as translations into English are to be included, engaging the tradition at all levels — whether by introductions that show the contemporary philosophical force of certain works, or in collections that explore an important thinker or topic, as well as in significant contributions that call for their own critical evaluation.

Blanchot

Extreme Contemporary

Leslie Hill

London and New York

First published 1997
by Routledge
11 New Fetter Lane, London EC4P 4EE

Simultaneously published in the USA and Canada
by Routledge
29 West 35th Street, New York, NY 10001

Typeset in Perpetua by Routledge
Printed and bound in Great Britain by TJ International,
Padstow, Cornwall

British Library Cataloguing in Publication Data
A catalogue record for this book is available from the British Library

Library of Congress Cataloguing in Publication Data
A catalogue record for this book has been requested

ISBN 0–415–09173–X (hbk)
ISBN 0–415–09174–8 (pbk)

The aim here is simply to test out to what extent it is possible to follow a text and at the same time to lose track of it, to be simultaneously the person it understands and the person who understands it, the person who, within a world, speaks of that world as though he or she were outside it; all in all, to take advantage of the strangeness of a dual work and an author split into two – into absolute lucidity and impenetrable darkness, into a consciousness that knows all and yet knows not where it is going – in order to feign the illusion of a commentary solely preoccupied with accounting for all and yet entirely aware of being able to explain nothing.

Maurice Blanchot, 'L'Expérience de Lautréamont' (LS, 59)

Contents

Contents

Acknowledgements

This book is the third, and final, volume in a series devoted to some of the most challenging areas in contemporary writing in French and essentially concerned with the relationship between the singularity of the proper name and the possibility of literature. Like its two predecessors, on Samuel Beckett and Marguerite Duras, this book has taken many years to finish, and there are many people, friends, colleagues, and others, to whom it owes a debt of some kind or other which it is not possible for me to repay except in words. For their assistance and support at different stages in the writing of this book, I should like therefore to record here my particular thanks to Andrew Benjamin, Geoffrey Bennington, Malcolm Bowie, Saskia Brown, Didier Cahen, Howard Caygill, David Constantine, Simon Critchley, Jonathan Derbyshire, Carolyn Gill, Darren Green, Michael Holland, Alan Jackson, Ian James, Ann Jefferson, Mig Kerr, Philippe Lacoue-Labarthe, Roger Laporte, Peter Larkin, John Lechte, Dionys Mascolo, Philippe Mesnard, Jean-Luc Nancy, Tony Phelan, Douglas Smith, Simon Sparks, Richard Stamp, Chris Turner, and David Wood.

I am grateful to the University of Warwick for the granting of study leave and for the provision of funds that enabled me to carry out the research on which this book is based. I wish in addition to acknowledge further financial assistance from the British Academy during the spring of 1996. I must also thank the University of Nebraska Press, the University of Minnesota Press, the State University of New York Press, and Stanford University Press for permission to quote from copyright material. Finally, I would like to dedicate this book to Juliet, whose very existence is just about as much a surprise to me as the completion of this book.

Acknowledgements

Extracts from *The Step Not Beyond*, by Maurice Blanchot, translated by Lycette Nelson, reprinted by permission of the State University of New York Press.

Excerpts from *The Work of Fire*, by Maurice Blanchot, translated by Charlotte Mandell, reprinted with the permission of the publishers, Stanford University Press. Translation ©1995 by the Board of Trustees of the Leland Stanford Junior University. Original edition ©1949 by Éditions Gallimard.

Extracts from *The Space of Literature* by Maurice Blanchot, translated, with an introduction, by Ann Smock, reprinted by permission of the University of Nebraska Press, ©Éditions Gallimard, 1955. Introduction and English-language translation ©1982 by the University of Nebraska Press.

Extracts from *The Writing of the Disaster* by Maurice Blanchot, translated by Ann Smock, reprinted by permission of the University of Nebraska Press, ©Éditions Gallimard, 1980. Copyright 1986, 1995 by the University of Nebraska Press.

Extracts from *The Infinite Conversation* by Maurice Blanchot, translated by Susan Hanson, reprinted by permission of the University of Minnesota Press. English translation ©1993 by the Regents of the University of Minnesota. Originally published as *L'Entretien infini*, copyright 1969 by Éditions Gallimard.

Abbreviations

All references to Blanchot's published writings will be given in the text, using the abbreviations listed below. Titles of English translations, where they exist, are provided in parentheses. In general, page numbers supplied in my text refer to the standard French editions of Blanchot's work; where two figures or sets of figures are cited, the second, wherever possible, refers to the available English translation. At times, for reasons of consistency or accuracy, it has been necessary to modify or revise these versions. Unless otherwise indicated, all additional translations are my own. Full details concerning both texts and translations used may be found in the bibliography of texts by Blanchot at the end of the book.

A	*L'Amitié*
AB	*Aminadab*
AC	*Après coup, précédé par Le Ressassement éternel* (*Vicious Circles, followed by 'After the Fact'*)
AM	*L'Arrêt de mort* (*Death Sentence*)
AO	*L'Attente L'Oubli*
BR	*The Blanchot Reader* (contains a number of uncollected articles and a selection of essays from *FP, PF, LS, LV, EI, A,* and *PA*)
CI	*La Communauté inavouable* (*The Unavowable Community*)
CLP	*Comment la littérature est-elle possible?* (*BR,* 49–60)
CQ	*Celui qui ne m'accompagnait pas* (*The One Who Was Standing Apart From Me*)
DH	*Le Dernier Homme* (*The Last Man*)

ED	*L'Ecriture du désastre* (*The Writing of the Disaster*)
EI	*L'Entretien infini* (*The Infinite Conversation*)
EL	*L'Espace littéraire* (*The Space of Literature*)
FP	*Faux Pas* (some of the essays collected in *Faux Pas* may be found in *BR* and *GO*)
FJ	*La Folie du jour* (*The Madness of the Day*)
GO	*The Gaze of Orpheus and Other Literary Essays* (contains a selection of essays from *FP, PF, EL, LV,* and *EI*)
IM	*L'Instant de ma mort*
K	*De Kafka à Kafka* (reprints a series of essays already collected in *PF, EL, EI, A*)
LS	*Lautréamont et Sade*
LV	*Le Livre à venir* (a selection of essays from this volume may be found in *BR, GO,* and *SS*)
MF	*Michel Foucault tel que je l'imagine* (*Michel Foucault as I Imagine Him*)
MV	*Au moment voulu* (*When the Time Comes*)
PA	*Le Pas au-delà* (*The Step Not Beyond*)
PF	*La Part du feu* (*The Work of Fire*)
RE	*Le Ressassement éternel* (*Vicious Circles*)
SS	*The Sirens' Song* (contains a selection of essays from *PF, EL, LV,* and *EI*)
TH	*Le Très-Haut* (*The Most High*)
TO1	*Thomas l'Obscur* 1941
TO2	*Thomas l'Obscur* (nouvelle version) 1950 (*Thomas the Obscure*)
UV	*Une voix venue d'ailleurs*

1

An intellectual itinerary

Why Blanchot?

> To write *on* is, in any case, without propriety. But to write on the event that is precisely designed (among other things) to make it no longer possible ever to write *on* – by way of epitaph, commentary, analysis, eulogy, or condemnation – is to distort it in advance and to have always already missed it.
>
> 'Tracts, affiches, bulletin' (*BR*, 204)

There is little doubt today that the name Maurice Blanchot signs some of the most challenging and influential literary and philosophical texts of the last fifty years. Dispersed across a variety of different genres, Blanchot's writings are extensive and numerous. They include countless critical essays on literary and philosophical topics, three full-length novels, ten or more shorter narratives or *récits*, as well as a significant amount of political journalism, not to mention a host of other fragmentary texts that resist all attempt at stable classification. Despite a reputation for sparseness and impenetrability, they display a matchless lucidity and relentless commitment to explanation, self-commentary, and gloss; taken as a whole, they constitute perhaps one of the most remarkable and enduring of monuments in the whole of recent intellectual history to the perseverance and assertiveness of thought itself.

Blanchot is a writer whose work eludes easy categorisation. His writing straddles literature and philosophy, which is to say that, while it belongs to both, it falls subject to neither. This is not to claim for Blanchot's writing a position of extraterritorial neutrality or metalinguistic immunity; nor is it to suggest that Blanchot's own texts are somehow able to arbitrate authoritatively and decisively on the question of the relation between literature and philosophy as such.

1

Indeed, the case is almost exactly the reverse. While asking fundamental questions of philosophical and literary texts alike, Blanchot's own writing is itself characterised by an awareness of its own irremediable and necessary incompletion, and by the knowledge that, just as all legislation is a response to lawlessness, so limits too are always but a tribute to the limitlessness that inhabits them as an ineluctable and indelible condition of their possibility. Blanchot here pushes philosophy and literature towards the unspoken margins that constitute them as what they are. In so doing he deconstructs and transforms them, radically altering the terms in which today it is possible, indeed necessary, to think not only the question of literature, but also the deeper question of which Blanchot writes in *L'Entretien infini* (*The Infinite Conversation*) that it is the questioning that eludes and outstrips, precedes and exceeds the question of the whole (*EI*, 16–21; 14–17).

Blanchot's intervention, then, is fundamental. What changes, with Blanchot, is not just a localised sector of the literary critical or philosophical landscape, but the manner in which the relationship between literature and philosophy, writing and thought is articulated at all. Blanchot, one might say, is the thinker who has most consistently shown the relevance of philosophy for the practice of literature as such; but he is also the writer who has demonstrated most powerfully the radical extent of the questions addressed in its turn by literature to philosophy as a whole. As a result, Blanchot in his writing has renewed the critical debate concerning the ontological – or non-ontological – status of literature and art in general, and profoundly transformed the manner in which it is necessary to think the question of the ethical demand to which writing is a response. Philosophy, Blanchot contends, cannot escape the words that make it possible, but neither can literature do without philosophy; indeed, as Blanchot puts it in *L'Écriture du désastre* (*The Writing of the Disaster*),

> to write in ignorance and without regard for the philosophical horizon, a horizon punctuated, gathered together or dispersed by the words that delimit it, is necessarily to write with facile complacency (the literature of elegance and good taste). Hölderlin, Mallarmé, so many others, do not allow us this.
>
> (*ED*, 160; 103)

Blanchot is probably best known as a critic of literature. As such, he is the author of some of the most perceptive and probing essays of the last fifty years. His texts on Sade, Kafka, Hölderlin, Mallarmé, Rilke, Bataille, Char, Beckett,

Duras and many others, make him one of the most distinctive and cogent analysts of modern and contemporary literary culture. But Blanchot's contribution does not stop there. He is also an incisive reader of many of the central philosophical texts of the last two centuries, an astringent commentator of Hegel, Nietzsche, Heidegger, Levinas, Foucault, Derrida, and others, while as a novelist he is the author of some of the most trenchant – and intractable – of modern literary texts, texts which, in their limpid clarity and irredeemable obscurity, give voice, as Georges Bataille once wrote, to the vertiginous extremity of that which is itself without limits and which, as Derrida has shown, remains radically uncontainable within the bounds of discourse, including the genre of narrative itself.[1]

For all his exemplary centrality within twentieth-century thought, Blanchot remains a figure of irreducible and striking singularity. Like others of his generation, Blanchot was never an academic, preferring instead to derive his livelihood from his activities as a journalist and from his publications as a literary critic and novelist.[2] As a thinker, Blanchot is in any case a writer deeply alert to that which all systems of thought necessarily repress or exclude and which, more often than not, turns out to be the dissimulated basis of whatever it is they in fact seek to propound. Consequently, Blanchot's critical or philosophical writings are most often couched in the form of fragmentary commentary, and frequently present their arguments by way of a complex movement of citation, paraphrase, and gloss. As a philosopher or critic, Blanchot writes, so to speak, within the margins of other texts, within the interstices of the writings that, by chance or necessity, he encounters as a reader. One might claim as a result, and with some justice, that Blanchot in his own right is therefore not an original thinker at all. He produces – and this is one of the radical departures characteristic of Blanchot's writing in general – few, if any, authentically philosophical or theoretical concepts that may be called his own. Indeed, the terms with which his name is associated, words such as worklessness (désœuvrement), the outside (le dehors), the neuter (le neutre), or disaster (désastre), are precisely not terms, not stable points of anchorage, but, as it were, fragments of a singular, still unspoken or long forgotten other language, or language of otherness, made up of words or traces constantly being effaced from within by the strange displacements to which they silently bear witness, always already undoing the discursive oppositions within which they function.

Blanchot's literary or philosophical project, then, like that of Bataille in L'Expérience intérieure (Inner Experience), is precisely not a project. This is in part

3

what gives it its singular force and compelling originality. For Blanchot attempts something more essential than simply the task of devising yet another theoretical discourse or conceptual frame within which to arraign art or literature and domesticate the questions it poses to both philosophy and thought. Instead, by persistently occupying the texts of others – from Hegel to Heidegger, Mallarmé to Paulhan, Nietzsche to Rilke – Blanchot tires out these discourses, pushes them to the limit of their endurance. Exhausting them in this way, he is then able to begin to address the fundamental otherness lying dormant within them or having been excluded from them. The consequences here are dramatic. For what comes to be inscribed in Blanchot's writing, both within and beyond philosophy, both within and beyond criticism and literature, is the radically ineliminable character of that – without origin or identity, beyond memory and meaning – which paradoxically both enables and disables the totality of thought as its simultaneous condition of both possibility and impossibility.

One may begin here to measure the scale of Blanchot's importance and the reasons why, in France and beyond, his work has come to exert a decisive influence over literary critics, novelists, and philosophers alike. For Blanchot's remarkable achievement is not only to have written some of the most demanding fiction of the age and to have challenged and displaced many of the basic assumptions that continue to inhabit modern philosophy and literary theory; it is also, in the words of Jacques Derrida, in a double gesture, to have both maintained the necessity of philosophy and yet to have questioned philosophy itself from a site – the site of poetical thinking and writing – which has always resisted the endeavours of philosophy to assign to it its particular – always already philosophical – truth.[3]

'Waiting for us, still to come, still to be read and re-read by the very ones who have been doing so ever since they first learned to read and *thanks* to him': with these words, in 1976, Derrida once paid homage to Blanchot.[4] What they serve to indicate today is both the urgency and the disjoined temporality with which we contemporary readers are each addressed by Blanchot's writing, enjoined in our turn to transform reading – and reading Blanchot – into what Pierre Madaule once hoped, in a homage of his own, would be a – deadly – serious task.[5]

An ethics of discretion

Discretion – reserve – is the place of literature.
'Le Rire des dieux' (*A*, 194)

Despite his undoubted stature as a key intellectual figure in France from the 1950s onwards, Blanchot is a writer who, for many years, has consistently and single-mindedly resisted the gradual appropriation of literature (especially in France) by the mass media, maintaining as a result an anonymity and a reserve of quite exceptional integrity. There are few photographs of the author, no published accounts of his life, little in his work that would seem to warrant biographical extrapolation. For all that, his intellectual itinerary has often had a fiercely public dimension, and indeed, as though to acknowledge as much, albeit in fragmentary ways, in response to readers' inquiries, in occasional published letters, and in one or two rare autobiographical asides and unprompted vestigial narratives of his own, Blanchot in recent decades has been concerned to disclose, deliberately but allusively, some of the historical circumstances surrounding the turning points in his writing life.

Yet while knowledge of these events does make it now possible to begin to describe some of the pivotal stages in Blanchot's complex and lengthy intellectual career, there remain many areas of the author's life about which little, if any, information is available. Blanchot himself has rarely departed from an overriding commitment to what one might call an ethics of discretion: an ethics that shuns the risk of indiscriminate self-exposure in order to affirm the value of distance and silence and by so doing preserve what in 1984 Blanchot termed 'the right to the unexpected word' ('le droit à la parole inattendue').[1] As a result, Blanchot's autobiographical moments are never confessional or introspective, nor do they seek to accredit the authority of a single, all-embracing narrative. Memory, Blanchot has often suggested, is itself a function of forgetting; and it is as though, through the fragmentary ways in which he has divulged some of the facts of his autobiography, Blanchot is concerned to remind his readers that a necessary condition of all acts of recollection is the effacement of much else that is essential, and that indeed the essential may in fact best be respected by patient attention to the infinite reserve of forgetting itself.

In Blanchot's fragmentary curriculum vitae, scenes of friendship loom large. So, too, do moments of political hiatus. Both have in common, on Blanchot's reading, their fundamental resistance to the teleology of narrative presentation. Political upheaval and fidelity to friendship belong to history but, more importantly, also interrupt it; they allow the opening of a space in which a relation with otherness intervenes to defer historical closure. Blanchot's discretion, then, both translates a desire for privacy and implies a belief in historical discontinuity; and it is as though, when writing his name into history, Blanchot is more concerned to display, in the margins of that history, the anonymity that precedes the inscription of any name. So when for instance in 1973, in *Le Pas au-delà* (*The Step Not Beyond*, PA, 9; 2), in one of his earliest covertly autobiographical digressions, he may be found reflecting elliptically on the radical discrepancy between his duties as a professional journalist and his experiences as an apprentice novelist in the years leading up to the publication of *Thomas l'Obscur* in 1941, Blanchot's purpose is not to provide the reader with a reassuringly linear narrative frame. It is rather to underline that fundamental dissymmetry between workaday activity and artistic non-activity which marked his career at its inception. The effect is to compel the reader to reconsider the relationship between history and writing in such a way that what now becomes primary is not so-called historical truth in its apparent (and misleading) self-evidence, but rather the irreducibility and alterity of that which is exterior to historical narrative because it is what has always already preceded the construction of history *as* narrative.

In this regard, it is no accident that elsewhere in the same book, in pages first published the previous year in homage to Edmond Jabès, Blanchot also raises the question of how to address the historical – yet more than historical – event of the Holocaust (PA, 56–7, 156; 38–9, 114).[2] For here, as in Blanchot's reflections on his own beginnings as a writer, what is at stake is a requirement that one attend, not to the meaning of history, but to the limits of historical understanding, not to the teleology and so-called objectivity of history, but to the burden of responsibility that history imposes, willingly or not, on those who are its actors or protagonists. For Blanchot in *Le Pas au-delà*, rather than explaining writing by recourse to narrative history, it is more a case of mobilising the resources of writing itself in order to bear witness – impossibly – to that in history which escapes historical representation. It is to uncover, within memory, a question not of history, but of writing, and within that question of writing, an ethical question that is not a question of history as such, but of political responsibility and of experience.

This issue of the relationship between writing and history is at the heart of much of Blanchot's thinking during the 1970s and 1980s. In 1983, Blanchot returned to the topic in another discreet autobiographical self-commentary, where, uncharacteristically, arguably by way of a response to recent controversy surrounding his early involvement with the nationalist right, he acceded to a demand – one he describes as also originating somewhere within himself (*AC*, 91; 63) – to supply, under the title *Après coup* (*After the Fact*), a retrospective commentary to a reissue of *Le Ressassement éternel* (*Vicious Circles*), a collection of two early short stories from the mid-1930s that first appeared in 1951. Rereading these texts, Blanchot used the occasion to reconsider the connection between those stories and the historical events – more precisely the event of the Holocaust – that at least one of the narratives, 'L'Idylle', in its evocation of a penitentiary workhouse, may be seen to parallel, if not indeed eerily to predict (*AC*, 94–6; 65–7). Blanchot, however, remains resistant to this apparent convergence between text and history. 'History', he concludes, 'does not control meaning [ne détient pas le sens], any more than meaning, which is always ambiguous – plural – may be reduced to its historical realisation, were this the most tragic and weightiest imaginable' (*AC*, 96; 67).[3] History, then, is not established truth, and provides no authorised translations; indeed, in some cases, Blanchot implies, history itself may turn out simply to have borrowed, in an act of plagiarism, the totalising impetus sometimes to be found within literary narrative itself. But equally, if history is at times just a displaced version of an oppressive, all-inclusive fiction, so, too, in the encounter with historical experience, fictional narrative sometimes also meets its limits. A story such as 'L'Idylle', writes Blanchot – indeed, any story whatever – will only ever fall short of the irreducibly singular historical event of those years, which in his text Blanchot names simply as: Auschwitz. 'No matter when it may be written,' we read, 'every story will henceforth be before Auschwitz' (*AC*, 99; 69).

These reservations with regard to narrative representation do not amount to a withdrawal from political exigencies, nor an abandonment of the obligation to bear historical witness. Rather the reverse. To read history, as does Blanchot, as a discontinuous space, irreducible to chronological narrative, is, by rejecting temporal closure, to affirm the necessary futurity of politics and political responsibility. Indeed, it was clearly to reinforce this very point that, some months after *Après coup*, at the age of 76, Blanchot followed up that book with another short text, *La Communauté inavouable* (*The Unavowable Community*), based on a discussion of recent work by Jean-Luc Nancy and Marguerite Duras, in which he undertook to draw the philosophical and political lessons of three significant moments in his own political itinerary: the pre-war commitment to action in small volatile groups existing outside of mainstream political parties, the struggle against the Algerian War, and the Paris *événements* of May 1968. In retracing that history, Blanchot's aim was not primarily to engage in an exercise in retrospective justification or self-criticism, but, more importantly in his view, to affirm the vital actuality of what he describes as 'the demand of communism' ('l'exigence communiste', *CI*, 9; 1). Indeed, by invoking the promise of communism in these terms, at a time when the word itself had become, in the eyes of almost all other commentators, arguably the most threadbare term imaginable in the whole political lexicon of the West, Blanchot's intention was not just to acknowledge the sorry legacy of a discredited word, but to reaffirm his hope and fears for the future. It is in this sense that Blanchot's discretion – his refusal of historical, autobiographical narrative – demands not to be viewed as a retreat from the political. It is rather that Blanchot chooses to suspend a certain avowable narrative history in order to address his text to the future, with an eye to the risk that in fact makes hope possible at all, to what he describes as '*the always uncertain end* inscribed within the destiny of community' (*CI*, 92; 56, Blanchot's italics).

This same insistence on the determining effects of the future and on both the risks and compelling decisions that are a necessary and indispensable element of any politics whatever also lay behind Blanchot's contribution, the following year, under the title 'Les Intellectuels en question' ('Intellectuals Under Scrutiny'), to the continuing debate in France about the tasks of the intellectual under the socialist presidency of François Mitterrand.[4] In this long retrospective piece, motivated in part by a desire to defend Bataille against the charge of complicity with fascism and sympathy with Vichy France – criticisms which, in their turn, have both been levelled at Blanchot as well – the author gives a personal account of the political challenges that faced intellectuals in France, and elsewhere in Europe, from the Dreyfus Affair to the time of the Algerian War and May 1968. He lingers here and there on the cases of Heidegger and Valéry, and it is by way of conclusion to a discussion of the latter's support for the anti-Dreyfus campaign that Blanchot remarks that: 'In this cursory examination . . . I can find nothing that justifies him [i.e. Valéry] for adding his own name to the list of those who, in the worst possible terms, were calling for the death of the Jews and the destruction of those who sought to defend them.' And Blanchot adds, with obvious disbelief: 'There would thus seem to be, in every life, a moment when the unjustifiable prevails and the incomprehensible is given its due.'[5] These are solemn words for more reasons than one; what they show in 1984, as he reviews the historical circumstances of his own political commitments, is a

8

Blanchot simultaneously aware of the infinite demand of justice and the precarious fragility of all ethical injunctions as such.

In the article, Blanchot also takes the opportunity to recapitulate, obliquely, many of the key turning points traversed or witnessed by him in the course of his own political evolution from the late 1920s to the present and which, taken as a whole, read like a résumé of the principal dilemmas and decisions faced not only by Blanchot in his own political life but by France as a whole from the early decades of the century onwards: the general loss of faith in parliamentary democracy in France that followed the First World War and which, paradoxically, the very methods of military rule that assured victory in 1918 served only to exacerbate; the subsequent discredit into which parliamentary democracy in France continued to fall as a consequence of its instability and weakness; the dangerous impatience with which, in the imperious name of justice, some called for an immediate war against Hitler in the mid-1930s; the dismal failure of the French government to act on 7 March 1936, when, in flagrant contravention of the Locarno Pact, Hitler's army remilitarised the Rhineland and set in train the events that were to culminate in the outbreak of the Second World War; the spineless abjection displayed by the Western democracies when they acceded to Hitler's demands at Munich in September 1938; the decision – in spite of all – on the part of some dissident intellectuals (including Blanchot himself) to defend the republic in the ensuing years; the painful period of the Resistance and the difficult choices that needed then to be made; and, after a lengthy hiatus, the campaign against the Algerian War in 1960, followed by the *événements* of May 1968; and finally, to close, the fateful year 1943 of which Blanchot writes, justifying the outline sketched in the preceding pages, that 'its return is always possible'. Lessons must be learnt from the past, Blanchot suggests, but it is the future – a future without present or presence – that is the only properly political dimension. This explains Blanchot's persistent watchword, reiterated during the 1980s in relation to the memory of Auschwitz, and inevitably addressed to himself as well as to each of his readers: 'N'oubliez pas!', 'Do not forget!', 'sachez ce qui s'est passé, n'oubliez pas, et en même temps jamais vous ne saurez', 'know what happened, do not forget, and at the same time never will you know' (*ED*, 131; 82).[6]

A share of biography

For me, what mattered was the encounter with others, where chance becomes necessity. The encounter both with people and with places. That is my share of biography.

(Pour moi, ce qui a compté, ce sont des rencontres, là où le hasard se fait nécessité. Rencontre des hommes, rencontre des lieux. C'est ma part de biographie.)

'Les Rencontres (1984)

Retracing these events, Blanchot offers little in the way of private testimony; his concern is rather to show how the flow of history is repeatedly interrupted by so many moments of necessary decision, so many dilemmas, so many failings or slippages, and that it is these that prompt the many sideways turnings that go to make up a single life's itinerary. These moments are not just public ones, for private experience is shaped by them too, with the result that it is the separation between the public and the private that is the most fragile division of all. So it would seem at any rate from the vestigial outline of Blanchot's own personal life given in a rare autobiographical sketch, published in *Le Nouvel Observateur* in November 1984. In the piece, more aide-mémoire than intimate record, Blanchot dramatises his life's progress in terms of a sequence of dated meetings with a small number of unique and singular others whom he names as: Emmanuel Levinas, Georges Bataille, René Char, and Robert Antelme.[1] As well as a discreet mark of a personal friendship, each of these names, in turn, functions as shorthand for a larger philosophical or political or literary encounter.

As the two men have often recalled, each in his own way, on numerous occasions, Blanchot and Levinas first met as fellow students of philosophy in Strasbourg in 1925. The two had very different backgrounds: Levinas, slightly the older, and a liberal, was recently arrived from Lithuania, while Blanchot, by all accounts still a monarchist, was from a well-off family from Quain in the Saône-et-Loire; yet, almost immediately, the pair swore a pact of friendship to each other whose longevity, terminated only by the death of Levinas in 1995, is at all events remarkable: 'it happened,' wrote Blanchot two years before Levinas's death, 'not because we were both young, but by a deliberate decision, a pact I hope never to break'.[2] The two quickly shared their respective intellectual enthusiasms. Blanchot introduced Levinas to contemporary French literature in the shape of Proust and Valéry, while Levinas for his part helped Blanchot with Husserl and Heidegger, particularly the recently published *Sein*

und Zeit. This last encounter in 1927 and 1928 alongside Levinas was one
Blanchot still recalled sixty years later as a veritable intellectual shock.[3] Both left
Strasbourg at about the same time; and though relations were more distant
during the years that immediately followed, it has recently been suggested that it
was of Levinas's youngest brother, Aminadab Levinas, who died in Lithuania at
the hands of the Nazis shortly before, that Blanchot was thinking when in 1942
he gave the unusual title of *Aminadab* to his second published novel. It was at any
event to Blanchot, at around the same time, while himself still a prisoner of war
in Germany, that Levinas entrusted his immediate family, and Blanchot who was
instrumental in finding a safe haven for Levinas's wife and daughter in a
monastery near Orléans, where they remained until the Liberation.[4]

The second major encounter in his life, Blanchot writes, was his meeting
with Georges Bataille. This took place in Paris late in December 1940; again,
the friendship between the two was immediate and absolute.[5] Against the
background of the Occupation, despite the hardships of the time, the two men
maintained a semblance of intellectual activity. Bataille, for his part, was still
committed to pursuing, if with diminishing resolve, the experience of
community begun before the war by means of such singular, heterodox groups
as the Collège de sociologie, or Acéphale; and it was within a similar collective
context that much of the discussion took place that was finally to lead to the
publication of *L'Expérience intérieure* in 1943. As Bataille openly acknowledges
throughout that text, Blanchot was a major participant in these exchanges, and it
is evident that the meeting with Blanchot had a galvanising effect on Bataille.[6]
The reverse is no doubt also true, and it may be argued that many of the changes
that took place in Blanchot's thinking and writing during the early or mid-1940s
may be attributed to his own encounter with Bataille. Their friendship was
evidently a two-way relationship; and just as Bataille, in writing *L'Expérience
intérieure*, drew openly on conversations with Blanchot and on the latter's two
recent novels, *Thomas l'Obscur* and *Aminadab*, so Blanchot, in his first essay
collection in 1943, *Faux Pas*, paid ample tribute to Bataille in return, recalling,
apropos of *L'Expérience intérieure*, Nietzsche's own description of *Also sprach
Zarathustra*, which Blanchot was to remember again, some twenty years later, in
L'Entretien infini (*EI*, 313; 211): 'this work is entirely apart' ('cette œuvre est
complètement à part') (*FP*, 52).[7]

Coupling Bataille's name, in 'Les Rencontres', with that of René Char, a
notable and early active member of the Resistance, Blanchot summarises the
war years under the following, highly elliptical headings: 'The call to

irregularity. The limit-experience. Opposition to the occupation and the Vichy regime. Underground activity' ('Appel à l'irrégularité. L'expérience-limite. Opposition à l'occupant et au régime de Vichy. Clandestinité'). But today, despite these unambiguous remarks, much obscurity still surrounds Blanchot's wartime activities, and Blanchot's silence about them has rarely passed the bounds of absolute discretion; indeed, it was only in 1994, in a short third-person autobiographical narrative entitled *L'Instant de ma mort*, that Blanchot finally yielded to his readers, after years of rumour, the sketch – little more than a suspended fragment – of how, fifty years previously, in July 1944, a young man, the 36-year-old Blanchot, faced – for his involvement in the Resistance? – a German military firing squad, and yet unpredictably, unaccountably, and in the end (says Blanchot) unjustifiably, was allowed to escape, allowed to survive the very moment of his own dying. Thus Blanchot's vestigial testimony of the war, the silent murmur of which resounds through much of the fiction and many of the essays published by Blanchot after the war and gives to their exploration of the impossibility of the experience of dying much of its singularity and insistent urgency.

Within a few years of the war's end, Blanchot quickly established himself as one of the most distinctive voices in French post-war literary criticism. He published widely, at times regularly, at times on a more occasional basis, in a host of literary journals and periodicals of diverse political hues. These included *L'Arche*, which, launched from Algiers early in 1944, was one of the first independent literary monthlies to emerge after the war, and on whose editorial committee, alongside Gide and Camus, Blanchot served for a brief time, as well as more enduring publications such as Sartre's *Les Temps modernes*, and Paulhan's *Cahiers de la Pléiade*. Probably most important of all among the journals to which Blanchot was a regular contributor in the period following the war was *Critique*, the monthly review founded by Bataille in 1946 and edited by him, with substantial support from Blanchot in its early years, and in which Blanchot published many of his most influential post-war essays, including a number of celebrated texts on Sade, Char, Hölderlin, Rimbaud, Hegel, Kafka, and Rilke.

In 1947 Blanchot left Paris for Èze-Village, a small town on the Mediterranean coast between Nice and Monte-Carlo, which, as he recorded in 1989 (*UV*, 13), faces out to Corsica to the south-east and over Cap Ferrat to the south-west. The decade that followed was a period of astonishing productivity. By May 1947, Blanchot had already completed his third, and last novel, *Le Très-Haut* (*The Most High*), on which he had been working since at least 1945. When it finally appeared, in July 1948, it did so simultaneously with *L'Arrêt de mort* (*Death Sentence*), Blanchot's first major short narrative or *récit*; the previous year had seen the first publication of 'Le Dernier Mot' ('The Last Word') and 'L'Idylle' ('The Idyll'), the two stories later collected in *Le Ressassement éternel* and *Après coup*. Some months before, in mid-January, Blanchot had also finished work on a second, dramatically shortened version of *Thomas l'Obscur* which, when it was published in 1950, turned out to be no more than a third of the length of the original 1941 text.[8] In 1949, too, Blanchot brought out two volumes of critical essays, *La Part du feu* (*The Work of Fire*) and *Lautréamont et Sade*, which together reprinted the bulk of his critical output over the previous four years.

The period between 1948 and 1950 saw the appearance of five major books; but Blanchot in the years that followed was scarcely any less prolific. He continued to publish fiction as well as literary criticism. In 1949 the journal *Empédocle* had published a short *récit* entitled simply: 'Un récit';[9] and three more short narratives quickly followed: *Au moment voulu* (*When the Time Comes*) (1951), *Celui qui ne m'accompagnait pas* (*The One Who Was Standing Apart From Me*) (1953) and *Le Dernier Homme* (*The Last Man*) (1957). These, in their turn, were followed, in 1962, by *L'Attente L'Oubli*, a book that is sometimes cited as Blanchot's last *récit*, though the text itself contests any simple attribution of genre; essentially unclassifiable, it is a work in which fictional representation finally seems to have become indistinguishable from meditative, philosophical prose, and vice versa.

In January 1953, the *Nouvelle Revue française*, France's most prestigious pre-war literary journal, was adjudged to have served out the post-war quarantine imposed upon it for continuing publication between 1940 and 1943 under the collaborationist banner of Pierre Drieu La Rochelle, and the journal began reappearing under the pre-war editorship of Jean Paulhan. The first issue carried an essay by Blanchot entitled 'La Solitude essentielle' ('The Essential Solitude'), which was later to become the opening chapter of *L'Espace littéraire* (*The Space of Literature*); from this point on Blanchot settled into what was to become, until Paulhan's death in 1968, a pattern of regular monthly contributions to the journal. The effect on Blanchot's work as a literary critic was impressive. The freedom he was allowed by Paulhan to write in whatever way he chose about literature in general released him from the constraints of conventional book-reviewing, which had gradually become a source of some frustration to

13

Blanchot. Indeed, it was largely the writer's impatience with the requirement that he discuss topical work by other writers, the format adopted by *Critique*, that lay behind Blanchot's reluctant withdrawal from active involvement in that journal after 1953.[10]

This left Blanchot able to pursue more radically what he had already begun to do in the latter years of the 1940s, and develop a different kind of critical language – more an oscillating syntax of irreducible paradox than an exhaustive system of totalising concepts – with which to address the question of literature, that fundamental question that Mallarmé, in 1894, had first formulated by inquiring: 'Does something like Literature exist?' ('Quelque chose comme les Lettres existe-t-il') to which he had supplied the answer: 'Yes, Literature does exist and, if you will, it alone, except for everything else' ('Oui, que la Littérature existe et, si l'on veut, seule, à l'exception de tout'), and the consequences of which Blanchot, in 1952, sought to clarify by asking, in more explicitly Heideggerian terms: 'What are the implications for being of the statement that "something like Literature exists"?' ('Qu'en est-il de l'être, si l'on dit que "quelque chose comme les Lettres existe"?', *EL*, 35; 43).[11] So when in 1955 *L'Espace littéraire* came out, based on work published in *Critique* and the *Nouvelle Revue française* over the previous four years, it was apparent that Blanchot had at his disposal a critical idiom that, alongside its redoubtable philosophical sophistication, manifested, as the publisher's blurb put it, an experiential or experimental dimension entirely its own. The comment is one that holds true for all the essays Blanchot published in the course of the next fifteen years, and it is those texts, published for the most part in the *Nouvelle Revue française*, that provided Blanchot with the material for the three further ground-breaking volumes that appeared over the next twenty years and on which his reputation as a critic and thinker now largely rests: *Le Livre à venir* (1959), *L'Entretien infini* (1969), and *L'Amitié* (1971).

In 1957, after ten years of solitary writing, Blanchot returned to Paris. One of his first points of intellectual contact in the capital was Dionys Mascolo, whom Blanchot had first met in the early 1940s and who, in July 1958, together with Jean Schuster, was responsible for launching the paper *Le 14 Juillet*, the main purpose of which was to co-ordinate intellectual resistance to the return to power of General de Gaulle that had occurred two months earlier. The deep fear at the time, as expressed by Mascolo and Schuster in a flier they produced on 17 May 1958, was that de Gaulle's unconstitutional *coup*, carried out with the support of the right-wing French military, was the first step towards the setting up of a – fascist – military regime not very different from that of Franco in Spain. Blanchot, on receipt of the first issue of the paper, replied to Mascolo immediately. 'I want to tell you I am in complete agreement,' he wrote. 'I refuse the whole of the past and accept nothing of the present.'[12]

In two subsequent pieces for the paper, 'Le Refus' and 'La Perversion essentielle' (BR, 167–73), Blanchot developed the substance of his own opposition to the regime. This had essentially to do with de Gaulle's claim – in Blanchot's eyes disturbingly reminiscent of Pétain's self-proclaimed personification of France in 1940 – to embody in his own person the national destiny of France; for by so doing the so-called providential leader of 1958 was seeking to lend his name and prestige to a dangerous, quasi-religious politics, a politics of nationalist mystification that sought mainly to fill the vacancy of power – the necessary void at the centre of politics – with a spurious, authoritarian ideology of national salvation. And in the face of such an 'essential perversion' of the political process the only response that Blanchot deemed to be adequate was one of absolute and categorical refusal.

Blanchot's contribution to the campaign against de Gaulle ushered in an intense period of renewed political activity on his part. Events came to a head when, in September 1960, the philosopher and journalist Francis Jeanson was put on trial, together with twenty-three others, French and Algerians alike, for aiding and abetting the FLN (the Front de Libération Nationale) in the struggle against French colonial involvement in Algeria. To coincide with the trial, Mascolo, Schuster, and Blanchot, with a small group of other intellectuals, issued a solemn declaration supporting the actions of those who had made common cause with the struggle for Algerian independence, and endorsing the right of French conscripts to refuse the draft; the statement concluded with the assertion that 'the cause of the Algerian people, which is making a decisive contribution to the ruin of the colonial system, is the cause of all free men'. After the initial number of signatories, the document soon became known as the 'Manifeste des 121'. It was allowed to circulate, however, only in clandestine form; and indeed the two mainstream journals that sought to print it, Les Temps modernes and Les Lettres nouvelles, were promptly confiscated by the authorities, while those who had signed, under new measures adopted by the government, risked being sentenced to between one and five years in prison.[13] But by then, enough had been done by those involved, activists and intellectuals alike, to discredit France's continued pursuit of the war, which was eventually brought to a close by the Évian accords of March 1962.

Blanchot's hope, already by the Autumn of 1960, was that the 'Manifeste des 121' would be not just an isolated endeavour, but the beginning of a new broadly based intellectual initiative. The vehicle for this longer-term project, he proposed, should be a new journal, a 'journal of *total criticism*' ('revue de *critique totale*'), as he explained in a letter to Sartre, one which, by combining literary output and criticism with current political and scientific discussion, would demonstrate the necessary interrelation of each of these different areas of thought. The intention was also that the journal should have, as Blanchot put it, an 'essentially collective' existence; to this end it was to be an international enterprise, based on the activities of at least three different national editorial committees, which necessitated lengthy discussions involving potential collaborators from Germany and Italy. But more important still for Blanchot, if the initiative was to succeed, was the need to elaborate a new form of writing, mingling the literary with the political in a coherent but critically open-ended manner, that would allow the journal's commitment to plurality, multiplicity, and collective exchange to find a specific rhythm of its own. The form Blanchot identified as the one best able to achieve this was the fragment; and it is no exaggeration to say that this turn to the fragment was to leave a deep imprint on everything Blanchot was subsequently to write. But by early 1964, despite the efforts of Blanchot, Mascolo, Louis-René Des Forêts and many others, the project for an international journal had failed. But if it did so, Blanchot noted at the time, it did so utopianly; and the very impossibility of success was proof, if any was needed, of the radical necessity of the enterprise.[14]

Within Mascolo's circle in 1958, and as a constant presence in all the different initiatives of the years that followed, Blanchot had encountered another important friendship, that of Robert Antelme. Antelme was by all accounts a remarkable man, and best known at the time as the author of *L'Espèce humaine*, a powerfully moving account of his experiences during his arrest and deportation to Buchenwald and Dachau for Resistance activity in 1944.[15] First published in 1947, the book made a strong impact on Blanchot, who writes about it at length in an important essay of April 1962 collected in revised form in *L'Entretien infini* (*EI*, 99–103, 191–200; 70–2, 130–5). And when in 1968, as though simply in resumption of the struggle against de Gaulle begun ten years earlier, the whole of France stood paralysed by students' and workers' demonstrations, it was with Antelme, together with Mascolo, Duras, and countless others, indeed – as Blanchot phrases it in 'Les Rencontres' – 'with everyone' ('avec tous'), that Blanchot played what was no doubt a significant if discreetly anonymous part in the May *événements*. Blanchot's main activity, it seems, was as a member of the 'Comité d'action étudiants-écrivains', that fervently anti-authoritarian group of revolutionary students and writers that met from 20 May 1968 till the following spring and which produced in October 1968 a semi-clandestine magazine, entitled *Comité*, in which over half the texts, although unsigned, were, according to Mascolo, all written by Blanchot.[16]

Admittedly, the committee had eventually foundered by the following March amid fierce internal dissension; around the same time, too, Blanchot himself also abruptly withdrew from the movement, explaining in a letter to Levinas that the reason for his action was the position taken by the extreme left in favour of Palestine and against Israel. Though he acknowledged that the move was not motivated by anti-semitism, he nonetheless took the view that the end result was little different: 'It would seem', he wrote, 'that anti-semitism from now on can count among its allies those who are, as it were, free of anti-semitism'. And he went on to ask: 'Isn't this a strange reversal, one that proves that the absence of anti-semitism is simply not enough?'[17] As though in response to that very question, from 1971 Blanchot began in his writing explicitly to address the issue of the Holocaust.

Pas de récit?

A story? No. No stories, never again.
(Un récit? Non, pas de récit, plus jamais.)
La Folie du jour (*FJ*, 38; 18)

The story that Blanchot tells in the course of these various autobiographical and semi-autobiographical texts is incomplete, fragmentary, discontinuous. Everything that is divulged is communicated obliquely. As a result, while these partial narratives are significant for what they affirm, they are also, as Blanchot himself would no doubt concede, equally revealing for what it is they prefer to leave unsaid. It is perhaps unsurprising, therefore, that on the part of some commentators Blanchot's very obliqueness has been viewed with the very greatest of suspicion; and on more than one occasion the writer has been pressed by his critics to begin recounting in more detail what the autobiographical fragments to which I have referred so far leave largely unmentioned: the writer's pre-war involvement with the extremist, nationalist right.

Knowledge of this unfamiliar past was first brought to the attention of the vast majority of Blanchot's readers in 1976 when the journal *Gramma* published an extensive bibliography of the writer's early published texts.[1] Since then, numbers of readers, at times polemically, at times more dispassionately, have raised the question of the relationship between these pre-war political writings and Blanchot's post-war criticism and fiction. The author's own response to inquiries addressed to him personally has been twofold. On the one hand, he has refused to justify, or even comment in much detail on his pre-war political choices, while on the other hand, particularly regarding specific points of controversy, he has clearly been concerned to preserve the factual accuracy of the historical record. A number of Blanchot's various letters of clarification have found their way into print.[2] Even so, they have failed to satisfy the anxious – inquisitorial – demand for narrative on the part of some of Blanchot's critics who have implied that the writer's objections to historical narrative are a screen behind which to conceal a deeply rooted – and culpable – evasiveness with regard to the past.[3]

It is indeed the case, as we have seen, that Blanchot at times goes to surprising lengths to avoid narrating explicitly the detail of his own particular – albeit far from uncommon – evolution from extreme nationalism to dissident communism.[4] It must be acknowledged, however, that obliqueness or indirection is not in itself proof of historical evasiveness; and in any case, it is simply not true that in his later texts Blanchot eschews all autobiographical self-scrutiny. In *Le Pas au-delà*, for instance, as mentioned above, Blanchot may indeed be found recalling, indirectly, aspects of his experience as a journalist and writer during the period leading up to the completion of *Thomas l'Obscur* in May 1940. But in such passages Blanchot's concerns are not anecdotal ones; for what the author is doing is to elaborate a model for a very different understanding of the relationship between writing and history from that enshrined in traditional, retrospective autobiographical narrative, a model that explains not only Blanchot's personal reluctance to satisfy the requirement for autobiographical narrative addressed to him by his detractors, but also the very impossibility of meeting any such demand. This is why it is worth examining in some detail the passage from *Le Pas au-delà* I have mentioned. Blanchot writes as follows:

> I will attempt in vain to represent to myself the person I was not and who, without willing it, began writing, writing in such a way (and thus realising) that the pure product of doing nothing was thereby penetrating into the world and into his world. That took place 'at night'. In the day, there were

the acts of the day, the daily words, the daily writing, declarations, values, habits, nothing of importance and yet something that dimly had to be called living. The certainty that by writing he was putting precisely this certainty into parenthesis, including the certainty of himself as a subject of writing, led him slowly, yet immediately, into an empty space whose emptiness (the heraldic, barred zero) in no way prevented the twists and turns of a lengthy itinerary.

(PA, 9; 2)

Writing of his own past in this way, Blanchot resists the temptation to present his experience as a process of teleological maturation. The author's signature endorses neither the fulfilment of a career nor the accomplishment of an artistic project. The emphasis falls instead on difference and incommensurability. Memory becomes split between at least two competing, dissymmetrical pronouns, each instantiating a different textual figure, including, on the one hand, the anonymous narrative voice of *Le Pas au-delà* itself, which speaks in the first person, while referring to itself (as only a few lines earlier) in the second person, and, on the other, the writer of fiction of the early years, to whom the fragment refers in the third person. Crucially, however, this temporal or historical dichotomy does not engender narrative; it serves rather to repeat or re-enact the distance that already, prior to *Thomas l'Obscur*, separated the author's everyday duties as a journalist from his night-time activities as a writer of fiction. A difference in time introduces a difference in temporality; and there opens up between day and night, between living and writing, a radical – infinite – separation, an interruption which itself does not belong to narrative and which no narrative form can claim as its object nor indeed successfully mitigate or repair, since to do so would be to substitute for the gaping void or futurity that presides over all historical experience a teleological fiction that would serve merely to occlude the very opening of history to itself as an experience of the future. During the 1930s, Blanchot tells the reader, the day was given over to politics, and writing fiction was what – literally – took place at night. But there is no story that can tell the truth of this interval, no narrative that can embrace it, with the result that what counts most, in retrospect, is not the apparent complementarity between the acts of the day and the experience of the night, but the irreducibility of the – futural – void dividing them from each other.

What writing introduces into the world, according to *Le Pas au-delà*, is a nothing, a gap in intelligibility and an abeyance of all certainty, a vacancy in meaning which alone gives writing its chance. Writing, here, for Blanchot submits to a more exacting requirement than that of telling linear stories. It becomes a response to the disjunction between languages and within language without which writing itself would not in fact be possible at all. In this way, even as it lends itself to a guarded autobiographical digression, Blanchot's text is impelled to question the possibility of any autobiographical contract dependent on the stability and self-identity of a signature. Instead, as a result of its fragmentary structure, a text such as *Le Pas au-delà* is constrained, by dint of its own conditions of possibility, to bear witness to the very interruption of sense that alone gives it its chance as a text. This is why, in Blanchot's texts, writing and narrative are always, so to speak, in inverse proportion, and why what is asked of writing is that it always contest the power of narrative to capture the meaning of history. This in turn is why Blanchot's diffidence regarding autobiographical narrative asks to be read not as a repression of the past, but rather as a response to the demand that writing itself respect the void or disjunction in language without which, of course, writing itself would not occur at all. In turning discreetly from historical narrative, then, Blanchot not only holds open the promise of the future, he also enjoins the reader perpetually to reconfront the past, not as established story but as futural writing, not as teleology but as eschatology, not as embodied truth, that is, but as pressing injunction.

What matters, then, for Blanchot, is not autobiographical confession or avowal, but the responsibility to writing. This, in turn, is but another name for responsibility to the Other and to justice for the Other. In this context, Blanchot's own principle is clear: it is to respect in language the fundamental disjunction or plurality without which there would be no language, while at the same time rigorously taking responsibility for his own writing, a responsibility that, as Blanchot acknowledges, is incumbent on him alone. As he wrote in 1984 to Roger Laporte, by way of introducing the fullest account yet of his own pre-war political itinerary, 'You know my principle. Let each express himself according to his own responsibility' ('Vous connaissez mon principe. Laissez chacun s'exprimer selon sa responsabilité').[5] If these words mean anything, it is that the question raised by Blanchot's own particular political evolution is not a question requiring autobiographical disclosure, but, more abruptly and more trenchantly, a question that is inseparable from the issue of ethical and political responsibility.

The acts of the day (1)

There is no such thing as good nationalism. Nationalism tends always to integrate everything, all values, that is how it ends up being integral, i.e., the sole value.

(Il n'y a pas de bon nationalisme. Le nationalisme tend toujours à tout intégrer, toutes les valeurs, c'est en cela qu'il finit par être intégral, c'est-à-dire l'unique valeur.)

'Sur le nationalisme' (1991)

It is now well known that, during the major part of the 1930s, Blanchot was principally active as a political journalist. As such, he contributed to a wide range of nationalist newspapers and periodicals. By far the most influential and important of these was the *Journal des débats*, a traditionalist, staunchly conservative evening daily, whose principal share-holder at the time was the iron and steel magnate François de Wendel, and which had as its *directeur*, whose responsibility it was to determine editorial policy, a long-standing associate of de Wendel, Étienne de Nalèche. By the 1930s, by all accounts, the *Journal des débats* had known better days. Despite a prestigious history reaching back to the time of the French Revolution, it had entered into a phase of irreversible decline, though in the eyes of the right-wing intelligentsia who made up the paper's main readership it still enjoyed considerable respect for the literary distinction of its articles and editorials.[1] Blanchot's earliest signed contributions to the newspaper date from 1931 and 1932. Relatively soon, however, he had progressed to the position of *rédacteur en chef* on the paper; in that capacity, working in close consultation with de Nalèche, Blanchot would have been primarily responsible for writing front-page leader articles and generally making sure the paper went to press on time and in good order.

The 1930s in France were of course turbulent and difficult years. Looking back from the perspective of September 1939, Georges Bataille commented: 'The inter-war years is a time when lying was no less necessary to living than drink. The absence of solution defies expression.'[2] At home, growing economic crisis, government instability, corruption in high places, and the increasing militancy of both the left and the extreme right, all left parliamentary democracy in a notoriously weakened state, while internationally the political stage was still largely dominated by the legacy of the First World War, and the fundamental issue for France was still felt to be the question of what policy to adopt in the face of the German threat. As for France's mainstream political parties, these were divided between two different and incompatible approaches to many issues, including foreign policy. On the one hand were those radicals

21

and socialists who, like Aristide Briand, France's ever-present Foreign Minister during the period from 1925 to 1931, had become, after the end of the First World War, the enthusiastic proponents of a foreign policy founded on the League of Nations and on what Prime Minister Édouard Herriot described in 1924 as the threefold principle of arbitration, security, and disarmament. Implemented by successive governments during the latter part of the 1920s and the early 1930s, the policy took shape as a series of gradual revisions or renegotiations of the Treaty of Versailles of 1919, probably the most successful of which, as it seemed at the time, was the conclusion of the Locarno Pact of 1925, by which, in return for admission to the League of Nations the following year, Germany agreed to recognise the Western borders imposed by the Allies at Versailles and accept the demilitarisation of the Rhineland.

Inevitably, this policy of détente was not without its critics. Indeed at the other end of the political spectrum in France were those conservative nationalists who, following the example of Clemenceau, Prime Minister between 1917 and 1920, remained bitterly hostile to any retreat from the provisions of the Treaty of Versailles – irrespective of how unworkable or destabilising they might in reality turn out to be – and who viewed with deep mistrust the attempt to substitute the juridical, contractual framework of the League of Nations for a more traditional diplomacy founded on military strength and a system of alliances between states rooted in mutual self-interest. And it was here that the *Journal des débats* was to be found, acting for the most part as a daily mouthpiece of the 'Comité des forges', that powerful association of the owners of all the major French steel-producing factories, presided over by de Wendel, which the propagandists of the Popular Front in 1936 were to attack most fiercely, charging it with representing – as it did – the oligarchic might of France's 200 wealthiest and most influential families.

From the outset, in some of his earliest contributions to the *Journal des débats*, Blanchot displayed an abiding interest in the question of the relationship between force and law. The concern is one that was fundamental to all Blanchot's political thinking of the period, and he went on to rehearse the position time and time again. Politics and violence, for Blanchot, were not irreconcilable opposites, but the two sides of a single coin. All political legitimacy, he argued, rested necessarily on a founding act of force; force, however, was not an abstract entity to be seen in isolation from the interests it sought to promote. Force in politics – for Blanchot the two terms were largely synonymous – could be either beneficial or prejudicial, according to whether –

22

put crudely – a particular state of force was in the service of peace or of war; and it was in any case incumbent on national government to secure the peaceful survival of its own national community by recourse, where necessary, to acts of appropriate force. The practical consequences of this position are not hard to see. It followed for Blanchot that, in both the national and international sphere, the recourse to force was both necessary and legitimate if the purpose was to maintain peace; and it further followed that legal or juridical principles that were not adequately defended by appropriate force could only give the illusion of security and were to that extent worse than nothing. In the context of France's struggle first against Germany and then, from 1933, against Hitler, the debate, Blanchot contended, centred not on the speculative question of how war might be avoided between nations, but on the more fundamental issue of how best to defend France's national interest, which began of course with the need to secure a stable long-term peace. The choice facing France was a brutal one: did it want peace, or did it want war? If the answer was peace, as it was for Blanchot, it followed necessarily that the government had to translate that choice into decisive and effective action by recourse to all appropriate means; and though this would begin with tried and tested diplomatic methods, it might end, in the last resort, with military deployment. To precipitate the threat of war by failing resolutely to defend the peace was in this perspective the height of irresponsibility. But to shrink from such action in the belief that war might thereby be avoided was absolutely disastrous, and would serve in fact only to make the prospect of war itself more certain.

This basic political philosophy finds expression in Blanchot's early journalism in a number of ways. In 1932, for instance, he contributed an unsigned obituary to the *Journal des débats* on the death of Aristide Briand, the main architect of France's post-war foreign policy, writing of Briand that 'his speeches were always triumphs and his actions failures'.[3] The point here was that in politics a fundamental dissymmetry separated words and acts, and that noble sentiments on their own were unable to effect political changes that might be achieved only by decisive commitment to forceful action. Blanchot, however, was far from a cynical apologist for political violence. Indeed, as he contended elsewhere – this was his conclusion to a discussion of Malaparte's celebrated treatise of 1931, *Technique du coup d'État* – acts of force had to be judged within a specific political context; and acts of revolutionary violence, for instance, would succeed politically – as they had in Russia in 1917 – only when sanctioned by a prior political project enjoying at least some degree of

23

popular support or when the politics of a regime had lost all credibility or coherence.[4] So if the question of politics for Blanchot was inseparable from the question of force, it was also inseparable from the question of the legitimacy of such force. What was fundamental to successful political action, for Blanchot, was an understanding of the necessary reciprocity between force and law, the fact that laws to be respected relied on the recourse to force, but that force itself, if it were to result in stable government, had to be legitimised by reference to the proper interests of the nation; and it was its endemic inability to confront this issue that gave rise to Blanchot's virulent opposition to the woolly internationalism of the League of Nations, which he saw as an organisation motivated more by wishful thinking than by proper understanding of political realities, and blinded to unpalatable truths by its obstinate belief in abstract and fanciful internationalist conventions which it had neither the means nor the will to defend.

Once Blanchot had begun to serve as *rédacteur en chef* on the *Journal des débats*, reflecting the fact that the views he was expressing were those of the paper rather than necessarily his own, his contributions to the paper mostly went unsigned. Nevertheless, his statements of opinion on behalf of the journal were no less incisive than those published earlier under his own name; and in the course of the years that followed, though political circumstances varied significantly, the main policies advocated by the paper changed little and the newspaper remained resolutely committed throughout to the nationalist, conservative cause. Being in favour of strong national government, economic stability, the free market, and law and order, the *Journal des débats* was implacably opposed, as a result, not only to the French Communist Party (the PCF) and Socialist Party (the SFIO), both of which it claimed to be in the pay of the Soviet Union, but also to those sections of the Radical Party who, alongside the socialists and communists, formed between May 1936 and June 1937 the Popular Front coalition that was to carry the hopes of many working people for social reform and peace, and which was to prove the target of some of the paper's most incisive polemic.

In the realm of foreign affairs the single most important political question for the *Journal des débats*, as for the French right in general, was the threat to security posed by German expansionism. As a result, while the paper displayed, for instance, much affection for Britain, it maintained a consistent and unyielding hostility to Germany, opposing each of the concessions made to Germany by successive governments in the effort to promote better

Franco–German relations. The reasons for this were given in the form of a withering critique, on both theoretical and practical grounds, of the internationalism of the League of Nations. An editorial of 17 January 1935, for instance, noted with some irony that, in demanding a plebiscite in the Saar, which eventually resulted in the return of the region to Germany, Hitler (who had taken Germany out of the League of Nations in the autumn of 1933) was merely making profitable use of the Wilsonian principle of national self-determination, and that by endorsing such an abstract juridical convention the League of Nations had done little more than hand Hitler on a plate the means to extend German territorial and economic power and thereby fatally weaken the League of Nations itself. The paper went on to accuse the League of Nations of naivety. Whoever enacts a legal principle, the *Journal des débats* argued, ought first to consider the question of the force that will ultimately determine the use – or abuse – of that law; as the editorial put it: 'In the beginning was the Word, claim the Geneva parliamentarians. In the beginning was the act, says Adolf Hitler, repeating Goethe's Faust.' ('Au commencement était le Verbe, disent les parlementaires genevois. Au commencement était l'action, répète après le docteur Faust Adolf Hitler.')

Matters came to a head, when, on 7 March 1936, Hitler's troops, in clear breach of the Locarno Pact, reoccupied the Rhineland, and the French government, with its partners in the League of Nations, did nothing. (It is of course now known that Hitler's military commanders had orders to pull back if they encountered French troops crossing the border, adding considerable force to the view, reiterated by Blanchot in 1984, that the real turning point in the West's capitulation to Hitler occurred in March 1936 rather than in September 1938.) Two years later, on 18 March 1938, in the face of another defeat for the cause of peace – Hitler's annexation of Austria – the *Journal des débats* described the events of 7 March as marking the beginning of a new era, the era of France's squandering of its victory of 1918. In fact, already in 1936, three days after Hitler's army had moved into the Rhineland, the message was much the same: while, as far as the rest of Europe was concerned, it had broken a solemn contract, Germany in its own eyes was only availing itself of an opportunity those other countries had given it in the first place. What the event proved, for the *Journal des débats*, was the bankruptcy of the internationalism embodied in the League of Nations. Peace, the paper argued, simply could not be guaranteed by contractual or juridical means; as an editorial of 13 March 1936 damningly observed:

If there is one truth that is slowly dawning, ten years too late, it is that the problem that exists between Europe and Germany is not a juridical problem, but a problem of force.... Europe and America ... have believed in a juridical organisation of the world. This novelty implied equal good will on the part of all nations, prepared to accept the map of the world and work together for a better international future. This was to suppose the problem already solved.

(Journal des débats, 13 March 1936)

The logic of contractual responsibility embedded in French foreign policy after 1924 presupposed in Germany, as in all other states, a reliable subject fully committed to honouring its promises; it assumed that, if a country breached international rules, such a rogue state could be arraigned before the tribunal of other nations and persuaded to act otherwise. However, if that state refused to acknowledge the jurisdiction of the court, there was little the tribunal could do about this, except resort to force. But the recourse to force was what the contractual system was specifically set up to eliminate; and while the juridical framework of the League of Nations did allow for the use of sanctions, what this implied in reality was that there was an increased risk of local conflicts escalating to the larger international community and that, accordingly, individual states would be more than reluctant to become involved at all. Indecision and inaction were the only outcome. So the result of reliance on the League of Nations, according to the *Journal des débats,* was not to lift the threat of war, but in fact to make war more likely by showing the government to be unwilling and unprepared for a properly robust defence of its national interest. This was why, to the paper's ears, the history of Franco–German relations since 1918 sounded like a litany of defeat, with each reversal leading inexorably down the road to war: thus France's early military withdrawal from the Rhineland in 1930, thus the failure of the London conference of 1933 to settle the question of reparations, thus the plebiscite restoring the Saar to Germany in 1935, thus Hitler's remilitarisation of the Rhineland in 1936, thus the Anschluss of March 1938, and thus, finally, the Munich accords of 1938. The lesson seemed clear. The nation had to look to its own moral and material strength to defend itself; in the last resort, enjoying the prospect of a stable long-term peace meant preparing for war; as one leader, dated 16 March 1936, put it, using a tried and tested nationalist formula: 'the only guarantee of peace and security lies in moral and material strength [la force morale et matérielle]'. 'Peace', it added, 'is a question of force.'

Blanchot remained with the *Journal des débats* until the defeat of France, in June 1940, in the war with Germany against which the newspaper had so often warned. Long before then, however, it must be remembered that, in addition to his work at the *Journal des débats*, Blanchot was also the author of another, parallel, political discourse, one he pursued in a variety of short-lived extremist publications – titles such as *La Revue française*, *Réaction*, *La Revue universelle* or *La Revue du siècle* – that existed on the further fringes of mainstream right-wing politics. As early as 1931 and 1932, while starting out with the *Journal des débats*, Blanchot was writing political articles and book reviews in various magazines and journals belonging to what soon became known at the time as the Jeune Droite.[5] This was a loosely defined, highly volatile, disparate ideological movement that was largely the preserve of disaffected younger members of the French monarchist movement, *Action française*, who, tired of the circumspection and inertia of that party's traditionalist leadership, had turned to more extreme measures in the desire to overcome what they saw as France's decline into mediocrity; indeed, alongside its virulent nationalism, hatred of Marxism, and contempt for parliamentary democracy, what mainly distinguished the Jeune Droite was its diagnosis that France was in the grip of a profound spiritual and ideological crisis that might be remedied only by recourse to radical and violent means that demanded immediate mobilisation.

In some respects, the distance between the Jeune Droite and the more traditionalist French right was less one of substance than tone and emphasis, and, on occasion, the ideas Blanchot could be found expressing in 1932 and 1933 in, say, *La Revue française* were not far removed from what he had written, in a personal capacity, in some of his early pieces for the *Journal des débats*; indeed the article 'Les Années tournantes', based on an influential book of the same title by Daniel-Rops, with its evocation of the moral bankruptcy of the current political system in particular and the spiritual emptiness of the modern world in general, turned out, when it appeared in March 1933, to be no more than a digest of a much longer article from *La Revue française* published some months earlier.[6] And there are strong parallels, too, between the arguments put forward anonymously in the *Journal des débats* during the middle years of the decade and those contained, for instance, in such extended pieces as Blanchot's two articles on French foreign policy for *La Revue du XXe siècle* in 1935, in which Blanchot took the opportunity of developing simply at greater length, and in his own name, the same swingeing polemic against the ineffective, juridical, moralistic thinking of the League of Nations as was already in evidence in editorials for the *Journal des débats*.

At the same time, as his thinking moves between these two types of publication, from the mainstream, nationalist press on the one hand to the journals of the Jeune Droite on the other, Blanchot's prose acquires a new, more radical inflection. When writing for *La Revue française* or *La Revue du siècle*, what Blanchot does is to articulate in a much more far-reaching way the ultimate implications of the critique of government policy presented in the *Journal des débats*. Writing under his own name, Blanchot accelerates and intensifies, so to speak, the discourse available to him within the columns of the traditionalist press. In that process, the political stakes are raised very rapidly, and Blanchot begins to call into question, in the strongest possible terms, not only the wisdom or effectiveness of a whole range of policies carried out by successive radical and centre-left French governments, but also – at least in the form known to him in the early 1930s – the fundamental legitimacy of French parliamentary democracy as such. (As he did so, it has to be remembered that Blanchot was doing no more than to echo the sentiments of many of his contemporaries, on the left as well as the right; indeed, for many witnesses at the time, the most emblematic event of all was the night of anti-parliamentary rioting of 6 February 1934, sparked off by a series of notorious financial scandals penetrating to the very heart of government, when activists of the far right and France's war veterans' organisations marched on Parliament, and the authority of the National Assembly hung in the balance.)

From Blanchot's own perspective, the reason for his radicalisation of the constitutional stance defended by the *Journal des débats* was a logical one. It was that the system of parliamentary democracy was based on similar abstract, juridical assumptions as the League of Nations itself; in both cases, Blanchot suggested, traditional pragmatism, tried and tested over the years, had given way to a politics based on the idolatry of abstract principles. Just as enthusiasts of the League of Nations were prepared to abandon the healthy scepticism of traditional diplomacy in preference for a dream of contractual harmony between states, so the proponents of parliamentary democracy seemed prepared to sacrifice the overriding need to defend the national interest on the altar of the increasingly vacuous principle of political representation. By clothing politics in a fog of moralistic unreality, the argument ran, legalistic principles served not to promote greater security, but merely to exacerbate the inherent weakness of

28

parliamentary democracy by compromising the need for decisive action. It followed therefore that if one rejected the juridical internationalism on which French foreign policy relied, one also had to refuse parliamentary democracy as well; in either case, the key point lay in recognising the existence of a prior imperative, more compelling than the attachment to fetishised conventions, which was the necessity to defend the future of the national community as such. And in order to meet that objective and to restore proper strength and authority to that community, it was essential not only to transform France's political relations with its neighbours, but also to rid the nation, by violence if necessary, of the debilitating effects of a system of parliamentary democracy which reduced the national interest to a sorry charade of factional, party rivalries. What was needed, unambiguously, was a radical, national, possibly violent revolution. This, at any rate, was the conclusion to which Blanchot came in a series of pieces published in the extremist press from 1932 to 1937.

It is important to realise here that Blanchot's relationship to political discourse throughout the 1930s was always, at least, a dual one. On the one hand, he maintained a regular – though anonymous – presence within the *Journal des débats*, defending with vigour a constitutional politics that, however dismissive it might be of government policy, always stopped short of recommending the violent overthrow of the régime. On the other hand, in a variety of marginal publications, Blanchot attached his name to a rather different discourse whose purpose was to challenge the very legitimacy of parliamentary democracy and to promote the cause of radical, violent revolution. Between these two discourses the relationship was a complex one; though plainly irreducible to one another, they were evidently not mutually exclusive, and it would be misleading to identify Blanchot himself, so to speak, simply with one rather than the other of these positions. In this respect, Blanchot was neither simply a revolutionary nor a constitutionalist, but in some sense always already both. To some extent, the preference for the one rather than the other at any one moment was probably a tactical one. It also has to be remembered that Blanchot was subject to the usual economic constraints of having to earn a living by his writing. But crucial to Blanchot's political evolution throughout the 1930s is the fact that, by holding simultaneously two divergent, dissymmetrical political discourses, he was able to appeal in his writing at one and the same time to two differentiated, incommensurable concepts of the political, which meant that neither discourse ever came to have hierarchical superiority over the other. Never, one may conclude, did Blanchot fall victim to the temptation of only ever subscribing to one single – totalising – political discourse; and it was this that arguably left him relatively immune to the lure of that vision of totalising immanence that some of his nationalist contemporaries found so compelling when they saw it embodied in the total (and totalitarian) states of fascist Italy or Nazi Germany.

Yet the continuity between these two political discourses professed by Blanchot was hardly seamless. Indeed, rather the reverse. Of the two, the first, which was massively present, though not exclusively so, in the editorials for the *Journal des débats*, corresponded to a concept of politics defined and understood as the day-to-day administration and management of the life of the community; while the second, mainly to be found in some, though not all, of the articles written for extremist journals, embodied a very different concept of politics, of which perhaps the most that can be said is that it functioned as an interruption or suspension of politics in that previous sense. What might be construed there, say, as a politics of the possible, founded on national memory, tradition, and continuity with the past, was interrupted here by a politics of the impossible, turned towards forgetting, refusal, and violent disgust with the present, and investing its enthusiasm in the promise of the future. There were inevitably many areas of antagonism between these two concepts of politics; but the most revealing difference had probably to do with the question of political force or violence. To justify the recourse to force, for instance, Blanchot, according to the first of these two concepts, needed only to refer the question to the criterion of the national interest: force was legitimate to the extent that it was exercised in the resolute defence of peace and for the benefit of the continuing survival of the national community. But the Blanchot of the second of his political discourses was not bound by such prior principles as these. Revolutionary violence is necessarily in excess of any existing legitimising, constitutional framework; its very function from Blanchot's perspective was to introduce into politics a hiatus within which everything might be founded anew; it had therefore to repudiate all existing constitutions in order to perform or invent the future and thereby (re)constitute, so to speak, a new politics, one that, before being established, had to pass through the stage of being a violent refusal of politics, an anti-politics and a non-politics, therefore, since the goal it fixed for itself was not that of safeguarding the present, but summoning up the future by invoking the infinite potential of revolution.

At this point, Blanchot's political project, like that of others among his contemporaries, becomes as daring as it was full of risks. While still preserving

– elsewhere – his resolute commitment to a politics of the present, he undertook to imagine the founding of a new politics. The responsibility for this new, revolutionary departure, based on revulsion at the debased character of the present, he entrusted in his writing, as did many others at the time, to youth, for only young people – no doubt like the 26-year-old Blanchot – were deemed to have the enthusiasm, appetite, grandeur, and potential for violence that might release them from the shackles attaching them to the present and the past. This revolution, in Blanchot's eyes, was a revolution whose spiritual and cultural potential far outstripped what, for instance, the Soviet Union had to offer, if only because the USSR by now had become, he argued, an enemy of radical revolution, a bureaucratic and totalitarian power dedicated to state tyranny.[7] For Blanchot the whole purpose of revolution was to introduce into politics and into history a violent hiatus; it was to suspend the claims of possibility by affirming the impossible, and it was to restore to the nation the effervescence it had lost by its acceptance of a decaying regime of parliamentary democracy. That such an act of political refoundation should be presented as necessarily violent was no more than logic or honesty demanded; and the risks this involved were ones that, at any rate in his political writing, Blanchot at the time thought it essential to confront.

In 1933, Blanchot became *rédacteur en chef* for a short-lived, polemical, independent nationalist daily called *Le Rempart*, which ran from mid-April till late August 1933. Owned and edited by Paul Lévy, *Le Rempart* was closely associated with the anti-government and fiercely anti-German policies of the maverick nationalist député Georges Mandel, who, it is said, supplied the paper with much of its inside information.[8] Throughout its brief duration, Blanchot contributed to *Le Rempart* a series of editorials and news items ranging widely over matters of internal and external policy. But two main motifs are typical of almost everything Blanchot published in the paper. First was a vehement insistence on the ever increasing threat to peace posed by the rise to power of Hitler. Blanchot was unyielding in his total and unconditional hostility to Hitler – whom he was to describe in 1935 as the 'representative of an unacceptable political doctrine' ('le représentant d'une doctrine politique inadmissible') – not only on the grounds that Hitler was pursuing the traditional objectives of German imperialism since Bismarck, but also because National-Socialism itself was no more than a 'perverted nationalism' ('un nationalisme perverti'), based on a 'mystical apotheosis of the nation' ('l'apothéose mystique de la nation'), owing more to religion than to politics and finding expression in many different

31

manipulative and demagogic initiatives, including, wrote Blanchot as early as May 1933, 'the barbarous persecution of the Jews' ('les persécutions barbares contre les juifs').[9] The second key topic present in Blanchot's contributions to *Le Rempart* was a deep-seated anger and disgust at the inadequacy of the response to the German threat made by France's centre-left government. And it was this in part that impelled Blanchot to call upon his readers to overthrow not only that government but the whole French parliamentary system of which it was an inevitable and natural product. Revolution here was no longer just desirable; it had become a necessity.

It was under that title, 'La Revolution nécessaire', that Blanchot published, in June 1933, one of the more programmatic and better-known pieces from *Le Rempart*'s brief existence. In it, in typically vitriolic vein, Blanchot lambasts the current parliamentary regime for its weakness, its sectarian divisions, and its irresponsibility in conspiring to squander the peace won at such cost in 1918. In these circumstances, he argued, France had only one chance of salvation; no hope could be placed in a corrupt parliamentary democracy, nor in materialistic capitalism, nor in dictatorial socialism, nor in communism, but only in spiritual revolution, or national revolution. Blanchot concluded:

> The spiritual revolution, the national revolution is no longer an image nor a symbol. With every day that passes, events bring it nearer, each day makes it ever more necessary. And, bit by bit, they tell us what it will be: hard, bloody, unjust, our last chance of salvation [dure, sanglante, injuste, notre dernière chance de salut].[10]

These are startling and, for some, shocking words. On one level, no doubt, their vehemence simply measures the degree of Blanchot's anger and impatience in 1933. But it is also important to understand the function of the violence Blanchot invokes here with such unproblematic zeal; for there are at least two reasons why Blanchot's article culminates in the way it does. First, it has to be recognised that Blanchot's words belong less to an established political discourse as such, than to a revolutionary, anti-political, even extra-political one. In writing words such as these, Blanchot's aim is not to describe but to prophesy, not to state but to perform; it is, in anticipation of real events, to effect already, by linguistic means, the political hiatus, the abeyance or vacancy of power that he identifies here as revolution. While that abeyance lasts, however, it can be subject to no constitutional principle or legal system; and this is why the revolution will necessarily be unjust, but also the reason why the purpose of radical revolution is to embody both a hope and a promise: as Blanchot had put it only a few lines before: 'our greatest hope today is that for a free nation, for the defence of man, for culture, will rise up the magnificent promise of revolution' ('notre plus grande espérance aujourd'hui, c'est que pour une nation libre, pour la défense de l'homme, pour les biens de l'esprit, se lève la promesse magnifique de la révolution').

There is also a second reason for this rhapsodic invocation of revolutionary violence; this is directly related to the question: what revolution? In *Le Rempart* and elsewhere, Blanchot is quick to state what this revolution is *not*: it is not, for instance, a Marxist transfer of power from one class to another based on 'the myth of collectivism' ('le mythe du collectivisme') and culminating, Soviet-style, in 'the monstrous dictatorship of the State' ('la monstrueuse dictature de l'État'); but neither is it a fascist or Hitlerite irrationalism imposing on its subjects the 'idol of all-powerful community' ('l'idole de la communauté toute-puissante') and whipping up their frenzied enthusiasm in the name of the 'mystical apotheosis of the nation' mentioned earlier.[11] All that can be said about Blanchot's revolution of 1933 is that it will be animated by a violent, visceral refusal of all forms of servitude and of representation, and carried out in the name of national freedom, man, and culture. These words are of course empty ones; what they signal is that the ends of Blanchot's revolution, unlike the sham pseudo-affairs of Hitler or Stalin, cannot be prescribed in advance by political discourse. The revolution is nothing other than the violence of its own unmediated effervescence and the ferment of its own irreducible self-presence. The promise of revolution is precisely what it claims to be: a promise, and as such it cannot be converted into ready currency; for its only mode of existence lies in its futurity and its absence from any system of political representation. And this is why the appeal to violence looms so large in Blanchot's political journalism of the 1930s as a whole, for violence – or, more precisely, one particular kind of violence – is the only manifestation of futurity that political discourse will allow.

In February 1936, Blanchot's name appeared once more on the cover of an extremist nationalist monthly, edited by Thierry Maulnier and Jean de Fabrègues, both influential protagonists of the Jeune Droite movement some years earlier.[12] This new journal was entitled *Combat*, and it owed its launch in January 1936 to the tense political climate in France surrounding the forthcoming elections in April and May. With its extreme nationalism, its anti-materialism, its anti-communism, its anti-capitalism, its hostility to parliamentary democracy, its endorsement of social and spiritual revolution, and its intermittent anti-semitism, the journal, which by December 1936 was proudly claiming a thousand subscribers, has been described by some recent commentators as being largely fascist in intent, though *Combat* itself did not explicitly identify itself as such.[13] Inevitably, like many of the journals of the extreme right at the time, *Combat* was based on an unstable coalition between contending personalities and policies; indeed, Robert Brasillach, who contributed regularly to the journal during the first fifteen months of its operation, and who was already by 1936 a committed fascist and anti-semite, was to complain how the involvement of various liberal intellectuals in *Combat*, in his words, 'spoiled matters' and caused him to withdraw from the journal after March 1937.[14]

Blanchot's own contribution to *Combat* comprises a total of eight articles; published from February 1936 to December 1937, all belong to the first two of the journal's three-and-a-half years of existence. In many respects, Blanchot's articles were in much the same vein as those for *Le Rempart*. Violently polemical, full of paradox and rhetorical reversal, they pursue with undiminished vehemence many of the topics dealt with by Blanchot in his other journalism of the period, including the necessity of decisive action abroad to stem German expansion, and the call for radical, violent revolution at home. In 'La Guerre pour rien', for instance, of March 1936, Blanchot castigated the centre-left government for its illogicality in having concluded the previous May what he saw as a vacuous treaty of mutual assistance with the Soviet Union – a state with which France had few, if any, interests in common – with the result, in Blanchot's view, that France was being exposed, in defence of the Soviet Union, to the eventuality of a needless war in which France had no part.

Pursuing the same logic, the following month he lambasted the regime for its reliance – even after the crisis of 7 March – on a foreign policy based on continued support for the League of Nations. Such failings, Blanchot contended, were the inevitable consequence of a system of parliamentary government that lent greater weight to party intrigue than the national interest. By July, after the election of the Popular Front, in a notorious article entitled 'Le Terrorisme, méthode de salut public', Blanchot was arguing once more not only in favour of nationalist rebellion but violent revolution as well. This was the only course of action, he maintained, that was likely to reawaken the French nation from its slumber, and he defended the initiative by pointing to the collapse of all other forms of opposition to the government and by affirming that the interest of the many justified, on the part of the few, the resolute recourse to terrorist acts aimed at bringing down the regime. Was Blanchot's endorsement of violence more rhetorical than real? Was the purpose simply to shock, or was it to lend political support to the growing, menacing street violence of the period? This is difficult to say. Blanchot's invective, at any rate, fell on deaf ears, and by November 1937 he had concluded, in a piece entitled 'La France, nation à venir', that it was the French nation itself that had gone missing and lived on only as a ghostly memory and an ever vaguer hope. The future, it seemed, truly did now belong to the future, a future that was increasingly intangible or remote.

Between these two articles for *Combat*, from January till October 1937, Blanchot was involved, alongside Maulnier and others, in another journalistic venture. This was *L'Insurgé*, a weekly broadsheet that was funded by Jacques Lemaigre-Dubreuil, of the vegetable oil manufacturer Lesieur, but which had no titular *directeur* or *rédacteur en chef*, which was one reason for its often disparate and at times contradictory editorial stance.[15] Much like *Combat*, though with a more eager concentration on daily political events, *L'Insurgé* defended a violently nationalist, anti-parliamentary, anti-capitalist, anti-communist, revolutionary syndicalist agenda; and much like *Combat*, too, it printed, during its brief existence, its share of intermittent anti-semitic diatribes and cartoons, mostly directed at Léon Blum and his government.[16] Blanchot's involvement in the paper was constant and protracted. Throughout the virtual entirety of its ten-month existence, he wrote a weekly book review, as well as contributing, during the paper's first six months, a regular political column, which suddenly all but stopped after the fall of Blum's government in late June.

In his political texts for *L'Insurgé* Blanchot returns to many of the foreign policy issues discussed by him elsewhere; perhaps the only notable change, however, is in Blanchot's language, which, in *L'Insurgé*, becomes even more violently reactive and vitriolic than ever before. The shift in tone is revealing. Gone is the peculiar optimism of *Le Rempart*; gone, too, is the clear hope that by decisive action war might ultimately be averted. Their place is taken by an even more anguished and desperate polemic against France's parliamentary government. On one level the change is no doubt a direct measure – in Blanchot's estimation – of the ever-increasing probability of war, a war France seemed likely to lose; while on another it is a clear indication that, despite Blanchot's appeals for a violent national revolt to sweep away the government, there was no viable, alternative political force left in France that might fulfil that role. France, for Blanchot, was being precipitated headlong into war by the irresponsibility of its own elected government and there seemed little chance the threat might be avoided. It was as though France itself had now fallen into unknown depths of degradation and abjection, France itself that stood dishonoured and divorced from its past, France itself that had fallen victim to a sorry process of separation and decline. All that France now inspired was disgust; and disgust here, for Blanchot, like refusal, was still a revolutionary sentiment; the only hope it held out, however, was that of a violent rejection of what was, and there seemed little prospect of what might be in the future.

A question of responsibility

I will put it more precisely: that Céline may have been a writer in the grip of a delusion does not make him antipathetic to me, but this delusion expressed itself in anti-semitism; delusion, here, excuses nothing; all anti-semitism is in the last resort a delusion, and anti-semitism, even if it is a delusion, remains *the capital error*.

(Je dirai plus précisément: que Céline ait été un écrivain livré au délire ne me le rend pas antipathique, mais ce délire s'exprima par l'antisémitisme; le délire, ici, n'excuse rien; tout antisémitisme est finalement un délire, et l'antisémitisme, serait-il délirant, reste *la faute capitale*.)

Letter to Raymond Bellour (1966)

In recent years, as some readers will be aware, Blanchot has been severely taken to task by a number of commentators for his involvement in *Combat* and *L'Insurgé*; and the claim has repeatedly been made that in his political journalism of the period, in the unnecessarily coy words of Tzvetan Todorov, Blanchot 'assumed the role of spokesman for a certain anti-semitism'.[1] The charge is of course a serious one; if proven, it might be felt to damage irreparably the credibility of what Blanchot has to say on the subject of Judaism and about the Holocaust in his texts of the 1960s and 1970s. But what is most startling of all about the accusation that Blanchot himself professed anti-semitic views in the 1930s is that, to date, no evidence of any real substance has ever been produced to support it. At most, the charge rests on a particular interpretation of no more than four articles published by Blanchot in 1936 and 1937. In two of these cases (the articles entitled 'Après le coup de force germanique' and 'Le Terrorisme, méthode de salut public' that appeared in *Combat* for April and July 1936, respectively) what is at issue are two blunt, even crudely polemical references to the reckless impatience – as Blanchot saw it at the time – of those Jewish émigrés to whom Blanchot refers, with peremptory violence, as 'unbridled Jews' ('des Juifs déchaînés') who, in 1936, wanted to declare immediate war on Hitler, irrespective of the chances of success or the human cost of such a policy.[2] Elsewhere, there are a limited number of passages in L'Insurgé that it is possible to read as drawing in some measure on some of the standard themes of anti-semitic invective; this might be said to be the case, for instance when, in an article entitled, ironically, 'Blum, notre chance de salut . . .', Blanchot refers to Léon Blum – a Jew – as representing 'a backward ideology, a decrepit mentality, a foreign breed' ('une idéologie arriérée, une mentalité de vieillard, une race étrangère'), although, in the context in which the phrase appears, it is more immediately apparent that Blanchot is condemning Blum for his internationalism and support for the Soviet Union rather than attempting to make polemical capital out of his Judaism.[3]

It is true, of course, that there is another, more general dimension to the charge of anti-semitism, which has to do with Blanchot's overall involvement in at least two publications, Combat and L'Insurgé, which, on occasion, if not systematically, did give a platform to anti-semitic views. To some extent this is hardly surprising. Anti-semitism was endemic in the French right and extreme right at the time, and was of course far from unknown in left-wing circles as well; and one might argue in mitigation of Blanchot that having to face the possibility of finding one's own name printed alongside views with which one might, at times, violently disagree was one of the risks the writer had to take if he wanted to be a political journalist at all. In contributing to Combat and L'Insurgé Blanchot was plainly running this risk; and there is every reason to suppose he was both aware of that fact and, up to a certain point, prepared to accept that, in the eyes of his readers, his own name might become associated, albeit indirectly, with some form of anti-semitic discourse. This risk of contagion from anti-semitism was by definition always possible, and though there is no evidence whatsoever that Blanchot was even remotely sympathetic to the anti-semitism of some of the articles that did appear in L'Insurgé, it is clear that these did not discourage him from contributing to the paper in one way or another during the virtual entirety of its existence. Much the same could be said of Blanchot's texts for Combat; and though he eventually withdrew from the magazine after December 1937, Blanchot must nevertheless be reckoned to be fully responsible before that date for allowing his own texts to appear in that magazine, as they frequently did, alongside those of an anti-semite such as Robert Brasillach. Indeed, Blanchot himself concedes as much when he explained in a letter to Diane Rubenstein in 1983 that one of the conditions he laid down for his participation in *Combat* was the assurance that Brasillach would not be involved in it.[4]

Anti-semitism, then, as Blanchot was well aware, was always present in some form or another in *Combat* and *L'Insurgé*, if not over his signature, then at least sometimes alongside it; and this is the reason, as Blanchot implicitly acknowledges in his 1984 letter to Laporte, that it is of course possible to read as indirectly anti-semitic both the two references to the Jews in his pieces for *Combat* and the ambiguous language used in one or two further articles for *L'Insurgé*. To the extent that the threat of contagion by anti-semitism could never be contained, Blanchot must therefore be held responsible for acquiescing up to a certain point in the anti-semitic language intermittently used in those publications. The possible association of his name with some form of anti-semitic discourse seems therefore to have been a price that, up to a certain point, in 1936 and 1937, Blanchot the journalist was prepared to pay; and if this was the case, it is likely that it was because other political issues at the time seemed urgent enough to warrant the compromise.

But how far was Blanchot prepared to acquiesce in the anti-semitism of some of those around him? There is some evidence that when, in late October 1937, *L'Insurgé* closed down, it was Blanchot who was chiefly responsible for terminating the venture, and that one of his key motives for doing so was the increasing prevalence of anti-semitism in the paper, as evidenced, in what turned out to be the final issue of *L'Insurgé*, by one venomous, though hardly uncharacteristic diatribe by Charles Deleuze, the paper's sports correspondent, against Jean Zay, then Jewish-sports and education minister.[5] For his part, Blanchot's own last contribution to the paper, printed in this final issue, was by way of a more radical leave-taking: what it announced was the need for revolutionaries of all political hues to dismantle the binary paradigm of current political action in order to affirm a common future owing nothing to the nationalism of the nation state or the communism of the Soviet Union. Blanchot's involvement in *Combat* ended in much the same way some weeks later, in December 1937, with a piece which similarly put forward a proposal for a new politics based on a radical redefinition of nationalist as well as revolutionary thinking. Taken together, both pieces amounted to something of an abandonment of any kind of conventional politics, even of the kind espoused by the two publications in which the articles appeared. At any event, as far as the issue of anti-semitism was concerned, Blanchot had by then made his own

38

priorities clear by returning to work alongside Paul Lévy as *rédacteur en chef* of the satirical, independent nationalist weekly, *Aux écoutes*.[6]

The charge of anti-semitism is not the only one to be levelled at Blanchot's pre-war journalism. Some have argued that what is in fact more troubling is the extent to which, in his articles for *Combat* and *L'Insurgé*, Blanchot endorses extremist acts of anti-parliamentary, anti-democratic violence; and it is certainly true that he does show little restraint in calling for the overthrow – by whatever means necessary – of the regime, or, for instance, on one occasion, drily envisaging the violent dispatch of those Communist Party leaders pronounced guilty of betraying both the revolution and their country.[7] Perhaps most provocative of all in this respect – as the text of the article implicitly concedes – is the article entitled 'Le Terrorisme, méthode de salut public', published in *Combat* in July 1936. In the article, written at a time when – Blanchot argued – parliamentary opposition to the Popular Front was ineffectual, and real political debate had become stifled beneath a hollow and oppressive consensus, Blanchot felt justified in appealing, parsimoniously, to a limited campaign of violence which would put an end to the politics of parliamentary complacency and demonstrate the urgent necessity for a more robust defence of France's national interest.

It is important to note that the purpose of such violence was self-evidently not to install fascist dictatorship in France nor to impose a small nationalist clique in government, but rather to interrupt a specific type of oppressive parliamentary politics and thus to allow the possibility of a different political future. So if Blanchot endorsed acts of terror in the piece, it was solely in order to deliver, as he put it, to the very people who might be ready to condemn them – the French electorate at large – the benefits of such an interruption. The purpose was to perform remedial surgery on the body politic. This is why the benefits of such violent action, according to Blanchot, would be primarily therapeutic: a dead or decaying political system would be destroyed, root and branch, and the life of the national community as such would be restored to proper vitality. To this extent, the violence Blanchot was invoking was not directed towards any seizure of power as such; its goal was more symbolic than real, and consisted more in the need to provide the nation with a vivid token or figure of the fundamental illegitimacy of the elected democratic government and the regime it represented. What was clearly at stake here, in Blanchot's view, as it had been in *Le Rempart*, was the future of the nation as illuminated by the futurity of revolution; and it was no doubt a calculated move on the writer's part that the acts of terror he advocated in the article were justified – at least in Blanchot's presentation – by an unmistakable reference back to the memory of Danton, Robespierre, and St-Just, those earlier revolutionaries of 1793, who, in similar times of national crisis, set up a more famous Comité du Salut Public, or Committee of Public Safety, to defend the nation against the challenge from within and aggression from without, and eventually embarked on a campaign of terror whose purpose was the saving of the Jacobin revolution.

If Blanchot's article espouses terrorism, it was in order to effect a political or historical hiatus; indeed, such a hiatus was indispensable if politics was to be refashioned anew. But what kind of refashioning did Blanchot have in mind? Part of the answer comes in his farewell article to *Combat* in December 1937, which appeared under the title 'On demande des dissidents'. The conclusion is as follows:

> In reality what counts is not being above parties, but against them. It is not to take up the vulgar slogan: neither right nor left, but to be really against the right and against the left. It is evident in these circumstances that the true form of dissidence is that which abandons one position without ceasing to observe the same hostility towards the opposite position or rather which abandons it in order to accentuate this hostility. A true communist dissident is the one who leaves communism, not in order to move closer to capitalist beliefs, but to define the true conditions of struggle against capitalism. In the same way, the true nationalist dissident is the one who neglects the traditional formulas of nationalism, not in order to move closer to internationalism but to combat internationalism in all its forms, including the economy and the nation itself. These two specimens of dissidence seem to us to be equally useful. But they also seem equally rare. Dissidents wanted.[8]

Citing this passage, one influential commentator, Zeev Sternhell, describes it as 'a perfect definition of fascist thinking'; and Jeffrey Mehlman, quoting Sternhell, has taken it as conclusive proof of Blanchot's pre-war commitment to fascism.[9] Summarising the passage, however, Sternhell significantly misconstrues Blanchot's position in the article by portraying it as proposing a political synthesis between left and right, an interpretation he glosses by adducing a quotation from Drieu La Rochelle's *Socialisme fasciste* of 1934 to the effect that fascism is a politics not of equilibrium or oscillation between left and right, but of fusion.

This notion of fusion is supplied here, however, entirely by Sternhell, and is not to be found at all in Blanchot's actual text. Indeed, the very point of Blanchot's article lies in its rejection of all political parties – of whatever political colouration – as vehicles for radical political change. What it proposes, with some irony, is not fascism, therefore, but, to the extent that they rely on a principle of political representation, the destruction of all political parties in general. By describing Blanchot's article as fascist, it would seem that Sternhell is in some danger of entirely misrepresenting the politics of radical dissidence Blanchot attempts to put forward in the article. For what Blanchot envisages, and what marks, so to speak, his own entry into dissidence – and which is also the reason he specifically rejects the 'vulgar slogan' that gives Sternhell's book its title and main thesis – is not a transcending of right and left or a merging of right and left within some third force akin to the mystified nationalism of Nazi Germany. It is something more complex, that involves a radicalisation of the differences between left and right as well as a fundamental redefinition of all inherited forms of nationalism and communism.

One may doubt of course how and to what extent a programme such as this may be realisable at all in practical political terms; at any event it is clear that Blanchot's programme was designed not to consolidate the political synthesis between left and right that, according to Sternhell, is the hallmark of fascism or National-Socialism, but rather to shatter the totality which such an organic synthesis would aim to embody. The aim is not to fuse right with left, but rather to call into question the whole principle of political representation that would make such fusion possible. This, of course, is why rather than with the prospect of a new, unified political movement, Blanchot's article ends up not with one, but two disparate and irreconcilable forms of dissidence, and with an endorsement of the principle of critical rarefaction rather than of mass mobilisation. What Blanchot's parting manifesto sets out in this way, then, is not a recipe for fascism, as Sternhell maintains, but something more clearly resembling a destruction of representational politics in all of its received forms.

Any challenge on this scale to the stability of inherited political discourse, as Blanchot acknowledges, is necessarily founded on an act of radical, violent refusal. But violence, according to Blanchot, is inherent in politics; indeed, as I have argued, the two are for Blanchot like the two sides of the same coin. Admittedly, there are many different kinds of violence. But what is it, one may ask, about the therapeutically destructive violence of the kind recommended by Blanchot that distinguishes it from the violence being done to the nation by parliamentary democracy or from the violence of war itself? To these questions Blanchot provides in fact only a partial answer; for what justifies the revolutionary recourse to violence in Blanchot's texts is not so much the national interest, which necessarily has to be suspended by the hiatus in politics that the revolution effects, but rather the purity of the act of refusal itself (and this is why, in some of the later texts in *Combat* and *L'Insurgé*, Blanchot often seems to write not as a nationalist, but a violent anti-nationalist). 'Refusal tolerates no conditions,' Blanchot wrote in 1933, 'except that of never recanting.'[10]

However, with regard to some of the texts it is supposed to govern, the purity of this refusal is arguably far less radical than Blanchot's project required. For as Jacques Derrida has convincingly argued, any act of foundational or refoundational violence is necessarily always already iterative.[11] To the extent that the violence of refusal, by interrupting politics, offers itself up as the foundation and beginning for a new politics, it inevitably always already forms part of that new politics; the act of rebellion turns retrospectively into an act of foundation and the act of refusal becomes an act of assertion or endorsement. The implications of this reversal are serious ones for Blanchot's political project, for they show with what ease the violence of refusal may be inverted and take on the mantle of a very different type of violence, a violence committed not on behalf of the nation or its people but against it. What at one stage may be construed as a pure interruption *of* politics necessarily runs the risk of turning out to have been only an impure episode *in* politics. So, however much the article on terrorism, for instance, may be read as a defence of the promise of the future against the oppressive, dictatorial violence of a sham parliamentary consensus, it is always possible – and necessary – for the piece to be read or misread as endorsing a mode of violence that, far from interrupting a violent politics, turns out to have already been contaminated by that which it sought to oppose. At the very point he was evidently seeking to break out of the cycle of the repressive politics of representation, there was every danger that Blanchot might end up, in his extremist journalism, appearing merely to propose a mirror image of that politics. There is – and was – always the risk that the endeavour to put a violent end to a politics of violence might itself be metamorphosed into just another sequence in the violence of that politics. And rather than being the opponent of oppressive violence, it is therefore always possible – and necessary – for the Blanchot of *Combat* and *L'Insurgé* to be read in fact as simply another exponent of the self-same political violence.

42

A deep and worrying instability, then, affects the whole of Blanchot's revolutionary project; and this is surely one reason why that particular project was pursued by him only intermittently, in moments of great national complacency or crisis. The risks involved, however, were not contingent ones; for, as Blanchot recognised, there could be no politics at all without the necessary recourse to force or violence. So, while it is simplistic to describe Blanchot as an apologist for terrorism, it is evident that the unstable violence of *Combat* and *L'Insurgé* was far from an aberration on Blanchot's part. At any event, the uncontrollable political equivocation inherent in his texts for *Combat* and *L'Insurgé* marks a clear limit to Blanchot's revolutionary nationalist project of the 1930s. One symptom of that limit is the concept of the nation itself; and it is striking that throughout the 1930s, as he rejects all forms of political or parliamentary representation in the name of the promise of future revolution, Blanchot conceives of that future almost exclusively in terms of the self-presence of the nation, that is, beyond representation, the nation's self-identity and proximity to itself as political subject and origin. Throughout, it is the nation in arms that operates in Blanchot's discourse as the only acceptable or credible agent of political action and the ultimate source of legitimacy for any politics at all.[12]

Though understandable in the context of continental Europe after the First World War, this deep attachment to the nation as the subject of history nonetheless severely dates and limits the whole of Blanchot's thinking in that period, and inscribes it within a certain political, ideological, and philosophical closure, a closure in relation to which the other – the future – is thought of only in terms of the concept of nation as source of identity. What this suggests is that the crucial blind spot of Blanchot's politics throughout the 1930s was the failure to think of the question of community except in terms of homogeneous nationhood, and to conceive of futurity not in relation to the alterity of writing, as he would do later, but by recourse to a concept that, despite Blanchot's strenuous efforts to make it appear otherwise, it is difficult to understand in any other way than 'primarily as tradition, order, certainty, truth, and every form of rootedness' (*PA*, 9; 2), in short, in terms of those very concepts that, gathered under the rubric of the relation to being, writing itself will later put into question.

Which is why, on the one hand, Blanchot is right to disown the texts from *Combat* and *L'Insurgé* that carry his name; and why, on the other, it is nothing less than a measure of Blanchot's philosophical rigour and fundamental probity that the question that comes to dominate the whole of his post-war thinking, with regard to literature, philosophy, and politics, beyond the concept of subject or nation, is the question of the Other and the question of community, and the question of that responsibility to the Other and for the Other which founds, but thereby also precedes, the law.

The acts of the day (2)

[Drieu La Rochelle] renewed his previous offer to me [i.e. that Blanchot take over editorial responsibility for the *Nouvelle Revue française*]. I refused absolutely, saying: I could not ask writers to collaborate on a journal for which I myself would not wish to write. We went our separate ways, and I did not see him again, except once, in late '43 or early '44, when I came across him on the Champs Élysées. He told me: 'So it was you that was right. They really are too stupid' (I imagine he meant the occupying forces or the collaborators). I replied: it's not a matter of stupidity, but horror.

Letter to Jeffrey Mehlman (26 November 1979)

By early 1938, to all intents and purposes, Blanchot had abandoned the discourse of nationalist revolution he had been pursuing, at regular intervals, since the beginning of the decade; but he still continued to work as *rédacteur en chef* for both the *Journal des débats* and *Aux écoutes*. At any event, 1938 was a watershed for other reasons; for late in September that year Chamberlain and Daladier, though they pretended differently to their electorates, set the final seal on the policy of appeasement of Hitler and, as Blanchot and others had predicted, launched Europe on the inevitable path to war. Admittedly, this view of Munich was not universally shared at the time; the agreement which forced Czechoslovakia to cede to Hitler the German-speaking territories along its western border with Germany was hailed by many on the French right as a resounding success. Maulnier, in *Combat*, for instance, though still deeply critical of the parliamentary system as such, applauded the government for averting the immediate threat of war.[1] The *Journal des débats*, however, was much less sanguine. Though the paper was strongly in favour of closer Franco–British collaboration, and though it took the view that the issue of the Sudeten Germans could be resolved peacefully, it also recognised that Hitler remained a threat, and concluded that the most urgent priority was for the Western democracies to arm in expectation of war.

The response from *Aux écoutes*, which had formerly been sympathetic to *Combat* and had greeted its launch in January 1936 with some enthusiasm, was more outspoken still. One unsigned editorial, for 10 September 1938, complained that 'There have been too many gentle words when what was needed was robust language.' A fortnight later, Paul Lévy delivered the paper's considered verdict: in preparing to appease Hitler, he wrote, Britain and France had 'suffered the most serious defeat in their history'; elsewhere in the same issue, with evident approval, the paper cited Churchill's famous remark, pronounced before a group of Czech journalists a few days before, to the effect that 'France and Britain had to choose between war and shame. They chose shame, and they will get war, too.'[2] It is true that this hostility to Munich on the part of Lévy and Blanchot was hardly unexpected, for it was entirely consistent with everything the two men had written throughout the whole of the preceding decade; no-one was surprised, therefore, least of all *Je suis partout*, which could only think of accusing Lévy of being a war-mongerer.

Two-and-a-half years later, in the months leading up to France's defeat by the German army, Blanchot was still writing for the *Journal des débats* and *Aux écoutes*. But when defeat came, the *Journal des débats*, like many other titles, withdrew to Clermont-Ferrand. For his part, François de Wendel, writing to de Nalèche in a letter of 24 July 1940, made plain his wish in the circumstances to see the paper die a natural, honourable death, and withdrew his financial backing; the *directeur*, however, for private reasons, decided to keep the paper going and, after a brief interval, it began appearing again from offices in Clermont-Ferrand, from where, with financial support from the Vichy government, which it received together with all the other official Vichy newspapers, and in spite of the disapproval of de Wendel, it continued to appear regularly till mid-August 1944.[3] There is evidence that Blanchot too made strenuous representations to persuade de Nalèche to suspend publication; and though he persisted up until the fall of France in writing for the *Journal des débats*, he was increasingly to find his editorials censored or refused, leaving Blanchot little option than to withdraw at that point from all political involvement in the paper.

With *Aux écoutes*, the situation was initially much the same. It too retreated to Clermont-Ferrand and, by mid-July, began appearing again; however, instead of the (Jewish) name of Lévy, it now carried that of Blanchot (as *directeur*) on its masthead, and Blanchot continued in this role as Lévy's proxy till the end of the month, bringing out two further editions. Only three more issues appeared, however, in August, without Blanchot's name; and shortly afterwards the paper folded entirely, subject to a censorship order from Laval.[4] During the brief interregnum of late July, Blanchot, while paying lip service to the new Vichy ideology of national revolution, seems to have attempted to gain for the paper enough latitude to allow it to explain to its readers, for instance, how, a week before the armistice, high-level discussions had taken place between Churchill and the French Prime Minister Paul Reynaud concerning a plan for the creation of a single Franco–British Union under which France would be declared an integral part of Britain. Had it been accepted, the plan would have guaranteed what the paper referred to, approvingly, as the 'relentless pursuit of the struggle' ('la continuation acharnée de la lutte') against the occupier.[5] However, despite the support of Reynaud, the initiative failed, and France, instead, alone amongst the occupied countries of Europe, embarked upon a policy of overt collaboration with the enemy.

There is little public record of Blanchot's actions during the Occupation; but what is known suggests that throughout that period Blanchot followed a dual strategy of endeavouring on the one hand to maintain some kind of public role for himself within the literary and cultural sphere, while on the other safeguarding, as much as was possible, his intellectual independence. The result was a series of short-lived initiatives on Blanchot's part, such as his brief involvement early in 1941 with the Jeune France cultural association, and also, in 1942, his readiness, temporarily, to support Paulhan in his scheme to regain editorial control over the *Nouvelle Revue française*, which since the defeat had been under the collaborationist editorship of Drieu La Rochelle, a ploy which at the very least had the effect of destabilising the journal and hastening its demise by July 1943.[6] In both cases, it seems, though determined in the first instance to explore the possibilities for cultural intervention, Blanchot quickly withdrew his co-operation as soon as those limits became too constricting. And when, to a large degree for personal financial reasons, it seems, he agreed to resume writing for the *Journal des débats*, which he did for three-and-a-half years, from 16 April 1941 until 17 August 1944, eight days before the Liberation, it was to contribute only a regular weekly book review to the paper and not to endorse its generally enthusiastic support for the politics of Vichy. In December 1943, some fifty of these pieces, many extensively edited, together with three other articles and an unpublished introduction, and at least one article which had previously fallen foul of Vichy censorship, were brought together, at the suggestion of Gaston Gallimard, in what was to be Blanchot's first volume of critical essays, *Faux Pas*, a title chosen, Blanchot later wrote, to reflect the fact that *Faux Pas* really was a false move.[7]

A temptation?

> Literature contemplates itself in revolution, it finds its justification in it, and if it has
> been called Terror, this is because its ideal is indeed that moment in history when 'life
> endures death and maintains itself in it' in order to secure from it the possibility and
> truth of speech. This is the 'question' that seeks to realise itself in literature, and
> which is its being.
>
> La Littérature et le droit à la mort' (*PF*, 311; 321–2)

Writing in *Critique*, in November 1947, under the title 'Le Règne animal de
l'esprit' ('The Spiritual Animal Kingdom'), borrowed for the occasion from
Hegel's *Phenomenology of Spirit*, Blanchot speaks of a temptation (*PF*, 308; 318).
The temptation arises, Blanchot puts it, when literature and history appear to
coincide in one absolute, seemingly apocalyptic interval, when the suspended
event of writing finds itself mirrored and justified in the pure advent of
revolutionary Terror. At such a moment, writes Blanchot, freedom and death
are as one, the possibility of death becomes inseparable from the possibility of
life, and absolute negation speaks with the same authority as absolute
affirmation. Between Blanchot the revolutionary journalist during the 1930s and
Blanchot the literary critic of the post-war years, the parallels, as Blanchot
himself seems to imply, are compelling; and it may seem as though, obliquely
and in retrospect, Blanchot is seeking to legitimise some of his pre-war political
decisions by associating with them a belief in the radical, contestatory force of
literature itself.

But there is here a crucial difference. Though writing may find its justification
in revolutionary violence, its goal is in fact not justification, but justice; and
though it may find itself mirrored in the spectacle of the Terror, its aim is not
self-reflection, but disappearance. Literature is irreducible to the sovereignty
that comes from absolute power; the only injunction to which it falls subject is
that of its own effacement, absence, and radical exteriority to power and
possibility. If literature, for Blanchot, belongs to destruction, it is because its
role is not to assert authority, but to contest all authority, including its own.
Unlike the dangerously ambiguous texts of 1936 and 1937, always liable to find
themselves re-inscribed within a discourse reliant on the political self-presence
of the nation, literature here retains a reserve and distance that renders it
irreducible to the political simplification that threatens and ultimately
disqualifies those early political texts. For if it is true that literature, like
death, seizes itself paroxystically within the immediacy of a paramount moment
of absolute freedom, as the rhetoric of terror would suggest, it is also the case

that literature, like death, is an encounter with the limitless impossibility of that moment, and with the lack of power that leaves writing forever suspended as an absent event that can never properly come to be, since the only domain it occupies is the domain of worklessness, impotence, and disaster.

To compare Blanchot's extremist texts of the 1930s with the texts on literature written after the war is to be struck irresistibly by apparent similarity and irreducible difference. Here as there, a principle of representation or mediation is being challenged in the name of the effervescent immediacy of a terrible and sublime moment. But where the pre-war political writings fall victim to the contagious effects of an unmediated nationalism that, in its very appeal to the future self-presence of the nation, is in fact, though it may not itself be aware of this, just another discourse of political representation, literature turns aside from the temptation of such a moment to resist the lure of immediacy. Literature, so to speak, maintains a discretion that Blanchot's political texts, in their impatience to realise themselves, were never able or willing to display, which was why they were always vulnerable to compromise, liable to be contaminated by the very violence they claimed to challenge. For its part, literature refuses that contamination; and what Blanchot's account of literature and terror in 1947 shows is the extent to which, if Blanchot's polemical texts of 1936 and 1937 failed, it was not because they were extreme, but because they were in a sense never extreme enough; it was not because they refused a certain legitimate politics, but because their refusal of that politics was in fact never pure enough, and because the interval they sought to effect in politics was never separate enough from the politics of representation for Blanchot to envisage a politics no longer founded on the concept of nationhood and on the future self-presence of the nation as the model par excellence of community as such.

Between 1937 and 1947, much that defies words had somehow taken place: France's defeat and Occupation, the Second World War, the resistance, the discovery of the death camps, the beginnings of the cold war. During that period, Blanchot seems to have spent the bulk of his time writing: writing the weekly essays that were to be partially collected in *Faux Pas* and the numerous articles that established his reputation as a critic shortly after the war; writing too the novels *Thomas l'Obscur, Aminadab,* and *Le Très-Haut,* not to forget the thick manuscript confiscated in 1944 that Blanchot mentions in *L'Instant de ma mort* (*IM,* 15). This discrepancy between public script and private scribbling may appear immense. But it is also somewhat deceptive. For what Blanchot arguably

48

came to understand in the course of this protracted exposure to writing, from the late 1930s onwards, was not only the extent to which the political discourse to which he, like many other thinkers and writers of the non-conformist right, had appealed in his pre-war revolutionary texts had been covertly, indeed primarily, an aesthetic one; but also, more importantly, that this grounding of the political in aesthetics had relied on an ultimately untenable conception of the work of art as a form of deferred self-presence.

For such had largely been the view of literature put forward by Blanchot in the many book reviews he contributed throughout 1937 to *L'Insurgé*, the main purpose of which, he wrote at the time, was to deal with such works as were distinguished by 'a certain indifference to futile things, of which there are many, a certain pride which forces them to refuse common resources, a certain ruthlessness towards themselves and towards ourselves'.[1] As these lines suggest, the literary critical standpoint adopted by Blanchot at the time was primarily an aesthetics of refusal, an aesthetics that privileged in the work of art its ability to contest all forms of social and political representation by the immediacy of its own self-presence. The position was of course not merely an aesthetic one; much the same view informed Blanchot's political texts for *Combat* and *L'Insurgé*, which were also devoted to the attempt to discredit all current forms of political and social representation in order to affirm, beyond representation, the possibilities and potential of France's future self-presence as a nation. In both the aesthetic and the more properly political sphere, the message then was largely the same; and there is an evident logic in the fact that Blanchot, in his literary critical essays at the time, may be found affirming in the work of art the voluntaristic purity of a future act of politico-aesthetic refoundation.

But in Blanchot's case, aesthetic ideology and the practice of literature soon parted company. As Blanchot was quickly to discover in writing his own early novels, to rely on a view of literature that privileges foundation over the responsiveness to alterity and asserts the identity of a subject over the contestation that comes from the Other is to cling to an impoverished, and in the end untenable conception of art. It is to prefer an illusory idea of art's self-sufficiency and autonomy to the radical questions raised by the possibility – or impossibility – of the work of art as such; and it is to repress the realisation, as Blanchot himself was subsequently to demonstrate, that art and literature are necessarily deeply inimical to all notions of cultural foundation or beginning, all conceptions of artistic truth or essence. The years between 1937 and 1947 were plainly eventful ones. But perhaps the most decisive factor of all that makes the

49

Blanchot of 1947 no longer the Blanchot of 1937 is simply that, in the interval, the writer had begun at last to take seriously his own experience as a novelist, and to abandon the lingering commitment to the project of (re)founding, in literature, the self-presence of the French nation. The shift was no doubt not a chance event, but the result of much self-criticism and scrutiny; it was also not a sudden one, and the complex temporality of the change in direction that ensued may be seen to have left many marks on Blanchot's work, not least on the differing speed with which Blanchot the literary critic and Blanchot the political thinker caught up with Blanchot the writer of fiction.

Some ten years after 'La Littérature et le droit à la mort', in 1958, as he prepared to join the struggle against de Gaulle and the pro-colonialist military who had brought him to power, Blanchot found himself embarking on what was to be a new phase in his political itinerary. There seems little doubt that the writer was then brought to reflect upon the lessons to be learned from his own political past. As always, Blanchot did so obliquely, in an essay first published in August that year, by considering the fate of two other thinkers whose writings raise complex political questions of their own: Nietzsche and Heidegger.[2] Blanchot begins by reminding the reader how the texts of the first, however implausibly, re-interpreted, re-edited, and compiled anew by his family and heirs, were made to serve as philosophical or ideological justification for some of the most repellent policies of the Third Reich. But how, asks Blanchot, was such falsification possible? Blanchot's judgement is as scrupulous as it is unforgiving. Clearly, Nietzsche and the Third Reich had nothing in common; but Nietzsche, having at one point announced, in spite of himself, a forthcoming systematic work of philosophy, which he did not write, has to bear some responsibility for the fact that others were able, on the basis of that statement, to concoct such a work as 'The Will to Power' and, in so doing, give to Nietzsche, posthumously and no doubt against his will, the role he was made to play in the 1930s and 1940s with such dire political consequences.

Reading Nietzsche's fragments, then, Blanchot is aware that meaning is always contextual; and that by cynically manipulating the context of his writings, Nietzsche's heirs were able to ascribe to him views he surely would have found offensive. But while this shows that statements cannot be taken in isolation and are decisively bound to their context, it also confirms that contexts can and do change, and that texts whose meaning becomes contaminated in that process have perhaps some responsibility to bear for the possibility of such changes. Assuredly, Blanchot concedes, the principle may be reversed; and if the thought of Nietzsche is dangerous, he writes in *L'Écriture du désastre*, this may simply prove that danger is an essential element in the movement of thought itself and that, without such risks, thinking itself is no more than bland conformism (*ED*, 189; 123). However, Blanchot's analysis, if it applies to Nietzsche, must also be seen to apply to Blanchot; and it is at any event worth noting that in the principle of contamination which Blanchot invokes to describe Nietzsche's responsibility for the misreading of his own texts, there is at work precisely the same logic of re-inscription as that which affects Blanchot's own earlier political writings, a logic that dictates that statements made in one context can, unpredictably and uncontrollably, always be reread and misread otherwise than how they were intended, and even turn into something more nearly resembling their opposite. The responsibility for thought, Blanchot concludes, is infinite; as in the case of Nietzsche, it is from the very outset always at least twofold, since the responsibility of thought is responsibility not only to the contestatory violence of thought but also for the incalculable implications of that violence.

In a long footnote to the article, which was extensively reworked prior to re-publication in 1969, Blanchot turns to Heidegger's reading of Nietzsche, first pursued in Freiburg in a series of lectures and seminars during the period from 1936 to 1939. On one level, those lectures, as Blanchot freely admits, represent an important moment in Heidegger's endeavour to distance himself from the official philosophers of National-Socialism and from the regime he had first supported with such enthusiasm. Even so, there remains the question of how and why Heidegger had been willing to put his own philosophical writing to work in the service of a racist, totalitarian political system. Blanchot is attentive to the nuances of Heidegger's reading of Nietzsche; but as with Nietzsche, he is also rigorously unforgiving. Indeed, he concludes by observing how, in his public endorsement of Hitler shortly before the fateful plebiscite of November 1933, which took Germany out of the League of Nations and began the long road to war, Heidegger was guilty of committing his own philosophical language – the language of *Sein und Zeit* – to the cause of the Nazi state and of thus compromising his own writing by the politics it was used to defend.[3] The contamination of the one by the other remains irredeemable; and for having thus put his own philosophical probity into the balance, writes Blanchot, Heidegger's own discourse will henceforth always remain under suspicion (*EI*, 210; 451).

At this point, some readers of Blanchot have remembered Blanchot's own troubled political past. Are there parallels to be drawn between Heidegger and

51

Blanchot? Should one apply to Blanchot the strictures whose principle he clearly and convincingly articulates with regard to Heidegger? The question is without doubt a legitimate one. But to confuse Blanchot with Heidegger is also to neglect a number of essential, absolutely irreducible differences: Blanchot never endorsed Hitler politically, never held high office in a state institution with the explicit support of the Nazi Party, never threw the weight of his philosophy behind the inner truth of the Nazi movement, and consistently refused the temptation of silence when it came to responding to the question of the Holocaust. And from 1938 onwards he began the lengthy process of dismantling his own uncritical reliance on what Philippe Lacoue-Labarthe has termed national-aestheticism, and in articulating that turn to the ethics of alterity that was to be the main focus of all Blanchot's work in the years to come.

This is not to say Blanchot's early political writings do not run substantial risks; nor is it to suggest that Blanchot's readers should not, like Blanchot, be rigorous and unforgiving in questioning the implications of those early political texts. Respect for Blanchot's later writing demands nothing less.

2

The (im)possibility of literature

Founding fictions

Literature is perhaps essentially (but neither solely nor overtly) power of contestation: contestation of established authority, contestation of that which is (and the fact of being), contestation of language and the forms of literary language, lastly contestation of itself as power.

'Les Grands Réducteurs' (A, 80)

Blanchot's two early novels – *Thomas l'Obscur* (1941) and *Aminadab* (1942) – are arguably among some of the most compelling yet obscure of all modern literary texts. More than fifty years after publication, their resistance to interpretation remains undiminished.[1] This inscrutability, however, is not merely the product of unfamiliar contextual factors, nor does it derive simply from the systematic withholding of information by the author or narrator. Indeed, contrary to repute, these early novels of Blanchot are neither full of esoteric allusions nor obsessed with silence; they are, rather, outrageously garrulous and self-explanatory, and given to endless digressions designed to elucidate the import and purpose of the stories they tell. In that process, however, each of these texts persistently reveals itself to be more than the sum of its parts, with the result that what is most enigmatic of all is the extent to which, as one reads, the local and specific mysteries posed by Blanchot's writing give way to the larger, more intractable puzzle of the nature of the discourse that has somehow engendered them.[2] The only secret of such texts, one might say, is the secret of their own possibility; and the main question they raise, therefore, is the question of their foundation as works of literature.

Admittedly, one of the most obvious reasons for the obscurity of Blanchot's fiction is the sceptical disdain the texts themselves adopt towards conventional norms of novelistic verisimilitude or narrative coherence. These are texts that, unlike others, make little attempt to conceal the violence with which they interrupt what the reader is enjoined to consider, at least implicitly, as a previously stable state of affairs. The technique is one already exploited to challenging effect in Blanchot's two short stories 'L'Idylle' and 'Le Dernier Mot', written in 1936 and 1935 respectively. In the first of these, the tale begins with the sudden arrival of a foreigner within an (unnamed) city, without it ever being explained from where he has come or why, and what purpose his visit might have; yet this does not prevent the narrative from recounting his brief life in the city, oppressed by the terrible – and terribly ambiguous – spectacle of a sham life of happiness, until he is eventually punished for attempting to escape from the city and dies as a consequence, only then to enjoy the hollow privilege of a grand funeral, after which everything returns to the dubious normality of domestic routine. 'Le Dernier Mot', in turn, commences in a similarly abrupt way, with an unexplained exchange of conversation between anonymous interlocutors about some presumably metatextual password, or watchword, of indeterminate character ('le mot d'ordre', *AC*, 57; 39) that is somehow no longer available; pursuing this half-hearted theme into something more akin to allegory or myth, the text keeps going up to the point where, like the Tower of Babel to which Blanchot's text refers in conclusion, everything in the story collapses into ruins, bringing to an end, among other things, this particular story.

But the uncompromising anti-realism even of stories such as these appears tame and unexceptionable when set alongside the outlandishness of the first version of *Thomas l'Obscur*. Part philosophical inquiry, part *Bildungsroman*, part inner experience, part self-reflexive *mise-en-abyme*, part Pentecostal fable, part apocalyptic rhapsody, part ironic romance, part stylistic *tour de force*, this is a work that displays few, if any, of the standard features of conventional novels of the time. True, it retains a residual narrative structure that follows a vaguely circular pattern; and while at the outset the protagonist, Thomas, is found slipping into the sea, embarking, in the mist, on what is described, no doubt self-referentially, as a new and unfamiliar itinerary on his part, and which leaves him bereft of all previous points of orientation, so he is discovered at the end of the novel by the side of the sea once again, hurling himself, at least metaphorically, into what the book describes in closing as 'a flood of crude images' (*TO1*, 232; cf *TO2*, 137; 117). Between these two rhyming moments, each detailing the protagonist's self-possessed immersion into the watery deep, little of consequence seems to have taken place, except for the dispatching of Thomas, this 'keeper of the impossible' (*TO1*, 231; cf *TO2*, 136; 116), along with the reader, on a bizarre sequence of fantastical textual experiences and encounters, involving love, death, destruction, and re-creation, and which, while they may remind the reader of much that belongs to the literary past, endeavour nonetheless to affirm their absolute autonomy from conventional expectations and hold within themselves the irreducible mystery of their unfolding.

Published one year after *Thomas l'Obscur*, *Aminadab* presents what seems to be the next stage in Thomas's story; it opens in the broad light of day with a scene in which the protagonist, after passing by an unassuming shop and resisting the invitation to go in, then, for no clear reason, responds more positively to an enigmatic gesture – invitation? sign of friendship? farewell? or warning? – from a woman waving from one of the windows of the building opposite, somewhat resembling a run-down boarding house. In a decision that is lightly taken but heavy with consequences, Thomas enters this second building. But by launching him – like the reader – on an endless journey through the various rooms and floors of this allegorical establishment, about which nothing seems certain, and on an ultimately fruitless quest for the woman who appeared to signal to him, Thomas's initial resolve proves to be the source of all his subsequent misfortunes, misfortunes which are brought to an end – though not necessarily a conclusion – in the closing scene when Thomas at last submits to what is described as a necessary, if still enigmatic fate. All the while, in an explicit echo of the book's opening, the light in the room is shown to be slowly fading, as though to suggest that Thomas's life and the narrative have become synonymous and that the falling silent of the one serves to announce the extinction of the other.

Such textual moments of beginning and ending are evidently performative as well as descriptive; by invoking the fictional possibility of a particular finite world, they ground Blanchot's own narratives within the space of that possibility. By asserting their own freedom, so to speak, Blanchot's novels legislate for their own autonomy as literary artefacts. But in order to do so, and however strenuously they endeavour to carry out this project, they are necessarily faced with a fundamental paradox. Beginnings and endings can only be thought in their own absence. Any act of foundation, be it an act of aesthetic framing, of ontological grounding, or ethical injunction, has to confront the necessary circumstance of its own prior absence; indeed, for an act of foundation to be possible at all, it must first be preceded by an absence of foundation. Such prior absence is thereby a necessary condition of any possibility of foundation; however, to the extent that it insists, as it necessarily must, on the belatedness and fragility of any such moment of foundation, any such condition of possibility is also a condition of impossibility. The laying of foundations, as it were, is an activity that may take place only within a bottomless abyss; and it is the bottomless abyss that constitutes the only reliable foundation, albeit a foundation that is always already an absence of foundation. Such an absence of foundation is not just an ironic flourish: it is an essential condition that, to the extent that it enables the act of foundation, by that very token also disables it. The price of the possibility of foundation, one may say, is the impossibility of that foundation.

In this perspective, it is clear that none of Blanchot's narrative beginnings or endings functions unproblematically. Without exception, all these moments of narrative inception or closure prove in fact to be remarkably indeterminate; and, throughout, the self-certainty of the initial founding moment is tempered – if not indeed radically challenged – by the awareness that the world founded in this way fails to embody itself as an inaugural, fully transparent presence. Instead, the act of foundation remains irreducibly opaque; and it is as though the fictional world Blanchot's writing opens up already has its distant origin elsewhere, in an unspoken and largely irretrievable anteriority that resists narrative exposition and veils the clarity of the text in impenetrable but indeterminate obscurity. At times, as in the case of the perplexing sign from the third floor to which Thomas rashly responds in *Aminadab*, not knowing what it signifies, nor even if it signifies at all, the possibility of beginning, in the form of the presumed meaning of that gesture, becomes synonymous with the paradoxical impossibility of beginning that the gesture's failure to communicate seems to imply. And as a result, like Blanchot's other incipits, the opening of *Aminadab* remains suspended on the threshold of its own necessary violence, which the writer makes little attempt to mitigate or transform. The violence of the origin is never effaced; to the dismay, puzzlement, frustration, and ultimate fascination of the reader, the beginning of the text is displayed as pure interruption, as a hiatus in whatever is held to precede the beginning.

Much the same is true of Blanchot's endings. In *Thomas l'Obscur*, by way of bringing to a close an extraordinary scene of burgeoning vernal creation, albeit one that by the end undergoes a catastrophic fall into solitude, darkness, and tawdry imagery, Blanchot has his own protagonist cast himself into the waves of these images 'as if', writes Blanchot, 'shame had begun for him' (*TO1*, 232; cf

TO2, 137; 117). Put in these terms, the ending deceives as well as disappoints; Blanchot's prose, like Thomas himself, seemingly lingers on, surveying everything that has just taken place, delaying the closure the narrative already seems to have reached, and thus outliving itself, so to speak, echoing what the 1950 version terms the 'empty word of Thomas' (*TO2*, 135; 116). The reference to shame in this context, though, is revealing; what it recalls is Levinas's early contention that 'what manifests itself in shame is . . . precisely the fact of being chained to oneself, the radical impossibility of fleeing from oneself in order to hide from oneself, the irredeemable presence of the self to itself'. [3] The ending of *Thomas l'Obscur*, then, is not the ending of Thomas; rather it is like an ultimate condemnation of both Thomas and the literary discourse that carries his name, the final proof, so to speak, that the only possible end to writing is in fact the interminable impossibility of such ending.

Such paradoxes are also much in evidence in *Aminadab*. There, at the very moment Thomas is busy receiving from Dom, his erstwhile and future companion, the news that it is time for them to leave, he hesitates, prolonging once again the questions that have never ceased to be asked in pages gone by, yet never answered; even at this late stage, as Thomas hovers between life and death, silence and speech, the threat of darkness and the yearning for light, he seems still to be hoping for a response to the question that will allow him to throw some illumination upon all that has occurred (*AB*, 227). Unabashed by the information (of indeterminable purport and unverifiable accuracy) given by the young woman Lucie, to the effect that he was not the one to whom the inaugural sign was intended in the first place (*AB*, 220), and told that at any event, as far as the boarding house was concerned, according to Dom (*AB*, 212), he would have been better advised going down to the basement rather than up to the floors, Thomas brings the novel to an end with an unanswered, still almost preliminary question, which he addresses to Lucie, unless it is to the light itself (assuming the two to be different): 'Who are you?' (*AB*, 227). The question is one Anne, in *Thomas l'Obscur*, had already asked of Thomas, only to regret having done so a moment later; and as the Thomas of *Aminadab* echoes it once again, it becomes evident that this novel too, like its predecessor, can only end on a sentence that is more a repetition that a resolution, more a rehearsal than a moment of closure. The failure to reach conclusion, in both texts, is a token of the extent to which both novels, as they seek to convert the violence of beginning or ending into the self-sufficient law of their own necessity, cannot escape the realisation of their own irredeemable excess; they remain traversed

57

to the very end by the enigma of everything that, by necessity, cannot in fact be spoken and which yet seemingly constitutes the only reason for their existence.

Blanchot's two novels, then, begin without beginning, and end without ending. Their possibility as autonomous, self-bound artefacts is traversed by the impossibility of such self-legislation; and what is at one moment a condition of possibility is at another a condition of impossibility. Beginnings are a function of the absence of beginnings, and endings an interval imposed on the endlessness of language; each and every point that claims self-presence is shown here to be already inhabited by the other from which it derives, on which it depends, and which therefore has the potential to disable its claim to be what it is. For all that, Blanchot's novels do not lapse into anti-mimetic playfulness. Rather, a new kind of monstrous logic – an ante-logic as well as an anti-logic – takes over within Blanchot's writing, one whose effects are signalled from the outset, in *Thomas l'Obscur*, by a series of strange and mind-numbing paradoxes and inversions by which clarity turns to obscurity, plenitude to void, presence to absence, decision to paralysis, and freedom to constraint. Standing for instance on the shore again, Thomas looks on intently, with increased acuity, at the distant sight of another swimmer – perhaps his own doppelgänger – appearing and disappearing off the horizon, and is filled with a feeling of boundless freedom, somewhat akin to the freedom of beginning itself. But already the euphoria of his telepathic intimacy with the far-off swimmer becomes mingled with discomfort and distress; and it is as though boundless freedom has suddenly turned into something more nearly resembling opaque compulsion, in much the same way that, in the pages that follow, it is by closing his eyes that Thomas sees more deeply into the darkness, and while refusing to walk that he finds himself imperiously being propelled along.

From this point on in Blanchot's text, writing becomes inseparable from what might be described as an experience of nothingness. Necessarily, however, *Thomas l'Obscur* challenges the adequacy of such terms. Like the inner experience of Georges Bataille, Blanchot's project can be described only in antithetical or paradoxical terms; and just as, like that of Bataille, Thomas's experience is an experience that is not an experience, so nothing in Blanchot's novel is not nothing. Or so it would seem from what is one of the novel's most famous passages, Thomas's encounter with the night. Blanchot writes:

> The night soon appeared murkier and more terrible to him than any other
> night, as though it had really come forth from a wound in thought that

could no longer be thought, thought treated ironically as an object by something other than thought. It was night itself. Images that made up its darkness flooded over him, and his body, changed into a demonic mind, sought to picture them to itself. He could see nothing, and, far from being overwhelmed by this, he made this absence of vision the culminating point of his gaze. Useless for seeing, his eye took on extraordinary proportions, grew beyond measure, and, stretching to the horizon, let the night penetrate to its centre in order to create for itself an iris. So it was, by virtue of this emptiness, that his gaze and the object of his gaze mingled together. Not only did the eye which could see nothing apprehend something, it apprehended the cause of its vision. It saw as an object that which prevented it from seeing.

(TO1, 14–15; cf *TO2*, 17–18; 14–15)

This night – night 'as such' – is not the luminous night of the concept nor of dialectics, but the night before the concept and before dialectics; it is the night that precedes the night, the night that is itself impenetrable to the thought of night but which is the necessary prior condition of that thought. As such, its status is uncontrollably paradoxical. In so far as it is irreducible to dialectical reason and logical negation, Thomas's night before night cannot be thought as night, nor can it be addressed as a prior cause of night; it remains foreign to all forms of identity as well as all narrative chronology. This night is not a night, therefore, nor does it occur before night; it is the night thinkable only as that which is external to the concept of night, and, to that extent, may be described only as a radical impossibility of night. And yet because this is the night which does precede the night, it is necessarily also that which enables the night – both word and thing – to appear as such; and to that degree it must logically already hold within itself the possibility of the appearance of night.

The night 'itself', then, in Blanchot's description, features here as both possibility and impossibility; indeed possibility at one level is entirely dependent on impossibility at another. This explains the peculiar experience undergone by Thomas as he peers into the depths of night. For as he gazes on, in the darkness, with his unseeing eye, at his own inability to see, all he can make out, in the lack of any visible object, are the circumstances that might make vision possible. However, those circumstances do not themselves constitute an object of vision; what they do is rather to present Thomas with the spectacle of an absence of vision, with the result that Thomas, blinded by this absence of sight, is faced, so to speak, with the vision of the circumstances that prevent him from seeing anything at all. So as Thomas stares on, unseeing, into the night, what he finds himself looking at is not just the absence of a particular visible object, nor simply the absence of visibility as such, but, more radically, the presence of that darkest of other nights (as Blanchot terms it elsewhere) which is the only truly nocturnal night of all, the night that is impenetrable to all visibility and synonymous with an originary impossibility of vision which is nothing other than the prior condition of visibility as such.[4]

Throughout *Thomas l'Obscur*, possibility in general is retraced, as here, to the originary impossibility that must be excluded or negated in order for possibility to be constituted as such. Blanchot dramatises this here with regard to vision; elsewhere he does so in relation to language. The logic is much the same. For the night before night that confronts Thomas in the darkness is both irreducible to the word night and yet its necessary condition of possibility. The night 'itself' is both prior to the word night and the word's most original inspiration; yet while the other, darker night, to which the word night pays silent homage, cannot itself be incorporated within language, the – impossible – attempt to name that night before night is nevertheless, in Blanchot's account, what constitutes the purpose of literature as such. According to this Orphic logic, by which possibility is only ever a function of prior impossibility, and an object only ever grasped at the very moment of its ineradicable loss, the unnamable night before night constitutes the only (im)proper object (or absence of object) that literature may claim as its very own, even though for it to do so is for literature to be reminded all the while that what counts as its own is also that which is irrepressibly alien to it. The paradox is one that has radical implications for Blanchot's fiction. On the one hand, the night 'itself', by tracing the limit that passes between language and that which is irreducible to it, is evidently – as mystery or enigma – what enables narrative to take place at all; on the other hand, however, in so far as it cannot be enclosed within the bounds of narrative, such a night necessarily also transgresses those bounds, disables narrative, and throws the very possibility of narrative into question. Narrative is no longer in control of itself, and is left instead, as in the case of *Thomas l'Obscur*, to grapple with the impossibility of naming that constitutes it as narrative. Such self-reflexive turns are crucial to Blanchot's fiction, as the example of *Thomas l'Obscur* shows; and just as the impossibility of vision reveals what is arguably most extreme and fundamental about sight itself, so the most radical and far-reaching of novels for Blanchot are those that pursue narrative to their originating point, which is that of their own dissolution.

As all readers of Blanchot's fiction know, the impact of this bizarre yet rigorous logic on Blanchot's work is persistent and dramatic. What it does to *Thomas l'Obscur*, for instance, is to turn the novel into a monstrous and heterogeneous infusion of oxymoron, aporia, and paradox; and it is from this potent verbal brew – more central than one might think to mainstream literary thinking in the twentieth century – that flow the many baffling figures and tropes that litter Blanchot's text. Witness, for instance, the eerie spectacle of Thomas, this very first of human beings (*TO1*, 133), who, in the depths of night, finds himself

> grappling, in dreadful solitude, with something absolutely inaccessible, absolutely foreign to all being, absolutely inconceivable, something which he could say did not exist, yet which filled him with terror and which he could sense lurking within the space of his own solitude.
>
> (*TO1*, 24; cf *TO2*, 30; 27)

Thomas, we read, is a character who, were he to be seen with his own eyes, 'would have appeared in the form of an entity that existed only in so far as it did not exist entirely' (*TO1*, 41); who is thus 'really dead and yet at the same time excluded from the reality of death' (*TO1*, 48; cf *TO2*, 40; 36), and is 'in every circumstance anonymous and entirely without history' (*TO1*, 64; cf *TO2*, 56; 55).

Thomas it is, the novel adds, who is 'in each human act the dead person that simultaneously renders it possible and impossible' (*TO1*, 212; cf *TO2*, 106; 93); who is at bottom a figure 'whose true essence was not to be, on whom the fact of not being conferred neither a diminution nor an aspiration to being, who could not be considered as lacking but as superabundant' (*TO1*, 216); and who, to close, avers: 'I am indeed the origin of that which has no origin' (*TO1*, 226; cf *TO2*, 129; 108). And all these attributes are not limited to Thomas; many of them are found, too, in the figure of Anne, the novel's Eurydice, who, at the moment of her own death, is one of the few to realise to what extent 'death, destroying everything, could also destroy the possibility of annihilation' (*TO1*, 204; cf *TO2*, 96; 85). As she does so, she demonstrates clearly how the preoccupation with dying, throughout Blanchot's work, is less in the service of negativity or nihilism than of radical passion, irreducible extremity, and boundless affirmation.

In the language of Heidegger, the nothing ('das Nichts') that Blanchot stages in this way in *Thomas l'Obscur* is of course not nothing, because the question it raises, as Heidegger maintains, is the question of Being itself.[5] One is reminded here of Blanchot's early review of *La Nausée*, in which he described Sartre's novel as aspiring – with only partial success – to the status of 'a kind of novel of Being' ('une sorte de roman de l'être') and went on to recall the importance of Heidegger for a proper assessment of the challenges facing modern art. Texts such as the recently translated 'What is Metaphysics?' of 1929, claimed Blanchot, 'allow one to gauge the force and creative will of [Heidegger's] thinking which, in the infinite contest between laws, under-standing and chance, offers art a new point of view from which to contemplate its necessity'.[6] This endorsement of Heidegger in the review explains why Blanchot was somewhat critical of what he describes as Sartre's undue concessions to traditional psychological analysis and conventional plotting. Blanchot was evidently both too much and too little of a philosopher to be tempted by the project for an existential anthropology implicit in *La Nausée*, and when *Thomas l'Obscur* appeared, three years after *La Nausée*, it accordingly made only minimal concessions to the demand for either character or plot. But despite the profound differences between them, *La Nausée* and *Thomas l'Obscur* share a similar objective, which is that of pursuing within fiction a project that has all the signs of a foundational philosophical enterprise. But where Sartre was ultimately to rely on the self-transparency and self-reflexive freedom of the narrating subject, Blanchot was to pursue some of the implications of the Heideggerian 'nothing' in a more radical way, one that, as we have seen, begins gravely to compromise the foundational possibilities of language and literature as such.

Blanchot's first move in *Thomas l'Obscur* is in fact not to adhere to the economy of Heideggerian Being at all, but rather to transpose or translate the Heideggerian principle of the 'nothing' into the rather different language of Emmanuel Levinas, more particularly into the Levinasian topos of the *il y a*, that phrase signifying 'there is', which, for Levinas, replaces the originary generosity of the Heideggerian gift of Being (as expressed in the German phrase: *es gibt*) with the horror and anonymity of being.[7] This use of the phrase *il y a* was not exclusive to Levinas, however, for it was cited in much the same way by Blanchot in his story 'Le Dernier Mot', where it is identified – by the story's first-person narrator – as constituting 'no doubt' the last word mentioned in the title (*AC*, 66; 45). But if for Blanchot's story *il y a* is that last word, the narrator

62

explains, it is because 'the last word cannot be a word, nor the absence of a word, nor anything other than a word' (*AC*, 77; 53). In this respect, the *il y a* is a strangely ambiguous moment of ontological foundation; on the one hand, since the *il y a* is logically prior to all propositions, including negative ones, and cannot itself be negated, it necessarily serves as a moment of foundation for being; but, on the other hand, as Levinas insists, if the *il y a* necessarily precedes the constitution of any world whatever, be it a fictional or non-fictional one, it follows that the *il y a* poses an implicit, ineliminable challenge to the autonomy and stability of that world. Considered from the point of view of the *il y a*, the world derives its possibility from prior impossibility. So if the *il y a* is a founding moment, what it founds is in fact an absence of world; what it inscribes is a series of always anterior repetitive traces whose origin is always lost. Accordingly, when the *il y a* does reveal itself, Levinas argues, it does so in the form of eternal wakefulness; and what it dramatises is not self-presence nor originary giving, but the necessary intrication of being and otherness and the irreducible dependence of all giving on what is a prior and thus infinitely irredeemable debt.

To the extent that it becomes synonymous with the necessary failure of all beginnings and endings, the *il y a* demonstrates what Levinas describes in *De l'existence à l'existant* as 'the impossibility of death, the universality of existence even in its annihilation'.[8] But if absence is always already a form of presence, presence itself must be at some risk of forfeiting the very proximity and nearness at hand that make it what it is. Presence is always already marked by its own alteration and by the inherent possibility of non-presence. Ineluctable alterity threatens from the outset; and being becomes inseparable here from its own boundless absence and impossibility of foundation. The implications of *Thomas l'Obscur* are much the same. What Blanchot's novel suggests is that, if the attempt is made in the language of fiction to grasp being for itself, so to speak, then being turns out necessarily to be always already inhabited – and thereby dissolved – by alterity, loss of origin, infinite repetition, absence, nothingness, the impossibility both of beginning and of ending. By a dizzying and outrageous paradox, being comes to function like an instantiation of its own groundless absence. As far as Blanchot's writing is concerned, the result is both poverty and plenitude, nothingness and infinity, a radical emptiness that, by interrupting the all, finds itself facing the fact of its own boundless exteriority. Literature, here, oscillates uncontrollably between that which is and that which refuses to be; what writing founds as possibility at one moment, it dismantles as impossibility at another.

If *Thomas l'Obscur* is a novel of the impenetrability of night 'itself', *Aminadab*, the second novel involving Blanchot's Thomas, is a novel of unremitting daylight. This is what is stressed in the novel's opening sentence, which reads: 'It was broad daylight' ('Il faisait grand jour', *AB*, 7). Compared to *Thomas l'Obscur*, *Aminadab* is a novel of mimetic representations and artefacts. But from the outset, this mimetic impetus in the novel is sharply and ironically curtailed. This becomes clear very soon after the beginning of the story, when Thomas, having boldly entered the boarding house, is invited to select a room for himself. Shortly after, in typically uncanny fashion, Thomas finds himself in a place containing a strange painting contraption, comprising, among other things, a complicated assemblage of pullies and ropes, several stools, an easel, a mirror, a spotlight, a sundial, and a collection of palettes dripping paint on to the floor. Thomas sits down on one of the stools, and, looking at the unfinished painting, realises that much of the detail of the room he is in has already been faithfully copied on to the canvas, including the very stool on which he is sitting. Eventually the painter completes Thomas's portrait; and though the painter seems most satisfied with his work, Thomas for his part can find no resemblance at all between his own face and the portrait; and it is as though Thomas, his features aged and blurred by the painting, has been incorporated into the picture under false pretences, as an effaced simulacrum of himself.

In the course of this description, the narrator remarks: 'It was difficult to tell what was there to do the painting and what was there to be painted' ('Il était difficile de savoir ce qui dans cet ensemble devait servir à être peint ou à peindre') (*AB*, 19). A similar reversibility or indecision applies to Blanchot's description as well; for over and above the story of Thomas, it is apparent that what is being depicted in this scene of mimetic reproduction is the process of mimetic reproduction as such. On Blanchot's part, the description of the studio is plainly a novelistic *mise-en-abyme*, whose purpose is to dramatise and test out whatever claim might be made by this novel – and all other novels in general – to be adhering to some form of mimetic realism. But Blanchot's text rapidly shows that the theory of mimesis, like much else in the novel, rests on a fundamental paradox. The only perfect imitation of an object would be in fact that object itself. Such redoubling would produce, however, not resemblance, but repetition. Before any object may be perceived as an exact, mimetic copy of another, a margin of alterity must first have differentiated object from copy in order that the relation of resemblance between the two may be instituted at all. But in so far as resemblance is founded in differentiation, mimesis in the true

64

sense proves to be an impossibility. Mimesis, it transpires, only functions at all in so far as the imitation is an imperfect one. Indeed, it may be said that it is only because of the impossibility of mimetic identity in the true sense that mimesis is possible at all. But, by that token, the relationship between object and copy falls subject to a logic that necessarily escapes the concept of mimesis, with the consequence that any theory of mimesis is left with the insurmountable problem of accounting for the existence of the mimetic process itself, since that process, though it may produce objects that are judged to be mimetically accurate, is not itself an imitation. An ineliminable residue remains, which necessarily exceeds mimesis; like the question of the inaugural light that illuminates – without clarifying – the world depicted in *Aminadab* itself, something radically other than the fictional world itself continually survives, intelligible only as an obscure enigma defying translation into anything other than itself.

Throughout *Aminadab*, the reader is faced with ineluctable, aporetical impasses of this sort. The result, as far as the text is concerned, is radical uninterpretability. Moreover, Blanchot's text is itself largely made up of conjecture, commentary, interpretation and gloss, attributed to a variety of characters, all claiming to make sense of the internal workings of the enigmatic world of the boarding house in which the novel is set. Paradoxically, the sheer number of these often contradictory internal commentaries makes interpretation not easier, but harder. Indeed, one of the ways in which the novel resists interpretation is by already incorporating within its textual fabric numerous other, already available mythological, philosophical, religious, literary, or rhetorical discourses. On one level, these serve to exacerbate the apparent interpretability of Blanchot's narrative; at the same time, by overlaying the narrative with a palimpsest of rival interpretations or commentary, they also obliterate the narrative and leave the reader, as it were, with little hermeneutic business of his or her own. Yet these internal discourses, though they may exhaust the text, are themselves never exhausted by it, if only because, to a large degree, they are what constitute the text as such. The bizarre result is a writing in which everything already seems to possess somewhere in the novel its own implicit or explicit interpretation, except for the process of commentary itself, which remains uninterpreted and, one might add, boundlessly uninterpretable, with the result that what seems lucid at one stage becomes quite opaque at another. The inhabitants of this boarding house, Thomas reflects at one point, in free indirect speech, are many of them liars and rogues (*AB*, 33). What could be more lucid? We are reminded, however, elsewhere in the text,

65

that this is only Thomas's – negligent and entirely short-sighted? – interpretation of what is going on, in which case that thought too is just as likely to be completely false. So as far as the reader is concerned, all Thomas's opinion might be held to show is how far Thomas, too, is nothing but a liar and a rogue.

But it would be wrong to conclude from this kind of hermeneutic paralysis that all in the novel is equally mendacious or arbitrary. To do so would be to ape Thomas's own fondness for unreliable generalisation and fall, with the protagonist, into the trap of negligence and misrepresentation (assuming for a moment – *concesso non dato*! – that the house is not indeed full of liars and rogues). In place of this kind of lazy relativism, what Blanchot's text suggests instead – and this is the particular inflection that *Aminadab* gives to the question of the *il y a* – is that when it comes to interpretation it is always already too late. Reading, writing, speaking are weighty obligations, from which it is impossible to withdraw, that remain incumbent on all of us, whether we wish it or not. Like Thomas during most of the early part of the novel, to go anywhere at all is always to be accompanied by the irksome, inevitable presence of that other who, in the form of the character Dom – whose name evokes the Lord to whom Thomas is forced continually to play the part of reluctant bondsman – is literally chained to him as his very own special, alien companion. Just as Thomas himself is a sometimes unwilling reader of the discourses he encounters on his journey through the house, which he cannot elude, so the reader, too, so long as he or she is a reader, cannot avoid becoming entangled in this text, enchained to a narrative and a controversy that may be without resolution but are not without making their own urgent, ineluctable appeal for the reader's attention.

But within or beneath the text, disturbing its foundations, just as the basement – according to Dom – runs under the house, offering a possible space of freedom far from the light of day, there is always the lure of something else, an outside, which seems to offer hope of escape. To suggest this finally is perhaps the purpose of the title of *Aminadab*. The name, unexplained until some fourteen pages before the end, arrives suddenly, referring only to some perhaps legendary gatekeeper whose role it is to guard the great gate leading below the house to the basement. But the existence of such a figure, the reader is told, is probably a myth, and the great gate only a wooden fence; in any case, if Thomas were to leave by the basement, all he might find would be the impossibility of dying and the cruel torment of rebeginning. Better, says Dom, to stay inside the house. But to do so would of course be not to find rest, but to remain, like Aminadab the mythical gatekeeper, hovering between house and basement, inside and out, fiction and truth, legend and reality, always embarked, like at least one of his earlier, Biblical namesakes, on the endless journey out of Egypt, together with the other children of Israel, towards an ever distant promised land. This novel, like history, fails to conclude, and the light the novel throws on such events remains obstinately opaque.

Throughout the whole of both *Aminadab* and *Thomas l'Obscur*, the question arises of how these texts are to be read. Neither book allows one to entertain for long the possibility of reading them as conventional realist texts; and the reader is obviously tempted instead to attempt to decode, if not perhaps *Thomas l'Obscur*, then at least *Aminadab*, as Sartre was the first to propose, as an allegory. But if *Aminadab* is an allegory, it is not because – as Sartre contends – the novel is simply a coded, fantastical representation of the metaphysical dereliction of modern man. If *Aminadab* is readable at all as a second-degree, allegorical narrative, one that incorporates within itself, so to speak, the perpetual possibility of another, figurative layer of interpretation or legibility, it is because, by its very resistance to interpretation, the novel implicitly appeals at every turning to the possibility of there being another text, another interpretation, another commentary able to frame the text and somehow efface its startling indeterminacies.

However, nothing in Blanchot's novel allows itself to be deciphered in this way. That other, parallel discourse into which the novel might be translated is nowhere accessible, and the logic of allegory, ironically conceding its own failure in the form of the novel's refusal to be paraphrased or translated except into the text it always already is, serves here only to reaffirm the impenetrable clarity and radiant obscurity of Blanchot's writing. In Paul de Man's phrase, allegory supplies here only the story of an 'impossibility of reading';[9] it operates not as a trope of self-reflexive interiorisation or self-representation but as a figure of exposure to what Foucault, glossing one of Blanchot's later essays on Kafka, terms the outside, that alterity that can never be included within conceptual thought because, like the night before night of *Thomas l'Obscur*, it is what constitutes the unspeakable condition of thought itself. If it is an allegory, *Aminadab* is at best an ironic or impossible one, and the phantom, parallel, other reading that the novel may be thought to propose is in fact nothing other than the novel itself perpetually repeated and continually reread, with the result that the relationship between the text and its own reading is a relationship of radical strangeness, both infinite proximity and infinite distance.

As the story of Aminadab the gatekeeper serves to illustrate, there is in

Blanchot's novels no exit from the labyrinth of language and fiction. Reading here is possession of the reader by the text, not interiorisation of the text by the reader. Early in *Thomas l'Obscur*, Blanchot dramatises this strange reversal. As Thomas sits at his desk, reading, he is devoured by the text before him as though by a praying mantis; and in this singular sexual aggression, it is not just a case of Thomas reading the text, but rather of the text reading him. The Thomas of *Aminadab*, as his decisions too become the object of conjecture and interpretation by the other inhabitants of the boarding house, undergoes a similar mutation; and the effect, in both fictions, is not just to portray Thomas as an obstinate reader, but to transform the reader into a double of Thomas, unable to withdraw from the strangely circular, empty obligation of always being a reader of words continually read by words. Reading here is a process of endless submission to language. Indeed, it transpires that even to interrupt reading is still to be caught in the act of reading words as well as being read by them. The only option that remains is to repeat, recite, re-invent words with a view not to reasserting the apparent presence of words to themselves, but by responding to their fundamental absence from themselves. Which is what Blanchot did in 1950 by signing a second version of *Thomas l'Obscur*, one that, by virtue of the many changes it makes to the 1941 text, itself has the status of a detailed reading or interpretation of the earlier work, but which, for all that, is also a restatement of the previous version in its fundamental difference from itself. In this rereading of *Thomas l'Obscur* by Blanchot there is thus no progress towards clarification, no lifting of ambiguity, no added profundity. All the new version of the novel does is to add further to the burden of reading. By so doing, what it shows is that works such as *Thomas l'Obscur* are always other than what they seem, and that if they seem to belong to impenetrable night, to the impossibility of beginning and the impossibility of ending, they respond to that condition with the unrelenting persistence of an act of limitless affirmation.

In this way, as they tirelessly endeavour to found their own possibility as fictions, Blanchot's novels are impelled by the logic of that ambition to contest without end the possibility of all such acts of temporary foundation. Literature is not an entity coincident with itself and possessed of the purity of self-presence, as Blanchot's pre-war or wartime criticism might lead one to believe; it is more like a constant movement of disappearance and effacement that is perpetually put into crisis by its own lack of stability, identity, or definition. In the end, what Blanchot's novels demonstrate is the fundamental aporia and impossible possibility of literature 'as such'. For literature founds itself only upon the abyss; and whatever literature founds, therefore, including literature itself, is necessarily without foundation. The implication, too, is that the proper name Thomas, that doubter and twin to his own other self, is only ever a mark of the writer's anonymity, a lingering trace of the original namelessness that for Blanchot the novelist represents both the appeal and necessity of literature as such.

How is literature possible?

On one of its sides, poetry makes sense, but on another it unmakes it. It distances speech, and if it restores it to us, it is from afar. It binds dangerously the possibility of speaking to an impossibility that becomes, as it were, its very condition. It allows us to write 'I am unhappy', but this *initial* expression of unhappiness, by depriving us of already-formed, familiar, and reliable thoughts, exposes us to an experience full of risks, and more than that, to a silent drone, a stammering, whose perfection does not prevent us from acknowledging it as a lack.

'Le Paradoxe d'Aytré' (*PF*, 75–6; 71)

Blanchot's first published texts as a literary critic date from his earliest years as a political journalist. The two functions, in Blanchot's case, often overlapped; they did so most extensively in 1937, when, for almost the entirety of its ten-month existence, Blanchot contributed to *L'Insurgé*, alongside his better-known political pieces, a regular literary column in which he reviewed, among others, a host of recent books by such authors as Julien Benda, Georges Bernanos, Drieu La Rochelle, Aldous Huxley, Marcel Jouhandeau, Thomas Mann, François Mauriac, Charles Maurras, Victor Serge, and Virginia Woolf. But while Blanchot's work as a critic began in a space determined by political activity, it would be wrong to conclude that his criticism was in a narrow sense political. The truth is rather the reverse. It was Blanchot's consistent belief during that early period that in the contest between the literary and the political it was literature that enjoyed foundational status, and not politics. For Blanchot, only literature – not politics – was in a position to tell the truth about the political as such, while politics, in its dealings with literature, was destined always to encounter the limits of its power and authority. Which is to say that, alongside many of his nationalist contemporaries, Blanchot's own critical writing of the late 1930s and early 1940s – and this was arguably to remain the case until the end of the war – was profoundly indebted to what Philippe Lacoue-Labarthe, commenting on Heidegger's withdrawal from active politics after his disastrous endorsement of Hitler and the National-Socialist state, has termed national-aestheticism, the idea, that is, that art, to the extent that it is what founds all community, is what founds the political too.[1]

Blanchot's own pre-war version of national-aestheticism, however, unlike that of other, more conservative writers, was bound to a project that was explicitly (re)foundational and to that extent profoundly and resolutely contestatory. This is clearly demonstrated not only in Blanchot's literary journalism, but by his early fiction as well. In 'L'Idylle' of 1936, for instance, the city – the *polis* – seems able at best to provide its citizens with the terrible (and suspect) spectacle of happiness; literature alone, in the form of Blanchot's own narrative, might be seen to embody Alexandre Akim's irreducible yearning for freedom and his desire to quit the city for good. First articulated in a work of fiction, this principle of the supremacy of art as both political and metapolitical foundation soon became a central theme in Blanchot's literary journalism. So when in January 1937 he entitled his programmatic opening article for *L'Insurgé*: 'De la révolution à la littérature' ('From Revolution to Literature'), this was plainly not a call for writers to put their work in the service of (national) revolution, but more an appeal to the boundless revolutionary potential of literature as such, which he proposed to measure, significantly enough, by the capacity of works of literature not only to found a higher order of reality, but to give rise to other art works too. Far more important, at any event, than the oppositional sympathies of the individual writer, Blanchot asserted, was

> the oppositional force [la force d'opposition] expressed in the work of art itself and measured by its capacity to do away with other works or abolish a section of ordinary reality, as well as the capacity to summon up new works, as forceful or more forceful than itself, or to determine a higher reality.[2]

Blanchot's activities as a literary critic for *L'Insurgé*, like that paper itself, were to be short-lived, and it was not until April 1941, in a very different political context, that Blanchot embarked on what was to be his second sustained period of activity as a literary journalist: the three-and-a-half years spent at the *Journal des débats* as one of the paper's regular reviewers of current novels and essays. In that role, Blanchot was clearly intent on pursuing the literary critical project he had begun before the war. Indeed, despite the changed circumstances brought about by the Occupation and the setting up of the Vichy government, Blanchot's writing about literature, though it had to be voiced more discreetly than ever

70

before, had lost none of its fundamentally oppositional impetus. From the outset, Blanchot's concerns in the texts for the *Journal des débats* were at least threefold. First, in the abeyance of all normal public and political life, Blanchot was clearly committed to the notion that, in so far as it represented a veiled sign of national (and nationalist) resistance, cultural activity under the Occupation should carry on in spite of all; and it was in these terms that he justified in his own column, albeit discreetly, his own preoccupation with contemporary cultural matters.[3] There were other reasons, too, which had to do with Blanchot's own work as a novelist; and it is more than likely that, in such pieces as 'Mallarmé et l'art du roman' (*FP*, 189–96; *BR*, 43–8), and in the essay on Lautréamont published in Maulnier's *Revue française des idées et des œuvres* in April 1940 (*FP*, 197–202), Blanchot was seeking to provide his readers with something like an implicit commentary on his own novelistic practice. More generally, too, Blanchot in his articles was clearly aiming to articulate in detail, and for the first time, a coherent aesthetic discourse of his own, one that combined a vigorous opposition to literary realism with a defence of what Blanchot thematises initially as the foundational autonomy and purity of the literary work.

Throughout the 1940s the name Mallarmé was one of Blanchot's most important points of literary reference for such a foundational view of literature, and in the articles for the *Journal des débats* the legacy of the poet looms large. But at the time, this choice of Mallarmé as the founding poet of French modernity was scarcely a neutral one. For the monarchist right, in the words of Maurras, Mallarmé was no more than a belated, backward romantic ('un romantique attardé'), a symbol of politico-cultural as well as poetical anarchy, and one of the sources of the sickness afflicting the modern French nation. As far as anti-semitic, collaborationist circles were concerned, the diagnosis was much the same; for Robert Brasillach, writing in June 1940, shortly before France's capitulation to Germany, Mallarmé was an alien presence at the heart of the nation ('un étranger dans sa nation', as Brasillach put it), while Drieu La Rochelle, the following year, for his part declared Mallarmé's poetry a masterpiece of onanism and inversion, and attacked the poet for sinking to the lowest depths of physical, i.e. sexual, degradation ('le dernier degré de la déchéance du corps, la déchéance sexuelle').[4] Admittedly, hostility of this kind was not universal. Some years before, the influential *Nouvelle Revue française* critic, Albert Thibaudet, though a staunch supporter of Maurras, had written more warmly, if still somewhat faintly, of Mallarmé's heroically self-denying decadent preciosity, while Thierry Maulnier, in his

71

Introduction à la poésie française of 1939, similarly paid tribute to Mallarmé's gifts as a verbal alchemist.[5]

For Blanchot, however, Mallarmé was far from the poet of the coruscating – or barbaric – word. Initially, Blanchot's own position was more closely aligned with that of Paul Valéry, for whom the lesson of Mallarmé lay in the realisation that poetry, though it might use the same words as everyday discourse, functioned according to entirely different demands and constraints, and that if prose-writing resembled walking, as Valéry was wont to explain, poetry itself was more like dancing. In Mallarmé's case, the poet's exemplary lucidity and total mastery over the resources of language gave his texts an unequalled purity of purpose and effect.[6] Blanchot's account, though in many respects similar, radicalises this argument. Mallarmé in his poetry, Blanchot contends, raises the status of the work of art to that of an absolute, pure creation that obeys its own necessity and embodies its own law. All true literature, he argues, aspires to the status of myth and founds itself in the effort to overcome chance; it eschews all facile concessions to the expectations of the audience, including the demand for conventional realism or verisimilitude; it offers a radical challenge to the degradation, mediocrity, and inauthenticity of everyday life, taking instead as its essential theme the communal destiny of a national people in particular and of humanity in general.[7] At this point, as we shall see, Blanchot's account of Mallarmé takes on a markedly Heideggerian tone; and there are a number of evident similarities between the role ascribed to Mallarmé in these texts of the early 1940s and that played by Hölderlin in Heidegger's writings on poetry (or 'Dichtung') during the previous decade.

But of all Blanchot's wartime articles perhaps the most significant were those devoted to Jean Paulhan's critical essay *Les Fleurs de Tarbes* in the autumn of 1941.[8] In that book Paulhan had set about diagnosing what he described as a characteristically modern sickness or neurosis: the claim, originating with nineteenth-century romanticism, that rhetorical commonplaces – clichés, ready-made expressions, banal statements and received platitudes as well as established literary rules and conventions – were an impediment to original thought and should be purged from all genuine literary work. Because of its belief in the essential purity of thought and its profound mistrust, even hatred of words, Paulhan described this attitude as a form of Terror; and in *Les Fleurs de Tarbes*, by demonstrating its internal contradictions, what he sought to do was to dispel the effects of Terror and rehabilitate what he referred to as Rhetoric, that now discredited, classical view of the relation between language and thought that held that linguistic commonplaces were a necessary and integral part of all communication and expression, including literature itself. While Paulhan's rhetorician was willing to affirm that literature was a matter of adhering to proven, well-established norms, his terroristic opposite number refused all rhetoric in the name of the purity of thought and the authenticity of original poetic expression.

'In short,' as Michael Syrotinski explains, 'Terror is the precedence of thought over language, and Rhetoric the priority of language over thought.'[9] Paulhan in his book has few difficulties in illustrating the inconsistencies in the terrorist case. Not only did Terror display an impoverished understanding of the poetic potential of commonplaces, he argued, but it was self-contradictory even in its own terms; indeed the terrorist who, by waging war on words, sought by his words to establish the priority of thought over language was at best only likely to win a Pyrrhic victory. In the debate between thought and language, Paulhan concluded, all was a question of perspective; and what may be proof of the priority of thought over language for the writer of a text, may be for the reader of the self-same text exactly the reverse, and vice versa. But as Paulhan pursued this argument, he slowly became aware that the opposition between Terror and Rhetoric was less clear-cut than it first appeared; and in the end it is even as though the terrorist protesting against his dependence on a given state of language has more in common with the rhetorician than the rhetorician himself. Despite their seeming incompatibility, then, it transpires that Terror and Rhetoric have far more in common than seemed to be the case; and Paulhan, even as he promotes the hope of a (rhetorical) reconciliation between Rhetoric and Terror, is also left in conclusion quizzically undermining the foundations of his own argument. What had begun as a crusade against Terror ends up following a vicious circle of its own making; for Rhetoric rediscovered, as Paulhan concedes, is not far removed from Terrorist purism reaffirmed.[10]

The main source of the peculiar self-defeating or self-questioning paradoxes running through Les Fleurs de Tarbes is not hard to find. For the crux of Paulhan's book turns on the peculiar logic of linguistic commonplaces themselves; and it is this that lies behind not only the inconsistencies of Terror that Paulhan exposes, but also the aporias and self-inverting paradoxes of his own demonstration. For all commonplaces, as Paulhan points out, are by nature uncontrollably duplicitous, which is why they provide ammunition for both rhetorician and terrorist alike. To the extent that they can be repeated in any and every circumstance, they are proof of the precedence of

73

language over thought; but in so far as they may be used in each case as though for the very first time, they are evidence of the inventiveness of human thought in its encounter with language. Being common, their purpose is to enable communication; but being unoriginal, they just as easily defeat it; they are a prime instance of the poverty and insufficiency of everyday speech; but they are sometimes full of the most surprisingly florid turns of phrase or figures. Commonplaces, it would seem, can function simultaneously in each of these contradictory registers. As such, they follow a peculiar logic of hyperbolic paralysis reminiscent of that described by Lacoue-Labarthe in his reading of Hölderlin's fragmentary texts on tragedy. Indeed in Paulhan, as in Hölderlin, it is as though sense relations themselves have begun to behave according to a strangely aporetic pseudo-dialectic of hyperbolic intensification that, far from accrediting the mediating power and all-embracing unity of sense itself, instead has the effect of ruining the possibility of mediation at all. Statements are inverted into their opposites without transition, and paradox becomes the only viable figure of thought at all. In the case of Paulhan's commonplace, the effects are impressive: the more transparent a commonplace seems, the more impenetrable to thought it becomes; the more communicative it is, the more uncommunicative it proves; the more unambiguous it is, so the more ambiguous it turns out. And vice versa.[11]

Reading Paulhan, however, Blanchot is not primarily concerned to assess the validity of the critic's case. As with the work of other writers, Blanchot's strategy is twofold: it is first to generalise the essential proposition of the text to its fullest possible extent; and second to radicalise that argument to the point where it becomes consumed by its own impossibility. It is immediately evident in this context that Paulhan's Terror is not a simple romantic aberration. Rather, it follows from Blanchot's own post-symbolist view of literature as an act of pure, absolute creation that what Paulhan is addressing as Terror is in fact the essence of literature as such. The so-called sickness of words, Blanchot rejoins, is inseparable from the health of words; and any authentic literature, as it seeks to found itself within the terms of its own freedom, affirms itself necessarily, according to the logic of Paulhan's Terror, as a radical refusal of literature, a hatred of language, and a repudiation of all established literary conventions.

But as literature embarks on this contestatory project, it has to negate its own conditions of possibility, for it is clear that without language and without the existence of previous texts, and without the conventions regulating and enabling

74

them, there can be no recognisable thing such as literature at all. If literature chooses to exist only on the basis of the purity and originality of its endeavours, it is soon faced with the realisation that on those terms it cannot exist at all, except as endless banality or mute silence. In such circumstances, Blanchot asks, how is literature possible at all? Only, he replies, by virtue of a double illusion: if literature claims to be pure or original, it is because language has already proven it wrong: the purity of literature is already an impurity, and its alleged originality already a lack of originality. The essence of literature, Blanchot concludes, lies in its radical non-essentiality; the purest and most original texts, one might say, are those that expose themselves with utmost purity to their absence of purity. Literature here becomes affected with the same vertiginous logic as Paulhan's commonplace, and it becomes increasingly clear for Blanchot, in the texts written for the *Journal des débats* during the Occupation, that the essence of art lies not so much in the foundational purity of the work, but rather in the aporia that turns that act of foundation into no more than the impossibility of a possibility. As a result, writing in Blanchot comes increasingly to be described in terms of the contestatory extremity of the inner experience – experience without experience – of writing as such, and it is here that one may sense the crucial importance for Blanchot not only of his own work as a writer of fiction, but of his friendship with Georges Bataille. At any event, the Kantian project adumbrated by Paulhan in *Les Fleurs de Tarbes*, namely that of placing literature on a more secure, rhetorical footing, as Blanchot shows, and as Paulhan was himself no doubt aware, inevitably founders. As it does so, the attempt to produce a coherent aesthetic based on the purity of the work of art gives way to a teeming array of uncontrollable paradoxes that deprive Paulhan's would-be Copernican revolution of any intelligible foundation, and announce to Blanchot, in respect of literature, the radical inadequacy of all transcendental arguments as such.

The exchange between Paulhan and Blanchot turns principally on a question of literature. But there is more here at stake also. It would be to trivialise matters unduly simply to assume, as some have done, that Blanchot in his account of Paulhan's Terror was primarily concerned with settling an account with his own guilty, pre-war activist past.[12] But it is nevertheless evident that the debate between Blanchot and Paulhan about the possibility of literature also touches crucially on the political question of the future of the (national) community in its time of distress. Both for Paulhan and for Blanchot, in their differing ways, it is clear that the question of writing was inseparable from the question of its relation to the wider political and cultural community at large. It is this that gives Blanchot's account of Paulhan its particular urgency in the context of the France of 1941. Indeed, the paradoxical status of literature in Blanchot's essay depends largely on its simultaneous appeal to the future of the community and its resistance to all established, current and prior forms of that community. Literature itself, in these texts, so to speak, is the real, yet always contestatory commonplace of the community; it grasps itself, in Blanchot's account, as an impossible interval, one that belongs necessarily to the language to which it is addressed, but which also projects itself beyond the present state of that community to voice what is nothing less than a promise of radical futurity. Blanchot says as much explicitly, by way of conclusion, when he reminds his readers that in order to imagine the future of literature 'all that is needed is to conceive that *true* commonplaces are words torn apart by lightning and that the rigours of the laws found the absolute world of expression, beyond which chance is nothing but sleep' (*FP*, 101; *BR*, 60).

In their capacity to contest all that is external to them, such *true* commonplaces, as Blanchot calls it, are the works of literature themselves. The role imparted to them here is impressive; but what is perhaps most striking of all is the extent to which, by committing literature to a politics of opposition to the status quo, Blanchot endeavoured still to entrust to literature the capacity to found anew the national community it sought to address. In the France of 1941 this was of course an unambiguous message, and one that provided little comfort for supporters of the Vichy regime or the Occupation. But it meant that Blanchot also found himself in the rather contradictory position of claiming for literature a capacity to refound the current political and cultural order, while also having to acknowledge elsewhere that the only foundation of which literature was capable was an impossibility of foundation. The realisation that literature's boundless power of contestation derived from its necessary and irredeemable antagonism to all acts of foundation was one that was already implicit in *Thomas l'Obscur* and *Aminadab*; but it was arguably to take Blanchot the literary critic several years more before he was able fully to draw the necessary philosophical conclusions from this. But this was no doubt why, once the Liberation did come, one of the writer's first tasks was to embark on a detailed philosophical explication with one of the most influential philosophical sources of his thinking at the time: the writings of Heidegger.

'Naming the gods': from Heidegger to Hölderlin

The just relation to the world is in turning aside, and this turning aside is just only if it is maintained, in separation and distance, as the pure movement of turning aside.

(Le rapport juste au monde est le détour, et ce détour n'est juste que s'il se maintient, dans l'écart et la distance, comme mouvement pur de se détourner.)
'Le Rire des dieux' (*A*, 194)

The reference to Heidegger is rarely explicit in Blanchot's wartime texts for the *Journal des débats*, but its importance is hard to underestimate. In 'Mallarmé et l'art du roman', for instance, first published on 27 October 1943, and chronologically the last of the articles to be collected in *Faux Pas*, Blanchot writes as follows:

Language is what founds human existence and the universe. Man who reveals himself in dialogue and finds in dialogue the event of his foundation, and the world that is put into words by an act that is its fundamental origin, both express the nature and dignity of language. The mistake is to believe language is an implement man has at his disposal in order to act or manifest himself in the world; language in reality has man at its disposal to the extent that it guarantees him the existence of the world and his existence in the world. Naming the gods, transforming the universe into discourse, that alone is what founds the authentic dialogue that is human existence, and that too provides the fabric of such discourse, its shimmering and mysterious figure, its form and constellation, far from the everyday expressions and rules that apply in ordinary life.
(Le langage est ce qui fonde la réalité humaine et l'univers. L'homme qui se révèle dans un dialogue où il trouve son événement fondamental, le monde qui se met en paroles par un acte qui est sa profonde origine, expriment la nature et la dignité du langage. L'erreur est de croire que le langage soit un instrument dont l'homme dispose pour agir ou pour se manifester dans le monde; le langage en réalité dispose de l'homme en ce qu'il lui garantit l'existence du monde et son existence dans le monde. Nommer les dieux, faire que l'univers devienne discours, cela seul fonde le dialogue authentique qu'est la réalité humaine et cela aussi fournit la trame de ce discours, sa brillante et mystérieuse figure, sa forme et sa constellation, loin des vocables et des règles en usage dans la vie pratique.)
(*FP*, 191; *BR*, 45)

From his use of the expression 'la réalité humaine', introduced in the 1930s by Henry Corbin as a way of rendering Heideggerian 'Dasein' into French, it is evident that, in this passage, as elsewhere in *Faux Pas*, Blanchot is quoting.[1] He does so, however, as is often the case, both approximately and anonymously. Happily in this instance, the source of the quotation is not difficult to identify: it is Heidegger's famous lecture, 'Hölderlin und das Wesen der Dichtung' ('Hölderlin and the Essence of Poetry'), delivered in Rome in April 1936 and first published in French in 1938, though it is clear that Blanchot subsequently read the text in the German original.[2] In the lecture, Heidegger quotes at length from Hölderlin, notably from a fragment usually held to belong to a preliminary draft for the unfinished poem 'Friedensfeier' ('Celebration of Peace') and which runs:

> Viel hat erfahren der Mensch. Der Himmlischen viele genannt,
> Seit ein Gespräch wir sind
> Und hören können voneinander.

Michael Hamburger gives the following English version:

> Much men have learnt. Have called by their names many of those in Heaven
> Since we have been a discourse
> And able to hear from each other.[3]

Glossing these words in the lecture, Heidegger explicates them in the following terms, providing Blanchot with much of his own emphasis on the foundational role of language with respect both to human Dasein and the opening of a world:

> From the moment language happens authentically as discourse, so the gods come to speak and a world appears. It is important, on the other hand, to see that the presence of the gods and the appearing of the world are not just a consequence of the happening of language, but are simultaneous with it. So much so that it is in the naming of the gods and the becoming word of the world that consists the authentic discourse which we are ourselves.
>
> (Seitdem die Sprache eigentlich als Gespräch geschieht, kommen die Götter zu Wort und erscheint eine Welt. Aber wiederum gilt es zu sehen: die Gegenwart der Götter und das Erscheinen der Welt sind nicht erst eine Folge des Geschehnisses der Sprache, sondern sind damit gleichzeitig.

Und das so sehr, daß im Nennen der Götter und im Wort-Werden der
Welt gerade das eigentliche Gespräch besteht, das wir selbst sind.)

(E, 40)

Late in 1943, then, in a deliberate and sustained manner, Blanchot can be
found paraphrasing Heidegger who is himself paraphrasing Hölderlin.[4] To
understand what is at stake here it is perhaps worth recalling the particular
weight that, in 1943, for Blanchot, attached to the two names of Heidegger and
Hölderlin. Heidegger, of course, thanks to Levinas, had been familiar to
Blanchot since the late 1920s; and by the early 1940s, as the passage cited above
attests, he had evidently become for Blanchot the thinker most deeply and
purposefully engaged in articulating philosophically the question of the
foundational nature of language in general and poetic language in particular,
and in challenging the inherited presuppositions of aesthetic theory as such,
including received notions of literary mimesis or traditional beliefs regarding the
duality of form and content. In raising these issues, Heidegger, for Blanchot, was
clearly setting the agenda for modern literature and art in general; and this was
why, in formulating his own view of the foundational dimension of language,
Blanchot needed in fact to do little more than simply transpose into French
Heidegger's central contention, contained in the 1936 lecture, that 'language is
not an implement to be had at one's disposal, but that very event that has at its
disposal the highest possibility of being human' ('die Sprache ist nicht ein
verfügbares Werkzeug, sondern dasjenige Ereignis, das über die höchste
Möglichkeit des Menschseins verfügt') (E, 38).

In the lecture, Heidegger went on to reverse the traditional hierarchy
between ordinary language and poetic language, arguing that poetic language –
which Heidegger reformulates, in a more originary turn, as 'Dichtung', i.e. as
that which necessarily precedes, as their common origin, all such derived
notions as poetry or literature – was what opened, not only the very possibility
of everyday language as such, but also the possibility of the coming of a people
– notably the German Volk – into the knowledge of its historical destiny and
its own particular task within the history of Being. 'Dichtung', according to
Heidegger, is thus, as he puts it, the originary, foundational tongue of a
historical people:

Poetry is the founding naming of Being and of the essence of all things –
not just any saying whatever, but the saying by which everything which we
subsequently discuss and deal with in everyday language first comes into

79

the open. That is why poetry never treats language as material that is present-at-hand, but poetry itself first makes language possible. Poetry is the originary language of a historical people.

(Dichtung ist das stiftende Nennen des Seins und des Wesens aller Dinge – kein beliebiges Sagen, sondern jenes, wodurch erst all das ins Offene tritt, was wir dann in der Alltagssprache bereden und verhandeln. Daher nimmt die Dichtung niemals die Sprache als einen vorhandenen Werkstoff auf, sondern die Dichtung selbst ermöglicht erst die Sprache. Dichtung ist die Ursprache eines geschichtlichen Volkes.)

(*E*, 43)

Developing this account, Heidegger argues, with specific reference to Hölderlin, that the proper task of the work of art, by virtue of the foundational dimension of poetic language, is to articulate for the historical community what he calls the between ('das Zwischen'), that median space or time that separates, while thereby connecting them, both gods and humans; the vocation of poetry is thus to integrate as one, as Heidegger puts it, the signs that come from the heavens and the voice of the people (*E*, 46–7).

It was Hölderlin, for Heidegger, who most radically dedicated his poetic word to this task, by describing in his poetry the task of mediation ascribed to 'Dichtung' at the very moment he endeavoured to perform that task. Hölderlin, for Heidegger, was the poet who most intently aimed to understand the necessity of poetry and carry out its demand in the time of distress that is the time of modernity. Hölderlin in his work, Heidegger affirms, thereby 'puts into poetry the essence of poetry' ('dichtet das Wesen der Dichtung') (*E*, 47). This is what gave Hölderlin, in Heidegger's eyes, his crucial philosophical importance; the work of Hölderlin constituted an essential turning point in the history of the West, a turning point that, as Heidegger was wont to remark, had been all but overlooked by the West itself. But no matter, even in his solitude, indeed no doubt because of that very solitude, Hölderlin remained for Heidegger quite simply the essential poet (the poet's poet, 'der Dichter des Dichters', *E*, 47); and the phrase is one Blanchot in his turn cites approvingly, noting for instance of René Char, Heidegger's friend, in October 1946, that 'his poetry is the revelation of poetry, the poetry of poetry, and, as Heidegger says more or less of Hölderlin, the poem of the essence of the poem [comme le dit à peu près Heidegger de Hölderlin, poème de l'essence du poème]' (*PF*, 105; 101).[5]

But the importance of Hölderlin for Heidegger was not just philosophical or poetological; it was political as well. Heidegger began lecturing on Hölderlin in the winter of 1934, soon after his resignation, in April, from the post of Rector of Freiburg University, a position that, as is now well known, he took up in April 1933 as part of a co-ordinated campaign to win over the German university system to National-Socialism.[6] The context of Heidegger's turn to Hölderlin was therefore crucial, and there is little doubt that on one level it was undertaken by Heidegger as a means of redefining and defending – philosophically as well as politically – his own disastrous political venture of 1933 and his own particular commitment to Nazism (of whose 'inner truth', it is now clear, Heidegger was to remain convinced for many years to come). Some of the actions of this political Heidegger were no doubt familiar to Blanchot by the early 1940s.[7] In any case, the figure of Hölderlin was itself no stranger to political controversy. Already for some years, since the end of the First World War, the poet had been viewed by some – including the Nazi ideologue Alfred Rosenberg – as Germany's own national poet, an identification that Heidegger arguably sought to cultivate in his own way by dedicating his 1936 lecture to the memory of Norbert von Hellingrath, Hölderlin's early editor, killed in the trenches in 1916, and which culminated in June 1943 in celebrations throughout the Reich, including Paris, on the occasion of the centenary of the poet's death, under the patronage, amongst others, of Josef Goebbels.[8]

In the dialogue between Heidegger and Blanchot about the poems of Hölderlin, then, there are many different issues at stake; these bear not only on the question of the relationship between literature and philosophy, between metaphysics and its other, between poetry and ethics, but also on the debate about language, community, nationhood, and great art. At the same time, however, it is also noticeable how little explicit engagement with these broader issues is visible in Blanchot's recourse to Heidegger in the essays of the early 1940s from which I have quoted so far. In 1942 and 1943, it is as though Blanchot was content simply to incorporate Heidegger's reading of Hölderlin into his own thinking without much reservation. It was not until three years later, in 1946, that Blanchot began explicitly to articulate in his published critical work the outlines of a more thorough, and more demanding engagement with Heidegger. This he did in an essay entitled 'La Parole "sacrée" de Hölderlin' ('The "Sacred" Word of Hölderlin'), first published in Critique in December 1946, and collected, in revised form, in La Part du feu three years later (*PF*, 115–32; 111–31). The essay is in effect a detailed commentary on Heidegger's essay of 1941 devoted to Hölderlin's famous poem about the role of the poet, 'Wie wenn am Feiertage . . .' ('As on a holiday . . .', in Hamburger's translation).[9] It was written at impressive speed. As late as mid-October Blanchot was confessing in a letter to Bataille, who had evidently suggested he review Heidegger's article for *Critique*, that though he was tempted by the proposition, he had still not yet seen the recent issue of the magazine *Fontaine* containing the French translation of Heidegger's text; by December, though, Blanchot's article had been delivered to the publisher and was already on sale in bookshops. All of which suggests that, even before the essay was written, Blanchot had spent considerable time reconsidering his relationship to Heidegger and rereading Hölderlin.[10]

As elsewhere in his work, in the essay 'La Parole "sacrée" de Hölderlin', Blanchot proceeds indirectly. He writes largely alongside Heidegger, that is to say, with Heidegger, but also, simultaneously, against him. This is a common strategy in Blanchot, who in all his writing, rather than endorsing or opposing a philosophical argument, tends instead to accompany it through its various twists and turns in order then to prise it apart by confronting it with the limits of its own possibility. In reading Blanchot's article on Heidegger, therefore, it is less important to attend, in themselves, to the overt conceptual statements that occur in the essay, many of which can be traced back to Heidegger, than to examine the particular, often paradoxical treatment to which Blanchot subjects some of those formulations. So while the essay does open with a series of circumspect criticisms regarding the legitimacy of Heidegger's style of commentary, including his prosaic neglect of Hölderlin's poetic rhythms and his reliance on etymology as a mode of argument, most readers of the article have declared Blanchot's account of Heidegger's reading of Hölderlin to be extremely faithful to Heidegger, so much so, for instance, that Herman Rapaport, in a discussion of the relationship between Heidegger and Derrida, credits Blanchot – somewhat ironically in the circumstances – with being little more than a particularly astute, foresightful 'mediator of Heidegger'.[11]

If one reads Blanchot's text with greater attention to detail, however, there are signs of a more deep-seated disaccord with Heidegger. This is borne out by the minor modifications that Blanchot incorporated into the essay when revising it for inclusion in *La Part du feu*, as, too, do many subsequent remarks made by Blanchot about Heidegger's account of Hölderlin.[12] Admittedly, as far as the 1946 article is concerned, the evidence for Blanchot's departure from

Heidegger's reading is at times very faint. This does not of course make it any the less real. Indeed, as though to illustrate this very point, Blanchot at one moment offers a sly reflection on the elliptical nature of his own intervention. Heidegger, in his 1941 piece, is glossing Hölderlin's use of the word *Natur* (Nature) and quotes the following lines from the poem 'Am Quell der Donau' ('At the Source of the Danube'):

> Wir nennen Dich, heiliggenöthiget, nennen
> Natur! dich wir, und neu, wie dem Bad entsteigt
> Dir alles Göttlichgeborne.

> (We name you, under a holy compulsion we
> Now name you Nature, and new, as from a bath
> From you emerges all that's divinely born.)[13]

Heidegger points out that, in the manuscript, these lines are in fact crossed out; this is taken to support the contention that the Latinate term Nature (*natura*) is no longer sufficient to Hölderlin's purpose, but has silently begun to bear witness to Greek φύσις in its capacity as original, founding word or *Grundwort* ('This overcoming', says Heidegger, 'is the consequence and the sign of a more original saying' ['Diese Überwindung ist die Folge und das Zeichen eines anfänglicher anhebenden Sagens'] *E*, 58). This is, of course, in Heidegger's thinking, a recurrent strategy, one that consists in the re-translation of so-called founding words back into their original Greek forms.[14] Blanchot's rejoinder to this move is to repeat it, but at the same time also invert it: 'That nature', he writes, ' . . . owes to the Sacred its most essential qualities . . . is something that is affirmed by these lines from "At the Source of the Danube", lines that, although subsequently crossed out, were nevertheless still formulated' ('Que la nature . . . doive au Sacré ce qu'elle a de plus essentiel . . . c'est ce qu'affirment les vers d'"Aux Sources du Danube" qui, quoique biffés par la suite, n'en ont pas moins été formulés') (*PF*, 123; 119).

The point is more than a philological nicety. For Blanchot follows up his remark almost immediately with the claim, which is at the centre of his disagreement with Heidegger, that by interpreting the Sacred as chaos, even chaos suitably redefined as an originary gaping and the opening or awakening of nature itself to the light, Heidegger falls victim to a misleadingly traditional view of the poet. The darkness of original night, Blanchot objects, mourned by the poet as he is illuminated by nature's awakening, has no place in Hölderlin's experience. (Throughout the essay, this emphasis on Hölderlin's experience is a significant feature of Blanchot's reading, and one that places his essay within the context of an exchange not only with Heidegger, but also Bataille.) For Blanchot, paradoxically, it is at the very moment when Heidegger begins reading Hölderlin as though the text were written in a language closer to the pre-metaphysical origins of Western thought, that he succumbs to a misreading that fails to do justice to Hölderlin's originality. The point may seem trivial, but more is at issue than a question of poetical interpretation; for while both Heidegger and Blanchot agree that the Sacred precedes both humans and gods as their common space of possibility, they differ sharply as to the relationship between the language of poetry and this necessarily unapproachable and incommunicable origin.

For Heidegger, the Sacred, seen either as originary chaos or as the very essence of nature itself, marks the very opening of being to itself. For the poet, it is like a moment of originary quickening that, like the nature – $\varphi \acute{u} \sigma \iota \varsigma$ – that is his all-inclusive and prescient companion, ushers him into the light of both world and work. Hölderlin, in this way, appears in Heidegger as the poet who, out of darkness, receives the vision of light clarified, transformed, shaped and mediated through poetry; he is the poet who, as Heidegger puts it in his 1943 postface to 'Was ist Metaphysik?', in naming the Sacred, fulfils the same task as the thinker who speaks Being.[15] The figure is that of the poet as mediator; yet though Blanchot acknowledges the importance of that role in at least some of Hölderlin's poems, he is quick to see its limitations (PF, 118; 114). Indeed, his own account of the poet could not in fact be more different; for Blanchot's Hölderlin is not the poet of the burgeoning origin, but of the origin dispersed, not the poet of the night transfigured, but of the day affirmed, not the poet of the lighting of Being, but of the light which precedes the light. In Hölderlin, Blanchot writes, 'night and chaos always end up vouching for law, form, and light' (PF, 123; 120); and he continues as follows:

> The Sacred is the light of day: not the day as contrasted with the night, nor the light as it shines from above, nor the flame that Empedocles searches for below. It is the light of day, but prior to the day, and always prior to itself, the day before the day, a light before light to which we are closest

when we grasp the dawn, the infinitely far-off distance of daybreak which is also what is most intimate to us, more inward than inwardness itself.

(*PF*, 124; 121)

In their account of the Sacred, Heidegger and (after him) Blanchot both cite a prose commentary by Hölderlin on a translation of a fragment from Pindar.[16] The text, which Hölderlin titles 'Das Höchste' (and which an exactly contemporary Blanchot work suggests one might venture to translate into French as 'Le Très-Haut', 'The Most High'), seeks to formulate the dichotomy between what Hölderlin terms the immediate or the incommunicable ('das Unmittelbare', that which cannot be mediated) and the law, as he puts it, of rigorous communicability ('die strenge Mittelbarkeit'). While the first of these, Hölderlin maintains, is impossible for both gods and mortals, since both are subject to the need to make distinctions (i.e. mediate contrasts or oppositions) in order to judge or to know, the second imposes on both mortals and gods, by the most elevated of laws, the stringent obligation to communicate or to mediate between the two realms of heaven and earth. Hölderlin's words are elliptical and enigmatic, and pose formidable problems of interpretation. For his part, Heidegger resolves these by aligning Hölderlin's distinction with the concept of ontological difference, i.e. the difference between Being ('Sein') and beings ('das Seiende') that is at the centre of all Heidegger's own work. On this reading, Hölderlin's paradox of communicability and incommunicability may be reformulated in such a way as to refer to Heideggerian Being, to the extent that being, for Heidegger, necessarily resists all mediation or communication because it is precisely what enables all communication or mediation to take place at all. And it is this logically prior realm, which is not in itself an entity, but the condition of existence of all possible entities that, in Heidegger's view, constitutes the essence of Hölderlinian $\varphi\upsilon\sigma\iota\varsigma$; and it is this that Hölderlin's Sacred word is held to name. As Heidegger explains:

Immediate all-presence is the intermediary for all that is communicated, i.e. that which is communicable. The immediate itself is never something communicable, but on the other hand the immediate, in the strict sense, is communication, i.e. it is the communicability of the communicable, because this makes it possible in its essence. 'Nature' is all communicating communicability; it is 'the law'.

(Die unmittelbare Allgegenwart ist die Mittlerin für alles Vermittelte und d.h. für das Mittelbare. Das Unmittelbare ist selbst nie ein Mittelbares, wohl dagegen ist das Unmittelbare, streng genommen, die Vermittelung, d.h. die Mittelbarkeit des Mittelbaren, weil sie dieses in seinem Wesen ermöglicht. Die 'Natur' ist die alles vermittelnde Mittelbarkeit, ist 'das Gesetz'.)

(*E*, 62)

In his own paper, Blanchot rallies initially to much the same view, and cites Heidegger accordingly: 'What is the Sacred?', he asks. 'It is the immediate, says Heidegger, taking his lead from a prose fragment by Hölderlin, the immediate that is never communicated, but is the principle of all possibility of communicating [l'immédiat qui n'est jamais communiqué, mais est le principe de toute possibilité de communiquer]' (*PF*, 123; 120).

At this point further difficulties arise. For if the Sacred is that which by essence cannot become an object of communication or mediation, and if it is nonetheless the task of Dichtung to name the Sacred, how is the poem possible? Does it not, in an act of fatal hubris, simply turn the Sacred into an object, the very reverse of itself? This danger exists, Heidegger concedes, and the law of the Sacred is thereby necessarily threatened. But in the last resort, Heidegger rejoins, that which is derived from the origin is powerless against that origin ('So vermag das dem Ursprung Entsprungene nichts gegen den Ursprung') (*E*, 74). The Sacred – $\varphi \acute{v} \sigma \iota \varsigma$ or Being – is that which makes the poetic act possible; poetry, which owes its existence to the Sacred, cannot change the Sacred into what it is not, if only because the Sacred already includes its own opposite. Though the poet may suffer at the hands of the Sacred, he belongs to its opening and is given, by that opening, both the duty and the means to speak it in its constancy or permanence, and submit to its law. The poet's part, for Heidegger, corresponds to a kind of originary fervour, and his stance is one of silent, prescient absorption in the all-enclosing presence of Being. Whatever the anguish of the originary chaos represented by the incommunicability of the sacred, the poet, on Heidegger's submission, is nevertheless able to domesticate it by his silence and transmute it into the gentleness that characterises all poetic disclosure. As Heidegger writes, in a famous passage:

> The violence of chaos, that offers no pause, the terror of the immediate, that thwarts all access, the Sacred is transformed by the silence of the sheltered poet into the gentleness of the communicable and communicating word.
>
> (Die Erschütterung des Chaos, das keinen Anhalt bietet, die Schrecknis

des Unmittelbaren, das jeden Zudrang vereitelt, das Heilige ist durch die Stille des behüteten Dichters hindurch in die Milde des mittelbaren und vermittelnden Wortes gewandelt.)

(E, 71)

For Heidegger, then, the poem is possible, in Hölderlinian terms, on condition that the incommensurability or discontinuity that exists between the demand for poetic communication and the elusive nature of the incommunicable object can somehow be transmuted into a relationship that admits of mediation, a mediation whose purity is vouchsafed both by the suffering of the poet and the intensity of his silence.

Despite appearances to the contrary, Blanchot refuses this moment of reconciliation between Dichtung and Being. Blanchot insists, with more radical commitment than Heidegger, on the irreducible incommensurability of the relation – the relation without relation – that binds the necessity of poetic communication to the incommunicability of the Sacred, and vice versa. Hölderlin's poem, he argues, is the site of what can only be described as a fundamental aporia, an impossible possibility. As Blanchot asks Heidegger:

How can the Sacred, which is 'unexpressed', 'unknown', which is what opens only on condition that it is not unveiled, which reveals because it is itself unrevealed, how can it fall into speech, let itself be alienated into becoming, itself pure interiority, the exteriority of song? In truth, indeed, this is not possible, it is impossibility itself [à la vérité, justement, cela ne se peut pas, c'est l'impossible].

(PF, 128; 126)

While Heidegger spirits away the incommensurability between the communicable and the incommunicable to discover in that relationship a movement of gentle mediation, Blanchot insists instead on the groundless impossibility of such mediation. The poem, for Blanchot, remains the place of an irretrievable tension, one that cannot be unified within any kind of dialectic or within the totalising embrace of Heideggerian Being; instead of being construed, as it is by Heidegger, as an inaugural act of historical or ontological foundation, what Hölderlin's poem affirms, for Blanchot, is the irresolvable double bind that imposes on poetry the obligation of writing while confronting it perpetually with the impossibility of writing. Hölderlin's text, throughout, is read by Blanchot as a dramatisation of this aporia. Thus, for instance, the disabling circularity that dogs Hölderlin's project to name in poetry the wholeness of nature, a wholeness that comes into being only by the act of poetic naming that constitutes it, but which cannot come into being because, in order for there to be a poet to carry it out, the act of naming needs already to have taken place. The poet is the product of the poetic work, which confers on him his existence; before the work is written, therefore, the poet has no proper existence; but if that is so, no poetic work can in fact be produced, with the result that the poet survives only in a ghostly future perfect, divided from himself and without necessity, confronted with the aporia of an act that cannot accomplish the task which it is called upon to fulfil.

Such aporias, Blanchot insists, are the price as well as the condition of poetry as such; for, as Hölderlin's work attests, poetry somehow, in spite of all, remains a possibility. But this possibility rests on its own necessary impossibility; and this is what Blanchot's essay raises in objection to Heidegger: the question of the impossibility of the possibility of poetry. (In later texts, alongside Levinas, Blanchot will ask of Heidegger a very similar question, not in respect of Dichtung, but in relation to what, in a celebrated passage of Sein und Zeit, Heidegger addresses as the question of Dasein's 'ownmost possibility', the possibility of its impossibility, that is to say, the question of death.)[17] To press home the point, Blanchot cites Heidegger once more, offering his own version of the passage from the commentary on 'Wie wenn am Feiertage...' given above. Blanchot writes:

> Directly, the Sacred cannot be grasped, even less can it become speech, yet through the silence of the poet, it supposedly lets itself be pacified [il se laisserait apaiser],[18] transformed, and finally transported into the speech of song. Possibly so. But what has become of the problem? It has taken another form, but it still remains a problem; or rather, it has now been replaced by a double enigma: how and why can 'the violence of chaos that offers no pause, the terror of the immediate that thwarts all access, the Sacred' ['l'ébranlement du chaos qui n'offre aucun point d'appui et d'arrêt, la terreur de l'Immédiat qui fait échec à toute saisie directe, le Sacré'] let itself be transformed and attained by silence? And, in turn, how and why can silence let itself be attained by speech?
>
> (PF, 128; 126)

Crucially, here, at the very moment he incorporates into his own text this description of the poetic act, Blanchot truncates, interrupts Heidegger's sentence.[19] The move is an emblematic one; for as he does so, Blanchot signals the decisive moment of his own intervention into Heidegger's discourse, that moment where Heidegger's own discourse founders on the impossibility to which it fails to do justice. It is important to note here to what extent Blanchot's interruption of Heidegger is founded not only on a poetological difference, but an ethical one as well. Crucial to Blanchot's divergence from Heidegger is the question of the law, of that which Hölderlin in his Pindar commentary names as 'das Höchste', the Most High. For Heidegger, the question of the law is simple, since what is at stake in Dichtung for Heidegger is the law of Being itself; it is this of course that enables Heidegger to treat poetry as enacting a gesture of political inauguration by telling a historical people the truth about its historical, ontological destination. (And it is worth recalling here Heidegger's notorious claim, made in 'Der Ursprung des Kunstwerks' ['The Origin of the Work of Art'] of 1936, that, in its relation to truth, poetry takes its place alongside a number of other such moments, including the act of founding of the state and of essential sacrifice.)[20] But for Blanchot, however, the question of the law is never simple; it is always double, it always involves having to respond, beyond the possibility of the law, to the impossibility that both founds and exceeds the law: the law beyond the law, so to speak, that, beyond being, formulates a demand that, by definition, can never be satisfied. As Blanchot writes, giving his own version of the Most High: 'Speaking is what is required, that, that alone will do. And yet speaking is impossible' ('Parler, il le faut, c'est cela, cela seul qui convient. Et pourtant parler est impossible') (*PF*, 129; 127).

From this ethical difference between Hölderlin and Heidegger flow all the other points of divergence touched on by Blanchot in his article: the emphasis on poetry's resistance – as poetic rhythm – to the totalising designs of philosophy; the distrust of Heidegger's confident reliance on the truth of etymology; the insistence on the specificity of Hölderlin's own poetic experience; the wary reminder, contra Heidegger, that any poetic act is confronted from the outset with the impossibility of beginning, and that poetry as a result cannot serve as a moment of stable ethical or political foundation; and the repeated affirmation, as Blanchot puts it, 'Le Grand Refus' ('The Great Refusal', *EI*, 69; 48), that while poetry may name the possible, its task is to respond to the impossible, and that, in the guise of the immediate, what Hölderlin's poetry is forever in the process of encountering is not Being, but, as Blanchot formulates it in 1969, in a heavily reworked passage from *L'Entretien infini*, the 'infinite presence of what remains radically absent, presence always infinitely other in its presence, presence of the other in its alterity: non-presence' (*EI*, 54; 38). Hölderlin's poetry, for Blanchot, founds no homogeneous community possessing within itself the truth of its own future destiny. Contrary to what Heidegger explicitly and implicitly uses Hölderlin to assert from 1934 onwards, the community that poetry installs for Blanchot is a community that exists outside of truth, in the interruption of history, in its exposure to the worklessness of the outside.

Blanchot ends 'La Parole "sacrée" de Hölderlin' with a reference to the impossible possibility, and with a final quotation:

> In its very impossibility, the reconciliation of the Sacred with speech demanded of the poet's existence that it most nearly approach non-existence. It was then, for a moment, that itself seemed possible, when, just before foundering, it allowed itself to be affirmed in song, in words issuing from an already silent body and uttered by a dead voice, in such a way that the hymn alone, worthy of the essence of the day, rose from the depths of the vanished day, and that spirit was glorified by its own distraction, but not because the most high is darkness, nor because in the end the spirit must be bound to its own destruction, but, as the All made itself language to say: because whoever wishes to encounter darkness must seek it in the light of the day, stare at the light of the day, and become the light of the day for themselves:
>
> > Enigma is the pure surging of what surges forth
> > The deep that shakes all, the coming of the day.
> >
> > [Énigme est le pur jaillissement de ce qui jaillit
> > Profondeur qui tout ébranle, la venue du jour.]
>
> (*PF*, 132; 131)

These closing two lines, cited as though from Hölderlin, with which Blanchot more or less concludes his article, bring together three key motifs from Blanchot's account: poetry's pure affirmation of the impossibility of its own possibility, the absence of foundation that puts everything into question, the always prior arrival of the light. Yet despite appearances to the contrary, these two lines are in fact not from Hölderlin at all; or, more precisely, they are on Blanchot's part both more and less than a quotation.[21] In reality, only the first

90

line is from Hölderlin, namely from the fourth stanza of the poem 'Der Rhein' ('The Rhine'), which reads: 'Ein Rätsel ist Reinentsprungenes'.[22] The second line that Blanchot reproduces is not however the verse which follows, nor is it easy to locate at all in the whole of Hölderlin's published work. It is more readily interpretable as Blanchot's own summary and apocryphal anthologising of two powerfully recurrent Hölderlinian motifs: the plunging abyss, the coming of the light.

What should one make of such slapdash scholarship? Laziness? Negligence? The result of writing too fast? Or just a poor memory? All this, no doubt. But also: the implicit affirmation, on Blanchot's part, that philosophers – such as Heidegger – have for too long endeavoured to interpret Hölderlin's poems; the task now is to rewrite them.[23]

The limitlessness of the limit

But if we call the day to account, if we manage to cast the day aside in order to discover what lies before or beneath it, we find that the day is already present, and that what is before the day is always already day, in the form of the inability to disappear rather than the power to make things appear, as obscure necessity and not radiant freedom. The nature, then, of what is before the day, of existence prior to the day, is the dark side of the day, and that dark side is not the undisclosed mystery of its beginning but its inevitable presence, a 'There is no day' [un 'Il n'y a pas de jour'] which merges with a 'There is already day' [un 'Il y a déjà du jour'], its appearance coinciding with the moment when it has not yet appeared. The day, in the course of the day, allows us to escape from things, it lets us understand them by making them transparent and, so to speak, null – but the day itself is what one cannot escape: in it we are free, but itself the day is fatality, and the day as fatality is the being of what is prior to the day, the existence from which it is necessary to turn aside in order to speak and understand.

'La Littérature et le droit à la mort' (*PF*, 318; 329–30)

The relation between Blanchot's critical essays and fiction is complex and multiple. The two series of texts do not belong to a single homogeneous space, but possess a different rhythm and temporality, a divergent external history and an incommensurable set of internal constraints. For this reason alone, it would be short-sighted to impose on the relation between Blanchot's discursive prose and fictional writing a secure hierarchical structure or polarity. Indeed, particularly in Blanchot's case, where the divisions between essay and fiction are less clearly demarcated than in other writers, there is arguably little reason to attribute special qualities – of originality, profundity, or subversive potential –

91

to one group of texts rather than another. Often it is the similarities between the essays and fiction that are more striking than the differences between them; and, frequently, motifs that first occur in a fictional context return as subjects of discussion in Blanchot's criticism, while issues debated in the literary essays often subsequently feature in barely modified form in fictional works.

This apparently easy circulation of meaning is deceptive. It ignores the effects of the peculiarly suspensive violence with which literature, Blanchot argues, interrupts the workaday continuity of meaning and causes a banal sentence such as Kafka's: 'the head clerk rang' (*PF*, 79; 74) to take on a very different set of functions according to whether it appears in a work of fiction or is used in the course of daily office routine. The argument is one that has often been put forward by theorists of literature inspired by phenomenology or by the structuralist neo-formalism that in many respects is its heir. Admittedly, it is no doubt essential for literary criticism to do justice to the disruptive force – the difference – that is put in play by the fictional deployment of language in literary texts. All too often, however, on the part of literary critics, the result has been to confer on the work of art the status of a superior, ideal, or idealised object whose principal distinguishing feature lies in the extent to which it is hoisted clear of so-called everyday discourse. The consequence of this, in turn, has been to determine the specificity of literature purely from the perspective of the very norms literature on this account is in fact deemed to transgress; at which point literature finds itself, albeit negatively, entirely reliant after all on the very rules and conventions that it is one of writing's main characteristics most strenuously to challenge.

The originality of Blanchot's own approach to the issue of the specificity or distinctiveness of literature, though it has often been misrepresented, may be measured by the extent to which he resists these pitfalls. Indeed, Blanchot refuses to see literature as being essentially transgressive if by that what is implied is that the fate of literature is entirely bound, dialectically, to societal or discursive norms; and he similarly rejects any idea of the work of art as an autotelic, intransitive, or self-referential entity entirely devoted to the aesthetic closure of its own essential self-presence. The so-called specificity of literature, for Blanchot, if indeed it exists at all, is not to be found in this concept of the self-legislating autonomy of literary language, nor in the idea that literature displays a richer potential for communicativeness than so-called ordinary speech; nor does it lie in literature's greater veracity or truthfulness to experience, nor

– as a neo-formalist critic might claim – in its greater awareness of its own inherent falsity as a verbal artefact.

In Blanchot's terms, what is singular about literature – to the extent that the question: what is literature? is susceptible of any determinate answer whatsoever – is rather the infinite paradoxicality of its essential non-essentiality and the boundless peculiarity of its relation to its own limits. Limits, of course, as Jacques Derrida has shown, obey a disconcerting and duplicitous logic that might be said to be entirely their own, were it not for the fact that limits, by their very nature, are endowed with infinite scepticism whenever it comes to determining the limits of that which is proper or improper to them.[1] Limits in this sense are not figures of authority or power, but evanescent traces traversed by an abysmal and aporetic logic. Once they are traced or inscribed, they serve to discriminate between a certain order and a certain disorder; and what falls within a given limit is declared to be subject to a law that does not hold for what is beyond that limit. Limits, however, can be instituted or proclaimed as such only by an authority that exists beyond the limit to be determined and which is itself not subject to the law to be enforced. To institute a limit therefore is not only to circumscribe and contain, but to yield paradoxically to the fragility of any such attempt at circumscription or containment; and it is to make the limit itself a function or effect of the limitlessness on which it is necessarily premised. The limit, then, no longer operates as a term in its own right, but rather only as a response to the interminability that thereby comes to inhabit it. And though its existence is implied by the limit, the limitlessness beyond the limit obeys a different law to that limit, a law that cannot of course be named from the perspective of the limit, except on condition that the limit itself be suspended. The limitlessness beyond the limit limits the limit by turning its law into a secondary, derived entity, and affirms its own necessity as an always prior demand, a demand that is thereby infinitely at odds with the law of the limit.

At this point it appears that the limitlessness beyond the limit itself constitutes something resembling a law, albeit a law that is necessarily irreducible to any law of the limit and infinitely dissymmetrical with it. Yet though the two exigencies – that of the limit and that of the limitlessness of the limit – are disjoined from one another, they do not exist in isolation from each other; and while the limitlessness beyond the limit belongs to the limit, so to speak, as its very condition of possibility and impossibility, the reverse is also true, for without the interval inscribed by the limit the limitlessness that lies beyond it would not be possible either. In this way, the limitlessness beyond the

93

limit may be said both to follow and precede the limit; just as the demand of limitlessness exceeds that of the limit, limitlessness itself is inseparable from its own necessary interruption. As Blanchot insists, the limitlessness is itself inherent in the limit; what it implies is not the lure of an effusive, all-embracing totality, but the rigorous necessity of infinite fragmentation, boundless discontinuity, and endless finitude. This logic is both bizarre and paradoxical, but it is absolutely fundamental to Blanchot's account of literature and of the literary. For Blanchot, one might say, literature is what arises when the relation between limitlessness and the limit is pursued to the point of its limitlessness. In literature, so to speak, limits are simultaneously maintained and suspended, and their effects intensified as well as effaced. What literature names is the strange movement by which, without ever gathering itself into dialectical unity, language poses limits and affirms meaning, but even by doing so silently reaches beyond those limits to respond to the limitlessness that is inseparable from those limits and which those limits in turn necessarily serve to punctuate and interrupt.

Three years after the publication of 'La Parole "sacrée" de Hölderlin' in 1946, there appeared in a literary journal a short story by Blanchot with a puzzling double title. The work was announced on the cover of the periodical as 'Un récit?'. In the table of contents, however, and on the first page of the text, it was simply called 'Un récit', until eventually, in 1973, the story was reissued under the now more familiar name of La Folie du jour (The Madness of the Day).[2] As Derrida has convincingly shown, the slippage between these two – subsequently three – titles is more than a case of localised lexical permissiveness. The effects extend to the story or text as a whole, which may thus be read not only as a protracted commentary on the hesitation inherent within its own title(s), but also as a radical questioning of its own unity and wholeness as such. Indeed, in that each proposed title doubles both as a naming of the text and an integral part of it, as an address to the text and a quotation from it, Blanchot's story puts itself in the double and dissymmetrical position of placing itself at one and the same time under the jurisdiction of one law, the law of literary genres and of narratives, while also responding to another law, the law of the text's own original namelessness and irredeemable madness. The result is to shatter the apparent self-identity or self-presence of the story as such.

Indeed, throughout the text of La Folie du jour, Blanchot exploits to radical effect the many paradoxes – governing the relationship between inside and outside, first and second, general and particular – that are produced by the structure of the limit, the frame, and the margin. The result is that complex structure of repeated self-imbrication that Derrida has famously described as 'chiasmic double invagination'.[3] This is not in itself the product of any particular subversive decision on Blanchot's part; as Derrida maintains, it is an uncontrollable consequence of the general structure of framing as such. What is distinctive, however, about Blanchot's text is that it pushes the paradox of the limitlessness of the limit to the extreme point of its necessary impossibility; and it is at that point – that limit – that everything changes, and the reader of Blanchot's story is faced with the task of interpreting – or, better, not interpreting – a textual space which no longer allows one to discriminate with finality between what is inside and what is outside, what is general and what is singular, what is subject to the law and what is beyond it.

Texts published in periodicals, however, as Derrida points out, always carry at least one supplementary title in the shape of the magazine's own, and it is worth noting that the journal in which 'Un récit' (or 'Un récit?') did first appear in 1949, edited by René Char, Albert Béguin, and Albert Camus, was the literary monthly *Empédocle*, which had taken its own name from the eponymous hero of Hölderlin's unfinished – and probably unfinishable – tragedy of 1797–99, *Der Tod des Empedokles* (*The Death of Empedocles*). Admittedly, this encounter between Hölderlin's Empedocles and Blanchot's *récit* may be entirely coincidental; but, as Blanchot argues elsewhere, apropos of Mallarmé's 'Un coup de dés', chance is not without its own – unpredictable – necessities. (Indeed, one might ask, was the hesitation between 'Un récit' and 'Un récit?' not itself the result of an inspired misprint?) And if the law is one of chance, chance will of course make its own irresistible demands. Which is why there is perhaps some justification for reading *La Folie du jour* from the edge or margin of its Hölderlinian resonances, and as an attempt at fictional exploration of the issues at stake in 'La Parole "sacrée" de Hölderlin'. By doing so it will be possible not only to examine more closely the relationship between Blanchot's essays and fiction, but to understand better, also, the impact on Blanchot's fictional writing of the engagement with Heidegger examined above.

Hölderlin's Empedocles is a figure who, combining intense hubris with intense devotion to the gods, aims to embrace the All in an act of willed self-destruction. In writing the play, which went through three different versions, each more fragmentary than the last, it is now generally accepted that Hölderlin was exposing himself to enormous artistic as well as personal difficulties. But as

95

Blanchot argues in a later essay on Hölderlin in *L'Espace littéraire* (*EL*, 283–92; 269–76), the project for the play also ran another risk, namely that of falling victim to an inauthentic illusion, what Blanchot describes there, recalling much of his earlier analysis, as the lure of the immediate, the impossible. In all his subsequent work, however, the temptation, Blanchot writes, was one Hölderlin strenuously resisted. 'The more Hölderlin is subject to the ordeal of "the fire of the heavens", ' Blanchot writes, 'the more he expresses the necessity of not surrendering to it immeasurably [sans mesure]' (*EL*, 288; 273). There is here, in Blanchot's reading, a further instance of what Philippe Lacoue-Labarthe has described as Hölderlin's 'hyperbologic', that strange pseudo-logic of indefinite exchange between contraries in the movement of their limitless intensification.[4] Fidelity to gods and to men for Hölderlin is purchased only by infidelity to both; and poetic purity is at the price of turning aside from both the heavens and the earth to maintain intact the interval that separates them and challenges their immanence or self-identity; indeed, writes Blanchot, it is as that pure, rendingly empty distance of separation between the gods and humankind that the Sacred may most properly – improperly – be formulated (*EL*, 289; 274).

Blanchot's reading of Hölderlin turns crucially on an awareness of the oscillating tension between two dissymmetrical forces: between that which is without limits and always threatens to overwhelm meaning, and the artistic – prosodic – measure needed to contain the limitlessness while also being interrupted by it. The affirmation of this dual logic is a crucial priority in Blanchot's account of Hölderlin; but it is also an essential element in all Blanchot's critical writing on literature in general. Indeed, it may also be said to be at the centre of a fictional text like *La Folie du jour*; and for this reason it is not difficult to perceive many striking similarities or convergences between Hölderlin's poems and Blanchot's own *récit*. Both depend, for instance, on the double contention, first, that the only proper goal of literature as such – precisely because it is not an object but the prior condition of any subject or object at all – is the limitlessness of the impossible; but, second, that the boundlessness of what is unlimited can only be manifested in literature by rigorous insistence on separation and difference. These are the terms within which Blanchot's reading of Hölderlin moves; but they characterise the thematic and narrative structure of *La Folie du jour* as well.

Indeed, *La Folie du jour* begins, as though in homage to Hölderlin's Empedocles, with an extraordinary testimonial to the limitless extremity of both living and dying:

I am neither clever nor stupid. I have known joys. That is saying too little: I am alive, and this life gives me the greatest of pleasure. Death, then? When I die (perhaps shortly), I will feel immense pleasure. I am not talking about the foretaste of death, which is insipid and often disagreeable. Suffering numbs the mind. But such is the remarkable truth of which I am sure: I experience boundless pleasure in living and will find boundless satisfaction in dying [j'éprouve à vivre un plaisir sans limites et j'aurai à mourir une satisfaction sans limites].

(FJ, 9; 5)

These are impressively powerful and affirmative words. But they are less transparent than might at first appear. Despite the text's suggestions to the contrary, living and dying, like pleasure and satisfaction, are not absolute events or experiences; for they may be grasped or determined only within the limits that circumscribe them and constitute them as what they are. Necessarily, then, Blanchot's references to living and dying, pleasure and pain, inscribe those limits, but they do so seemingly in the absence of those limits. No sooner are the limits of experience implied than they are overwhelmed by the boundlessness of the affirmation that spills beyond them. The opening sentences, with their cautious clauses of denial, their moment of self-confessed understatement, and the allusion to the impending (impossible?) possibility of death, all serve to mark the limits within which the narrator is speaking; but paradoxically, by the very fact of marking these limits, Blanchot's sentences place themselves beyond them. To draw attention to such limits is to efface them, and the principle of limitation turns unaccountably into one of excess. Writing itself, of course, neither lives nor dies; and it is that very impossibility that enables it to locate itself, as here, within the space between the possibility of living and the possibility of dying as they present themselves to the narrator. But if writing can occupy the ground between life and death, it is only because of its essential limitations; for it is the essential irrelevance and impossibility of the difference between life and death as far as writing is concerned that allow Blanchot's text to test to the extreme the possibilities embodied in those two equally impossible states. Writing is an experience of the limit; and precisely because of this it is also an act of limitless affirmation. In other words, it is the limitedness of writing that is the key to its limitlessness. And the experience of dying, when it too comes, serves as an instantiation of much the same logic, as both a realisation of inescapable finitude and an occasion for boundless gaiety (FJ, 12; 7).[5]

97

Blanchot's text experiments throughout with this strange, mutual implication of the experience of the limit and the limitlessness of experience. Telling stories, for instance, is a task that, as Blanchot's narrator reminds his readers at the end, falls only to those capable of reasoning with distinction (*FJ*, 37–8; 18); and it is indeed clear that, for a narrative to be articulated at all in a text, that text must endow itself with recognisable limits. The condition is one to which *La Folie du jour* subscribes without difficulty; indeed it does so to excess, with the result that the narrative structure of the *récit*, shot through with interruptions of one kind or another, remains painfully discontinuous and, as the 1973 title implies, seems never far from seeming quite deranged. At many points the *récit* is like a long sequence of fragments, of disconnected scenes, elliptical beginnings, and moments of charged apostrophe, which the impressively staccato, incisive rhythm of Blanchot's prose manages to carry along with a violence all its own. At one stage, the narrator has a brief vision, but what promises to be an all-embracing moment of plenitude turns out to be no more than a peculiarly truncated – limited – glimpse of a man half entering, half leaving the entrance to a courtyard, allowing a woman with a pram to pass between him and the gate. 'This brief scene', comments the narrator with beatific enthusiasm, 'whipped me into a frenzy [me souleva jusqu'au délire]' (*FJ*, 19; 10).

Some pages later, with more dramatic effect, at the exact mid-point of the text, a telling fissure interrupts even this precarious account: the protagonist has glass crushed into his eyes, and he is briefly blinded by the excessive exposure to the light that ensues. With his eyes wrapped in bandages for the apocalyptic duration of seven days, he is forced to contend, not with the illumination afforded by the light (which has to be limited if normal vision is to take place), but with the blindness caused by the limitlessness of the light. Light here is what enables the narrator to see but also prevents him from seeing; and much the same double bind confronts the narrator when he attempts to narrate the event of the destruction of his sight: such an event, standing as it does at the centre of the *récit*, is what allows the text to aspire to story-telling at all, except that such an event, no longer belonging to the realm of the visible, refuses to be narrated, and leaves the text of Blanchot's *récit*, like the light itself, oscillating madly between being a condition of possibility and one of impossibility, simultaneously opening and closing the narrative itself (*FJ*, 22; 11).

What follows, however, serves only to intensify the narrator's desire to re-experience the boundless extremity of this impossible encounter, this encounter with the impossible:

Even when I was cured, I doubted this to be the case. I could neither read nor write. I was surrounded by Northern mists. But what was strangest of all was this: despite the memory of my awful encounter [le contact atroce], behind curtains and dark glasses I was slowly wasting away. I wanted to see something in broad daylight; I had had my fill of the ease and comfort of the shadows; I had the same desire for the daylight as for water and fresh air. And if seeing was fire, I demanded the plenitude of fire, and if seeing was an encounter with madness, I madly desired that madness.

(FJ, 23–4; 12)

From this point on, *La Folie du jour* begins to supply to its readers, almost for the first time, something resembling a continuous narrative thread; but, in order to do so, it is as though the text has to accomplish, after Hölderlin, a categorical return of its own, and turn aside from the fire of the heavens to speak with the sobriety and restraint of a Northern twilight.[6] Indeed, the protagonist's brush with the madness of the light can only be narrated thanks to these belated, if piecemeal concessions to story-telling. And at this stage, the story falls victim to a double bind reminiscent of that experienced by Hölderlin in his struggles with Empedocles: on the one hand, to the extent that the story to be told hangs essentially on the limitlessness of the event that is, so to speak, its focal centre, the narrative must endeavour to speak of that which is immediate and impossible; but, to the extent that the limitlessness of that event is what makes the story impossible to narrate, the narrative must also turn aside from what lies at its centre to linger on its problematic margins, fissures, and borders. Such, for Blanchot, is literature's inescapable demand and its infinitely challenging resource: its affirmation of the limit and its responsiveness to the limitlessness beyond the limit.

But at no point do these two competing demands ever become reconciled by Blanchot within a unified dialectical structure. The light in Blanchot never turns into an originating moment able to incorporate within itself both its limitlessness and its own limits; it behaves instead according to an aporetical logic of originary repetition. The light, like the *il y a*, always precedes itself both as what it is and as its own absence. The light, therefore, is always already something other than light; in itself, so to speak, it neither illuminates nor makes dark, since it is what enables these founding ocular metaphors to appear at all, and thereby relieves them of any other foundation than that of their own prior absence. In its very madness, Blanchot's *récit* refuses the law of narrative in its everyday demands for clarity, luminosity, and illumination. While it repudiates this familiar figure of the law, which is 'severe and unpleasant' ('rigoureuse et peu agréable') (*FJ*, 29; 15), it does not transgress the law to encounter lawlessness, for it responds to the demand of another law, one that is glimpsed lurking behind the doctors' backs. This other law is very different from the repressive authority represented later in the *récit* by the ophthalmologist and the psychiatrist who come to interrogate the narrator and demand from him a story. Personified as a singular, sexually differentiated, explicitly female character, this other law is a seductive and impulsive figure, whose persuasiveness rests, paradoxically, not on a set of legitimate and authoritative principles, but is strangely contemporaneous with the language of the narrator and his text; as the law herself declares: ' "The truth is, we can no longer go our separate ways. I will follow you everywhere, I will share the same roof, we will enjoy the same sleep" ' (*FJ*, 31; 15).

This encounter with the law constitutes what might be described as the *récit*'s transgressive moment. Transgression here is not a simple movement beyond the jurisdiction of the law of narrative accounting (or recounting), identified with the ophthalmologist and psychiatrist, towards the institution of a better, more authoritative statute. For one thing, as Blanchot's narrator discovers, there already is beyond that law of accounting another, more compelling figure, who calls herself the law and has little in common with the repressive authority of the state. The law, so to speak, is itself not single, but always at least double, which is one reason why this other figure of the law encountered by Blanchot's narrator is not described in terms of a universalising abstraction, but as a sexually differentiated, singularised female character. (As we have seen, it is this knowledge of the irreducible division at the heart of the law that constitutes for Blanchot one of the lessons of the Hölderlinian topos of 'Das Höchste', the Most High.) Whatever her frivolity and impenetrability, the demands of this other law are both inescapable and unanswerable. But rather than showing the remorseless uniformity and self-identity of the law, these twin traits more nearly draw attention to the essential insecurity and fragility of the law, its insatiability and persistence. This is arguably why, in *La Folie du jour*, though the figure of the law is the one constantly harassing the narrator and inciting him to action – though without prescribing or imposing upon him what that action might be – it is the figure of the law who feels terrified and under threat, not the narrator. If the law is the Most High, she is also that which is most vulnerable; and if the law is both of these, this is because her demand for justice is always absolute, always singular, and as such can never be satisfied.

100

As a result, in *La Folie du jour*, as in the poems of Hölderlin, the law always expresses itself as an irreducible double bind. The requirement, in Blanchot's case, is for the text to testify to the madness of the day by simultaneously supplying a narrative and doing justice to what escapes narrative; and while it is between these irreconcilable demands that Blanchot's *récit* comes to be written, it is the result of the dissymmetry between them that it proves impossible for the text adequately to satisfy either one. This affirmation of impossibility is the measure of Blanchot's paradoxical enterprise; and it is by respecting the essential incompatibility between the two requirements that *La Folie du jour* demonstrates the necessity of responding simultaneously and dissymmetrically to the need for narrative and the demand for justice. If literature is an act of transgression, one might argue, it is only to the extent that transgression is understood not as a breach of the law in the spuriously anarchic name of lawlessness, which results only in a reinforcement of the law, but rather as an act of contestation of the repressive authority of psychiatrists, ophthalmologists, and police super-intendents, in the name of a more exacting demand, one which traverses literature without being identical with it, and which requires – impossibly – that one respect simultaneously both the limit and the limitlessness of the limit.

One can perhaps say now why *La Folie du jour* is not simply an illustration of the arguments Blanchot presents in his critical essays on Hölderlin, and also why Blanchot's fiction is radically irreducible to the idea that the work of art is founded on anything other than its own impossibility. To have succeeded in either of these aims, *La Folie du jour* would have to have been deducible from a single authoritative law, embodying a homogeneous structure of representation, based on the fundamental equivalence between the two moments or instances of the law portrayed within the story. However, the relation in Blanchot's text between the limitlessness of experience and the experience of the limit makes such a structure untenable. The paradox here is not solely decorative, nor does it serve simply to express scepticism; it is a response to the sheer impossibility of subordinating difference, discord, or contradiction to any single totalising concept. Paradox in Blanchot, one might say, is not the sign of a dialectical imagination, it is rather the proof that dialectical synthesis or unity is no longer even imaginable. The madness of the day, in this way, does not belong to the order of representation but effects a pure interruption of all representation. Like a Hölderlinian caesura, it intervenes into narrative as a vacant interval, a syncope that suspends representation in order to respond to the law beyond the law, the law that enables but also disables representation as such.[7] If literature

101

here proves transgressive of philosophical discourse, it is not because it can more, but rather because it can less; not because it confronts the law of representation from a position of greater authority, but because it turns aside from representation in order to affirm the other law – the law of the other beyond all law – that interrupts all representation.

3

Writing the neuter

From work to worklessness

The time of the absence of time is not dialectical. In that time, what appears is the fact that nothing appears, the being that grounds the absence of being, which is when there is nothing, and which already is no longer as soon as there is something: as if there were beings only by virtue of the ruination of being, when being is lacking. The reversal which, in time's absence, constantly refers us back to the presence of absence, to this presence as absence, to absence as the affirmation of absence, an affirmation in which nothing is affirmed, in which nothing does not cease to be affirmed, with the monotonous insistence of the indefinite, this is not a dialectical movement. Contradictions do not cancel each other out, nor do they become reconciled; only in time, for which negation is power, is the 'unity of contraries' possible. In time's absence what is new renews nothing; what is present is no longer of the moment; what is present presents nothing, represents itself, and belongs henceforth and for all time to the movement of return.

'La Solitude essentielle' (*EL*, 21; 30)

In November 1947 and January 1948 Blanchot published, in two parts, what still remains his most programmatic philosophical account of literature in general. The first of these two papers was called 'Le Règne animal de l'esprit' ('The Spiritual Animal Kingdom'), the second 'La Littérature et le droit à la mort' ('Literature and the Right to Death'); and it was this latter title that Blanchot was subsequently to re-use for the essay as a whole when it appeared largely unchanged as one continuous text in 1949 in *La Part du feu*. The two original titles were not without significance. For while the phrase 'La Littérature et le droit à la mort' was loosely based on a quotation from Hölderlin's Empedocles,[1] the title 'Le Règne animal de l'esprit', for its part, was explicitly borrowed, via

Bataille and Kojève, from Hegel, namely from the first section of the third part of chapter five of the *Phenomenology of Spirit*, the section entitled: 'Das geistige Tierreich und der Betrug oder die Sache selbst' ('The Spiritual Animal Kingdom and Deceit, or the "Matter in Hand" Itself').[2]

As commentators have acknowledged, Hegel is the initial source of much of Blanchot's thinking in 'La Littérature et le droit à la mort'. Blanchot's own reading of Hegel is closely based on that of Kojève, whose *Introduction à la lecture de Hegel* also first appeared in 1947 and to whose general thesis – that Hegel's philosophy is a philosophy of death – Blanchot subscribes with little, if any qualification.[3] Moreover, Blanchot's specific interest in the section on the 'spiritual animal kingdom' in the *Phenomenology* was itself prompted by Kojève's remarks on the passage in his *Introduction*, and reinforced by Georges Bataille's own earlier response to Kojève which, in a famous draft letter of 1937, later reprinted in *Le Coupable* (*Guilty*), he himself describes as 'that of an animal caught with its leg in a trap'.[4] The reason why Blanchot chose to focus his attention on the implications of this particular section from the *Phenomenology* is not hard to see. For on Kojève's submission, within the general framework of the teleological movement of Hegelian spirit through history, what Hegel's account of the 'spiritual animal kingdom' sought to address was the moment of the inactive and uncreative literary intellectual.

'Man,' declared Kojève, 'the real presence of nothingness in being (time), is action, i.e. struggle and work: – this and nothing else.'[5] But in Kojève's scheme, the literary intellectual fell far short of human destiny as defined in these terms. The artist, for Kojève, fails to engage in work in the everyday, real world; as a result, he is incapable of negating and transcending himself and remains only ever able to express his naturally given talent in a solitary manner; and this failure was what condemned him, in Kojève's eyes, to a purely individual, unmediated, animal-like existence. The literary intellectual, for Kojève, though he might claim to sacrifice his own private interests to absolute, timeless values such as truth and beauty, was thus destined to miss the appointment with history and misunderstand the nature of the matter at hand. What he did instead, according to Kojève, was to perpetrate on himself and the world what amounted to a deception; he was thus guilty of what Hegel termed 'Betrug', and what Kojève – followed by Blanchot – rendered into French as: 'imposture', or fraud (the term recurs at a number of crucial moments in Blanchot's text). And Kojève concludes:

104

the Intellectual negates nothing, therefore creates nothing; he displays only his 'nature': he is a 'spiritual' animal (the spiritual animal kingdom). . . . The ideal universe he sets in opposition to the world is merely a fiction. What the Intellectual offers to others has no real value; he is therefore deceiving them.[6]

In his letter to Kojève reproduced in *Le Coupable*, Bataille on one level largely accepts this diagnosis; but, as befits a writer who famously describes himself elsewhere as having been 'broken, crushed, killed a thousand times over' ('rompu, broyé, tué mille fois') by Kojève's lectures,[7] he dramatises the implications in a very different manner. One has to realise, Bataille observes, that Hegel himself also belonged, to a certain degree, to the spiritual animal kingdom. By accentuating the discrepancy between Hegel's authorship of the *Phenomenology* as a relative and particular individual and the claim of his thought to enact the movement towards absolute knowledge, the remark was the occasion for a more far-reaching challenge. For if history was at its end, or at the very least finite, as Kojève maintained on the basis of his reading of Hegel, and if the essential driving force in history was, as Kojève asserted, what Hegel had conceptualised as negativity, then the problem remained of the ultimate fate of such negativity once history was over. On logical grounds, Bataille objected, history itself could not be relied upon to eliminate the negativity that, having provoked it into existence at the outset, necessarily exceeded its closure at the end. Negativity, he continued, was thus in fact irreducible to the dialectic of history it was meant to propel; instead of history's obedient servant, it more closely resembled a form of inescapable, originary violence.

From Bataille's perspective, the problem of the end of history was not an abstract or fanciful one; nor was it to be taken literally. Rather, by delimiting the restricted economy of the historical dialectic, it raised a fundamental question as to the status and significance of whatever fell short of that economy. More specifically, as Bataille suggested in his letter to Kojève, it threw into sharp new focus the issue of the meaning and necessity (or lack of meaning and necessity) of inner experience in particular, and art, sacrifice, and religion in general. These were the things, according to Bataille, that, having appeared at the dawn of history, were more than likely to survive its ending. From Bataille's perspective, Kojève's imperious dismissal of the literary intellectual served, then, only to dramatise more acutely still the puzzle as to the relationship between philosophy and art, history and experience, a puzzle Bataille formulated in response to Kojève by coining the – for Kojève – entirely self-contradictory notion of unemployed negativity, 'negativité sans emploi'.[8] Such negativity, Bataille explained, is without historical purpose or justification; if it remains thinkable as negativity at all, it is a mode of negativity emptied of content and without possibility of absorption, negativity that has become synonymous with the impasse of its own violence, ineliminable excess, uselessness, and absence of truth.

Approaching this debate in his turn, Blanchot's own concerns in 'La Littérature et le droit à la mort' were at least twofold. First, there was an evident polemical purpose. This involved the need to formulate a critical response to one other important or influential account of the relationship between the literary intellectual and history put forward in the course of 1947: Sartre's *Qu'est-ce que la littérature?*.[9] In that essay, Sartre had sought to portray the writer of prose (though, symptomatically, not the poet) as an agent of history, subject to the necessity of choice and thus responsible for all his actions, including literary ones. 'Speech is action' ('Parler c'est agir'), wrote Sartre;[10] and it is no exaggeration to say that the whole doctrine of 'engagement' or commitment was designed to assert this identification of prose writing with action in the world, and thereby assimilate literary prose to a moral project founded on intersubjective freedom and existential authenticity. In response to this, Blanchot for his part aimed to enlist the support of Kojève and Hegel in challenging the philosophical basis of Sartre's position; and Blanchot's essay may in some ways most easily be read as a sustained attack on Sartre's endeavour to equate literature with action in the world, and as a refusal of the normative implications that flowed from this subordination of literature to moral propaganda.

Like Sartre, Blanchot took from Hegel the basic principle that all action is negation; but, unlike Sartre, he went on to distinguish between the negativity characteristic of literature as such (and not just, in an impoverished version, of lyric poetry, as Sartre had allowed) and the negativity governing work in the world. If literature was action, Blanchot rejoined, it was action of a very different kind to the work performed by the ordinary citizen in the course of his or her daily labours. The main difference lay in the immediacy or absoluteness with which literature as a whole negated the totality of the world as such. Literature, Blanchot argued, was not subject to the same dialectic of progressive and necessary mediation as work that takes place in the world; it obeys instead a dialectic – or, more exactly, a pseudo-dialectic – that knows not an infinite number of mediated and graduated positions, but only two: All or Nothing. For Blanchot, literature is in fact not dedicated to producing meaning in the world; its goal is rather to abolish the world absolutely in order to put in its place an absolute absence of world and thereby to substitute for real, functional objects a series of imaginary, absent objects. By definition, literature could not be made subject to worldly, moral criteria such as authenticity or intersubjective freedom; to be a writer at all, for Blanchot, was to be committed to what, for Sartre, made sense only as verbalism and bad faith.[11]

The only truly committed literature, Blanchot maintained, was the literature of Kafka or Sade, for theirs was a literature committed to the absoluteness of literature's negation of the world and, by that token, to the absoluteness of its self-affirmation in the face of the world. The fatal contradiction of Sartrean 'engagement' was that, by conceiving of writing as mediated action, it was unable to take seriously the peculiar specificity of writing as absolute negation (and affirmation). By imposing on literature a moral goal outside of literature, all Sartre's theory demonstrated, in spite of itself, by its failure to control reading and convince the audience of the truth of its position, was the inherent unreliability and ambiguity of literature, its propensity to turn into objects of fundamental irony the most fervently defended of moral or political beliefs. As Sartre was to discover in the ensuing decades, 'engagement' was thus at a cost: not of ruining literature, as Sartre's traditionalist critics had charged, but, more disturbingly, as Blanchot had argued, of fatally weakening those very values Sartre wished literature to embody, and which literature, by virtue of its ineliminable bad faith, was never able unambiguously to endorse. (Thus began, according to Blanchot, the irresistible process of disengagement recounted in Les Mots, by which Sartre was finally to abandon literature altogether.) Literature and worldly action, for Blanchot, if they were to converge at all, might meet not within the pages of Sartrean 'littérature engagée', but, as we have seen, only on those rare, extreme occasions when the absoluteness of the negation and affirmation embodied in literature coincided with a similarly radical moment in the political sphere, as it did for instance at times of convulsive, revolutionary upheaval. This was the logic, as far as Blanchot was concerned, behind Sade's support for the Jacobin revolution and his contempt for all reformist half-measures; and it was the ever future prospect of further instances of this unmediated convergence between All and Nothing that testified to the solidarity that existed, for Blanchot, not between literature and day-to-day political struggle, but between literature and revolution, between that writing that could no longer recognise itself in the literary institutions of the past and the political transformation that is premised on radical refusal of what had hitherto been accepted as politics as such.

But if Blanchot was ready, in 'La Littérature et le droit à la mort', to exploit Kojève's account of Hegel's 'spiritual animal kingdom' for his own purposes in the polemic with Sartre, he was willing to accompany the Hegelian dialectic only up to a certain point. Ultimately, like Bataille in *Le Coupable*, Blanchot turns Kojève's Hegel against himself. The work of the literary intellectual, rather than marking a failed moment within the progressive unfolding of the dialectic, comes to figure instead a recalcitrant impasse testifying to the failure of the dialectic; what for Kojève had turned into a tribute to the teleological possibility of the dialectic, is for Blanchot more like the affirmation of its necessary interruption. This strategy of inversion and displacement is one Blanchot uses throughout 'La Littérature et le droit à la mort'. At the outset, Blanchot reiterates the claim, made by Hegel towards the beginning of the chapter on the 'spiritual animal kingdom', that individuality is initially caught in a vicious circle, in which, Hegel argues, in order to know what the purpose of action is, individuality must first know what it is itself, but where in order to know what it itself is, individuality must first have acted.[12] Blanchot in his text applies the paradox to the figure of the author, who is placed by way of a similarly vicious circle in the predicament of being unable to be a writer until he has written a work, but unable to write a work until he becomes a writer. In the end, of course, in order to begin at all, both Hegel's individuality and Blanchot's author are forced simply to act; yet what for Hegel is construed as a paradigmatic case of dialectical mediation and passage remains for Blanchot an encounter with the impossibility of beginnings and the interminability of writing; as Blanchot puts it elsewhere: 'In order to write, it is necessary already to write' ('Pour écrire, il faut déjà écrire') (*EL*, 184; 176). Hegelian Aufhebung turns here into a – literally – aporetic impasse, one Blanchot resolves in 'La Littérature et le droit à la mort' only by abrupt rhetorical fiat: 'Let us suppose', he writes, 'the work to be written: with it the writer is born' (*PF*, 297; 305).

Elsewhere, much the same pattern is repeated, with the result that Hegel's dialectic of spirit is rewritten by Blanchot as a series of discontinuous and incompatible demands rather than a progressive ascent towards absolute knowledge. As Blanchot observes of the writer:

The difficulty is not only that the writer is several figures in one, but that each of these moments negates all the others, demands everything solely for itself and accepts neither conciliation nor compromise. The writer must respond simultaneously to several absolute and absolutely different commands, and his moral code is made up of the encounter and opposition between implacably hostile rules.

(PF, 303; 312)

In this way, what may appear at first sight to be a respectful homage to the logic of Hegel's text proves at a second look to more closely resemble a parody of Hegel, with the result that the Hegelian dialectic comes to be doubled in Blanchot's text with a pseudo-dialectic that is more like a logic of paralysis than of progression. What the word literature comes to name in Blanchot, therefore, is not a moment in the unfolding of the dialectic but rather an interruption or suspension of the dialectic. Indeed, as Rodolphe Gasché has convincingly argued, the more one reads Blanchot's essay, the more one is aware of how little in fact remains, despite appearances to the contrary, of Hegel's original project: no essence, no spirit, no Aufhebung, no resolution of contradictions, indeed no contradictions at all.[13]

Blanchot, for his part, concedes in a footnote that his reading of Hegel does not aim to give a faithful presentation of the author of the *Phenomenology of Spirit* (*PF*, 295; 302). But it would be wrong to conclude that Blanchot is pleading guilty to the charge of wilful misreading. With Hegel, Blanchot's strategy is much as it was with Paulhan or Heidegger: it is to accompany the text along a certain trajectory in order to propel it into an aporia of its own making. With regard to Hegel, the principle is one Blanchot formulates only much later, in *L'Écriture du désastre*. There, he points out the danger of opposing Hegel directly; for to do so is inevitably already to endorse Hegel. This means of course that the only way to read Hegel's text, as it were, is to read it without reading it and, as Bataille had suggested almost forty years previously, to take as the guiding principle of that reading the necessary complicity between Hegel and the fraudulence of the 'spiritual animal kingdom':

It is not possible to 'read' Hegel, except by not reading him. Whether to read him or not read him, to understand or misunderstand, or reject him, all this is Hegel's doing or else does not happen. Only the intensity of this non-event [ce non-lieu], in the impossibility of there being one, readies us for the death – of reading, of writing – that leaves Hegel alive, in the

109

fraudulence of finished Meaning [dans l'imposture du Sens achevé]. (Hegel as the fraudster [l'imposteur]: this is what makes him invincible, mad with his own seriousness, a counterfeiter of Truth [faussaire de Vérité]: 'putting one over on us' to the point of becoming, without realising it, a master of irony – Sylviane Agacinski.)

(ED, 79; 46)

In 1947, then, Blanchot's purpose in reading Hegel (and Kojève) was not to use Hegel as a foundation for his own thinking, as has been too quickly assumed by some; his project was rather to explore the margins of Hegel's text and put the dialectic of history into relation – albeit necessarily a relation of non-relation – with what it forcibly excluded. This is why 'La Littérature et le droit à la mort' is written simultaneously as a commentary on Hegel and as an interruption of Hegel, and why Blanchot positions himself obliquely both inside and outside Hegel's system, which is to say neither inside nor outside, but along its margins and borders. It is no accident in this respect that Blanchot comments on the strategic infidelity of his essay to Hegel only from the edge of his own text, that is to say, from the window of a footnote. Indeed it is indicative of Blanchot's trajectory in the essay as a whole that of the text's five footnotes the first is devoted to Hegel (and Jean Hyppolite), the next two to Hegel and Kojève, and the last two to Levinas, whose name appears here for the first time in Blanchot's published work, as though to bear witness, from below the page itself, to at least one of Hegel's exclusions.[14] The appeal to Levinas is a key move in the argument; for it allows Blanchot to deploy, with regard to the relationship between philosophy and literature, the deconstructive force of what, after Levinas, Blanchot calls the *il y a*, and which he summarises in 'La Littérature et le droit à la mort', citing *De l'existence à l'existant*, as

> the anonymous and impersonal flow of being that precedes all being, the being that at the heart of disappearance is already present, that in the depths of annihilation still returns to being, being as the inescapability of being, nothingness as existence: when there is nothing, *there is* being [quand il n'y a rien, *il y a* de l'être].

(PF, 320; 332)[15]

The *il y a* functions as an important crux for the whole of Blanchot's argument in 'La Littérature et le droit à la mort'.[16] Its implications are many. First, as far as the reading of Hegel is concerned, the effect is to delimit the Hegelian dialectic and open it up to what in *L'Espace littéraire*, speaking of Kafka, Blanchot calls the outside, and which has to be understood as that which precedes or exceeds the limits of the dialectic, yet which does not belong to the dialectic as a moment of necessary transgression. According to Levinas, as Blanchot reminds the reader, the *il y a* affirms simultaneously both the presence of being and the presence of the absence of being. The *il y a* always presents being, Levinas argues, and cannot itself be negated; indeed, since the necessity of affirmation always precedes the possibility of negation, any attempted negation of the *il y a*, however it may begin, will always end, by an inescapable necessity, as a perpetual recapitulation – a 'ressassement éternel' – of the *il y a* itself. Similarly, since it cannot itself be negated, the *il y a* cannot therefore be assimilated within the mediating logic and ascensional dynamic of Hegelian Aufhebung. It remains irreducible to Hegelian conceptuality, and has to be seen as constituting a radical challenge to the totalising pretensions of dialectical thought itself. Like Bataille's 'négativité sans emploi', the *il y a* refuses incorporation within the totality of history or time; and to the extent that it may be described as occurring in time at all, it is an event or absence of event that may be situated, in the vocabulary of *L'Espace littéraire*, only in the time which is the time of time's absence, the time that is not the substance of spirit's culmination but of futurity, of deferral and return, recurrence and difference.

There is a second reason why the *il y a* threatens the totalising closure of the Hegelian dialectic. For not only is the *il y a* irreducible to Hegelian conceptuality, it is itself indispensable for the very possibility of dialectical thought as such. Indeed, precisely because the *il y a* presents to thought the original possibility of both being and non-being, it is – like Heidegger's 'Nichts' in 'What is Metaphysics?' – what enables logical negation to be formulated at all. Without the *il y a*, therefore, it is hardly conceivable how the dialectic might itself be possible. In 'La Littérature et le droit à la mort', then, as in the early texts of Levinas, the *il y a* occupies an important double function; it is both unassimilable within the dialectic, yet necessary for the dialectic to begin; it both allows logical negation to occur yet refuses to comply with it; it is at one and the same time both what enables and what disables the possibility of the dialectic. It is the rock on which the dialectic is founded but also founders; it is in that respect not so much a concept as a pre-concept, or pseudo-concept, a trace or inscription that is itself, like that to which it refers, irreducible to the distinction between spirit and body, idea and matter, concept and thing.

The *il y a* was derived by Levinas, in the first instance, from Heidegger's celebrated distinction between being (Sein) and beings (das Seiende); and like Heideggerian ontological difference, the *il y a* also belongs to both philosophy and something other than philosophy.[17] This is clear from the self-contradictory, impossible status of the phrase; for what the *il y a* seeks to name, in its total generality, is the pre-conceptual singularity of being. The condition is a peculiar one, but crucially, for Blanchot, it is a condition that the *il y a* shares with literature. Indeed, Blanchot argues, what literature, in its turn, seeks as its object or goal is not the reality of the world as limply described by language, nor is it the pure concept brought into being by the annihilation of things by words, nor is it the sonorous echo of words released from the obligation to mean, but something more radical and originary still, since it is the very condition of all these other operations: the pre-conceptual singularity of things as they were before their destruction by words. As Blanchot writes:

> [S]omething was there, which has now gone. Something has disappeared. How can I retrieve it and look over my shoulder towards what comes *before*, if all my power consists in turning it into what comes *after*? The language of literature is a quest for this moment that precedes it. Generally, it gives this the name of existence; it wants the cat as it is, the pebble seen *from the side of things*, not man in general, but this man and, in this man, what man rejects in order to speak of him, which is the founding of speech and which speech excludes in order to speak, the abyss, Lazarus in the tomb and not Lazarus returned to the light, the one already beginning to smell, who is Evil, Lazarus lost and not Lazarus saved and raised from the dead.
>
> (*PF*, 316; 327)

Literature here, for Blanchot, like the *il y a*, dedicates itself, not to the resurrection embodied in conceptual thought, but to the unthinkable singularity that precedes the concept as its simultaneous condition of both possibility and impossibility.

Blanchot's position in 'La Littérature et le droit à la mort' is never simple, always double. Throughout, the purpose is to demonstrate that Hegel's famous thesis – that language, as Blanchot paraphrases it, is 'the life that bears death and maintains itself in death' ('la vie qui porte la mort et se maintient en elle') (*PF*, 324, 336) – is susceptible of two radically divergent readings, depending on whether death is seen as triumph or defeat, as the apotheosis of the labour of negation, or the rending apart of being by its own unmasterable limits.[18] Such ambiguity, Blanchot insists, cannot be resolved, since ambiguity is always already its own only answer. Death here is the ultimate example – the example that cannot by definition be an example – of such radical ambiguity. Throughout Blanchot death insists, at one and the same time, as a figure both of extreme possibility and radical impossibility. Indeed, if the philosophy of Hegel, according to Kojève, is a philosophy of death, this is because death in Hegel is what supplies the key to all possibility as such; and Blanchot documents at length in his essay the implications of this argument, which are that language, and thus humankind in general, find their truth in the finitude embodied in death, because death is the source of the negativity that separates sign from object and by making language possible makes both humanity and literature possible, too: 'It is therefore entirely accurate to say that when I speak,' as Blanchot puts it, 'death speaks in me [la mort parle en moi]' (PF, 313; 323).

But if death in this way for Blanchot, as it was for Hegel and for Heidegger, is on one level the most proper of human possibilities, it is also something irreducibly other: it is an experience that is never accessible as such for any human self or subject, who is effaced in dying and unable to address dying as in any sense an individual, personal experience belonging to any self-present subject, self, or agency at all. Moreover, if death is the origin of all human possibility, it is an event that has as its own paradoxical outcome the very withdrawal of death from the realm of possibility. If death is possible, then, it is only with the effect of making death impossible. Death as possibility is abruptly inverted here, without mediation or transition, into death as impossibility; and the possibility of death becomes a limitless non-experience of the impossibility of dying. The encounter with finitude becomes an encounter with infinity, and the relation to the limit a relation with immeasurable alterity, a relation only conceivable, as Levinas will later argue, as a relation of non-relation.[19] Death here quits the realm of the possible; it requires no ability, or power, or authenticity on the part of whoever dies, who forfeits all possibility in the act – which is not an act – of dying itself. Both as experience and performance, then, death is impossible. For Blanchot, as for Levinas, it ceases here to be a symbol or proof of humankind's humanity; it ceases even to be the possibility of impossibility that it was for the Heidegger of Sein und Zeit; it becomes instead, simultaneously but non-contemporaneously, the impossibility of all possibility.

Pursued to the limit in this way, the entire dialectic of possibility conceptualised by Hegel and by Kojève, accompanied at length by Blanchot in

113

his writing, becomes unhinged. On one level, Blanchot's commentary ironically leaves much of the dialectic in place, while wildly exacerbating its effects in order to turn it into an unwieldy and lop-sided embodiment of its own partial logic; but, on another, it serves to announce the arrival of an alterity – the alterity of 'désœuvrement', of worklessness or unworking – which is irreducible to all dialectic, and survives only as a residue that cannot be taken up into the process of negation, mediation, and work. Literature stands here divided between possibility and impossibility, between its ability to name things in their absence and conceptual immateriality, and the impossible obligation to respond in words to the pre-conceptual singularity of existence as it once was before language made this possible. Writing is traversed by fundamental ambiguity, split apart by two (or more) competing requirements, two demands, so to speak, that recur in one form or another throughout the entirety of Blanchot's work, but whose differences cannot ever be equalised, reconciled, or mediated by any dialectic whatsoever, be it of history or of being, but only ever affirmed in their fundamental incompatibility, dissymmetry, and discord. And it is to this that literature in Blanchot is called upon to bear witness.

The worklessness of being

But what might be the difference (if there is one) between death by suicide and death by other means? The first of these, by entrusting itself to dialectics (entirely founded on the *possibility* of death, the use of death as power), is the obscure oracle which we cannot decipher, but with whose help we can sense, while constantly forgetting it, that whoever has pursued to the limit the desire for death, invoking the right to death and having power of death over himself – thereby opening what Heidegger has called *the possibility of impossibility* – or alternatively, believing himself to be master of what is beyond all mastery – allows himself to be caught in a sort of trap and is immobilised for all time – if only for an instant, obviously – at the moment when, ceasing to be a subject, losing his stubborn freedom, and as an other to himself, he comes up against death as that which does not happen or as that which (giving the lie to the dialectic, as in a fit of madness, by letting it reach its goal) reverses itself into *the impossibility of all possibility.*

L'Écriture du désastre (ED, 114–15; 70)

In *L'Espace littéraire*, his fourth collection of critical essays, published in 1955, Blanchot develops the problematic opened up in 'La Littérature et le droit à la mort'. Like the 1947 essay, *L'Espace littéraire* as a whole is framed by the question posed to being by the existence of literature as such; and like the earlier text too, it stages a prolonged encounter between a post-Hegelian dialectic of possibility and action in the world and the paradoxical logic of Levinas's *il y a*, that ineluctable apprehension of the presence of the absence of being that Blanchot thematises not only as an interruption in the dialectic, but also as an inescapable demand and impersonal affirmation synonymous with the language of literature itself.

The question posed to being by literature is in the first instance, according to Blanchot, a question literature poses to itself; and it is for this reason that *L'Espace littéraire* is principally concerned with the drama of literature's self-questioning in what, after Hölderlin, Blanchot terms a time of need or distress (*EL*, 258; 245). Blanchot's approach is driven, however, less by system and concept than by acute attention to the writing experience of a number of exemplary yet irreducibly singular literary figures, such as Mallarmé, Kafka, and Rilke. These are the protagonists in the drama Blanchot unfolds, and which begins, as it were, with a remark like that of Mallarmé, made in 1891 in a famous letter to Vielé Griffin, that the whole mystery of poetry lay in a word: the word '*c'est*', 'it is' (*EL*, 35; 43). But this abrupt insight into the mystery of poetry, Blanchot contends, gives rise in Mallarmé not to a single realisation, but an experience of being that was necessarily divided. Mallarmé's poetic experience commences, then, like that of Hölderlin, not simply with the realisation of being, but with an awareness of the inescapable dissymmetry between the existence of the work of art as an object or entity that is, and the vast generality of being which necessarily withdraws from all particular determination, but alone suffices, precisely because it is not an object, as the properly intangible, mysteriously unavailable object of poetry as such.

The dichotomy at issue here is a familiar one to readers not only of Blanchot but of Heidegger too. For the dichotomy within being that Blanchot articulates in response to Mallarmé's remark is plainly derived from a reading of Heideggerian ontological difference. In *L'Espace littéraire*, however, Blanchot does not linger for long with Heidegger; instead, much as he had in the late 1940s, he follows Levinas in recasting Heidegger's account of ontological difference as a relation between existence and the existent, between on the one hand the worldlessness, anonymity, and neutrality of the *il y a* and, on the other, that suspension or interval in the *il y a* which, in his post-war texts, Levinas refers to as hypostasis, and which marks the event-like emergence of time as an evanescent present and brings in its train the possibility of being in the world, positionality, subjectivity, consciousness, and freedom.[1] Hypostasis introduces a break into the namelessness of existence by turning existence into an attribute able to be embodied by a speaking self; from within the impossibility of negation that is existence, it hosts the arrival, so to speak, of an existent, who comes to be by asserting responsibility for itself as a necessary consequence of its dependence on the inescapability of existence.

As far as *L'Espace littéraire* is concerned, it is clear that much the same structure of difference and dependence as obtains between existence and the existent also governs the relation between the work of art and the worklessness that is the concealed origin of the work; and, indeed, Blanchot dramatises the genesis of the work of art in a manner that very closely echoes, in content if not necessarily in its vocabulary, Levinas's description of the emergence of the human existent from the anonymity of existence. In order to produce the work, for instance, Blanchot writes, the work that is an inaugural event as well as a possibility of communication, the poet must impose silence on the sterile repetitiveness of the origin and thereby master its interminable chatter; and the writer too must affirm from within the debilitating circularity of existence the possibility of a limit and a measure with which to sustain the work as such. In that movement, Blanchot continues, the work is born; yet, as it emerges into the world, the work has also to recognise its precarious vulnerability and its dependence on the very worklessness to which it owes its existence and which will, in the last resort, always ruin its own demand to exist (*EL*, 29; 37).

But though Blanchot adopts as his own much of the conceptual framework of Levinas's early writings, this is not to say he reproduces Levinas's argument without some characteristic shifts in emphasis. Blanchot, for instance, unlike Levinas, tends to assimilate the thought of hypostasis – and of all that is posterior, so to speak, to the moment of hypostasis – to a regionalised or delimited version of the Hegelian dialectic, which obviously, as a result, ceases to be a totalising dialectic at all, but survives nonetheless in Blanchot's text as a thought of being and non-being, of the necessity of death and freedom in the world. In addition, Blanchot underscores with arguably much greater force than Levinas not only the logical circularity of the *il y a* but also, despite the negative terms in which it is thematised, the inescapably affirmative character of the *il y a*; writing for instance, at one point, of the powerlessness of the work of art, Blanchot rejoins that the work, in its very weakness, points to a realm in which impossibility is a mark not of privation, but affirmation (*EL*, 232; 223).

116

Though Blanchot's borrowings from Levinas (and Heidegger) are extensive, not all Blanchot's thinking in *L'Espace littéraire* can be attributed to their influence. At least as much in the book is the result of a continuing debate between Blanchot and Kojève's Hegel (and, occasionally, Marx), largely mediated through the seemingly marginal but in fact crucial figure of Georges Bataille. As a result, in so far as Blanchot's writing may be presented in systematic fashion at all, it has to be said his position in *L'Espace littéraire* is manifestly and deliberately heterogeneous. What Blanchot defends in the book is not systematic theory, but a persistently double logic which finds difference, discord, and extreme reversal at every stage in the argument it puts forward. On one level, *L'Espace littéraire* puts forward a post-Hegelian dialectic of being and non-being, negation and affirmation, death and freedom, which is largely reminiscent of the dialectic left in place, if only partially or parodically, at the end of 'La Littérature et le droit à la mort' in 1947. On another level, however, the book disables and delimits this dialectic by showing it to be necessarily dependent on the – non-dialectical – impossibility of negation embodied in the *il y a*, and which persists within the work, as the neutral force Blanchot terms worklessness, from where it continues to act both as a prior condition of the work's emergence and as a force of dissolution that cannot be embodied in the work, and therefore undoes the work and ruins its very possibility. As Blanchot writes, for instance, in a passage that appears convoluted only because of the extreme hypotactic intricacy of his thinking:

That the work should necessarily be the sole light of what is extinguished and by which all is extinguished, that it should come to be only when the extremity of affirmation is verified by the extremity of negation, this is a demand we can still understand, though it is contrary to our need for peace, simplicity, and sleep, indeed, it is a demand we understand intimately, as the intimacy of the decision that is ourselves and that gives us being, only when, at risk only to ourselves, we reject, by fire and the sword, by silent refusal, its permanence and favour. Yes, we can understand that in this the work is pure beginning, the first and last moment when being presents itself as the precarious freedom which in our sovereignty has us deny being [l'être], without, however, yet including it in the appearance of beings [dans l'apparence des êtres]. But as for the demand that makes the work into what declares being at the extreme moment of the break – 'the very word: *is*' ['ce mot même: *c'est*'] –, the

117

point it brings to incandescence, even as the demand is itself consumed by the flame, this too we must grasp, and learn that it makes the work impossible, because it is what never allows the work to be reached, is what precedes the work, is the point at which, of being, nothing is made, at which nothing is fulfilled, and is the deep recess of the worklessness of being [la profondeur du désœuvrement de l'être].

(EL, 39; 46)

Two demands, the demand for the work and the demand of worklessness, vie with each other within the non-dialectical movement of art's self-affirmation; the conflict however is unequal, and the outcome, though unexpected, is also a foregone conclusion. Despite this, the nature of the relationship between these two demands is crucial to Blanchot's thinking; and it is an issue he addresses explicitly in a paper entitled 'Le Regard d'Orphée' ('The Gaze of Orpheus'), which, in a prefatory note, he commends to the reader as the compelling yet elusive centre of *L'Espace littéraire* as a whole. This duality of status is in turn itself reflected in the paper's figurative, mythological complexion, which places it mid-way, so to speak, between the fictional experience of night – 'l'*autre* nuit', the *other* night (*EL*, 169–78; 163–70) – as dramatised in *Thomas l'Obscur*, and the philosophical account of literature as pre-conceptual singularity given in 'La Littérature et le droit à la mort'. By taking a detour through myth, 'Le Regard d'Orphée' aims to satisfy simultaneously the demand both for philosophical exemplarity and for literary singularity. However, by claiming to meet both requirements at once, it fulfils neither of them properly, with the result that, while on one level the story of Orpheus, as Blanchot configures it, indeed reprises and clarifies in theoretical terms many of the underlying arguments and themes common to Blanchot's work as a whole, it also functions transgressively as a *mise-en-abyme* of the excessive, paradoxical logic it aims to describe – which is none other than the logic of law and transgression itself – and thereby disables the claim of philosophy or literary theory to be able to rescue literature from the otherness of darkness and bring it into the light.

In the story of Orpheus, the poet descends to the underworld to retrieve Eurydice from premature death; this, exceptionally, he is allowed to do on condition that he not look at her again. This condition Orpheus of course fails to respect, and he loses Eurydice again, and is himself subsequently torn apart and destroyed. The tale, in one perspective, Blanchot argues, is an exemplary account of the necessity of obliqueness and indirection, since it is the detour through partial blindness and invisibility that alone allows Orpheus to penetrate to the depths of the other night, that night before night, in order to bring Eurydice back from the dead. This law of indirection that requires Eurydice remain invisible is inescapable; for it is the condition of Orpheus' successful return to the light and of the work as such. That which is immediate, Hölderlin might have said, is impossible, and can only be grasped by way of a detour or turning. Which is to say, for Blanchot, that the work is itself primarily concealment, dissimulation: 'the depths do not give themselves up directly,' he writes, 'but reveal themselves only through dissembling themselves in the work' ('La profondeur ne se livre pas en face, elle ne se révèle qu'en se dissimulant dans l'œuvre') (*EL*, 180; 171).

But Orpheus disobeys this law of necessary obliqueness. He gazes upon Eurydice, and destroys the work; and it is as though what Orpheus yearns to bring back to the light, and which is the reason he cannot not look upon her, is not the Eurydice who will be restored to life and visibility, but – like the figure of Lazarus already beginning to smell to which Blanchot refers in 'La Littérature et le droit à la mort' – the other Eurydice who belongs to the other night and thus will always remain invisible, dying of a death that is without possibility or end. And it is for this other, irreducibly invisible Eurydice that Orpheus squanders both the work and his beloved's resurrection. This act of betrayal and sacrifice, which carelessly forfeits the work and seals Eurydice's fate, according to Blanchot, is itself as unavoidable as it is necessary; it is a response to another, more demanding requirement, to the law of the origin and of worklessness itself, which asserts that what is essential is not the work, but the darkness without which there would be no work at all, and in relation to which the work itself, though it may be the most extreme test of Orpheus' power as a poet, is of lesser and almost negligible importance: 'The work is all for Orpheus,' Blanchot writes, 'except for that desired look in which the work is ruined, with the result that only in that look can the work reach beyond itself, be united with its origin, and be consecrated in its impossibility' (*EL*, 182–3; 174).

From the point of view of the work, Orpheus proves culpably impatient and should have settled for bringing back Eurydice in song. However, as Blanchot reminds us, even in Orpheus' song Eurydice was always already absent and Orpheus himself already about to be dismembered for his singing. Orpheus' impatient gaze was therefore necessary. Without it, Orpheus would not have been exposed to the patience that is but another name for the care or concern

119

for the origin of the work that is worklessness itself; had he remained patiently faithful to Eurydice, he would not have experienced the torment of limitless patience that is the origin of the work. Patience and impatience begin here, in Blanchot's text, to gather together and disperse according to a peculiar movement of similarity and difference, reciprocal intensification and abolition. At times, while it remains a calculated decision to refrain from precipitate action, patience seems like the very opposite of impatience; at others, when it is a refusal of the tempting lure of intervention, patience seems more like the only valid impatience that there is, the impatience that experiences to the limit the torment of the wait. Impatience also, though it too may take the form of a calculating act accomplished in order to abolish the necessity of waiting, may itself become transformed at the next moment into the most excruciatingly patient wait there is. And if at one moment he can write that 'true patience does not exclude impatience, it is intimacy with it, impatience suffered and endured without end' (*EL*, 181; 173), Blanchot too can go on to add, some three pages later, that 'impatience has to be the core of profound patience [le cœur de la profonde patience]' (*EL*, 184; 176).

Patience and impatience function here according to a pattern that is not without recalling once more the 'hyperbologic' of chiastic intensification found, as Philippe Lacoue-Labarthe has argued, at the centre of Hölderlin's theory of tragedy. Indeed, in this respect, Blanchot's Orpheus finds himself in an analogous position to Hölderlin's Oedipus: if patience is impatience deferred, it is also impatience intensified, and if impatience is patience deferred, it is also patience intensified. But though patience and impatience may seem here to function like dialectical contraries, all dialectic remains absent: there is no moment of synthesis or of unification, no time in which to reconcile the two, only the time of the absence of time which belongs not to progress but to return, not to work but to worklessness, not to the world, but to worldlessness. And this is why the movement of patience and impatience in Blanchot gives rise not to a dialectic of the work, but to an awareness of the fundamental dissymmetry between work and worklessness, as a result of which, in the rivalry between the demand for the work and the demand of worklessness, it is necessarily always the latter that prevails. Orpheus' sacrifice of Eurydice does not lead therefore to the work, but to the sacrifice of the work, and to the affirmation of the impossibility of the work as the secret of its origin.

Outside

What occurs [ce qui arrive] through writing is not of the order of that which occurs.
But, in that case, what gives you the right to claim that something like writing ever
does occur? Or is it that writing might not ever need to take place [advenir]?

L'Écriture du désastre (ED, 102–3; 62)

In the final section of *L'Espace littéraire*, under the heading 'La Littérature et
l'expérience originelle' ('Literature and the Original Experience'), Blanchot
turns to the question of the relation between the work and the origin. This
last chapter first appeared, in a substantially longer version, in two
instalments in *Les Temps modernes* in 1952. On one level – and this is probably
the reason it was initially published in that journal – the text is a
commentary on Hegel that covers many of the same issues as 'La Littérature
et le droit à mort' and offers a similar critique of Sartrean 'littérature
engagée' as that earlier article. In 'La Littérature et l'expérience originelle',
however, Blanchot does shift the terrain of the discussion to consider the
implications of Hegel's famous claim, put forward in the first of his *Lectures
on Aesthetics*, that, as far as the modern world is concerned, art is and
remains, in Hegel's words, 'from the point of view of its highest
determination, as far as we are concerned, a thing of the past' ('nach der
Seite ihrer höchsten Bestimmung für uns ein Vergangenes'). Hegel goes on to
explain that, having become divorced from its 'authentic truth and vitality',
art in the modern age has forfeited its inner necessity and lost its prominent
place within reality to become instead simply an object of literary critical,
aesthetic inquiry.[1] But while Blanchot explicitly cites Hegel's diagnosis as the
starting point for his discussion, it is clear that since 1947 the debate has
moved on; and there are numerous clues within Blanchot's text which
suggest that, as well as a contribution to the debate with Hegel, Kojève,
Sartre, and Bataille, this concluding chapter – particularly the sections
entitled 'Les Caractères de l'œuvre d'art' ('Characteristics of the Work of
Art') and 'L'Expérience originelle' ('The Original Experience') – should also
be read as an oblique response to Heidegger's recently published essay 'Der
Ursprung des Kunstwerks' ('The Origin of the Work of Art'), which
concludes with an Afterword devoted to a brief discussion of the self-same
passage from Hegel's *Aesthetics*.[2]

Admittedly, Blanchot mentions Heidegger's name, in a footnote, only once in
the 1955 version of the essay (and not at all in the 1952 article), and otherwise

121

refers to him, seemingly in passing in the body of the text, only as 'a contemporary philosopher' ('un philosophe contemporain') (*EL*, 251; 240). Indirection, however, is a law to which Blanchot subscribes not only as a critic of literature but as an essayist as well; and closer examination of Blanchot's essay clearly demonstrates how far 'La Littérature et l'expérience originelle' shares with 'Der Ursprung des Kunstwerks' a number of key emphases and formulations. Among others, these include the distinction drawn by Blanchot, here as elsewhere, between the work of art and what Heidegger terms equipment, and which is most likely derived, if not directly from *Sein und Zeit*, from Heidegger's early Hölderlin lecture of 1936. Similarly, the view that art has its origin in art itself and not in the work of art nor the person of the artist, has a clear Heideggerian resonance, as does Blanchot's account of the structure of the work as resting on a violent contest between what Heidegger, in 'Der Ursprung des Kunstwerks', thematises as earth (Erde) and world (Welt), and which Blanchot, in his essay, describes as the antagonistic coming together within the work of art of what he calls elemental depth (*EL*, 233; 223) and the presence of being (*EL*, 235; 225).

Elsewhere, too, Blanchot is at one with Heidegger in rejecting all aesthetic philosophy – which necessarily means any aesthetic philosophy – founded on the opposition of subject and object, form and content. Finally, when he refers to the reader as one who consecrates or preserves the work, or, even more explicitly, when he argues that 'the work is history, it is an event, the event of history itself, and this is because its most steadfast claim is to give to the word beginning all its force' (*EL*, 238; 228), Blanchot is obviously echoing some of Heidegger's most provocative and original formulations. At one point Blanchot even uses the same pseudo-etymological pun when he refers to the work as an original 'leap', or 'Ur-sprung' ('saut', *EL*, 257; 244); and in other places, even some of the same names recur, notably that of van Gogh, one of Heidegger's few – though problematic – examples, to whom Blanchot, with only the faintest of ironies, attributes the stolidly peasant-like, pseudo-Heideggerian pronouncement that 'My attachment is to the earth' ('Je suis attaché à la terre', *EL*, 234; 224).[3]

Of all these shared motifs that pass between Heidegger and Blanchot, the most important is without doubt the common reference to Hegel's *Aesthetics*. Indeed, for Heidegger and Blanchot, Hegel's remark that art today is a thing of the past identifies the essential predicament of modern art in time of distress. The two thinkers understand the thesis, however, in sharply differing ways.

According to Blanchot, art after Hegel, so to speak, finds itself divorced from the truth of history for the simple reason, as Kojève had testified, that history in its essence has now been accomplished. The present and future belong not to art, but to action in the world; and if there is a book to be written in these modern times, Blanchot quips, that book is most likely not *War and Peace* but *Das Kapital*. But though history has severed its relationship with art, and though art no longer belongs to the world and to the work and to truth, the question of art still remains; and it remains as an absolute question that can no longer be adequately met either by world, work, or truth. The time of distress may be a time of crisis for art, but it is a time in which, perhaps for the first time, the question of art is posed by art itself without immediately being referred back to some already established theological or philosophical discourse. Modern art's exteriority to world, work, or truth is grasped here not as a condition to be lamented, but rather as a chance for art. For if the time of distress is inseparable from the radical exteriority of art to world, work, truth, it is because, for Blanchot, that time has begun to resemble the time outside time of the origin itself, and because the origin of art is not to be found in the rootedness of art within the classical past, but in the worldlessness, worklessness, and truthlessness of the art of the future.

Heidegger, for his part, begins with what is in many respects a similar diagnosis of art's isolation in this time in which, as he puts it, following Hölderlin, the gods are both no more and not yet.[4] Glossing Hegel's remark in his turn, Heidegger rephrases it as follows: 'Is art still an essential and necessary way in which the truth occurs [geschieht] that is decisive for our historical existence [unser geschichtliches Dasein], or is art no longer this?'[5] The question, according to Heidegger, still hangs in the balance; and the time of distress is measured exactly by the uncertainty that grows for Heidegger, while the world hesitates between the truth embodied in a poem of Hölderlin's, to which, he complains, the moderns have failed to harken for already a century-and-a-half, and the benighted desolation that is the consequence of the world's domination by metaphysics and its monstrous offspring, modern technology.[6] Modernity for Heidegger, here, is synonymous with the world's inability or failure to heed the truth of art; indeed, so dire is this time of distress, contends Heidegger in 1946, that it is not just the gods that have departed, leaving behind only a trace of the sacred, but the traces of that lost trace itself that are now barely legible at all.[7]

Importantly, what for Hegel and Heidegger, for different reasons and in vastly differing ways, is evidence of the beleaguered autonomy or isolation of art, is for Blanchot the very beginning of art. For it is only when art is not reducible to world, work, or truth, Blanchot maintains, that the question of art can be asked at all, and asked not under the much diminished rubric of aesthetic pleasure and learned criticism, as Hegel had predicted in the *Aesthetics*, but with direct relevance to the question of being in the time of distress itself (*EL*, 224; 216). For his part, Heidegger's response to the retreat of art from truth is to seek to ground afresh the relationship between art and world, art and work, art and truth. This he does of course by elaborating a radically new account of truth, truth not as *homoiosis* or adequation, but *aletheia* or unconcealment. From Blanchot's perspective, the gain here is also loss; what is achieved by Heidegger's redetermination of the work of art as the 'setting-into-work of truth', the 'Ins-Werk-Setzen der Wahrheit', is obfuscation rather than clarification, in that Heidegger substitutes for the radical demand of art an answer founded in world, work and truth, which are the very things, in Blanchot's eyes, that the existence of the work throws into question. Blanchot insists that the question be left open, that art be affirmed in its extreme refusal of world, work, and truth. And it is this Blanchot no doubt had in mind when beginning his discussion of Heidegger with a sentence that might appear to have come unchanged from 'Der Ursprung des Kunstwerks', but which, from Blanchot's pen, takes on a very different, not to say diametrically opposed meaning, and reads: 'A just answer is rooted in the question' ('Une réponse juste s'enracine dans la question' (*EL*, 219; 211).[8]

A number of crucial issues divide Blanchot and Heidegger here. The first has to do with the relationship between art and the work. For Heidegger, though the two are construed as distinct, they are also treated as inseparable, with the result that, as 'Der Ursprung des Kunstwerks' testifies, the questioning of art by Heidegger inevitably culminates in a thinking not of art, but of the work. For Blanchot, however, to identify art first and last with the work, like Heidegger, is to place art exclusively on the side of worldly possibility, power, and truth, and to do violence to the very possibility of art, which lies in its fundamental absence from itself, its essential inessentiality, its paradoxical impossibility.[9] (And it is also, Blanchot implies, to do violence to the refusal of the world enacted by, say, the poems of Hölderlin by enlisting them in the defence of the German Volk in its so-called time of distress.) True, the work for Heidegger functions as a foundational beginning, as an inauguration of itself and of what it founds, and to an extent Blanchot agrees; but if the work begins by beginning in this way, it can only do so because it is itself grounded (without in fact being grounded at all) in a worklessness which is the measure of the sheer impossibility of its beginning: 'The work says the word: beginning,' Blanchot writes, 'and what it claims to give to history is that initial right [l'initiative], the possibility of a point of departure. But itself it does not begin. It is always prior to any beginning, it is always already completed' (*EL*, 239; 228).

For Heidegger, however, if the work is a beginning, it is because the work has a privileged relationship to truth. Here Blanchot protests, and does so at his most incisive. Admittedly, truth, in Heidegger's text, is a concept that is new and difficult. It must first be taken as *aletheia*, unconcealment; second, it has to be read not as established verity, but as the dynamic self-presentation of truth out of what Heidegger calls un-truth, *Un-wahrheit*. Truth, he writes, is in its essence un-truth.[10] This does not mean that truth is falsity, nor that truth is born from its dialectical opposite, but rather that the truth of a work cannot be derived from received knowledge: 'The setting-into-work of truth', Heidegger explains, 'thrusts up the awesome and at the same time thrusts down the ordinary and what we believe to be such. The truth that discloses itself in the work can never be proved or derived from what went before.' ('Das Ins-Werk-Setzen der Wahrheit stößt das Un-geheure auf und stößt zugleich das Geheure und das, was man dafür hält, um. Die im Werk sich eröffnende Wahrheit ist aus dem Bisherigen nie zu belegen und abzuleiten.')[11] And Blanchot comments:

> As soon as the truth it is thought to yield is brought into the light of day and becomes the life and labour of the day, the work closes upon itself as something that is alien to this truth and without meaning, for not only in relation to established and reliable truths does the work seem alien, the very scandal of what is monstrous and un-true, but always it refutes the true [car ce n'est pas seulement par rapport aux vérités déjà sues et sûres qu'elle paraît étrangère, le scandale du monstrueux et du non-vrai, mais toujours elle réfute le vrai]: whatever this is, even though it may come from the work itself, the work overturns it, takes it back, buries it and hides it away. And yet the work says: beginning, and matters powerfully to the day. It is the first light that may be said to precede the day. It is an initiation, an inauguration. 'A mystery that inaugurates', says Char, but the work itself remains mysteriously excluded from initiation, exiled from the light of truth.
>
> (*EL*, 239; 228–9)

125

Blanchot goes on, some pages later:

> In relation to the world in which truth founds and bases itself on decisive affirmation as a place from which it can arise, art is an original representation of the anticipation and scandal of absolute error [l'erreur absolue], of something un-true but where the prefix 'un-' does not have the incisive character of a limit [de quelque chose de non-vrai, mais où le 'non' n'a pas le caractère tranchant d'une limite], for it is rather the full endless indeterminacy on which the true has no purchase, which it has no power to win back, and faced with which it determines itself only by becoming the violence of the negative.
>
> (*EL*, 255; 243)

Un-truth, in Heidegger's sense, Blanchot argues, is a violence that belongs to truth in the world; for that reason alone it could not be more different from the absolute error – the absolute exteriority – of literature to all possible concepts of truth that Blanchot endeavours to address in the closing sections of *L'Espace littéraire*. Indeed, as Levinas points out, it is at those moments, when Blanchot seems closest to Heidegger, that he is at his most distant.[12]

Art for Blanchot is inseparable from the risk it represents not only to work, world, and truth, but also to the existence of the poet as such. Here, as in his discussions of Hölderlin, Blanchot shows himself sensitive in the extreme to the artistic experience of the writers he examines. In this questioning of experience, the fundamental point on which Blanchot's writing turns, as I have said, is the (non-)experience of death. Heidegger, in famous pages in *Sein und Zeit*, had written of death as the most extreme and proper possibility of Dasein; and in his account of Rilke in *L'Espace littéraire* Blanchot reflects at length on that formulation. But as Rilke's work suggests, if death is extreme possibility, it is also extreme impossibility. In dying, no authentic self comes to be; rather, death cannot be experienced as such at all, and only results in the withdrawal of the possibility of dying. If death is impossible, it is because in death *I* do not die; the one who dies is the impersonal, anonymous 'on'. With death no relation is possible; death is that which is radically other. Indeed, death is not a constant or self-identical experience at all, rather the space of a violent reversal that tips without mediation from possibility into impossibility. In articulating death in this way, Blanchot in effect disposes of one of the key hierarchies in *Sein und Zeit*, the distinction between Dasein proper ('authentic' Dasein) and the Verfallenheit of Dasein, that fallen anonymity that is life in proximity to third-person

Heideggerian 'man', Blanchot's 'on'.[13] Being here loses its relation to itself as possibility, authenticity, or propriety; it dissipates itself to a point of extremity where it becomes synonymous with the affirmation of its own impossibility; and this, most insistently of all, is what sums up the experience of the origin Blanchot dramatises in *L'Espace littéraire*.

Art, for Blanchot, in the time of distress, does not lapse into dereliction, for it is only then that it discovers itself as what it is (not): as the worldlessness, worklessness, and truthlessness of the origin. The time of distress is a time of double infidelity to both humankind and the gods, and though Blanchot borrows from Heidegger some of the phases in Heidegger's historical scheme – the presence of the gods, the absence of the gods, the absence of the presence of the absence of the gods – Blanchot's prognosis differs crucially from that of Heidegger. While for Heidegger it was an article of conviction, as he puts it in his posthumous *Spiegel* interview, that 'only a god can still save us', for Blanchot the time of distress is not a time of salvation or nostalgia for salvation, but the time of art, the time of the absence of time.[14] Far from humankind needing a new god and a new divine, it is for Blanchot only the absence of the presence of the absence of the gods that allows the question of art to be raised at all. Art in time of distress is inseparable from the questioning to which there was and still is no answer; and it is this persistence of the question and the radical absence of the answer that Blanchot's writing affirms in the imminence and alterity of what Blanchot names elsewhere: a turning.

'Will you accept the certainty that we have reached a turning?' asks one of the interlocutors in *L'Entretien infini*. '– If it is a certainty,' replies his partner, 'it is not a turning. The fact of belonging to this moment at which a change of epoch (if any such exists) is taking place also affects the certain knowledge that would wish to determine it, making both certainty and uncertainty inappropriate. Never are we less able to circle around ourselves than at such a moment, and the discrete force of the turning lies first in this' (*EI*, 394; 264).

Neutre

The Neuter, if it may be called neuter, could be said to be that which withdraws while withdrawing and withdrawing even the act of withdrawing [ce qui se dérobe en dérobant et dérobant jusqu'à l'acte de dérober], without anything appearing of what thereby disappears, an effect reduced to an absence of effect: the neuter, at the articulation of the visible–invisible, the inequality still of the equal, the answer to the impatient question (that classifies and determines in advance by incautiously dividing into two, asking: which one?), albeit an answer that immediately and imperceptibly, even as it seems to entertain the question, modifies its structure by its refusal not only to choose, but even to accept the possibility of a choice between two terms: such as the one or the other, yes or no, this or that, day or night, god or man. 'Which of the two?' – 'Neither the one nor the other, the other, the other', as if the Neuter could only speak in the form of an echo, yet thereby perpetuating the other by way of the repetition that difference, always included in the other, albeit even in the form of the bad infinite, ceaselessly calls forth, like the swaying of the head of a man exposed to endless commotion.

Le Pas au-delà (PA, 107–8; 77)

In 1963, in an essay on the use of adjectival nouns and substantival infinitives as expressions of the unknown in the poems of René Char, Blanchot wrote as follows:

Research – poetry, thought – relates to the unknown as unknown. This relation discloses the unknown, but in a disclosure that leaves it veiled; in this relation there is presence of the unknown; the unknown, in this presence, is rendered present, but always as unknown. This relation of presence must leave intact – untouched – what it conveys and not unveiled what it discloses. The relation will not consist in an unveiling. The unknown will not be revealed, but indicated.[1]

(La recherche – la poésie, la pensée – se rapporte à l'inconnu comme inconnu. Ce rapport découvre l'inconnu, mais d'une découverte qui le laisse à couvert; par ce rapport, il y a présence de l'inconnu; l'inconnu, en cette présence, est rendu présent, mais toujours comme inconnu. Ce rapport de présence doit laisser intact – non touché – ce qu'il porte et non dévoilé ce qu'il découvre. Ce ne sera pas un rapport de dévoilement. L'inconnu ne sera pas révélé, mais indiqué.)

Six years later, in the text of the essay reproduced in *L'Entretien infini*, the lines given above read as follows:

Research – poetry, thought – relates to the unknown as unknown. This relation discloses the unknown, but in a disclosure that leaves it veiled; in this relation there is 'presence' of the unknown ['présence' de l'inconnu]; the unknown, in this 'presence' [en cette 'présence'], is rendered present, but always as unknown. This relation [ce rapport] must leave intact – untouched – what it conveys and not unveiled what it discloses. The relation will not consist in an unveiling. The unknown will not be revealed, but indicated.

(*EI*, 442; 300)

From one version to the other, three changes have occurred: twice the word 'présence' has been replaced by '"présence"', while in the phrase 'ce rapport de présence', the word 'présence' has been deleted entirely.[2] These are not isolated cases. Elsewhere in the essay many similar modifications have been made. In 1963, for instance, using the infinitive form as a kind of hypothetical impersonal injunction, Blanchot had written of the requirement to 'relate to the unknown without unveiling it, by a relation of presence [par une relation de présence] that would not be a disclosure [qui ne serait pas une découverte]'; in 1969, however, while making the very same point, the sentence also came to state something more nearly resembling the opposite of what it initially asserted: it was essential, Blanchot wrote this time, to 'relate to the unknown without unveiling it by a relation of *non-presence* [par une relation de non-présence] that would not be a disclosure' (*EI*, 443; 300; emphasis mine).

Presence, then, in Blanchot's essay, between 1963 and 1969, becomes '"présence"', or non-presence, or else is silently erased. Why these bizarre, multiple shifts affecting the one, apparently self-identical term? One explanation is that Blanchot became aware only belatedly of the inconsistency in his text between the concept of presence and the Heraclitean logic of veiled disclosure he was endeavouring to describe, and amended his text retrospectively to translate more effectively into words his original thought. Equally, the converse might also be true, and it is arguable that in the intervening years Blanchot simply changed his mind and, as Roger Laporte has suggested, withdrew the word presence largely as a result of his encounter with the work of Derrida, particularly Derrida's deconstruction of the privilege conferred on presence by a long-standing and tenacious metaphysical tradition.[3] But historical or circumstantial explanations of this kind provide at best only a partial answer. For not only do they founder on the sheer impossibility of distinguishing between authorial intention and verbal expression, but also, more importantly, they fail to address the more fundamental issue as to what made Blanchot's rewriting of his text possible at all and thus enabled him, whatever the motivation, to rename as '"présence"', or 'non-présence', or by means of an erasure, what he had initially formulated as 'présence'.

On one level, Blanchot's deletion of the term 'présence' in 1969 was evidently not the result of an arbitrary decision; for it must have rested at the very least on the realisation that, from the outset, the word presence was deficient in some respect and already sufficiently lacking in self-presence, so to speak, for its inappropriateness to become manifest. Presence in 1963, one might conclude, was necessarily already sufficiently divided from itself for the precision and adequacy of its meanings to be queried; for only on that basis was it possible for the text to demand and then accommodate the alternative, antagonistic reading introduced by Blanchot six years later. Already in Blanchot's original text, then, the integrity of the word '"présence'" seems to have been fundamentally flawed; and one could go on to argue that 'présence' itself in Blanchot was thus already marked in advance in 1963 with the possibility of its qualification (or disqualification) as '"présence"' or as 'non-présence'. That this was so is already clear from the context of Blanchot's remarks at the time on the necessarily veiled character of the unknown. For it would follow from that account that what the author sought to indicate by the term 'présence' in 1963 was not in fact the fullness and immediacy of the present at all, but rather the withdrawal of presence from itself and the movement of self-differentiation that made such withdrawal possible and in turn allowed Blanchot in 1969 to overwrite the word 'présence' with the series of ghostly alternatives listed above.[4]

However, even this reading remains somewhat unsatisfactory, for it too is ultimately dependent on the self-presence of Blanchot as the author of his own text and the stability of Blanchot's own proper name. For what is at stake here is in fact the status of that name and of all names in general. Underlying the very possibility of the changes Blanchot makes to his text on Char is a more general issue that has to do with the degree of autonomy, self-identity, or self-coincidence enjoyed by any name, in any text, once the conventional link between the name and that which it purports to name is severed or loosened, as it is for instance by the substitution of a term such as 'non-présence' for the 'présence' that preceded it. As that example implies, the act of naming is a good deal less reliable or definitive than it might appear.

To give something a second name, if only obliquely, is always in effect to challenge the adequacy of its first name. What is true of renaming here is necessarily also applicable to naming in general. To supply any name is always tantamount to erasing a name; and any name, it would seem, can only ever exist in response to a prior absence of name, which is also a demand for a name. Any act of naming is dependent therefore on what one might call a condition of original namelessness. But any such condition is the source of an irreducible double bind. On the one hand, it implies the possibility, indeed necessity, of naming in general, without which there would be no names at all, and not only no meaning or sense available to discourse. On the other hand, if what presides over the giving of names is a principle of original namelessness, it follows that the relationship between a name and what it names can only ever be a secondary or derived one, with the result that every name, so to speak, is only ever a name in name only. Indeed, if namelessness is what generates the obligation and possibility of naming, it must also be responsible for all those cases – which might in principle include all cases – where the names in question turn out merely to be provisional, false, or assumed ones. In this circumstance, there would seem to be little difference – other than a purely conventional one – between a proper name and an improper one. A fundamental aporia would come to affect the relationship between the name and its referent, with the result that the whole stability of conceptual discourse as such might be called into question, leaving the reader with no reliable criteria, other than purely linguistic ones, to distinguish between that which is simply 'presence', in Blanchot's text, and that which is ' "presence" ', even though the difference between the two, irreducible as it is itself to any received concept of presence, is indispensable – *as* difference – to the very possibility of thinking as such.

The act of naming behaves here according to two counterbalanced, but irreconcilable conditions. At one moment, in responding to the demand for naming, words are required to confer identity on what they name; at the very next, however, they find themselves compelled to yield to the lack of identity that gives rise to the name and inhabits it as a condition of its deployment. To the extent that they are meaningful, one might say, words are necessarily also meaningless. Namelessness is a condition that is exacerbated rather than appeased by the imposition of the name; and the fate of each and every name is thus to be ravaged to the core by the namelessness to which it owes its existence. If they are to function as names at all, one may conclude, names necessarily remain precarious and arbitrary, subject to endless multiplication and revision; rather than providing any stable point of anchorage in reality, what they trace in language is both the possibility and necessity of a process of constant slippage from one word to the next.

Namelessness itself is, in turn, of course only a name, and without the prior existence of names there would be no state of namelessness at all. To this extent, the original namelessness to which I have referred is in fact not original, nor is it indeed nameless. It functions in discourse not as a prior state of mute self-coincidence, but more like a dubious spectre of originality, whose status is secondary rather than primary, and whose purpose is to challenge the adequacy of words rather than confirm their authority. Instead of a self-present origin, it operates, as far as words are concerned, rather as an endlessly excessive possibility of erasure and substitution, deferral and re-inscription. Paradoxically, it is by withdrawing identity from words that language provides for their constant displacement, alteration, and proliferation; indeed, as Blanchot has often suggested, what from one perspective seems like the sickness of words, from another is no more than the very principle of their health. Words in this respect behave according to a homeopathic principle, which is evidence of the strange circumstance that, within words and beyond words, there is an infinite reserve of language (in both senses of the word) that is a source both of plenitude and absence and which results in the fact that while on the one hand language delimits, suspends, effaces, and puts at a distance, so in that very same movement it displaces, supplements, disseminates, and transforms. Language is inseparable from a fundamental paradox, one that traverses both name and namelessness, that implies that language is always able to say more, and less, than it is capable of saying. Language and sense are never commensurate with one another; just as there are always too many words for too few meanings, so there are always too many meanings for too few words.

It is this principle of paucity and excess, suspension and alteration, effacement and proliferation, that in Blanchot comes to be called the neutre.[5] Despite the name, the neutre is not an entity, nor is it, properly speaking, a concept. It is rather a name for the namelessness of the name, a concept whose purpose is to conceptualise that which precedes all concepts. Neither immanent nor transcendent with regard to language, it is both a word and not a word, a modest trace that in its very discretion bears witness to the discretely nameless character of that to which it refers. In this way, like language itself, the neutre is perhaps best understood as a movement of perpetual effacement and re-inscription that is logically prior to all conceptual distinctions. It therefore cannot be subordinated to the opposition between the visible and the invisible, the present and the absent, the intelligible and the sensible, all of which it precedes, suspends and displaces. As such, it is in excess of all positionality, all principle of being (or non-being), subjectivity, or truth. But while being marginal to thought, it is also fundamental to it; for what it names, by a detour, in its own resistance to naming, is the unthinkable

132

and impossible margin of thought itself, the alterity that is at the origin of all thought as such.

As Blanchot's treatment of a term such as presence indicates, what the neutre names in particular is the capacity of words silently to suspend and re-mark themselves, to arrest and displace their function, so that they cease to mean what they mean, but begin to oscillate uncontrollably between what they still do mean and the always other possibility that they mean something different, something that inhabits them as their own fundamental alterity. Blanchot's responsiveness to this unrepresentable excess – which is never present in writing as itself, but only as a perpetual movement of withdrawal and re-inscription – is one of the most striking aspects about the changes he makes to the text on Char, and the reason why, contrary to appearances, Blanchot in that text is in fact not mainly concerned to revise his text and rectify its sense by imposing upon it, retrospectively, some subsequent, teleologically determined truth, but rather, by means of a detour of (re-)naming that silently invokes the namelessness that inhabits each and every name in his text, to produce a kind of abysmal demonstration of the silent and abysmal workings of what is in fact the neutre itself.

This, then, is what is most clearly at stake in Blanchot's peculiar re-inscription of the term presence as that which is always already less than present just as it is always already more than present. For ' "presence" ', in Blanchot's text, evidently does not quite mean the same as 'presence', but nor is it the same as 'non-presence'. It is, one might say, both presence itself, and something other (or less) than presence; it is presence mentioned rather than used, but thereby used rather than mentioned; as such, it is perhaps readable only as an enigmatic erasure of presence, as presence, so to speak, in its fragility as erasure, presence always already effaced and just about to be effaced, presence deferred and dispersed, transformed into a possibility of otherness, into a spectral ' "presence" ' or 'non-presence'. This other ' "presence" ' does not belong to presence, since it is what suspends presence, postpones it, and separates it from itself. In so doing, what it does is to introduce into the writing of the word (assuming that ' "presence" ' is still a word), in the form of a set of suspensive quotation marks and an invisible erasure, a supplementary trace that, being itself beyond presence, is by that token also beyond being and non-being alike. What it presents to thought instead is an alterity that is beyond ontology. So if the neutre in Blanchot functions on one level as manifestation and erasure, it also exceeds those concepts, which it suspends and defers. Manifesting itself as erasure, the neutre discreetly erases that manifestation; erasing itself as manifestation, it manifests itself as an absent erasure that has always already disappeared.

The neutre, however, is not just a name; it is a response to that which always exceeds the name, which is why it gives rise in Blanchot to a discursive strategy or syntax founded on the movement of withdrawal and re-inscription to which one can also attribute each of the other rhetorical displacements – substitution, deletion, and interpolation – employed by Blanchot in rewriting 'René Char et la pensée du neutre'. As in the case of naming, these are not the preserve of rewriting as such, but are inseparable from writing in general. Here the neutre in Blanchot, to the extent that it serves to formulate the non-coincidence of language with itself, also operates as a name (without name) for writing itself, and just as the resources of the neutre are infinite, and infinitely oblique, so too are the possibilities – and impossibilities – of writing, and it is these, in response to the infinite alterity of the neutre, that Blanchot in his later texts explores at length, by fragmenting the page, by suspending generic boundaries and pushing them to the limit, by the systematic use of paranomasia to displace the borders between words and reconfigure the relations between them, and by dividing words from themselves in order to problematise such distinctions as that between use and mention, quotation and text, original and copy.

If the neutre is what makes words mean other than what they mean, it is arguably also what allows them to mean at all. And if meaning comes to be through the neutre, it follows that the neutre itself is beyond meaning. While the neutre is essential to the production of meaning, then, it also outstrips it; it refers both to the limitlessness of language and to the limit that gives rise to meaning. The neutre in this respect, Blanchot explains, is not diffidence or complacency, rather the reverse; indeed, he notes, the neutre is 'neutral' only 'in relation to meaning; not indifferent to it, but haunting the possibility of meaning and non-meaning by the invisible gap [écart] of difference' (*EI*, 448; 304). The neutre bears witness to the necessary excess of discourse over words, syntax over semantics, gesture over sense, saying over said, experience over subjectivity. By inscribing within writing the possibility of the always other word or non-word, the neutre is what turns any text – and not just Blanchot's own – into a palimpsest constantly divided from itself and dismantled from within by an alterity that it cannot internalise.

Words and names necessarily harbour within themselves the trace of their possible deletion and substitution by another name or word; by that very token, they also display in their inscription itself, and the necessary possibility of their effacement, the risk and chance of subsequent deletion, alteration, and transformation. For that reason, both as logic and as name, despite the singular number of the term, the neutre cannot be subordinated to the unity or totality of being. It therefore cannot be thematised as One, but only addressed as multiple exteriority and immeasurable alterity. This explains why ultimately the neutre cannot be contained in fact within the horizon of the possible, nor can the alterity it presents to thought be thematised in relation to possibility. The neutre necessarily invokes that which exceeds the possibility of names; it thus bears witness, in Blanchot's writing, not to the finite possibility of the other, but rather to the limitless alterity that, while it generates the infinite proliferation of names, is also beyond all possibility of naming. Intelligible neither as immanence nor as transcendence but infinitely other, the neutre is not just a name for the possibility of the other within being; it is a response to the namelessness and infinite alterity of the impossible beyond being.

Many are the words belonging to Blanchot's critical or philosophical lexicon that in 1969 come to be altered in response to the thought of the neutre. Indeed, the changes it prompts in Blanchot's texts, as they are revised and rewritten in detail, are far-reaching and systematic. On occasion, the word used to neutralise an earlier term is the word neutre itself. As such, the terms it displaces are most often words such as: 'impersonnel' (impersonal) or 'anonyme' (nameless or anonymous). Elsewhere, 'immédiat' (immediate) comes to be rewritten by Blanchot as ' "immédiat" ', 'être' (being) as ' "être" ', 'logos' (logos) as 'différence' (difference), 'authentique' (authentic) as 'juste' (just, valid, fair), and even 'désœuvrement' – suspected perhaps of being too easy a hostage to dialectical negativity – is deleted and re-inscribed as the phrase: 'absence d'œuvre' ('absence of work') (*EI*, 45; 32). But while these changes – together with the numerous other modification there is not space to mention – clearly demonstrate the extent to which, in the mid- to late 1960s, Blanchot embarked on a major reformulation of his critical and philosophical position, they also show, conversely, that what continues to count in Blanchot's text are not individual words or concepts, but, more profoundly, the very texture of his writing in the way it inscribes concepts only to displace and transform them. Blanchot is a writer of the oblique; and it is rarely a question of rejecting one set of concepts in favour of another, more a question of accompanying the available critical or philosophical discourses to the stage where they encounter – as indeed they must – the irreducible alterity that, albeit at different strategic points, inhabits each and every one of them. In the end, the only remarkable fact about Blanchot's rewriting of some of his own earlier articles in *L'Entretien infini* and *L'Amitié* is that the available discourse Blanchot seeks indirectly to question in this way is found not in the work of another but in texts signed by the nameless name of Blanchot.

As far as Blanchot's philosophical itinerary is concerned, the emergence of the neutre in the texts of the 1960s marks an important turning point. As we have seen, the thought of the neutre, like Derridean différance, with which it shares many features, marks an attempt to re-articulate in a compelling new way a host of issues relating to the question of being, language, and the history of philosophy which, in one form or another, had been at the centre of much of Blanchot's previous work. By introducing into his work the possibility of a new style of argument and new (non-)conceptual language, the thought of the neutre gave Blanchot's writing an astonishing fresh creative and critical impetus, which, among other things, allowed the writer radically to re-examine some of the longest-standing philosophical underpinnings of his own discourse. Most prominent of all in Blanchot's engagement with contemporary philosophy were, of course, his readings of Heidegger and Levinas; and it is no surprise therefore to find that one of the first topics against which the thought of the neutre comes to be deployed in Blanchot was the question of being itself.

During the 1940s and 1950s, as I have argued, Blanchot's critical writing was largely reliant on the impersonality and self-defeating paradoxicality of the Levinasian *il y a* to challenge the basis of Heidegger's foundational conception of Being. By the early 1960s, however, subsequent to his return from Èze and his renewed involvement in political activism, Blanchot, both in parallel with Levinas and independently of him, had begun to reformulate for his own purposes some of the implications of the thought of the *il y a*. Blanchot did this in terms that were somewhat different from those in which Levinas's own thinking had begun to develop, and this divergence is what was plainly at issue in an otherwise odd exchange between Blanchot and Levinas on the relationship between the neuter and Heideggerian Being. In a famous remark towards the end of *Totalité et infini* in 1961, in which he declared his complete break with what he termed the philosophy of the Neuter, using the expression to refer to the thought of Hegel and Heidegger, Levinas credited Blanchot with having drawn attention to the impersonal neutrality ('la neutralité impersonnelle') of Heideggerian Being of beings ('l'être de l'étant').[6] But already some years before, in an article of October 1958, responding to an earlier paper by Levinas,

'La Philosophie et l'idée de l'infini' ('Philosophy and the Idea of Infinity'), Blanchot had paid Levinas exactly the same compliment; but at the same time, while plainly endorsing Levinas's criticisms of Heidegger, Blanchot had nonetheless baulked at the use of the term neutre, on the grounds, as he put it, that Heidegger's neuter was 'un Neutre un peu honteux' ('a poor man's Neuter', even 'an apology for a Neuter').[7] And it is as though, despite their common polemic against Heidegger, Heideggerian Being is for Blanchot not nearly neuter enough, while for Levinas it is already too neutral by half.

On one level the difference here is simply one of terminology; and the apparent inconsistency between Blanchot and Levinas on the subject of the neuter is merely the result of two divergent concepts of neutrality. For Levinas, since the neuter names the conceptual totality of Being, it follows that the neuter is inseparable from a reduction of the Other to the Same. For Blanchot, however, as I have suggested, the position is almost exactly the reverse, since the neutre, in Blanchot's perspective, by its refusal of all conceptual self-identity, is indeed what effects an interruption of totality.[8] And as Levinas himself was later to admit, the neutre according to Blanchot is not an effacement of difference, but a mode of radical transcendence, more akin to what Levinas in later texts thematises as the infinite reserve of Saying ('Dire') as opposed to the Said ('Dit').[9]

It is true that there are a number of wider issues at stake here between Blanchot and Levinas which reach beyond these questions of terminology, and which have a significant bearing on Blanchot's response to Levinas's later work of the 1960s and 1970s. I shall return to these in due course. In the meantime, it is perhaps worth noting the impact of the thought of the neutre on Blanchot's writing in general. Indeed, in Blanchot's thinking between the late 1950s and 1960s, there is evidence of a remarkable shift, prompted no doubt in part by Levinas, the nature and extent of which may best be measured by a brief comparison between two versions of a passage from the essay 'Comment découvrir l'obscur?' ('How to Discover the Obscure?'), published in November 1959, and incorporated in revised form in L'Entretien infini ten years later. Reiterating the post-Hegelian notion that negation is possibility and that 'the struggle for possibility is the struggle against being' (EI, 67; 47), Blanchot then adds:

But should we not also say: impossibility is what in being has always already preceded being, being that always precedes itself and always ruins the decision of the point at which it may be said to reach completion? Certainly, we should! This would seem to imply that in possibility it is still being that lies awake, and that if it negates itself therein, it is in order the better to preserve itself from the *other* assertion that always precedes it and is always more primal than that which names being, and which is the assertion the Ancients revered as Destiny, that which turns aside from all destination.

(Mais ne devons-nous pas dire aussi : l'impossibilité est ce qui dans l'être a toujours déjà précédé l'être, l'être qui toujours se précède et toujours ruine la décision du terme où il s'accomplirait? Assurément, nous le devons! Cela revient à pressentir que c'est bien l'être encore qui veille dans la possibilité et que s'il se nie en elle, c'est pour mieux se préserver de cette *autre* affirmation qui toujours le précède et qui est toujours plus initiale que celle qui nomme l'être, affirmation que les anciens révéraient déjà sous le nom de Destin, cela qui détourne de toute destination.)[10]

In *L'Entretien infini* in 1969 the lines given above were revised as follows:

But should we not also say: impossibility, neither negation nor affirmation [ni négation ni affirmation], indicates what in being has always already *preceded* being [indique ce qui dans l'être a toujours déjà *précédé* l'être] and yields to no ontology [ne se rend à aucune ontologie]? Certainly, we should! Which would seem to imply that in possibility it is still being that lies awake, and that if it negates itself therein, it is in order the better to preserve itself from the *other* experience [cette *autre* expérience] that always precedes it and is always more primal than the assertion that names being and which is the experience the Ancients doubtless revered as Destiny, that which turns aside from all destination, and which we seek to name more directly in speaking of the *neutre*.

(*EI*, 67; 47)

Between these two versions of the 'same' passage, three important changes in emphasis and substance have been introduced. First, impossibility in Blanchot is no longer thematised as extreme affirmation, but redetermined, in accordance with the thought of the (non-dialectical) neutre, as that which escapes affirmation and negation alike and exceeds all such dialectical oppositions or contraries. Second, what is described in 1959 as that in being which precedes being, and is attributed by Blanchot to the interminable

138

self-preceding or self-anticipation of being itself, has in 1969 lost its self-precedence and been displaced into an anteriority that has already preceded being (the deletion of the present tense and italicisation of the past historic are both symptomatic here) and thus can barely be assimilated to it at all, which is why Blanchot can declare it irreducible to any ontology whatsoever, including, presumably, the residual ontology contained in the *il y a*. The forces that had given rise to the worklessness of being, so to speak, instead of persisting as a recalcitrant part of being, have now seemingly seceded entirely from the domain of being (and non-being) as such. As they do so, in what is the third important change to the text, they become testimony to what Blanchot describes in 1969 as the experience of destiny, an experience to which Blanchot gives here the name of the neutre, and which functions in the argument as a figure of non-ontological alterity.

As he deploys the neutre to redescribe Destiny in this way, Blanchot once more encounters Heidegger. Indeed, it is difficult not to read the reference to the figure of Destiny as a direct response to Heidegger's account of that which, in Parmenides, under the name Moira, is deemed to embody the presence of the present that is the destiny of Being, 'the gathered and thus unfolding destination of presence as the presence of the present' ('die in sich gesammelte und also entfaltende Schickung des Anwesens als Anwesen von Anwesendem').[11] But while Moira in Parmenides serves Heidegger as a means of developing the concept of ontological difference in terms of the twofold of presence and the present, and thus of thinking the manifestation of Being as such, Blanchot reads it very differently. Indeed, in its oblique resistance to destination as truth, the destiny that is the neutre is a turning aside from presence. Destination is thus not identified with the manifestation of presence and the truth of Being. Instead, as an instantiation of the neutre, the figure of destiny for Blanchot becomes a figure of limitless wandering beyond being or non-being, and a trace of that which has always already turned aside from itself and always already bears the mark or re-mark of an encounter not with being, but with impossibility and the other.

The thought of the neutre accelerates and reconfigures much that had been in preparation in Blanchot's writing of the 1950s, but had also remained implicit within it. In particular, it marks a decisive abandonment of all points of ontological principle, even one as precariously self-defeating as the *il y a*. The neutre in Blanchot is no longer here an apology for being; and as the centre of gravity of Blanchot's writing shifts, so the question of being – as simultaneously in the work of Levinas – becomes secondary, relegated as it were to subsidiary status by the question of the other.[12] This is the displacement in Blanchot's thinking that is most clearly responsible for the radical new emphasis adopted in many of the texts collected in *L'Entretien infini*. The thought of the neutre allows Blanchot not only to pursue the delimitation of Hegelian dialectics that the logic of the *il y a* had already allowed, but also to suspend the question of Being as formulated by Heidegger both in the fundamental ontology of the 1920s and 1930s and his subsequent critique of ontology, and, in so doing, to begin to dismantle the commitment to unity and totality that, for Blanchot, under the name of the One, remains the common and abiding legacy of the metaphysical tradition as such. Blanchot points this out in a footnote from 1969 which carries much of the philosophical weight of *L'Entretien infini* as a whole; as Blanchot writes:

> dialectics, ontology and the critique of ontology share the same premise: all three rely on the One, either because the One is what accomplishes itself as all, or because it understands being as a gathering, and as the light and unity of being, or because, above and beyond being, it affirms itself as the Absolute. Faced with these assertions, should we not say: 'the most profound question' is the question that escapes reference to the One? It is the other question, the question of the Other, but also the always other question.
>
> (*EI*, 34; 440)

No longer synonymous – unlike the *il y a* – with the unity of being, the neutre is necessarily irreducible to the truth of Being in its Heideggerian sense; indeed, from the very outset, as we have seen, the neutre is affirmed by Blanchot as that which is indifferent to the movement of concealment and unconcealment, veiling and unveiling, that is constitutive of Heideggerian *aletheia*. The neutre has nothing to do with being or non-being; it signifies without concealing or unveiling, and it does not belong to the realm of the visible or invisible. As Blanchot reminds his readers, speaking is not seeing; and there is little doubt that, in rejecting that optical metaphor, Blanchot was endeavouring to break not only with Heidegger's account of the manifestation of truth in particular, but also with Western metaphysics and Greek thought in general.[13] And it was to that end that Blanchot in all his writing began to reaffirm the radical primacy and irreducible alterity of that in language that was beyond language and belonged to the outside, by virtue of worklessness, poverty, errancy, fragmentation, or multiplicity.

The impact of the thought of the neutre on Blanchot's work was arguably threefold. First, from the mid-1960s onwards, it allowed him to articulate, within philosophy, what in retrospect has all the hallmarks of a distinctive deconstructive strategy. Second, the neutre gave him the means to reformulate the terms of the challenge put to philosophy by literature and writing as such. This Blanchot did in a sequence of essays written from the early 1960s onwards, principal among which were his two articles from 1964 on Kafka, 'Le Pont de bois' ('The Wooden Bridge') (EI, 568–82; 388–96) and 'La Voix narrative' ('The Narrative Voice') (EI, 556–67; 379–87), and a long essay on André Breton and Surrealism published three years later under the title 'Le Demain joueur' ('Tomorrow at Stake') (EI, 597–619; 407–21). In those essays, and others written during the same period, literature comes to be seen by Blanchot in a surprising new light. No longer is the fate of literature bound to the question of being in time of distress; instead, according to Blanchot, it now appears that literature has already intervened to suspend the alternative between being and non-being, and that, by passing beyond that alternative, writing has begun to respond to an urgency, a demand, that cannot be thematised in relation to being or non-being, but figured only as the infinite relation of non-relation with the Other. As Blanchot suggests, perhaps tentatively still, in 'La Voix narrative':

> all language begins by making statements and in making statements affirms. But it may be that to produce a narrative (to write) is to draw language into a possibility of saying that would say without saying being and without denying it either [qui dirait sans dire l'être et sans non plus le dénier][14] – or again, more clearly, all too clearly, to establish the centre of gravity of speech elsewhere, where speaking would neither affirm being nor need negation to suspend the work of being that is accomplished ordinarily in all forms of expression. In this respect, the narrative voice is the most critical of all, which, unheard, might give to be heard [la plus critique qui puisse, inentendue, donner à entendre].
>
> (EI, 567; 386–7)

This shift beyond being and non-being is an essential one for Blanchot. In its discretion and reserve, what it marks is the turning of a change of epoch. Under the impetus of the neutre, literature puts itself at a distance not only from all immediacy, but from all mediation too, according to the detour that constitutes it as always other to itself. Irreducible either to visibility or invisibility, writing here may be said neither to veil nor to unveil; it calls into doubt the logic of manifestation and all the optical metaphors that have hitherto dominated all philosophical thinking on truth, language, meaning, literature, art. As writing for Blanchot suspends here all relation both to being and to non-being, it dissolves the dependence of thought on the figure of the One. The multiple and the fragmentary in writing are what come to take the place of the unity of being or thought, effacing the appeal to the totality of presence in order to invoke a future without present or presence, a future that is dedicated, in Blanchot, not to identity, meaning, or self, but to the infinite alterity of that which is unknown, to a beyond that corresponds to an idea neither of transcendence nor of immanence.

The implications of this deep-seated displacement in Blanchot's thinking were not limited to his essays on literature; they had a dramatic effect, too, on Blanchot's own practice as a writer of literature. Indeed, just as the key turning point in Blanchot's early career was arguably the experience of writing *Thomas l'Obscur, Aminadab*, and *Le Très-Haut*, so perhaps the crucial moment in Blanchot's writing during the late 1950s and early 1960s was his protracted exposure to fragmentary writing forms, forms that, as in the case of *L'Attente L'Oubli* or *L'Entretien infini* itself, were no longer subject to generic distinctions such as the division between narrative and discursive prose. Under the attraction of the neutre, writing in Blanchot comes henceforth not only to be thought, but practised as well, according to a (non-)fundamental (non-)principle of radical fragmentation, fragmentation construed neither as dismemberment or failure, presence or absence, but as the only exacting response, beyond being and non-being, to the limitless infinity of the outside. To write the neutre is thus always to interrupt being and non-being alike, and announce in words the promise, the coming of the always irreducible, dissymmetrical other.

July 1948: writing, dying; dying, writing

Rilke's assertion that there is, so to speak, a double death, or two relations to death, one commonly called authentic and one inauthentic, echoed as it is in philosophy, only expresses the *doubling* within which an event such as death withdraws as though to preserve the emptiness of its secret. Inevitable, but inaccessible; certain, but ungraspable; that which gives meaning, nothingness as power of negation, the force of the negative, the end on the basis of which man is the decision to be without being, is the risk that rejects being and is history and truth, death as the furthest point of power, as my most proper possibility – but also the death which never happens to me, to which I can never say yes, with which no authentic relation is possible, which I evade at the precise moment I think I can dominate it through resolute acceptance, for then I turn away from what makes it essentially inauthentic and essentially inessential: in this perspective, death disqualifies 'being *for* death', it does not have the solidity to sustain such a relation, it is indeed that which happens to nobody, the uncertainty and the indecision of what never happens, to which I cannot give serious thought, for it is not serious, but is its own fraudulence, a crumbling away, a self-consuming emptiness – not the term, but the interminable, death not as propriety but as anonymity, not true death but what Kafka calls 'the sneer of its capital error'.

'Rilke et l'exigence de la mort' (*EL*, 161; 155)

In July 1948, some months after 'La Littérature et le droit à la mort', two works of fiction by Blanchot appeared simultaneously.[1] The first, *Le Très-Haut* (*The Most High*), was classified as a *roman*, the second, *L'Arrêt de mort* (*Death Sentence*), as a *récit*. This genre distinction, which has numerous precedents in French and in other European literatures, Blanchot glossed in 1954 in an essay entitled 'Le Chant des sirènes' ('The Sirens' Song') that, under the title 'La Rencontre de l'imaginaire', was later used to open the volume *Le Livre à venir*.[2] Crucial to the difference between the *roman* and the *récit*, Blanchot suggested, alongside all the more usual criteria concerning conventions of plausibility, complexity of plot, and narrative voice, was the relationship to time: while the *roman*, having its origins in the rich diversity and familiarity of the world of human experience, belonged to the time of the everyday, the *récit* on the other hand existed only in relation to another time, a time outside of time and at a distance from time, a time that is the time of the *récit* itself. As a result, Blanchot argued, the *récit*, unlike the *roman*, has the curious property of existing only as an enactment of the singular event that constitutes the *récit* itself; and this is why, as Blanchot put it, there is paradoxically no such thing as the *récit* in general, but also why there are so many *récits*. As Blanchot explains:

> The *récit* is not the relation of the event, but that event itself, the approach to the event, the location in which this event is called upon to take place, as an event still to come and by virtue of the attractive power of which the *récit* can itself hope to become reality.
>
> (*LV*, 13; *SS*, 62).

As Blanchot's publisher's note indicates, *Le Très-Haut* and *L'Arrêt de mort*, though very different, share some common threads. These range from numerous recurrent thematic motifs and similar narrative cruxes to broader philosophical and political concerns, all of which echo back and forth from one text to the

143

other like reciprocal quotations, though in point of fact the two works intersect explicitly on perhaps no more than one occasion.[3] *Le Très-Haut*, which is staged in the first instance as an ironic allegory of Kojève's end of history, begins by exploring the relationship – both discrepancy and interdependence – between political modernity and ancient familial myth, between the conceptual realisation of the state and the persistence of distant pre-historical origins which come to be expressed in graphic bodily or physical terms, as 'something very old, criminally old' ('quelque chose d'ancien, de criminellement ancien') (*TH*, 58; 54).[4] As the novel proceeds, this complex rivalry between modern reason and primordial myth comes to be figured as a relationship between the law and its outside, between the immanence of the political and the transcendence of death, disease, and love; and indeed, in its final stages, as Blanchot's would-be Kojèvian state is beset with arson, plague, and open rebellion, the novel finds itself dramatising the circular logic by which, in the novel, all opposition to the state ends up becoming, by dialectical reversal, a reassertion of the power of the state; and at the same time the novel endeavours also to transcend this circle by introducing into the fiction a relation of radical otherness, embodied at the end in the love between Jeanne Galgat, his carer, and the protagonist Henri Sorge, the Most High of the title, a love enacted in the mortal alliance which the pair contract at the end, at the very moment when death seems both absolutely inevitable and perpetually impossible.

By comparison, though it shares many of these concerns, *L'Arrêt de mort* is a far more elliptical and episodic work, and one that dispenses with even the residual paraphernalia of plot and counter-plot, character, and setting, found in *Le Très-Haut*. The result is both enigmatic discontinuity and infinite fascination, and this is arguably one reason why, of the two books, indeed of Blanchot's fiction as a whole, *L'Arrêt de mort* is the one text that has attracted by far the greatest volume of critical commentary.[5] The story is made up of two semi-autonomous first-person narratives. The first relates the death, then the apparent resurrection, and, finally, two days later, the second, now definitive death, brought about by a final injection administered by the narrator, of a woman friend named in the text simply as J. The second narrative, in which only the narrator and the subsidiary figure of the doctor in fact reappear, is apparently a continuation of the first, and tells of the narrator's subsequent relations with a series of women – named in the text as C(olette), N(athalie), and S(imone) – which culminate in a scene in the subway during the bombing of Paris, in which the narrator, entirely out of character, as he admits, finds

144

himself impelled to propose marriage to N(athalie) in a language not his own, in which he can barely make himself understood; there follows a strange and climactic encounter between the pair that night in the narrator's hotel room, until one week later, to the narrator's horror, Nathalie tells of having had a cast made of her hands and face the very day of the bombing by the same sculptor as J. had done in the earlier part of the book, and whose name Nathalie had found in the narrator's wallet, at which point, save for the brief, metatextual epilogue deleted from the 1971 version of the text, the narrative abruptly ceases.

Apart from the highly charged and deeply allusive character of the events in the book, what is most striking of all in *L'Arrêt de mort* is the strange logic of suspense and completion – of suspense as completion and completion as suspense – governing the narrative; this is reflected most obviously of course in the bizarre double meaning contained in Blanchot's title, which utilises an otherwise perfectly commonplace French expression – were it not, as Blanchot had put it seven years before, that commonplaces themselves might best be seen as words torn apart by lightning – and which is made here to signify both (idiomatically) a sentence prescribing death and (literally) a suspension in the enactment of death. The strategy is one Blanchot exploits to great effect in other ways too, and *L'Arrêt de mort* draws throughout, in an understated yet knowing way, on a vast range of commonplace intertextual material of mythical, biblical, historical, political, literary, and philosophical provenance. *L'Arrêt de mort*, in this respect, is very much a sum of many previous texts, and it is a text that seems to offer itself to the reader in several readily accessible ways: as fictional memoir, as ghost story, as love story, even as a *roman personnel* in the tradition of Constant's *Adolphe*.[6] But each of these angles of approach is quickly found wanting, and none of them proves persuasive enough to circumscribe Blanchot's text. Commonplaces, in *L'Arrêt de mort*, are less a source of clarification than of obscurity; read as a personal memoir, for instance, the *récit* soon turns into a memoir without a person; and the case is much the same with each of the other approaches: if the book is a ghost story, say, it is a ghost story without ghosts; if a love story, a story without lovers, and so on.

The effect is of a text in which literary conventions are simultaneously incorporated yet frustrated; each enigma proves, as the narrator puts it on one occasion, to be no more than the shell of an enigma, but all the more puzzling or fascinating as a result. This process of allusion and disappointment, withdrawal and displacement is everywhere in evidence in *L'Arrêt de mort*; but it is particularly striking in the numerous references made throughout, explicitly or implicitly, to specific historical dates. Of all Blanchot's *récits*, *L'Arrêt de mort* is the only one seemingly to be located at a particular historical moment, and there are many tempting parallels to be drawn between the events that unfold in the *récit* and the contemporary historical events mentioned in the book. Most suggestive of all among these historical references are those made, at the beginning of *L'Arrêt de mort*, to the Munich accords, signed at the end of September 1938, the aftermath and consequences of which seem to form the background to the events surrounding J.'s death and apparent resurrection in the early hours of the night between Monday 11 and Tuesday 12 October, and her second death twenty-four hours later, early on the morning of Wednesday 13 October 1938.[7] Also evoked by Blanchot's text, with a similar degree of historical precision, is the first bombing of Paris on 3 June 1940, during which the meeting in the subway between Nathalie and the narrator takes place, and the day on which, it is realised in retrospect, she had the cast taken of her hands and face.[8] And no doubt some significance too attaches to the fact that Blanchot's narrator, in a state of intense 'désœuvrement', first writes down his story, only then to destroy it immediately afterwards, during the aftermath of the Fall of France, in the first months of the Occupation, i.e. throughout July and August of 1940 (*AM*, 8; 1).

There are many other similar moments in *L'Arrêt de mort* when private or personal events seem in some way to be encoding a reference to events occurring on this broader historical stage. At one point, for instance, it is reported that J. had been sick for at least ten years, i.e. since 1928, much like France itself in the eyes of the early Blanchot (*AM*, 12; 4); that J.'s doctor had considered her dead since the time of the Popular Front (*AM*, 13; 5); and that, on the same authority, the narrator in 1940, who had been existing on borrowed time since Munich, had only six months to live (*AM*, 14; 5). To these possible parallels between the personal and the political may also be added a number of other, covert literary allusions, among which might be, as Michael Holland has argued, a reference to *Nadja*, André Breton's quasi-autobiographical *récit* of 1928, in which case Blanchot's *récit* may be read as a critical reworking of Breton's 'always future book', as Blanchot calls it (*EI*, 615; 419), which not only deals with the way in which Breton himself is literally haunted by a series of unexpected chance encounters, but also gives an important role in the plot to the afternoon of 13 October 1926.[9] And it is not impossible too, as Derrida and others have proposed, that Blanchot in *L'Arrêt de mort* is also drawing on a series of more esoteric, private allusions, perhaps including a reference to the life-story of Bataille's lover, Colette Peignot, better known under the name Laure, who died of tuberculosis at the age of 35 in November 1938, three-and-a-half weeks after the fictional J., and whose dying words – 'La rose!' – which Bataille recorded in a diary entry for 12 October 1939, are strangely reminiscent of J.'s in Blanchot's story (AM, 44; 25). The rose, as Blanchot notes some years later, was of course the Orphic emblem par excellence, the very symbol of poetical activity and of death (EL, 163; 157).[10]

There seems little doubt, then, that Blanchot in L'Arrêt de mort was seeking to set the events in the story within a much larger historical and intertextual frame; and the many readers who have endeavoured to decode the récit as an allegory containing a political or historical message are in this respect following an interpretative strategy already in part suggested by Blanchot's text itself. Indeed, the principle of convergence between private and public experience is itself clearly established from the outset by the fact that Blanchot's narrator, like the author himself in earlier years, is a political correspondent involved in the day-to-day writing down of historical events. Here, though, some of the ambiguities of the story begin. For in his capacity as a dutiful journalist, Blanchot's protagonist cuts a strangely detached and irresolute figure. He admits for instance that, as the events of Munich unfolded, instead of urgently hurrying back to Paris, as public and private responsibilities demanded, he for no obvious reason continued to linger in the holiday resort of Arcachon, with the result that, on this occasion at least, the narrator's involvement in history was, paradoxically, in the form of his absence from it.

For all its apparent arbitrariness, the incident is far from an isolated one, for a similar disjunction or dissymmetry between the narrator's private endeavours and the broad canvas of contemporary history is also in evidence when the narrator agrees to act for a friend in a duel arising from some purely private matter of the heart, on (or about) the very day in 1940 when, Paris having been abandoned by the government, the capital was declared an open city and left to the devices of the occupying forces (AM, 117; 73).[11] Elsewhere, too, the parallels between historical events and the events occurring in Blanchot's récit are more problematic than it might seem. Whereas an allegorical, historico-political interpretation of the text might require, for instance, that J.'s proposed cure be read as a symbol of the drastic remedy accepted by Chamberlain and Daladier at Munich, the fact is that Munich in reality delays J.'s treatment and makes it impossible for it to be administered at all. Munich in this regard is more condemnation than

147

salvation; and while this certainly emphasises to what extent, in Blanchot's own view, Munich, by vainly attempting to defer war, served only to hasten it, it also suggests that between historical events and private experience there are more discrepancies than there are correlations; indeed, in the light of J.'s heroic resistance in the weeks that follow Munich, and given that the narrator's voluntary absence from Paris, which, he claims, made the events surrounding her death possible (*AM*, 24; 12), was in spite of Munich and not because of it, one might equally conclude that personal experience serves not to confirm history, but rather to contest it, and that it is only a simplistic reading that attempts, reductively, to deduce the one from the other.

The relationship between public and private events in *L'Arrêt de mort*, then, needs to be examined with some care. But remarkably enough, in the haste to establish correspondences between the two series of occurrences, critics of Blanchot's *récit*, it seems, have ignored what is arguably the most peculiar feature of all regarding what, in the opening pages of *L'Arrêt de mort* (*AM*, 11; 4), the narrator claims to be the only date of which he is sure, and which marks the day on which J., having apparently already died once, dies again for the second time: Wednesday, 13 October [1938].[12] A cursory glance at the calendar quickly reveals that in fact 13 October 1938 fell not on a Wednesday at all, but on a Thursday. The date that is given in the text as the only one of which the narrator is certain is therefore decidedly uncertain. At the very moment when, by way of the date, Blanchot prompts the reader to scour the text in order to forge an encounter between private experience and historical reality, the possibility of that encounter, in the form of the calendar, is in fact withdrawn. History as such and the events in the *récit* prove irreducible to one another; and it is far from evident that J.'s death, to the extent that it takes place within time at all, occurs within the same temporal frame as that occupied by the historical record. This disjunction is not simply a case of metafictional playfulness on Blanchot's part, for it addresses a dissymmetry that is very much at the heart of J.'s whole existence; indeed, when, at one moment, commenting on the awkwardness with which she endeavours to die, her doctor is heard to exclaim: ' "Ah! par exemple" ' (' "Typical!" ', *AM*, 46; 26), what is immediately clear is that the life of J., like her forthcoming death, is exemplary or typical only because it is neither exemplary nor typical, and that her death, if it is interpretable at all, belongs not to the teleology of history, but to the unspeakable, the irremediable, and the impossible that exist only within the margins of history.

There were, and are, of course, many years when 13 October, the date mentioned by Blanchot's narrator, did fall on a Wednesday; these include, among others, the years 1937, 1943, and, most curiously of all, the one in which *L'Arrêt de mort* was itself published, 1948.[13] As far as the reader is concerned, the last of these is perhaps the one that disturbs the most, for at the very moment it appeared to be anchoring itself reliably in the past, Blanchot's *récit*, when first published, seems to have been looking forward, covertly, to its own ghostly repetition. Inevitably, as the contemporary reader knows, the future of that repetition was destined in its turn to become past; and what *L'Arrêt de mort* reminds us, by the use it makes of the ghostly date of Wednesday 13 October, is not only that the past is a condition of the future, but that the future is a condition of the past, and that in addressing the past *L'Arrêt de mort* was also addressing the futurity implicit within that past. Temporality here is repetition and recurrence, a factor that empties time of all presence and denies the narrative that is history any monopoly either on meaning or experience. Indeed, what seems clear is that, if it indeed takes place as claimed by the text, i.e. on Wednesday 13 October 1938, J.'s death cannot be said to take place within history, or in relation to any present moment at all; so if it does take place, then, it does so only within Blanchot's writing, in which it occurs without occurring, so to speak, as an event that is simultaneously made possible by the structure of repetition and difference that is the calendar and yet, equally well, rendered impossible by the calendar: Wednesday 13 October 1938 exists within time, one might say, only to the extent it exists outside of historical time. This is perhaps why, as far as *L'Arrêt de mort* is concerned, each event is also always already a non-event, and why what transpires in the *récit* is not only that the time of narration takes precedence over the time of the plot, but also that the time of reading takes precedence over the time of narration, with the result that reading itself, in its very futurity, becomes a re-enactment of the absent events of the *récit*. Whence, perhaps, in the closing pages of the 1948 version of *L'Arrêt de mort*, the fearsome warning, were the reader to supply an end to the text in exchange for its effacement, that the reader's end would be the narrator's beginning, and that there would cease to be any escape at all from this infinite round of inscription and erasure.

The temporality of writing implied here is a temporality that contests the teleology of history and of historical narrative. Writing instead is in the form of a series of repetitions or recurrences in which to advance is always already to return, and in which an event such as the death of J., though it marks a date and is marked by a date, belongs in fact neither to past nor to present nor future, but rather to another time, beyond presence, between past and future, in relation to which time itself, like the certain date of J.'s death, is continually, so to speak, beside, outside, or beyond itself. Blanchot's *récit* is thus not a story dedicated to memorialising the past in the belief that narrative is truth, nor is it a work bound confessionally to the future as a moment of deferred revelation. It is a text that belongs to a time outside of time which is the time of return. Return here, however, is not a function of permanence or identity, but of the alterity which is the possibility of time itself. So if *L'Arrêt de mort* is a text about historical events, it is not about the priority of history over experience, but about the repetitive futurity of events as such, their status as promise or condemnation, tragedy or hope. To adopt the terms of the narrator's encomium to the timeless moment that now concludes *L'Arrêt de mort*, if Blanchot's *récit* is about boundless unhappiness, it is also about boundless affirmation; if it is about the necessity of time, it also about the interruption of time. What it thus inscribes within time and finitude, so to speak, is the infinity of a timeless instant.

If the structure of temporal return is what is at stake in the dates everywhere to be found in *L'Arrêt de mort*, the same is also true of the narrative structure of the *récit*. This too is in the form of a series of potentially endless repetitive enactments which imply both finality and incompletion, time and timelessness. From the outset, the reader is told, Blanchot's narrator has tried several times, in novels and in other books, to give written form to the events of which he is required to speak (*AM*, 7; 1). But on each occasion the weakness and unreliability of words have conspired to undermine the writer's confidence in the possibility of ending. Instead of expressing truth, the narrator concedes, all words have ever done is to withdraw from truth. To write at all, for the narrator, is to write in the knowledge that the whole truth will always remain inaccessible; but if this is so, it is not because the truth is an embarrassing or unmentionable secret, but because truth, as far as words are concerned, is what has always already been lost. This implies no nostalgia, only the realisation that the absence of truth is the very secret of the possibility of words. The secret however is one that, by definition, cannot be uttered; it is in fact, to that extent, anything but a secret.

It is here, with the secret that resists words precisely because it is the secret of words, that Blanchot's *récit*, much like 'La Littérature et le droit à la mort', in fact begins. As it does so, it is necessarily obliged to provide a name, albeit a name without name, for that unspeakable secret. That name, however, is not hard to find, for it is the name without name of death itself. As elsewhere in Blanchot's work, death in *L'Arrêt de mort* is both extreme possibility and extreme impossibility, finitude and infinity, limit and limitlessness, experience and anonymity, meaning and meaninglessness. It is, as it were, the only secret worth revealing precisely because it is not a secret and cannot be revealed. The resulting paradox has many implications for language as such, and, in their dealings with Blanchot's narrator, words, in *L'Arrêt de mort*, behave accordingly. They are keenly aware of the limits imposed upon them by the simple fact they are just words; but they realise too that those limits are not only the end, but also the beginning of their very existence, the basis of both their possibility and their inexhaustibility, their impotence and endlessness. And this is why, as the past recedes from the narrator's grasp and refuses to be spoken, the absent past imposes itself upon him nevertheless as the condition of his very speaking; the events surrounding the dying and the impossibility of dying traversed by J. become like a repetition of a past that, lying beyond the limits of language, cannot be spoken but which, to the extent it gives rise to the limitlessness of language, everywhere has to be spoken, albeit therefore in its absence, in silence, and beyond possibility. The logic of Blanchot's text, like the remedy proposed to J. by her doctor, an eccentric versed in Paracelsus (*AM*, 19; 9), is not allopathic, but homeopathic. Death, like life, knows no opposite and cannot be cured except by itself. What is true here of dying is also true for writing; and the only antidote to the limitations of language proves to be the limitless exposure to those limits.

Writing here, then, becomes an insistent repetition of that which by definition it cannot say, and what Blanchot's *récit* does, in the inability to narrate the events of the past, is in fact to repeat them as a process of endless incompletion or limitless finality. Repetition functions accordingly as both failure and compulsion, worklessness and demand. The past, so to speak, is what never happens to the extent that it is what has always already happened, in exactly the same way that death, precisely because it always already belongs to the past, is only ever the non-event of its own impossibility. In the same way, the story Blanchot's narrator in *L'Arrêt de mort* is impelled to tell is a story that never happens as an event present to itself, and this is not only why none of the events in the story ever really takes place except as a ghostly occurrence or repetition of another event, but also why as a result the narrative is in fact more a narrative of the very limits of narrative, and why the narrator's story continues perpetually to take place as a constant repetition of itself. Whence, in *L'Arrêt de mort*, the elisions and interruptions in the narrative, the perpetual recurrences, and the process of replication or duplication that turns each

151

person or event into a version of another; each event, it seems, is like a memory or a premonition that is full of meaning only to the extent that it is simultaneously empty of all meaning.

Once Blanchot's *récit* begins, then, the story proves to be both singular and multiple, vestigial and compelling; and what takes place does so according to a movement of constant recurrence and repetition. Even before it is realised, for instance, that the *récit* as a whole is in two parts that mirror each other, the reader is introduced to a story involving two sisters, not just one. Later, the narrator, on a mysterious impromptu visit to S(imone), finds that she lives in an apartment comprising 'a single room, without a hallway, divided in two by a large curtain, with one side for the day, the other for the night [d'un côté pour le jour, l'autre la nuit]' (*AM*, 72; 43), and it is difficult in retrospect not to see the text of *L'Arrêt de mort* itself similarly split between day and night, *jour* and *nuit*, J. and N(athalie). The text as a whole is full of suspended vignettes of this kind; towards the beginning of the book, for instance, in similar fashion, Blanchot provides a *mise-en-abyme* of the story to come in the form of a brief scene, said to have taken place towards the end of 1940, which involves an unnamed woman and a mysterious object – perhaps the lifeless cast of J.'s once living hands, though this is nowhere confirmed – concealed in a wardrobe, the sight of which, as though by contagion, provokes in the woman a reaction – convulsive shaking and a deathly rattle – which recalls the process leading to J.'s death while, as far as the reader is concerned, also foretelling those earlier events. The effect is uncontrollable recurrence, a movement of return in which, as by the delayed action of some mysterious poison, the future turns into a ghostly premonition of the past and the past into a deathly repetition of the future.

To this temporal inversion is added even greater and more disturbing intensity as a result of the identity of the object glimpsed by the woman. Nowhere is it revealed what this is; and the only indication that the so-called 'living proof' relating (but how?) to the events in the story, and which lies hidden in the wardrobe, is indeed the cast of J.'s hands, is the narrator's admission that he can see those hands before him as he writes and, as he puts it, 'that they are alive [qu'elles vivent]' (*AM*, 21; 10).[14] But if the object in question is the cast of J.'s hands, the effect, if taken together with the closing invitation to the reader (in the 1948 version) to imagine the hand responsible for writing *L'Arrêt de mort* itself, is to frame the narrative as a whole with an enigmatic double reference to hands: to hands that are dead and alive because they have been uncannily re-embodied in statuesque effigy, and to hands which are alive and dead because they are the hands that write.

152

Writing features here in two guises, as extreme affirmation and extreme dispossession, as that which passes beyond the limit of living and that which exposes itself to the limitlessness of dying. Throughout *L'Arrêt de mort*, the motif of hands recurs time and again as a bodily figure of this double belonging of writing to living and dying and thus, in a sense, of its subservience to the demands of neither, its responsiveness instead to that which has no name except for the nameless name of the impossible. Thus, for instance, the statement of J.'s last wishes, scribbled down by her by hand, setting out what was to happen in her own final absence (*AM*, 13; 5); her handwritten correspondence with the narrator, possible only in his absence, but mysteriously sustaining her in the repeated encounter with death (*AM*, 24–5; 12); and the lines in J.'s hands, preserved in the cast as a monument to both life and death, but offering beyond life and beyond death not only a kind of physical inscription of her discontinuous life-story, but also a reminder of her final communication in death – never more alive, nor more lucid, says the narrator – which is to squeeze the narrator's hand 'with all the affection and tenderness she could' (*AM*, 51; 30). Thus, too, the scarred hand of Colette, full of mystery and significance (*AM*, 60; 35); and, most dramatic of all, in the dark, the exchange of hands, as from Orpheus to Eurydice, between the narrator and the unnamed N., sealing the pact of love that binds them to one another momentarily, eternally, across the foreignness of their languages, for the duration of a story that concludes with the knowledge that N.'s hands, too, like those of J., are alive only to the extent that they are also destined to die, and that, ominously, as though in advance of that end, N., too, has had a cast made of her hands in a procedure that, the narrator points out, is startling and dangerous when performed on living people (*AM*, 120; 75), no doubt because it changes them into the survivors of an impossible death, a realisation which is not limited to those who have casts made of their hands, but one that extends, by contagion, to all those who are subject to the temporality of return, be it through speaking, writing, or reading.

Early in the first part of *L'Arrêt de mort*, reference is made in passing to a photograph of the Turin shroud, hanging in the doctor's surgery, and displaying two overlaid or interwoven images, the one showing the face of Christ, the other that of Veronica, the woman credited traditionally with wiping Christ's face after the crucifixion, thereby imprinting on the cloth, in blood, the image of Christ's death. The description is another suggestive *mise-en-abyme*, and one that invites the reader of Blanchot's *récit* everywhere to seek within each seemingly truthful icon (the etymology of the name Veronica) the traces of

153

duplicity and otherness. For in this particular photograph, the features of Christ serve not only to confirm death and announce the possibility of resurrection, but also reveal in that very possibility the assertive force of a woman's face. The point here, however, is not to profess a belief in resurrection in any theological sense, but to indicate how, in death, uncontrollable contagious forces belonging neither to life nor death are inscribed within works of art, overwhelming limits and crossing boundaries, such as to undercut a traditional image of spiritual transcendence with a decidedly adverse image of earthly pride and beauty. The implications of this are not lost on Blanchot's *récit*, for not only does the story proper, relating the narrator's first encounter with J., begin with her mysterious appearance one night in his hotel bedroom, seemingly in response to a sense of the threat of dying hanging over him, an almost complete stranger (*AM*, 16; 7), but it continues with a whole series of similarly mysterious comings and goings in rooms at night, bearing witness to the fragility of spatial distance and the overwhelming force of unconscious desires: at one point, the narrator bursts in on Colette, his neighbour, apparently mistaking her hotel room for his own (*AM*, 59; 35); shortly after, a strange presence, that of Nathalie, materialises uninvited in the early hours of the morning in the narrator's own hotel room (*AM*, 64; 37); later still, for no good reason, the narrator finds himself in the middle of the night pushing open the door to S(imone)'s apartment in her absence (*AM*, 72; 43); until, finally, once again, the narrator's own hotel room finds itself mysteriously penetrated by N. who, having appropriated the key from the narrator, locks him out, only for him, to his manifest astonishment, to force the door open by striking it with his fist (*AM*, 107; 66), upon which there follows the climactic, almost immobile scene of the exchange of hands.

Moments of repetition, recurrence, or return of this kind are everywhere to be found in *L'Arrêt de mort*. But when textual motifs are repeated, what is it that repeats itself? 'Think about it,' says Henri Sorge, the protagonist of *Le Très-Haut*, when faced with a similar question, 'all the events in history are there around us, just like dead bodies [comme des morts]' (*TH*, 88; 88). Except, he adds, that 'Now, they are going to exist properly, now is the time, everything is reappearing, all is being revealed in clarity and in truth' (*TH*, 89; 88). Repetition here is not reinforcement, but a process of transformation by which events are stripped of identity and substance, and addressed in their singularity, intensity, and irreducible alterity. The finite possibility of death is turned into the infinite impossibility of dying, the possibility of time into the impossibility of time passing, and the reader is faced, as though in a premonition or repetition of an apocalyptic day of judgement, with what in *L'Arrêt de mort*, referring to the mysterious appearance of N(athalie) in his hotel room, in the guise of the dead J., the narrator, using the adjectival noun in the impersonal or neuter form, describes as: 'l'irrémédiable', the irremediable (*AM*, 65; 38). The irremediable, as the narrator explains, operates too according to the homeopathic principle; like death itself, it is that which cannot be remedied and which immobilises and interrupts all thought.[15] There is no remedy for the irremediable; but it can still be thought, albeit as an interruption of thought, as a thinking of that in thought which escapes thought. This is the trait of the irremediable that likens it to the thought of the *il y a* and the thought of the *neutre*; and if the irremediable can be thought, implies Blanchot's narrator, it necessarily therefore must be thought, if only because, as a thought, the irremediable not only falls subject to the necessity and the compulsion of that which knows no negation, but is in fact itself the thought which knows no negation. Accordingly, it can only figure in thought as absolute negation, which is why in turn it figures in thought as measureless affirmation, as the timeless invocation of the singular moment that, as Derrida has shown, Blanchot addresses here, as elsewhere, with the apocalyptic summons: 'Viens', 'Come'. It is this thought that *L'Arrêt de mort*, after all, is written to affirm.

The irremediable, here, interrupts meaning; like the *neutre*, it introduces into language a distance, neither internal nor external, neither visible nor invisible, that withdraws events or statements from themselves and re-inscribes them as other than what they are. The narrator explains how this occurs (without occurring) by recourse to a figure that is to be found increasingly in Blanchot's later *récits*. The figure concerned is that of the 'vitre', the window pane or glass.[16] Referring at one stage to his intermittent relations with S(imone), the narrator recalls one occasion when, after six years of absence, he suddenly caught sight of her through a shop window ('la vitre d'un magasin'); he comments: 'Whoever has disappeared completely and is suddenly there before you, behind a pane of glass, becomes a sovereign figure' ('Quelqu'un qui a tout à fait disparu et qui, brusquement, est là, devant vous, derrière une glace, devient une figure souveraine') (*AM*, 72; 43). The phenomenon – what Blanchot calls here, as in later texts, 'the phenomenon of the window-pane', 'le phénomène de la vitre' (*AM*, 79; 48) – functions here as a complex play of presence and absence, incompletion and finality; it inscribes within a scene or an event a difference that suspends or neutralises them, strips them of presence, and returns them to what the narrator next describes as 'a timeless past' (*AM*, 80; 48). All that takes place takes place, so to speak, within quotation marks, both as a vestige and as an alteration of itself; and the effect is to bring about a striking transformation in the narrator's relationship to the characters that feature in his narrative, whom he now begins to forget, or at least no longer to remember as beings, but rather as a series of interruptions in being. The first hint of this process occurs in the Paris metro, when the narrator realises that, as her name suggests, his neighbour C(olette) has suddenly become in his memory, as he puts it, 'a huge, impersonal hole, though still alive, a kind of living lacuna, from which she emerged only with difficulty' (*AM*, 63; 37).

In the case of C(olette), this particular dissociation seems to have remained largely without consequence; but when similar disturbances begin to characterise his dealings with Nathalie, this other Eurydice, with whom the narrator takes refuge in the underworld of the Paris subway on 3 June 1940, the effects are more startling. For it is here that words come to acquire a life and death — an absence of life and death — all their own, and it is this that is most clearly responsible for the narrator's impetuous proposal of marriage to Nathalie, a proposal he is able only to make in spite of himself, in words he only barely understands. Next, carried away by his violence, the narrator begins addressing N. in his own language, with the result — chance or fate? — that the pair lose contact in the crowd and each goes their separate way — Nathalie, it would seem, to the appointment with the sculptor, the narrator to the aimless wait that awaits him. The pair meet again, of course, that night, for the climactic exchange that has already been mentioned, but, unbeknown to them both, it is clear that something irremediable has happened in the meantime, were it not that what has happened had in any case always already happened in the distant past.

Now, though, the compulsion to repeat that irretrievable past takes on a more violent, less forgiving dimension, and while on one level the narrator forfeits any control over the words he still takes to be his, he is also compelled, with those words, to entertain the thought that those words demand of him; as he does so he is compelled to affirm that thought with all the force he can muster, for both the limitations of those words and the limitlessness to which they give rise are his thought and his thought alone. The legacy of words is violently double: while the finite nature of language offers only misfortune, the limitlessness of language makes it possible, by means of a word that is thereby no longer a word, to address the other, the loved one from whom the narrator, as from Nathalie, is infinitely distant and to whom, as to Nathalie, he is also infinitely close, with a single, solitary word, which, borrowed from the Book of

Revelation, puts an end to the world in order to speak to the other beyond all world. Repeated thrice over in *L'Arrêt de mort*, it is the word: 'Viens', 'Come', that, to the extent it belongs to no language at all, is both the final limit and the infinite boundary of writing as such.

What is at stake then in *L'Arrêt de mort* is the force of a demand that does not belong to the world, but precedes, traverses, and survives the world, allying itself to a dimension that may only be described as eschatological, and which, outside of history and outside of narrative, can only be thought as the relation of non-relation that thought itself entertains with that in thought that is always other than thought. This thought that suspends ontology, history, and temporality is an obligation that cannot be refused, in the sense that to refuse it is already to affirm it, to endow it with a force that is beyond being or non-being, making it intelligible perhaps only as a kind of singular, pre-conceptual trace, prior to being, prior to thinking, and even prior to language, though equally it is none of these things and may only be embodied by a pact, an alliance with the other, founded not on a statement of common destiny, not on a hierarchical injunction, not on the universal pretensions of a moral code, not on rules or norms or assertions of principle, but on a word that is not a word and which, in its endless repetition, can only ever be pronounced in the singular: 'Viens', 'Come'.

4

The absence of the book

Beyond philosophy?

'I reject these words with which you address me, this discourse into which you seek to entice me in such assuaging tones, and the duration of your words, one after the other, by which you delay me in the presence of an affirmation, and above all this relation you create between us by the simple fact of speaking to me even in my unresponsive silence.' – 'Who are you?' – 'The refusal to engage in discourse, to negotiate with the law of discourse.' – 'Do you prefer tears, laughter, the madness that does not move?' – 'I speak, but I do not speak in your discourse: by speaking I prevent you from speaking, by not speaking I oblige you to speak; there is no recourse for you, no instant in which to rest from me, who am there in all your words before all your words.' – 'I invented the great logos of logic to protect me from your incursions and to allow me to say and know by saying, according to the peace of well-developed words.' – 'But, in your logic, I am there also, denouncing the oppression of a coherence that takes on the role of law and I am there with my violence, affirming itself beneath the mask of your legal violence, the sort that subjects thought to the grip of understanding.' – 'I invented poetic irregularity, the errancy of broken words, the interruption of signs, and forbidden images in order to put you into words and, by putting you into words, silence you.' – 'I am silent, and straight away, in the hollowing out of day and night, you can hear me, all you do is hear me, no longer hearing anything, then hearing everywhere the distant murmur that, with every simple word, the cries of torture, the sighs of happy people, the spinning of time, the disorientation of space, has now passed into the world in which I speak.' – 'I know that I am betraying you.' – 'You are not in a position to betray me, nor be faithful to me. I do not know faith, I am not the unspeakable demanding secrecy, the uncommunicable that muteness would make manifest, I am not even the violence without words against which you might defend yourself with the violence that speaks.' – 'Nonetheless, affirming when I deny, denying when I affirm, ravaging in an ever

158

thoughtless act of wrenching separation: I denounce you as the word never uttered or
still too many that aims to except me from the *order* of language and tempt me with
another way of speaking. You torment me, it's true, even by leaving me in peace, but I
can torment you too: justice, truth, truth, justice, these terms you reject with your
pre-emptive sneer pursue you in their turn even to the point of the *other* into which
you reverse them. You do me Good by harassing me with the charge of injustice, and
I might even say you are the Kindness that is never caught doing anything kind.' –
'You can say this, I accept everything, confess my part in everything.'

Le Pas au-delà (*PA*, 159–60; 116–17)

Throughout the late 1940s and 1950s Blanchot's critical writing maintains a
close and privileged relationship with the philosophical work of Emmanuel
Levinas. But only rarely during that period does Blanchot explicitly refer to
Levinas; and it was not until 1961, when the publication of *Totalité et infini*
(*Totality and Infinity*) signalled an important new departure in Levinas's thinking,
that Blanchot began to address Levinas's work at all directly and in any detail,
eventually devoting to Levinas not only a sequence of three chapters in
L'Entretien infini, but also a substantial portion of the fragmentary texts published
in *L'Écriture du désastre* in 1980, as well as a lengthy tribute to Levinas, under the
title 'Notre compagne clandestine' ('Our Clandestine Companion'), later the
same year.[1] That Blanchot was drawn to address Levinas's work increasingly in
this way is an indication not only of the urgency for Blanchot of Levinas's
thinking, but it is also a sign of the distance between the two thinkers, a distance
that was a necessary and integral part of their friendship and which manifests
itself throughout in divergences of language and idiom, strategy and context.
Difference here, though, does not necessarily constitute opposition, nor should
one attribute the undoubted community of questioning that exists between the
two authors to the influence of the one upon the other. Instead, to read the texts
of Blanchot alongside those of Levinas, and vice versa, is to be aware – beyond
influence and beyond opposition – of the singular rigour of a response to infinite
debt, a debt that Blanchot, for his part, when speaking of Levinas, frequently
acknowledged with unalloyed personal affection.[2]

Infinite debt, however, does not imply slavish repetition, but almost exactly
the reverse. Properly to pay tribute to another means paying tribute to another's
difference; and this is achieved not by effacing distance but only by accentuating
it, not by faithful repetition but by recognising the necessity of infidelity. There
is here a peculiar double bind that governs all relations between texts and which
requires that fidelity, if it is to be possible at all, must necessarily be couched in

159

the form of infidelity. The paradox is one that is inherent in all commentary, and Blanchot describes its implications in detail when considering the challenge of writing about that other friend who was Georges Bataille. Fidelity, he writes, is not what it seems. 'A commentator', remarks Blanchot, 'is not being faithful when he faithfully reproduces; the words or sentences he quotes, by the very fact of being quoted, change in meaning and become immobilised, or else assume excessive prominence' (*EI*, 301; 203). Infidelity, it seems, is an unavoidable condition of all commentary. But if this is so, how then is it possible to respond faithfully to a text at all and repay, so to speak, the infinite obligation it thus imposes?

The – provisional – tactic Blanchot adopts in response to Bataille mingles modesty and respect with uncompromising defiance. Proximity, for Blanchot, is only possible from a distance.[3] To write on Bataille, he suggests, it is essential to avoid repeating the key words or concepts – terms such as despair, horror, ecstasy, rapture – that feature so powerfully in Bataille's work, in order to attend instead to the internal demand – the 'exigence' – of Bataille's writing, that which draws it outside or beyond itself and confounds the act of naming. To read Bataille in this way is to begin by suspending all the names the text provides itself and for itself, including that of the author, in order to affirm what escapes all naming and which is rather to be found in what Blanchot calls the 'surprise' of Bataille's language – both Bataille's surprise at language and the surprise of language at Bataille – and in the unique tone of the silent discourse of Bataille's text. The result is a practice of reading that refuses to privilege conceptuality, but instead allows itself to be led in the text by the repetitive movement of withdrawal and re-inscription, retraction and retracing, that Blanchot elsewhere addresses as the neutre.

Language, under the effects of the neutre, testifies here not to the stability of the name according to its status of universal particular, but, beyond all naming, to the nameless alterity inscribed in a singular movement of a writing, such as that of Bataille. Language here becomes synonymous with the movement that carries it beyond its own limits and, as a result, allows it to think more than it is able to think and to evoke an alterity whose only distinguishing trait is that, like dying, it is beyond all possibility. As Blanchot goes on to remark:

> what no existent can attain in the primacy of his or her own name, what existence itself, in the seduction of its chance individuality [dans la

séduction de sa particularité fortuite], in the movement of its sliding universality [dans le jeu de son universalité glissante], can in no way embrace, what therefore decidedly always escapes, all this language gratefully accepts; and it not only maintains it, but it is indeed by affirming it as such, as always other and always at a distance, as the impossible and the incommunicable, that language speaks and finds its origin, just as, in such language, thought thinks more than it is capable of thinking.

(EI, 312; 210)

Here it seems that, in order to respond faithfully to a text, it is necessary to respond, not to those elements in a text – concepts or arguments, topics or themes – which are easily repeated, and which, once repeated, in fact betray the text, but rather to that in the text – a tone, a slippage, an accident, or an incoherence – which cannot be named as such and thus seemingly resists repetition. The position is a paradoxical one, as Blanchot freely admits, in that what is thereby adjudged to be most singular or recalcitrant in a text is not that which is most original in it, but that which is already most repetitive in it and that by virtue of the displacements wrought by the iterative movement of writing itself marks the text with the trace of its irreducible difference from itself. What must be affirmed, in response to a text, one might say, is neither the letter of the text nor its spirit, but, beyond the binary saw of that alternative, that which constitutes a text's peculiar signature: its chance and its necessity, its displacements and detours, its obsessions and interruptions, its infinite difference from itself and irreducible alterity. In reading Bataille, then – and much the same is true of his reading of Levinas – what is at stake for Blanchot is not conceptuality but writing, not the ideality of meaning but the transformation effected in thought by textuality itself. And this is why, in considering Blanchot's texts written in response to Levinas, it is crucial to read those essays and fragments not simply for their argument, but with an attention to their own density and singularity as texts.

By the time Totalité et infini appeared, the association between Blanchot and Levinas had been a close one for already some thirty-five years. Shortly before 1961, as the debate on the question of the neutrality of Being in Heidegger suggests, there are signs that the philosophical relationship between the two men had entered into a new phase, one that served ultimately to redefine the nature of the accord between them. For in 1956, reviewing L'Espace littéraire, Levinas credited Blanchot, alongside many others, Hegelians, Marxists, and

161

Heideggerians alike, with the contention that philosophy was henceforth at its end: 'The present age', wrote Levinas, 'will have been the end of philosophy for everyone!' ('Ce siècle aura donc été pour tous la fin de la philosophie!').[4] And though Levinas went on to argue that Blanchot's interpretation of the work of art was fundamentally incompatible with that of Heidegger, he charged Blanchot – no doubt as a friend, but also (and for that very reason) with undisguised impatience – with the task of travelling further, nomadically, across the desert of the 'un-serious' and the 'un-true' that the Blanchot of 1955, in the footnote that concludes the main body of the text of L'Espace littéraire (EL, 260; 247), had presented as the source of art's so-called 'authenticity'. But if Blanchot was to respond to that exhortation, Levinas implied, it would mean confronting, not simply the question of being and non-being, but, more urgently, in Levinas's view, the question of ethics, a question that for Levinas was embodied in the biblical figure of Amalek, still waging war on the Jews, as he had first done at the time of the early Hebrews' journey out of Egypt, and who, Blanchot agreed in 1989, following ancient tradition, was the personification of Evil itself.[5]

In developing this argument, Levinas's main concern was to pursue a vigorous polemic against Heidegger, and in particular against Heidegger's subordination of justice to the question of Being, and total neglect of the philosophical legacy of Judaism. But by making the charge in a review of L'Espace littéraire, Levinas, if only indirectly, seems to have wanted to take issue with Blanchot too, not because Blanchot was at all close to Heidegger, as Levinas himself demonstrates in that same text, but rather because, in his opposition to Heidegger, according to Levinas, Blanchot nevertheless shared something with Heidegger, which was the refusal, common to both, of ethics, or, at the very least, of the concept of ethics.[6] For Levinas, this reluctance made little sense on Blanchot's part, particularly since ethics, for Levinas, was precisely that which was 'un-true' in the radical sense of not being subject to values of truth or falsity, however defined; and it is this that led him, referring to Blanchot's footnote, to issue the following challenge:

> If the authenticity of which Blanchot speaks is to mean anything more than an awareness of the un-seriousness of edification, anything more than a mockery – the authenticity of art must proclaim an order of justice, the slave morality that is absent from the Heideggerian city.[7]

Though Levinas had begun his discussion by suggesting how in Blanchot the impossibility of art radically transcends the realm of possibility that is philosophy, his review ended not by testifying to art's challenge to the philosophical order, but by demanding of philosophy – not of art – that it break with the truth of being and address the question of justice. As far as Levinas was concerned, what was beyond philosophy, so to speak, was not literature, but philosophy still: philosophy understood not as totality, but as a response to infinity.

A quarter of a century later, in 1980, writing in homage to Levinas in 'Notre compagne clandestine', Blanchot begins by repeating Levinas's remark – which Levinas had previously addressed to him – about the relation between literature and the end of philosophy implied in *L'Espace littéraire*. As he does so, however, Blanchot reaffirms the sceptical and ironic punctuation of Levinas's statement, which is enough, he suggests, to suspend and reverse its literal meaning.[8] Blanchot does not demur at the precipitate violence, even injustice of Levinas's earlier challenge regarding his residual affinities with Heidegger and his (implied) neglect of the question of ethics. Indeed, he endorses Levinas's conclusion by assigning to philosophy – and not to literature – the dominant place in the trivium of art, philosophy, and science: in the face of these its rivals, philosophy, claims Blanchot, answering Levinas, is what both has the last word and has no last word.

Philosophy in this context, for Blanchot, is not invoked in the guise of the systematic exposition of conceptual truth. Instead, it is presented under the auspices of the now fifty-five-year-long bond of friendship that first brought Blanchot and Levinas together as students of philosophy in Strasbourg in 1925. The gesture is an affectionate and personal one; but its significance is more than autobiographical. For Blanchot goes on to claim that philosophy itself, as he puts it, is in fact but another name for friendship:

> Philosophy [he explains, recalling the hopes shared by Levinas and himself as students] would forever be our companion, by day, by night, were it even to mean her losing her name, turning into literature, knowledge, non-knowledge, or absenting herself, the clandestine friend in whom we respected – loved – that which did not allow us to be bound to her, even as we sensed that there was nothing wakeful in us, vigilant even in sleep, which was not due to her difficult friendship. Philosophy or friendship. But philosophy is precisely not an allegory.[9]

Philosophy here is addressed both as philosophy and as something – someone

– more than philosophy, which – or who – can still be named as philosophy but also exceeds that name and stands, as it were, beyond philosophy. As Blanchot explains, reading Levinas for Blanchot means primarily having to respond to this dual status of the word philosophy, as though what was singularly repetitive in the texts of Levinas, his signature, so to speak, were his multiple relationship with the order and tradition of philosophy itself. In order to read Levinas, Blanchot argues, it is necessary to traverse philosophy; but Levinas also demands something more, which silently transcends the name of philosophy. This is why, though he reads Levinas philosophically, Blanchot pays Levinas the tribute of reading him not as a philosopher, but as a friend who is both more and less than a philosopher. Rather than endorsing or carrying out a critique of Levinas's conceptuality, Blanchot responds instead, within his own writing, but without mediating concepts of his own, to the singular inflection, the obsessive demand, the pressing urgency, the assault on philosophy that Levinas's own texts insistently rehearse. As he does so, Blanchot necessarily multiplies the slippages between his own thinking and that of Levinas, which are visible throughout Blanchot's philosophical homage in 'Notre compagne clandestine'. Whence, in that essay, the numerous borrowings from Levinas's own distinctive vocabulary, but at the same time, the admission that Blanchot is quoting from memory, and without authority, as is confirmed by the many only partially accurate quotations in the essay and by the lengthy paraphrases, often based on unidentified citations, which give the impression of a Blanchot haphazardly ventriloquising Levinas's discourse. The effect is deceptive. For while Blanchot speaks in the language of Levinas, he does so with discretion: by which I mean that he does so with both affectionate reserve and an awareness of the complex differences of both emphasis and substance that separate them from each other; with the result that Blanchot's account of Levinas, in its very fidelity to Levinas's language, also reads like a silent testimony to the fundamental dissymmetry between the two. In paying homage to Levinas, Blanchot does not write from a position of neutrality, but by borrowing extensively from Levinas dedicates his text to the impossibility of remaining faithful to Levinas, which is Blanchot's way of remaining faithful to Levinas, and to the divergences between himself and his friend, divergences that are all the more marked, in their discreet invisibility and silent suspension, by the fact that Blanchot writes in a language that is not so much his own as that of Levinas. Addressing the Other in this way, Blanchot remarks, is to speak not of the Other, but to the Other.[10]

By baptising philosophy as friendship, and by singularising the love of wisdom

164

that is philosophy itself, Blanchot turns aside from the idea of philosophy as conceptual totalisation. Friendship here, Blanchot writes in 1993, again echoing Levinas, is no longer thought on the model of Greek *philia*, but according to a logic of non-reciprocity and dissymmetry, in response to the disclosure of the other as unknown and the pre-eminence of the Other for whom one is responsible.[11] Friendship both implies community and throws the immanence and homogeneity of community into doubt. Never the property of an individual, always at least double, never general but always unique, beyond event or anecdote, the fruit of both chance and necessity, it is what inscribes the different and the multiple within all relation and escapes all possible gestures of totalisation. The friendship between Blanchot and Levinas is more than an external circumstance of thought, it is its persistent manifestation and metamorphosis. Philosophy here stands beyond in-difference and neutrality (in Levinas's sense of the word). It becomes instead the site of its own excess, its own alterity, its own difference with itself; and if philosophy is invincible scepticism, as Blanchot puts it, citing Levinas, it is because, as the thought of the neutre affirms, the borders and limits of thought are necessarily always suspended at the very moment they are determined, and because thought, as it puts itself in doubt, thereby finds itself in the disconcerting predicament of always thinking more than it thinks itself capable of thinking.

Philosophy and literature here are no longer in opposition. Not for Blanchot therefore the postmodernist enterprise of treating philosophy as a branch of literature, nor the temptation to abandon the austerity and rigour of thought in favour of the effusive figurality of the literary. Instead, Blanchot maintains the separation between philosophy and literature; but he does so not in order to preserve the autonomy and self-identity of each, but in answer to the namelessness of the demand of (and for) otherness to which both, in their divergent ways, give voice. For Blanchot, philosophy and literature have become oddly synonymous with the absence of their own name; and to the extent that they refuse that name, they persist as other than what they are and as a response – and responsibility – to what is beyond being and non-being. Across the divide that separates them, literature and philosophy answer, then, in common, but without communality, to and for the irrepressible infinity of language. And if Levinas is right to claim that it is 'indiscretion with regard to the unsayable [l'indiscrétion à l'égard de l'indicible] which is probably the very task of philosophy', what this says is that philosophy, by being bound to that in language which is beyond language, is also inseparable, like literature itself, from the

165

thought of the neutre, from what, using Levinas's words, but in a formulation unmistakably his own, Blanchot describes as the

> Enigma of a Saying [d'un Dire] as of a God speaking in man, man who relies on no God, for whom there is no such thing as dwelling [pour qui il n'y a pas à habiter], who is exiled from all world without afterworld [l'exilé de tout monde sans arrière-monde], and who finally does not even have language as his abode [comme demeure], no more than he may be said to have language to speak in either the affirmative or negative mode.[12]

Responding to Levinas's challenge about the ethical demand to which literature must give voice, Blanchot, it seems, accepts: literature is not other than philosophy, and thus cannot announce the death of philosophy or its abandonment in favour of those mystical effusions or solipsistic enthusiasms of which Blanchot, like Levinas, is so intensely wary. Literature remains, like philosophy, as a thinking which demands confrontation with evil, and if its fate is bound to the philosophy that is friendship, then what this suggests is that for literature, too, the question is one of responsibility. This indeed is what Blanchot himself underlines, at the end of 'Notre compagne clandestine', albeit less obliquely than Levinas in 1956, by invoking the name not of Amalek, but Auschwitz, citing as he does so Levinas's dedication of *Autrement qu'être* to the victims, Jews and non-Jews alike, of the Nazi camps.

The accord here between Blanchot and Levinas is real and unmistakable. But the friendship between them inscribes within that accord a necessary dissymmetry. As philosophical friends Blanchot and Levinas agree on many philosophical issues. But friendship cannot be reduced to that which is purely philosophical, for it is a response to what lies beyond philosophy in the singular address of friendship itself. It is here that the differences between Blanchot and Levinas emerge, as indeed they must if the relation between them is to occur as a relation of friendship at all. In Levinas's terms, the Other is what escapes thematisation; the Other can be named therefore only provisionally, by recourse to a glorious Saying – what Levinas calls 'le Dire' – that constantly erases what is said in order constantly to renew itself as always other than what it was. This is why all speaking to the Other, as Derrida has often argued, is irreducibly idiomatic. It is therefore not only unsurprising, but absolutely necessary that the thought of the Other, like the thought of the neutre, should give rise to irreducibly dissymmetrical thematisations. The possibility of language is itself on this condition. To respond faithfully to the Other means refusing – and refusing even in adopting – the language of the Other in the nameless name of the infinity and otherness of language.

That which is beyond philosophy – philosophy still, or literature one more time, in the refusal of the name that constitutes the necessity of both – is possible perhaps only as a singular writing that displaces, transforms, suspends, ignores, travesties, and erases conceptuality. On one level, such an enterprise may be criticised as philosophically naive, as Blanchot readily concedes on Levinas's behalf. But naivety here is better seen as a provisional, and unpredictable name for philosophical inventiveness. What counts is not the conceptuality of the Said, but the infinite movement of Saying that always insists beyond the Said. Blanchot and Levinas write differently of difference, and speak otherwise of the Other; but this is because the ground of their accord is also necessarily a ground of discord, their contemporaneity with each other a time of irreducible diachrony, and their undoubted community of thought a curved, dissymmetrical space where, as Blanchot puts it in *L'Entretien infini*, the distance from point A to point B is not isomorphic with that between point B and point A, 'a distance', adds Blanchot, paraphrasing Levinas, 'excluding reciprocity and presenting a curvature whose irregularity extends to the point of discontinuity' (*EI*, 104; 73).

Transcendence and the Other

The *il y a* is one of Levinas's most fascinating propositions: his temptation, too, the reverse side of transcendence, so to speak, and thus indistinguishable from it, which may be described in terms of being, but as the *impossibility* of not being, the incessant insistence of the neuter, the nocturnal murmur of the anonymous, that which never begins (and therefore an-archic, because perpetually eluding the decisiveness of a beginning), the absolute but as absolute indeterminacy: all this is bewitching, that is, it draws us towards the uncertain outside, speaking infinitely outside truth, like some Other we could not get rid of simply by calling him deceitful (the evil demon) nor because he might be said to be a mere mockery, since this speaking, which is only a laugh perfidiously suppressed, giving meaning while yet eluding all interpretation, neither gratuitous nor cheerful, grave, just as much, and the illusion of seriousness, so to speak, and thereby what disturbs us most, is also the movement most apt to deny us the resources of being as place and light: the gift perhaps of literature, without one knowing whether it enchants by disenchanting or whether its words that please and disgust do not ultimately attract us because it is a promise (a promise it keeps and does not keep) to illuminate what is obscure in all speech, what in speech eludes revelation and manifestation: the trace again of non-presence, the opaqueness of transparency.

'Notre compagne clandestine' (86)

Blanchot's explicit engagement with Levinas passes through a number of distinct phases. Shortly after publication in 1961, as already indicated, Blanchot devoted to *Totalité et infini* a series of three dialogues between unnamed interlocutors that were subsequently taken up, in modified form, in *L'Entretien infini*. These texts, however, should not be seen in isolation. The impact of Levinas's thinking on Blanchot extends well beyond the explicit mention of Levinas's own work, and is inseparable from the way in which *L'Entretien infini* is structured as a whole. Indeed, by adopting the expression 'l'entretien infini' as his title, and by presenting the three discussions of *Totalité et infini*, alongside the opening narrative, as the first texts in which the reader encounters the dialogue form in the book, Blanchot inscribes *L'Entretien infini* as a whole – composed of many diverse fragmentary forms as well as many seemingly traditional, discursive essays – under the sign of that peculiar dissymmetry between self and other that Blanchot, following Levinas, describes in the three chapters specifically concerned with *Totalité et infini*. In this respect *L'Entretien infini* is not a random collection of essays, but a work, painstakingly revised and rewritten, that in its complex compositional structure seeks to respond to the following question that Blanchot formulates from the outset and couches in largely Levinasian terms:

How might one speak in such a way that speaking is essentially plural? How may one affirm the search for a mode of plural speaking no longer founded on equality and inequality, hierarchy and subordination, or reciprocal mutuality, but rather on dissymmetry and irreversibility, so that, between two instances of speech, a relation of infinity would always obtain as the movement of signification itself? Alternatively, how may one write so that the continuity of the movement of writing allows the fundamental intervention of interruption as meaning and rupture as form?

(*EI*, 9; 8)

In the terms of this project, the infinite conversation dramatised in Blanchot's book is far from resembling what is usually understood as philosophical dialogue.[1] First of all, no single textual form predominates: fragment, essay, and conversation constantly delimit each other and challenge their relative priority. Furthermore, even within the dialogue forms themselves, there is no clear distinction between the two – perhaps at times even more than two – voices involved, and no progress towards synthesis or conclusion. Blanchot's interlocutors do not seek unity or homogeneity, but, in their intermingled voices, embody difference, separation, and withdrawal. Turning to *Totalité et infini*, they register on one level, perhaps unsurprisingly, a large measure of unanimity with Levinas. But this is not to say the voices necessarily agree with one another, and there is much in their conversation that remains unresolved or open to question, or is deferred necessarily till later.

In Levinas's book, we are told by one interlocutor, perhaps recalling the challenge addressed to Blanchot by Levinas in 1956, 'there is here a new departure in philosophy and a leap that it and we are being urged, so to speak, to perform' (*EI*, 74; 52). Accepting the invitation, Blanchot quickly makes his own the main articulations of Levinas's account of the irreducibility of the Other to the Same; and it is clear from this point on that Levinas's work provides Blanchot with the opportunity for addressing in very different terms than before some of the issues left in suspense by him at the end of *L'Espace littéraire*. Prominent among these, alongside the question of the relation of art to work, world, and truth, that Blanchot by the early 1960s had already begun to re-articulate by recourse to the thought of the neutre, was the demand of what Levinas insisted on calling ethics and to which Blanchot himself, by that time, had already begun to give a decisive and distinctive political inflection. Indeed, it would be misleading to conclude from Levinas's questioning of Blanchot in his 1956 review of *L'Espace littéraire* that during the 1950s Blanchot had somehow remained deaf to the question of ethics in its relation to literature. In some respects, nothing could be further from the truth. As the essays collected in 1959 in *Le Livre à venir* testify, Blanchot throughout the 1950s was seeking in his critical writing – while never formulating his project explicitly in these terms – precisely to address the ethical dimension of literature as such. In doing so, however, he refused to refer the demand of literature to the jurisdiction of morality or law and subordinate the act of writing to conventional concepts of duty and choice, freedom and responsibility, insisting instead, to the extent that the term of ethics was appropriate at all, that the only injunction to which literature fell subject was one based on its own impossibility and dispossessed anonymity and on the indigent challenge to universality that for Blanchot were the hallmark of writing as such.[2]

By the early 1960s it does seem that *Totalité et infini* supplied Blanchot with a fresh philosophical framework for taking this argument further. A rapid transformation takes place in Blanchot's critical writing with the result that what, for instance, had figured earlier in his texts under the rubric of impossibility, is henceforth reformulated in largely Levinasian language as an infinite relation to the Other, a relation beyond power or possibility and beyond being or non-being. The account Levinas gives, in *Totalité et infini*, of the relation of non-relation that obtains between the Same and the Other thus provides Blanchot with the means of re-inventing or re-articulating as the question of the Other the question of the impossibility of dying that is so crucial in his earlier work. Till now, for Blanchot, as *L'Espace littéraire* had made clear (*EL*, 106–7; 106), it had been the impossible embodied in death itself – its irreducibility to mastery by any subject present to itself – that had provided, in exemplary fashion, the model (beyond all possible models and models of possibility) of the relation of non-relation that for Levinas constituted the radicality of the Other's challenge to the Same and the Self. The impossibility of dying and the challenge from the Other become here, in Blanchot, the two sides of a radical rethinking of the logic of relation and of its implications both for the question of being and the question of ethics. For if death was alterity and alterity death, it followed that the key ethical question, perhaps indeed the only ethical question at all, was the question (beyond power or possibility) of the death of the Other, on which alone, as Blanchot put it in 1983 in *La Communauté inavouable* (*CI*, 21–2; 9), community – and thereby ethics as such – may be founded.

The question of the possibility or impossibility of death, in Blanchot, is never far from the question of language; indeed, the two in Blanchot are largely indissociable, if not in fact synonymous. In Blanchot's second dialogue on *Totalité et infini* one of the voices makes the connection explicit by claiming in turn that the question of the Other is in fact the question of language. Ethics here in Blanchot, as in Levinas, is reconfigured at the furthest extremity possible from moral legislation as a fundamental and inescapable dimension of language itself. 'The Other speaks to me [Autrui me parle]', one of Blanchot's interlocutors remarks pointedly, and adds:

> The revelation of the Other [la révélation d'autrui] that does not occur within the luminous space of forms is wholly speech. The Other expresses himself [Autrui s'exprime], and in this act of speaking puts himself forward as other [comme autre]. If there is a relation in which the other and the same [l'autre et le même], even as they hold each other in relation, *absolve themselves* from that relation, remaining as terms that are *absolute*

within the relation itself, as Levinas strikingly puts it, that relation is language.

(*EI*, 79; 55)[3]

Blanchot's interlocutors explain, in a passage added in 1969 that rehearses much that will be familiar to readers of *Totalité et infini*, there are at least three distinct ways of configuring the relation between the Same and the Other. According to the first type, one voice proposes, the law is that of the Same, and the aim of the process the incorporation of the Other within the unity and totality of the whole: this is the realm of the historical dialectic, the purpose of which is to assimilate the Other to the Same through the mediation of labour, by a process of negation, reduction, adequation, and identification. As far as the second type is concerned, rejoins his partner, none of this struggle is necessary. Unity here is achieved immediately, and the relation between the Same and the Other is one of ecstatic fusion; the Same, as it were, is magically absorbed into the Other, and unity and totality again prevail, with the only difference that here the law is that of the Other, but the Other functioning only as a mirror image of the Same that is always One.

Both voices wonder, obstinately though hesitantly, whether there is not in addition a third type of relation, and this is what Blanchot goes on to explore in the ensuing discussion. In this relation of the third kind, the Other is thought not as another Self, but as radically different, irreducible to the One or to the Same. This type of relation occurs, so to speak, beyond the horizon of world and being; it is relation without ratio, adequation, equality, symmetry, or reciprocity. This is relation without relation, relation in the form of a pure interval belonging neither to being nor non-being, irreducible to all thought of truth, visibility, veiling or unveiling, and figurable only as non-reversible dissymmetry, as a strange space in which the distance from me to the Other is not the same as the distance from the Other to me. Here, all topographical continuity is abolished. The Other is precisely not another 'I', but absolutely Other, beyond all unity or duality; as one of Blanchot's speakers confirms:

When the Other speaks to me [Quand Autrui me parle], he does not speak to me as an 'I' [il ne me parle pas comme moi]. When I appeal to the Other [l'Autre], I respond to that which speaks to me from no place, and am separated from him by a caesura such that the Other forms with me neither duality nor unity. It is this fissure – this relation with the other [ce rapport avec l'autre] – that we ventured earlier to characterise as an interruption of being; let us now add: between each human and the

171

next, there is an interval that may be said to belong neither to being nor to non-being, an interval borne by the Difference of speech, a difference that precedes all that is different or single.

(EI, 99; 69)

This third relation, Blanchot, some pages later, in another subsequent gloss, describes as a 'rapport neutre', a neutral relation (*EI*, 104; 73), and, despite their irreducible accord, the word signals here, between Blanchot and Levinas, just as it had in 1957 and 1958, the existence of a fundamental divergence. This is not simply a relic from that earlier period. Indeed, despite Levinas's explicit rejection of the neuter, and the effacement of difference it is taken to connote, Blanchot himself persists with the word; and, when revising his texts on Levinas for inclusion in *L'Entretien infini*, Blanchot in fact far extends its currency in his writing. For instance, in the original version of the chapter 'Tenir parole' ('Keeping to Words'), Blanchot had described the face of the Other, much in keeping with Levinas's own account, as being by essence that which was naked or bare ('nu', in Levinas's idiom); reworking the passage in 1969, Blanchot substitutes for this the word: 'neutre', so that instead of having, as in 1962: 'un rapport nu ou la nudité même du rapport' Blanchot's text now reads: 'un rapport neutre ou la neutralité même du rapport' (*EI*, 84; 59).

This diffident effacement of a important term in Levinas's conceptual vocabulary is not an isolated gesture. Throughout the discussion of *Totalité et infini*, Blanchot's interlocutors repeatedly cast suspicion on Levinas's attempt to formulate a language specifically his own, adequate to the project of grounding the possibility of ethics. At one point, for instance, the conversation turns to Levinas's use of the face ('le visage'), beyond all reference to the manifestation of Being in Heideggerian terms, as the most urgent embodiment of the presence of the Other as Other; and though the two interlocutors eventually agree that the face in Levinas is precisely that which is beyond representation, they do so despite the word rather than because of it, leading the reader to conclude that the word itself would be best withdrawn, precisely because it falls victim to the very logic of representation it seeks to transcend (*EI*, 77; 54). Elsewhere, in similar manner, on two separate occasions, it is the word ethics that is queried on the grounds of its generality and derivative character (*EI*, 78, 89; 55, 63); and in much the same way Levinas's concept of exteriority, which gives *Totalité et infini* its subtitle, is effaced in passing by one of the speakers only to be replaced instead by a reference to the pre-conceptual outside: 'le dehors' (*EI*, 78; 55).

Later, it is the turn of the privilege Levinas accords to the spoken word to be called into doubt also (*EI*, 80; 56), until finally it is the crucial term 'Autrui' (meaning: Others in general), that it is proposed be abandoned owing to its moralistic – 'altruistic' – overtones (*EI*, 100; 70).

As these examples suggest, Blanchot treats much of the conceptual language of *Totalité et infini* with a discreet but rigorous scepticism. Of all the minor disputes that arise as a result, perhaps the most revealing is the deep reservation expressed in *L'Entretien infini* by Blanchot about Levinas's persistent recourse in *Totalité et infini* to the name of God.[4] Levinas's use of the word, of course, is not gratuitous; it is a direct and unrepentant consequence of the project of rethinking the philosophical significance of Judaism. As such, its importance within Levinas's philosophical writing is difficult to underestimate. Indeed, as Blanchot reminds us, 'All true discourse, Levinas solemnly declares, is discourse with God, not a conversation between equals' (*EI*, 80; 56). 'The Other [Autrui]', for Levinas, he adds, 'must always be considered by me as closer to God than myself' (*EI*, 82; 57).[5] But despite the prominent part played by the name of God in Levinas's text, Blanchot makes equally clear his own uncompromising refusal of that name. As one of the voices in the discussion insists, 'Let us leave God to one side, the name is too imposing' ('Laissons Dieu de côté, nom trop imposant') (*EI*, 71; 50). The disagreement here is plain. For his part, Blanchot could well argue that it is he who is being more consistent than Levinas; for if it is the case, as Levinas contends, that the relation with the Other is without mediating concept or intermediary of any kind, so it would follow from this, in the compelling words of one of Blanchot's speakers, that henceforth 'there is therefore neither god, nor values, nor nature between man and man' (*EI*, 84; 59). To reinforce the point further, Blanchot leaves little doubt elsewhere in *L'Entretien infini* as to the resilience of his commitment to atheism.[6]

But more is at issue here than the difference between Blanchot's rigorous atheologism and Levinas's Judaism. For this debate on the question of God is not about religion as such. On numerous occasions, Levinas shows himself to be acutely aware of the fundamental differences between philosophy, religion, and theology, and is insistent that when he invokes God in his philosophical writings he does so not as a believer or theologian, but as a philosopher.[7] Moreover, in the exchanges between Blanchot and Levinas on the subject of Judaism itself, it is clear that, despite their considerably different relationship with Judaic tradition, both writers display a broadly similar understanding of its philosophical significance. This is perhaps not surprising. On his own admission,

Blanchot's access to Judaism was at the very least profoundly influenced by his friendship with Levinas, a friendship he described in 1968, in dedicating the text 'Parole de fragment' ('The Fragment Word') to Levinas, as being 'in a relation of invisibility with Judaism' ('en rapport d'invisibilité avec le judaïsme').[8] And this fundamental accord regarding the philosophical significance of Judaism was no doubt what allowed Levinas, in 1969, in the course of a lecture subsequently published in a volume of Talmudic readings, to claim confirmation from Blanchot, the non-Jew (who was, interestingly, left nameless by Levinas at the time) for the view that what was distinctive about Judaism was not only its universalism, but the fact that in Judaism there was also something else that was beyond universality, not in the guise of ethnic particularism, Levinas explains, but, transcending society and politics, what he describes as the holy burden of infinite responsibility for the Other.[9]

But despite this relative unanimity regarding the philosophical importance of Judaism, one central issue remains: the question of how to address the transcendent as such. Or as one of Blanchot's interlocutors formulates it in *L'Entretien infini*: 'Who is "the Other"?' 'Qui est "Autrui"?' (*EI*, 99; 70). As his partner immediately acknowledges, the question is an improper one, in that it risks substantialising the Other rather than responding to the unmediated challenge of his or her presence. However, Blanchot's text goes on to reiterate the importance of locating transcendence exclusively in the social field, outside of all theology. As one speaker had announced from the outset, speculatively, but with uncompromising seriousness: 'it may be that everything that may be affirmed of the relation of transcendence – the relation of God to his creature – ought primarily (for my part, I would say exclusively) to be applied to the social relation' (*EI*, 77; 54). In this way, while endorsing virtually without reservation Levinas's account of the transcendence of the Other and the relation of non-relation between the Same and the Other which it implies, Blanchot endeavoured to transpose into the political or social arena what Levinas articulates for his part as an ethical relation.[10] The implicit question, then, that is put to *Totalité et infini* by Blanchot, and which Blanchot himself formulates only obliquely in 'Notre compagne clandestine' in 1980, is to ask whether, by thematising transcendence by the use of religious vocabulary and thus equating transcendence with the name of God – albeit a God who, as Levinas insists, is not the God of onto-theology – Levinas does not run the risk of falling back into a notion of transcendence that, instead of being absolutely Other, is ultimately no more than the reverse side of humanistic immanence, and to that degree not absolutely transcendent at all but ultimately reliant on a travestied version of immanence.

As Blanchot and Levinas are both aware, much here turns on the referent of the word God: species or genus of supreme being, or proper name of that which is beyond being? The Christian God is traditionally seen as the former, while God in the Talmud, according to Levinas, is unmistakably the latter; and it is generally the case that the God Levinas invokes in his philosophical work is understood precisely not as (a) being at all, but as a name beyond being or non-being.[11] The name of God is fundamental for Levinas in this respect for it is what allows him to address his philosophical work not to the concept of the Other but to the Other as absolute singularity. To the extent that God is a proper name, it is the proper name par excellence; the invocation of God, therefore, is not a theological velleity on Levinas's part, but a philosophical necessity, one without which the whole edifice of Levinas's thinking would collapse, leaving behind only the necessary fixity of a conceptual framework that can do no more than reinforce being as representation.

But at the same time, the absolute transcendence of God, this alterity that, as Levinas writes, is always other than alterity itself, necessarily tends towards an extreme point which is that of its own absence, and the invocation of God must always be threatened by the possibility of this divine comedy of God's disappearance. Indeed, as Levinas admits in 'Dieu et la philosophie' ('God and Philosophy') in 1975, the reference to God must itself always be exposed to this danger, and the risk must always exist that it may turn into a mere doublet of the *il y a* and the immanent impossibility of not being.[12] The result is an ambiguity that is doubly worrying, for not only does it call Levinas's project into doubt, it also has the potential to transform Levinas's account of the transcendence of the Other into precisely one of those philosophies of the neuter (in Levinas's sense of the term) in which transcendence is never more than a mirror image of immanence, and vice versa. Which is to say perhaps no more than what Derrida suggests in 'Violence et métaphysique' ('Violence and Metaphysics') when he demonstrates how fraught with risks Levinas's project is, and necessarily not as sharply differentiated from that of Hegel as Levinas hoped or wished.

From Blanchot's perspective, it seems that God in Levinas is both impossible to accept for reasons of Blanchot's atheism, and yet, because of its importance in singularising Levinas's whole conceptuality, impossible to refuse. Faced with these difficulties, Blanchot adopts a characteristically bold and complex strategy. In *L'Entretien infini*, responding still to *Totalité et infini*, Blanchot replaces the question: who is the Other?, which he had withdrawn some pages before, with another question, bearing instead on what Blanchot describes, within neutralising quotation marks, as the problem of 'community'. The question Levinas's work leads one of Blanchot's voices to ask is therefore this:

What is the implication for human 'community' [Qu'en est-il de la 'communauté' humaine], once it is necessary for it to respond to that relation of strangeness between each man and the next which the experience of language leads one to sense, a relation that is both exorbitant and without common measure?

(*EI*, 101; 71)

To address this question, Blanchot implies, it is necessary to rethink transcendence not according to the model (which is necessarily anything but a model) of the relation between man and God, but solely within the realm of what, albeit misleadingly, is usually described by philosophy as intersubjective space, which is a space occupied, for Blanchot, contrary to what the name suggests, not by two subjects, nor by a subject and his or her other, but by what Blanchot terms a doubly dissymmetrical relation between two (or more) existents, irreducible to all dialectical reciprocity and equalisation, and without continuity or hierarchy.

In a remarkable shift, what throughout *Totalité et infini* Levinas addresses under the rubric of the asymmetry between the Same and the Other is reconfigured, in Blanchot's exposition, as the double dissymmetry between Self and Other (*EI*, 100; 70–1).[13] For the privative prefix 'a-', connoting absence, Blanchot substitutes the prefix 'dis-', meaning: two, and always at least double. In other words, what Blanchot proposes is that the relation of non-relation between the Same and the Other be redoubled by a second relation of non-relation passing from the Other to the Same, with the complication that now it is the Same – 'I', so to speak, albeit henceforth an 'I' without 'I' and without name – who, for the Other, is now nothing other than the Other. The hierarchical relation of non-relation between the Same and the Other described by Levinas is presented by Blanchot in such a way that the relation, beyond reversibility or reciprocity, is now seen always to be running in at least two distinct directions. The effect is to compromise the verticality of the relation to the Other as the Most High, and thus both secularise and multiply the relation as such.

The move, however, is not without its risks, and it is perhaps unsurprising that by some of Levinas's readers Blanchot has been severely taken to task for what is allegedly a gross misunderstanding of Levinas.[14] Indeed, as *L'Entretien infini* readily concedes, there is a danger that by redoubling the relation of non-relation one thereby allows the dissymmetry of 'community' to be recuperated precisely within the reversible logic of a dialectic of the Same for which the Other is only just another version of the Self. If that were the case, the only community to which Blanchot's double dissymmetry would give rise would be community founded on the immanence of communion and closure, that is, on the effacement of alterity and the assimilation of the Other within the Same, with all the dire – totalitarian – political implications, as Blanchot argues in *La Communauté inavouable*, that would follow. Blanchot insists, however, that his own redoubling of the Levinasian relation of asymmetry must be understood, according to the logic of the neutre, to be fundamentally and necessarily irreducible to any such equalising dialectic of reciprocity. On the contrary. As Blanchot explains,

> this redoubling of irreciprocity – the reversal that makes me apparently the other of the other [qui fait de moi apparemment l'autre de l'autre] – cannot, at the level we are describing, be incorporated into any dialectic [être pris en charge par la dialectique], for it does not tend to re-establish any equality whatsoever; on the contrary, it signifies a double dissymmetry [une double dissymétrie], a double discontinuity, as though the emptiness between the one and the other were not homogeneous but polarised, as though it constituted a non-isomorphic field, bearing a double distortion, both infinitely negative and infinitely positive, and such that one should call it neuter, so long as it is clear that the neuter does not annul or neutralise this double-signed infinity, but bears it in the manner of an enigma.
>
> (*EI*, 100–1; 70–1)

As Blanchot recasts Levinas's account of transcendence, he draws once more then on the conceptual resources of the neutre. Its intervention is twofold. First, it turns aside the threat of homogeneity implied by dialectical reciprocity and, exceeding the double bind of being and non-being, assertion and negation, imparts to the relation between humans an infinity that, beyond continuity or unity, radically reconfigures the possibility of social relations as such. Second, and more provocatively, the neutre allows Blanchot to suspend, though without negating or neutralising it, the vicious circle of transcendence and immanence within which philosophy as such is enclosed; and by both stepping beyond and not stepping beyond that fatal alternative, Blanchot's writing begins to address the human other, no longer in terms of either transcendence or immanence, but absolutely otherwise: that is, writes Blanchot, beyond the province of any name at all, 'not other as God, or other as nature, but as "man", more Other than all other' ('non pas autre comme Dieu ou autre comme nature, mais, en tant qu'"homme", plus Autre que tout ce qu'il y a d'autre') (*EI*, 102; 72). It is, so to speak, to this human other, other than all other other, to another than alterity itself, that the neutre in Blanchot, with its distinctive diacritical signature, makes its silent appeal.[15]

What Blanchot stages here is not an attempt to confound Levinas, or refute his work in any way; Blanchot's efforts are directed rather at producing a reading of Levinas that responds to the radical namelessness of the Other more readily than it does to the Other's proximity to God. This allows Blanchot, here and elsewhere, both in his writing and in the political domain itself, to broach a set of issues that, in Levinas's philosophical work, are for the most part either postponed or put to one side, and which bear on the relationship, within history and beyond history, not between humanity and the name of God, but among humans themselves, within what, for want of a better word, and with all due precautions, Blanchot, like Bataille and Jean-Luc Nancy, refers to as 'community'. Here, Blanchot's reading of Levinas has to be seen closely in relation with an exigency which is that of political activism, albeit an activism of an original and distinctive kind which, as Blanchot demonstrates in his own explicit political involvements in France, in 1958 to 1960, 1968, and since, turns aside from the pursuit of power as such to voice instead the infinite demand of refusal, of refusal maintained in the name – without name – of the Other.

This question of the political is not a marginal concern for Blanchot in his reading of Levinas. On the contrary, it continues to obsess Blanchot, and is a persistent preoccupation in the fragments making up the 'Discours sur la patience' ('Discourse on Patience') that Blanchot devoted in 1975 to Levinas's then recent books, *Humanisme de l'autre homme* and *Autrement qu'être*. In the 'Discours', as in *L'Écriture du désastre* as a whole, Blanchot subscribes virtually without reservation to Levinas's account of the infinite responsibility for the Other he had been elaborating philosophically since the late 1960s. Blanchot, however, also does something more, which is to exploit his own (non-)position, writing in the margins of Levinas's text (which is how Blanchot presents his

178

reading of Levinas in 1975) to ask, with infinite fidelity, but beyond all piety, a number of sceptical and challenging questions of Levinas's work. And Blanchot does so, as a marginal commentator, almost entirely within the terms of argument offered by Levinas, demurring only intermittently at Levinas's conceptual vocabulary, well aware that Levinas himself is struggling against the limitations of philosophical language as such, limitations which mean, for instance, that when Levinas speaks of passivity – of a passivity beyond all passivity – as that which precedes all being or non-being, the endeavour is inevitably dogged by the fact that philosophy accepts the term only by inscribing it within a binary paradigm that has always already privileged being as activity and thereby transforms passivity from the outset into not even the reverse, but more like the ghost of itself. And this is what Blanchot means when he remarks: 'Passivity as opposed to activity: such is the always restricted field of our thoughts' (ED, 30; 15).

The predicament is not new as far as Levinas's work is concerned. Blanchot does not use it as a pretext to relinquish his fidelity to Levinas; rather, by always seeking the more difficult and more exacting reading, as, for instance, when he accepts the invitation to think the notion of the immediate in Levinas in relation not to the present tense but the past (ED, 44; 24), Blanchot allows himself to be challenged by the text, obligated to it, and infinitely responsive to its strangeness. To read here is not to retain concepts, but, beyond conceptuality, to respond to the dissymmetry or interval that comes between the so-called letter of the text and the invincible scepticism of the writing. Indeed, the awareness of the gap between what is said in Levinas's text and the address to the Other enacted in the saying of Levinas's language – the distinction that Levinas himself thematises as the difference between 'le Dire' and 'le Dit', the Saying and the Said – does not relieve the reader of the responsibility of reading sceptically; on the contrary, it requires of the reader that he or she read with an ever increasing degree of vigilance: in other words, with infinite regard for the ever persistent namelessness of the neutre.

While allowing himself to be pressed by Levinas, as it were, Blanchot presses Levinas in return. In so doing, his responsibility is to scrutinise – as well as radicalise – the political implications of Levinas's thinking. And this is why, to the surprise of some readers, Blanchot asks of Levinas a question such as the following: if I am obsessed, persecuted by the Other, whose hostage I am, and to whom I owe infinite responsibility, to the extent of being separated from myself, abandoned to a passivity without present and burdened with a charge

179

that may never be fulfilled or relinquished, as Levinas's work both claims and affirms, how do I guard against the possibility I may simply be dealing with the paranoid will of an oppressive, sadistic Master (*ED*, 36–8; 20)? For if that were to be the case, the obligation that would fall to 'me' would not only be an obligation of infinite responsibility for and to the Other, but also the obligation to resist and struggle against the Other persecuting me and to do so by adopting all necessary and available means. What here is the relationship between infinite passivity (beyond passivity) and the highly determinate injunction to act? In Levinas's terms, it is clear that I am without power before the face of the Other; but it is precisely for that very reason, as Blanchot puts it at one stage, that 'justice demands refusal, resistance, even the violence whose purpose is to repel violence' (*ED*, 187; 121). Levinas himself points out that he is not putting forward in his work a prescriptive moral code but, more importantly, endeavouring to establish the ethical basis for the possibility of an ethics. He plainly insists that passivity beyond passivity does not mean passivity before evil; but if so, what then is the relation between that which belongs to being and that which is otherwise than being, between the dialectics of history, on the one hand, and, on the other, the burden of infinite responsibility for the Other? And if the second has priority over the first, how are these demands to be reconciled or mediated?

The questions are abrupt, even brutal in their implications; and the suggestion has been made that they are based on an error of reading, or are rendered inadmissible by the very spirit of Levinas's work. This may be true. But to disregard Blanchot's obstinate question in this way is to pay insufficient attention to Blanchot's unfaithful fidelity to Levinas; and it is to do violence to the suspensive motion of a fragmentary mode of writing in which every statement, assertion, or question in Blanchot's text is interrupted by the boundlessness of the neutre and its strange (il)logic of continuity and discontinuity, silence and infinity. Though on one level they may appear illegitimate, then, Blanchot's questions are compelling ones; and they address issues that are crucial if Levinas is to be taken seriously at all. For his part, Blanchot's own position with regard to the questions he raises is very clear. As Levinas's own work is the first to testify, it is that no single language or conceptual system can lay claim to total authority and that in the ethical or political domain, as in all others, there must be, simultaneously but dissymmetrically, always at least two languages, two voices, two demands in operation:

one dialectical, the other not dialectical, one where negativity is the task, the other where the neuter stands out beyond both being and non-being [où le neutre tranche sur l'être et le non-être], in the same way that it is essential both to be a free, speaking subject, and to disappear as the passive-patient traversed by dying and hidden from view [comme le patient-passif que traverse le mourir et qui ne se montre pas].

(*ED*, 38; 20)

What is essential in this relation, Blanchot adds, is that the ambiguity between these two languages be not resolved or equalised, and that the interval of dissymmetry and discord that passes – without passing – between these two demands be itself maintained and respected, in the manner of a void whose only obedience is to the neutre, indeed as that within thinking which infinitely exceeds the limits of thinking itself. As Blanchot puts it some pages later:

The necessity to live and die by this double language, and in the ambiguity of a time without present *and* of a history capable of exhausting all temporal possibilities (in order to accede to the satisfaction of presence): this is the irreparable decision, the unavoidable madness, which is not the content of thought, for thought will not contain it, any more than consciousness or unconsciousness provides a status by which to determine it.

(*ED*, 48; 27)

The lesson of the neutre, then, for Blanchot is that there is always an excess within language that is beyond language, and thus always an other otherness, so to speak, that not only exceeds all possible representations of the Other, but also effaces all possible names for the Other. To this extent, Levinas, whose own invocation of God could be described in much the same terms, is clearly right to conclude that the neutre in Blanchot is simply another name for transcendence; indeed, as Levinas observes in 1971, in an interview with André Dalmas, on the question of the neutre in Blanchot: 'this Neuter is not somebody nor even a something. It is only an excluded *middle* [un *tiers* exclu] which, properly speaking, not even *is*. Yet there is more transcendence to it than was ever disclosed by any after-world [plus de transcendance qu'aucun arrière-monde n'a jamais entr'ouvert]'.[16] But if the neutre is but another name for transcendence, this serves only to reinforce the fact that the neutre, neither negating transcendence nor affirming it, is both more and less than transcendence, and

181

that, if the neutre evokes a movement of thought at all, it is a movement irreducible to any dialectic of limitation and transgression, if only because the only law to which it bears witness is the law of its own limitlessness and reiterated effacement.[17]

Radically side-stepping all literary and philosophical classifications enforced by convention or by law, it is arguably as a lengthy commentary – and dramatisation – of this strange movement that Le Pas au-delà, published in 1973, may best be read. So much is already announced in the book's title. Embodied in the fragmentary mode that Le Pas au-delà explores as it returns and advances, here is an act of transgression that, turning aside from the temptation to sacralise the limit of thought and become locked in dangerous fascination with the figure of the law, suspends the law by suspending its own movement of transgression, with the result that the relation with the limit, like the relation with death, becomes an infinite relation of non-relation, one that gives rise not to another law, but the limitlessness of the outside as such, an outside that is thematised henceforth not as transcendence, but as the impossibility that (is) the neutre. As Blanchot writes in one fragment:

> Empty transgression, an image of the movement of all transgression that is preceded by no taboo, but posits no limit either by crossing beyond what cannot be crossed. No before, during, or after. It is as in another sphere, the other of any sphere. Within the realm of the day, what rules is the law, the prohibition it pronounces, the possible and the language of justification. Within the space of the night, are infringements of the law, the violence that breaches prohibition, the non-possible, the silence that refuses what is just. Transgression belongs to neither day nor night. Never does it encounter the law that is however everywhere. Transgression: the unavoidable accomplishment of what is *impossible* to accomplish – which might be called dying itself.
>
> (PA, 146–7; 106–7)

Transgression and transcendence are hereby effaced, pluralised, made radically other than the theological concepts that for Blanchot they once were and arguably still remain. Rewriting them as instantiations of the neutre, Blanchot reminds us that the neutre itself is in fact anything other than a concept. For if it is deployed by Blanchot, in Le Pas au-delà, in the guise of the fragmentary, the multiple, and the infinitely (dis)continuous, it is that the neutre, as the infinite movement of withdrawal and re-inscription, is already

a form of writing, and an antidote, so to speak, to both the fragility and the
fixity of words. As such, its infinite scepticism imperiously recalls what
Levinas thematises in his own texts as Saying, 'le Dire', which is a term
Blanchot at times borrows from Levinas as a version of what, in earlier
texts, he had addressed as the neutre of the narrative voice.[18] This explains
why the thought of the neutre in Blanchot is also the thought of literature,
and why literature or writing is what responds most exactingly to the
passivity beyond passivity that is the sign in Levinas of the infinite
responsibility to and for the Other. The point is made in *L'Écriture du désastre*:

> If there is some relation between writing and passivity, it is that both
> suppose the effacement, the extenuation of the subject: suppose a change
> of time: suppose that between being and non-being something which is not
> accomplished happens nonetheless as having long since already occurred –
> the worklessness of the neuter [le désœuvrement du neutre], the silent
> rupture of the fragmentary.

> (*ED*, 29–30; 14)

In many of his texts of the late 1960s and 1970s, Levinas, perhaps responding
in his turn to the strictures voiced by Blanchot the atheist, radicalises the terms
in which the appeal is made in his work to the name of God. In *Le Pas au-delà*,
belatedly, Blanchot provides what may be read as an oblique commentary on
Levinas's recourse to a non-theological, non-ontological God, suggesting that, in
so far as the name of God names nothing, the name is an empty name, a non-
name, a pure name naming only what is without name; but if this is so, it also
implies that the name of God, by bearing witness to the sickness of language, is
what allows language never to be cured of the malady that, as Blanchot once
rejoined to Sartre, is in fact the best available proof of language's unassuming
vitality. The name of God becomes here Blanchot's preferred – homeopathic –
antidote to all endeavours to cure language of its supposed sickness, an antidote
that, by maintaining the sickness of language, maintains the impossibility of a
word such as that of God, an impossibility that is of course the very condition of
possibility of the name of God itself (*PA*, 69–70; 48). Under the protection
(without protection) of the neutre, it is as though Blanchot is able here to
rewrite the name of God not as theological transcendence, but as the name for
that which in language always escapes language, which is one way of describing
the neutre itself. This rewriting of the name of God as an instantiation of the
neutre explains perhaps how in a series of later texts, the name of God finds its

way back into Blanchot's writing. It does so, however, not as evidence of a tardy abandonment of atheism, but on two conditions: first, that what it names without naming is not the God of Christianity but the God of the Talmud, and that the name of God, no sooner written, is immediately retracted and re-(de-)named as that of an Other.[19] Which, on Blanchot's part, is a way of affirming that, in the face of the absolute alterity of the Other, the only beginning of response, in the impossibility of its possibility and its withdrawal both of what is and of what is not, beyond immanence and transcendence alike, is what Mallarmé used to call: 'le seul acte d'écrire', the sole act of writing.

The demand of writing

(A primal scene?) You who live later, near to a heart that beats no more, suppose, suppose this: the child – aged seven, eight perhaps? – standing by the curtain, drawing it aside and, through the window-pane [à travers la vitre], looking. What he sees: the garden, the wintry trees, the wall of a house: yet as he looks on, no doubt as children do, at where he usually plays, he grows weary and slowly looks up towards the ordinary sky, its clouds and grey light, the dull day without depth.

What happens next: the sky, the *same* sky, suddenly open, absolutely black and absolutely empty, revealing (as though through the broken window-pane [la vitre brisée]) an absence such that everything has always and forever been lost in it, so much so that affirmed and dissipated within it is the dizzying knowledge that nothing is what there is and, to begin with, nothing beyond [rien est ce qu'il y a, et d'abord rien au-delà]. What is unexpected about the scene (its interminable trait) is the feeling of happiness that immediately engulfs the child, the ravaging joy to which he can bear witness only in tears, an unending stream of tears. People think he is just having a childish upset and try to console him. He says nothing. He will live henceforth with that secret. He will weep no more.

L'Écriture du désastre (ED, 117; 72)

At the end of *L'Entretien infini*, Blanchot summarises the arguments put forward in the volume as a whole by enumerating nineteen propositions of varying length and complexity under the general heading: 'L'Absence de livre' ('The Absence of the Book'). The title immediately recalls the phrase 'absence d'œuvre' (absence of the work) which, increasingly in his later writing, Blanchot comes to substitute for the concept of 'désœuvrement'. As with the expression 'absence d'œuvre', the syntax adopted for 'absence de livre' is not without some significance. For by depriving the book of any grammatical article, definite or indefinite, the phrase refers to the idea of the book as in effect always already under erasure; Blanchot's writing thereby endows the word absence with dynamic qualities that change it from a substantive into something more nearly resembling a verbal form.[1] The term, accordingly, comes to function like a new coinage. Absence does not imply nostalgia for an entity formerly present and now lost, but functions rather as a force of effacement and re-inscription that from the outset inhabits the book as its abiding, innermost principle (or absence of principle), albeit as a principle that in fact lies outside the book and presents itself to writing as the necessity of the book's past and future erasure. Absence here, then, is proffered as an exteriority beyond the book, and which the book, by definition, cannot incorporate within itself; and in this sense, once more, with regard to the book itself, the absence of the book, in Blanchot, functions as a simultaneous condition of possibility and impossibility.

In this closing chapter, which acts a moment of eschatological invocation, bringing a certain past to an end, and manifesting the infinite promise of the future, a gesture the writer redoubles by addressing his text to the absent books of anonymous friends, Blanchot begins with both an ending and a beginning: the one, falling at the end of history, bears the name of Mallarmé, while the other, at the very beginning of time, carries instead the mark of that mythic original man who first put tool to surface, tracing an inscription and inaugurating what was to become, as Blanchot puts it, the possibility of presence, meaning, and culture, in short, the history of the book as such in its threefold guise: as empirical object, pre-condition of all knowledge, and self-identical totality. At either end of the millennia, in Blanchot's account, two absent events seem to call to one other, opening and closing a history: first, an initial act of inscription, coming at the dawn of intelligibility itself, prior to all thought of the book, but giving rise to the possibility of the book, even as the act itself, preceding both the visible and the invisible, neither adding an object to the world nor removing one from it, installs within the horizon of the world – which it thus suspends – a gap in the universe, a universal void, a 'vide d'univers' (*EI*, 620; 422) that precedes and exceeds, enables and disables the book as such; then, many centuries later, a moment of completion in which the act of writing, bringing the order of the Book to a close, spills at last, once again, beyond closure, in order to enact, under the auspices of the absence of the book, its own double movement of erasure and re-inscription as a process of infinite dissemination, dispersion, and fragmentation. And between these two turning points, according to Blanchot, enabled but also undone by the sole act of writing: the theological history of the book, having now reached its end though enduring still, founded on the assurance of self-presence and temporal continuity, embodying in its dialectical unity and closure the arrogant self-certainty of a culture for which otherness is only ever an occasion for the demonstration of mastery.

While the law of the book demands of language that it remain subject to the dialectic of discourse – and the discourse of dialectics – writing is what is always already beyond the power and possibility of that law. Writing, so to speak, in refusing all posing, is radically opposed (or preposed) to any book. 'To write', argues Blanchot, 'is to produce the absence of the work (worklessness)' (*EI*, 622; 424); and he adds, some pages later, by way of explanation:

> The absence of the book: the prior deterioration of the book, its dissident play with regard to the space in which it is inscribed; the prior dying of the book [le mourir préalable du livre]. Writing, the relation to the *other* of every book, to what in the book would be de-scription [dé-scription], a scriptuary exigency outside discourse, outside language. Writing on the edge of the book, outside the book.
>
> (*EI*, 626; 427)

Though it always interrupts the rule of the book, writing is not simply a name for negativity, nor is it merely a function of the book's absence from itself. Writing is called forth not by the book, which is bound always to seek to re-incorporate writing within itself as presence, discourse, and sense, but by the attraction exerted on writing by the pure exteriority of the outside in its irreducible alterity and disseminated plurality. The outside in Blanchot, in that it precedes, exceeds, and traverses the book, is beyond presence. Lacking any principle of self-identity or permanence, it cannot as a result ever be construed 'as such'. Like the neutre, it resists the law of naming, which is why, if writing is a trace inscribed on the outside, what it traces, as it were, is not a trace of itself, but a trace that is always already other, always already multiple, and thus always already effaced. To the extent that it is of the outside, then, writing remains absolutely bereft of origin or beginning. Irreducible to the continuity or temporality of narrative, writing in Blanchot is thought only as irremediable repetition, infinite fragmentation, ineliminable excess, impossible alterity, which in turn explains why the figure of absence of the book, though it may work as a possible name for writing, cannot be read as a concept of writing, since what it seeks to name is prior to all concepts; it functions instead – impossibly – as a pre-conceptual trace that falls beyond the jurisdiction of all philosophical or critical discourses to the extent that all such discourses are necessarily founded on the self-presence and permanence of the law.

Crucially, if it is to be articulated or promulgated at all, the law itself must be written down; and it is for this reason that the possibility of writing necessarily precedes the law and cannot be coerced by it. This is also why writing, which nothing precedes, is dangerous and violent, and why, as Blanchot had learnt from the example of Hölderlin, the relation to writing, necessarily a relation of non-relation, must always be articulated obliquely and by means of a detour: the detour that, for Blanchot, constitutes literature itself. So while it is true, as Blanchot affirms from the outset, that writing is the greatest violence of all, because it exceeds both the law and its own law (*EI*, viii; xii), it is also the case that one of the functions of the law is to rescue human order from the violence of writing by affirming the necessity of the limit in the form of a second writing turning away from the outside, and which is the writing of the law itself (*EI*, 634; 432). But inevitably the limit instituted by the writing of the law has always already been transgressed; indeed, without such prior violence no law would be possible at all. Whence the law's awareness of its own dual status, for while it seeks to impose the limit that it values, properly, as its own, the law is also bound to acknowledge its fragility and impropriety in that, if it is to be written at all, it must always already have been breached.

In this sense, far from being beyond the law, transgression already belongs to the law, and in this perspective it is evident transgression is a necessary moment in the proper deployment of the law as such. But this solidarity between law and transgression, though it necessarily confirms the supremacy of the law, does not mean the law has no outside. On the contrary, what it implies is that the law and transgression have themselves already been transgressed, so to speak, in a more radical sense, by that which is already prior to the law because it is that upon which the law itself always already depends. Such, Blanchot argues, is the case of writing, which is why writing stands with regard to the law in a relation of exteriority, dissymmetry, and dissidence. The relation between writing and the law is a relation of non-relation; and it is from this that derives the 'transgressive' demand – the 'pas au-delà' – of writing, writing that is always other than the law, not because of its superior power or legitimacy in the face of the law, but rather because of its refusal, on grounds of impotence, impossibility, and weakness, to allow itself to be addressed by the language of the law and constituted by the law as a subject or hostage of that law. In other words, the transgressive extremity of writing is not the result of its ability to assert, against established law, and in competition with the law, the authority of a counter-law, but because, preceding the discourse of law, lacking all unity, presence, and identity, writing is a challenge to any authority whatsoever, including of course its own.[2]

For Blanchot, this is not to claim, against the threat of external censorship, that writing enjoys (or should enjoy) special privileges on the grounds that it is a vehicle for the all-conquering creativity of the imagination. It is to argue instead that writing must be thought as a response to a more exacting demand than that of the law, a demand which is that of limitless contestation; writing here is a response to the impossibility and infinite alterity of the outside. The ethics of writing, therefore, for Blanchot, have nothing to do with enforcing workaday societal norms, however desirable or just these may be; and it is this that founds Blanchot's consistent opposition to all forms of censorship, whether religious, moral, or political. With respect to all forms of authority – and this includes the principle of its own so-called aesthetic autonomy – writing is in a position of irreducible dissidence. Since literature does not and cannot obey external moral injunctions of whatever sort, it has no alternative but to affirm its essential dispersion and insubordination to all. What follows from this for Blanchot is not a retreat into aestheticism or art for art's sake. For it is precisely because writing is irreducible to any form of moral, political, or aesthetic authority, that it is able to constitute – or, better, de-stitute – itself as a response to the infinite demand that is the demand of the Other. Writing here for Blanchot does not simply have an ethical dimension; it has become absolutely inseparable from the exigency of the ethical as such. As Blanchot commented in 1983 in answer to a questionnaire:

> Writing is admittedly a form of work, but a perfectly insane one, which asks nothing, does not justify itself, and which no reward might possibly satisfy. Writing: a singular demand (let us call it bizarre), more ethical than aesthetic, since that to which it responds is an impersonal injunction without obligation or sanction [un 'il faut' sans obligation ni sanction].[3]

The argument presented by Blanchot in 'L'Absence de livre' is not a purely philosophical one; for it comes in the form of an impossible narrative that is itself in part a myth of origins. But while the text presents to the law of the book a narrative dealing with the donation and withdrawal of the law, it makes clear that its own narrative is a necessary concession to the detour of writing as such. The word writing in Blanchot is never simple, but always multiple; and here it becomes a name for that in writing which permits the formation of a pact, or alliance, between writing and the law and gives rise to the possibility of literature. Yet while Blanchot's essay provides for this narrative structure by narrating the genesis of that structure, it also neutralises and withdraws narrative from itself, with the result that narrative is maintained as a necessary detour but ultimately inscribed within a space that narrative itself cannot enclose and whose borders pass beyond and transgress the possibility of narrative. Narrativity is thereby suspended and put under erasure. So if 'L'Absence de livre' is in the form of a narrative, it is also at the same time an interruption of narrative; and while on one level it adopts a tabular structure reminiscent of the articles of the law itself, on another level it also fragments the law, pressing, within the fissures of the law, the claims of a demand that, not benefiting from the law's mediation, is in fact more rigorous still than the law itself.

This double movement of obliqueness and suspension, self-contestation and dissimulation is a structure that perseveres throughout the whole of Blanchot's writing. It recurs in especially persistent form in those narrative texts or *récits* that, alongside his more familiar books of literary criticism and philosophical analysis, Blanchot, since the early 1950s, had continued to write and publish: *Au moment voulu* (*When the Time Comes*), *Celui qui ne m'accompagnait pas* (*The One Who Was Standing Apart From Me*), *Le Dernier Homme* (*The Last Man*), and *L'Attente L'Oubli*. Admittedly, as noted before, this last title, published in 1962, was Blanchot's last free-standing *récit*; and, in any case, the book owed perhaps as much to metafictional essay as it did to conventional narrative. But this apparent falling silent of Blanchot's fictional writing after 1962 is deceptive, first because that silence was in fact not a silence, giving way as it did to a series of texts, notably *L'Entretien infini*, *Le Pas au-delà*, and *L'Écriture du désastre*, which, though not fictional works in any received sense, nonetheless contain extensive fictional passages that serve, at the very least, to challenge the ease with which these texts are usually categorised as works of philosophy and, moreover, to delimit the ambitions of philosophy by practising a mode of textuality for which the boundaries that pass between philosophy and its other(s) are neutralised and deprived of their title and identity. There is a second reason why the apparent coming to an end of Blanchot's fictional works in 1962 is deceptive, which is that for Blanchot, as *L'Arrêt de mort* testifies, the ending of fiction had in a sense always already taken place before that date, in that the endlessness of the end for Blanchot was inherent in fiction itself as a version of the limitless interruption that coincides with the inscription of the limit itself. What lies withdrawn in

Blanchot's apparent abandonment of fiction after 1962, then, is not the closure of fiction, but its always prior responsiveness to the limitlessness that is the reverse side of finitude and is inscribed most insistently by Blanchot in the heterogeneous, fragmentary manner adopted by him in his books from *L'Attente L'Oubli* onwards.[4] Here, the ending of fiction is as much a case of repeated return as perpetual effacement, and indeed it is both: effacement as return, repetition as perpetuity, impossibility as affirmation.

Like their predecessors, Blanchot's *récits* of the 1950s entertain complex, paradoxical relations with narrative structure. Though they submit in part to the constraints of narrative, these fictions follow, as they do so, a detour of dissimulation with the result that Blanchot's writing is constantly responding in narrative to that which is infinitely other than narrative. If the absence of the book is a token of the infinity of writing, so the limitations imposed on narrative in Blanchot's *récits* are like a tribute paid to the limitlessness of writing itself. This tension between finitude and the infinite, between possibility and impossibility is one Blanchot explores in all the *récits*, and it is what gives rise, clearest of all perhaps, to the peculiar oscillation between movement and paralysis, eventfulness and suspension that is characteristic of them, and which Derrida neatly sums up by punning on the closing sentence from *La Folie du jour*, reading Blanchot's 'pas de récit' both as that which is no narrative at all, and as that which is a step towards, along, or even beyond the path of narrative as such. The effects of this stumbling rhythm of advance and return, reprise and interruption, perseverance and paralysis, are everywhere to be found in Blanchot's texts; but such is the irregularity of the movement produced, in relation not only to the law of narrative in general but the structure of Blanchot's own writing in particular, that there are good reasons, ethical as well as literary critical ones, as Derrida has shown, for hesitating before applying to Blanchot's *récits* any all-purpose interpretative grid. Writing in Blanchot, one may say, is never the rule, always the exception.

But the singularity of writing, while it may contest the law of exemplification, is not solipsistic closure, and to read Blanchot's *récits*, as any text, is necessarily first to become entangled in a complex set of conventions and expectations governing the treatment of fictional space and narrative time. The paradox applies no doubt by definition to probably all literary texts; it is at any event what gives Blanchot's *récits* their peculiar status, as Derrida has argued, as examples without example, paradigms without paradigm, cases without law. In this regard, *Au moment voulu*, published in 1951, if not exemplary, is arguably no exception. Like the author's other fictions, the book is set almost entirely in an anonymous interior location – here, an apartment – whose most salient characteristic is its labyrinthine emptiness, and its strange spatial configuration that seems to accommodate both boundless immensity and sparse confinement. And though the text begins abruptly and incisively, with the unexpected surprise of the narrator's encounter with Judith, a woman of his acquaintance, on the threshold of her flat, the narrative barely proceeds much beyond this liminary metatextual event, about which much in the way of information is deferred or withheld, save to evoke a constantly suspended, forgotten, or abandoned visit to fetch a glass of water from the kitchen, with the result that the fiction as a whole remains suspended on an interminable scene that refuses to develop beyond this allusive beginning. Indeed, two years later, this request for a glass of water was still being rehearsed, or repeated, in identical words – 'Give me a glass of water ['Donnez-moi un verre d'eau'] – by the narrator of Blanchot's next récit, *Celui qui ne m'accompagnait pas* (*MV*, 12; 3; *CQ*, 96; 51).

'Nobody here desires to bind themselves to a story' ('Personne ici ne désire se lier à une histoire') (*MV*, 108; 47), declares Claudia, Judith's friend and companion, to the narrator at one stage, and the protagonist comments as follows:

> This sentence made a great impression on me. I thought I could see a light radiating forth from it, I had touched a point of startling luminosity. A sentence? more a slippage, a picture not yet framed, a movement of sparkling brightness that shone in quick dazzling bursts, and this was no calm light, but a sumptuous and capricious chance occurrence, the moodiness of light itself.
>
> (*MV*, 108–9; 47)

Claudia's pronouncements are endowed here with a powerful emblematic force, and Blanchot confirms as much when he re-cites them, eleven years later, in *L'Attente L'Oubli*, using them again to allude, as here, to the relation of non-relation passing – or not passing – between two sexually differentiated bodies or voices.[5] At this climactic point in the text, like the phenomenon of the window-pane – what Blanchot in *Au moment voulu*, as elsewhere, refers to as 'le phénomène de la vitre' (*MV*, 82; 35) – that separates inside from outside while also connecting them, transforming presence into absence and infinite distance into boundless proximity, Claudia's words interrupt the narrative to mark a suspension in the story that is also a suspension of the story. In the process, what

191

is revealed in Blanchot's protagonists, beyond narrative, is an avid commitment to desire that requires not the binding of narrative events, but rather their effacement, and an openness to capricious chance rather than stern necessity, in the knowledge that the former is no more than an ecstatic version of the latter, albeit with the risk that the narrator, for one, will find himself deprived of the protection afforded by narrative, and bound henceforth, as he puts it, not to story but to the poverty of dispossession that lies beyond and conditions it.

Shortly before *Au moment voulu* was published by Gallimard in 1951, Blanchot brought out a fragment of the text, corresponding to the first twenty-five pages of the book version, under the title 'Le Retour' ('The Return').[6] The term did not specify, of course, whether it was a case of the narrator returning to earlier, strangely familiar haunts, as the first paragraph of the text suggests, or, more disturbingly, whether the return more closely resembled the ghostly recurrence of another time, come to haunt the narrator's memory and confront him with what, beyond memory, constitutes the condition of possibility of recollection as such. At any event, and in either case, the term provides some clue as to how, in its suspension of narrative, Blanchot's *récit* may be approached; it also gives an indication of the nature of the book's reliance on a series of events that constantly resist designation as events, and which, if one concedes the term, are in fact more like absent events, events without event, in which case they demand most plausibly to be read as a form of all-pervasive metatextual commentary on the event without event that is the *récit* itself.[7] Residual though it is, it is certainly true that the narrative structure of *Au moment voulu* is dominated by this figure of return, which has its own recurrent motto in the form of the oft-repeated phrase: 'À nouveau! à nouveau!' (*MV*, 14; 4), meaning: again, again, once more, once more: once more as though for the very first time. The phrase, which is to be found in many other places in Blanchot's writings, is one that the author glosses himself in 'L'Expérience originelle' ('The Original Experience') from *L'Espace littéraire*, a text he was writing shortly after *Au moment voulu*, and in which he suggests: ' "Again, again!" ["A nouveau, à nouveau!"], is the cry of anguish grappling with the irremediable, with being [le cri de l'angoisse aux prises avec l'irrémédiable, avec l'être]' (*EL*, 256; 243).[8] And Blanchot explains:

It is in this sense that in the precincts of art there is a pact concluded with death, repetition, and failure. Beginning again, repetition, the inescapability of return, all the things evoked by those experiences in

192

which eeriness is allied with the strangely familiar, where the irremediable takes the form of endless repetition, where the same is given in the dizziness of replication, in which there is no cognition but only *recognition* [où nous ne pouvons pas connaître mais *reconnaître*], all this alludes to that initial error which may be expressed as follows: what is primary is not beginning, but rebeginning, and being is precisely the *impossibility* of being for the first time.

(*EL*, 255; 243)

In other words, what occurs without occurring, once more, for the first time, repeatedly but always differently, throughout *Au moment voulu* as well as Blanchot's other *récits*, is that which is irremediable: what in 'L'Expérience originelle' Blanchot describes as the impossibility of not being, but which in later writings is more frequently thematised by him as the impossibility not only of non-being, but of being as well, a radicalisation of Blanchot's thinking that belongs to the transformation in his thought brought about by the intervention of the neutre. The shift – arguably more one of degree than substance – was no doubt prompted not only by Blanchot's reading of Levinas during the latter part of the 1950s, but also by the experience of writing, for example, without example, a text such as *Au moment voulu*. For in that text, as the title suggests, the figure of return itself repeats – once more, as though for the very first time – Nietzsche's experience of eternal recurrence, an experience that is itself indeed the experience of 'once more, as though for the very first time', and which as such, as Pierre Klossowski was to remind Blanchot some years later, is in fact founded on an impossible aporia, in that, having first posited the possibility of revelation, it is then forced to negate that possibility by the very content of the revelation it imparts.[9] Understood in this way, the experience of return is properly unthinkable within the horizon of being; what it affirms, beyond being, is the impossibility of beginning, ending, meaning, presence, even finitude itself. Depriving the narrator of responsibility for his own story, it exposes him to the lack of origin and arbitrariness of a wheel of chance which is none other than the wheel of writing itself, for which all past is future and all future past, in a radical effacement of all possibility of presence.

The figure of return functions here as a paradoxical, but fatal and fateful exigency, one that reveals in the inevitability of death the impossibility of dying, in the law of repetition the excess of difference, in reason madness, and in the temptation to conclude, the necessity of infinite incompletion. Without the

193

promise or memory of the end, writing, like life or speech, cannot in fact begin, and to speak at all, in the words of *Celui qui ne m'accompagnait pas*, is always to be nailed to the spot; the end however is always out of reach, it can only ever be announced in advance of itself, and to write till the end and in view of the end is to submit forcibly to an endless circle where the end has always already taken place without taking place and remains infinitely deferred as the limit that gives rise only to its own limitlessness. Here, Blanchot's stumbling narrative leads narrator and reader into an experience where each step forward is necessarily a step back; where omnipotence is weakness and remembering forgetting; where the only illumination is darkness, and the only truth violence and passion; where the plenitude of the world gives way to emptiness beyond the world; where the only revelation lies in the infinite impossibility of revelation; and where the suspension of time embodies the demand of a unique moment that, across infinite distance, is both a thought to be affirmed and an Other to be addressed.

In this sense, the figure of return is not a figure at all, but more an evanescent trace, always already effaced, that, like the pre-conceptual singularity it is, addresses itself to thought as the trace of thought itself: thought, that is, not as self-identity, but as what one might call, with Blanchot, the giving withdrawing of the neutre itself, thought as both the necessity of death and the impossibility of dying, thought in the sense it has for Blanchot when he writes, in *Le Pas au-delà*, of its inadequacy in the face of death, an inadequacy that implies that thought itself is already a manner of dying, already a way of approaching the impossibility of dying which is but a name for the limitless impossibility of thought itself: 'Death', Blanchot writes,

> being that to which we are not accustomed, we approach it either as the unaccustomed that astonishes or as the unfamiliar that horrifies. The thought of death does not help us to think death, does not give us death as something to think. Dying, thinking, so close to one another that thinking, we die, if, dying, we dispense with thinking: each thought might be termed mortal; each thought a final thought.

(*PA*, 7; 1)

Alongside the neutre, the outside, and disaster, Blanchot writes in *L'Écriture du désastre*, the word return is one of the four names without name for what Blanchot describes as 'thought, whenever it allows itself to be unbound, by writing, to the point of the fragmentary [lorsque celle-ci se laisse, par l'écriture, délier jusqu'au fragmentaire]' (*ED*, 95; 57). As such, it is a vestige of what might be termed the language of the absence of the book, a language lost and never uttered, a language of infinite alterity. Eschatology here, if it is the language of the limit, is also the language of the limitlessness of the limit. This dual, ethical responsiveness to both the end and the endlessness of the end is what sustains the intensity with which Blanchot's *récit* challenges narrative order and pushes meaning to the brink of a catastrophe that is not an erasure of thought, but irremediable testimony of that which in thought always escapes thought. This in turn is what gives Blanchot's writing in *Au moment voulu* what Derrida has called its apocalyptic tone, which, as Derrida maintains, rather than a moment of ultimate truth, is what turns Blanchot's version of apocalypse into an apocalypse without apocalypse, an apocalypse of apocalypse. For what it brings, beyond truth, beyond falsity, is the experience of thought itself as an encounter with the extremity of the limit and with the limitlessness of the limit. In the absence of the book, then, writing for Blanchot turns aside from morality, law, being, and sense, to measure up to the immeasurable extremity of the outside. As it does so, what it affirms is its own infinite obligation to alterity, which requires of writing that it challenge and contest all law, all power, all sense, all identity, all stability of thought of whatever kind.

An uninterrupted questioning

Suppose a past, a future, without anything which would make it possible to pass from one to the other, in such a way that the line of demarcation, by remaining invisible, would demarcate them all the more: the hope of a past, the completion of a future. All, then, that would remain of time would be this line to be crossed, which, being always already crossed, is nevertheless uncrossable and, in relation to 'me', impossible to situate. It is perhaps only the impossibility of situating this line that we presumably call the 'present'.

The law of return, in supposing that 'all' may be said to recur, appears to posit time as closed: the circle beyond circulation of all circles; but in so far as it breaks the cycle in its middle, it puts forward a time that is not incomplete, but, on the contrary, finite, except at that point which is now, and which alone we believe we possess and which, lacking, introduces the break of infinity, obliging us to live as though in a state of perpetual death.

Le Pas au-delà (PA, 22; 12)

Writing, Blanchot maintains, though solitary, is not a solipsistic enterprise; indeed solipsists, he implies, much like pessimists, probably do not write at all (*ED*, 174; 113). For Blanchot, to write is instead always to address the unknown other: the other in so far as it is unknown, the unknown in so far as it is radically other. Writing, then, necessarily implies communication, community, even communism; and such were the terms, borrowed from Bataille, Jean-Luc Nancy, and others, with which Blanchot, in 1983, began the book that has most obvious claim to being the author's ultimate political testament: *La Communauté inavouable*. But while invoking these words, Blanchot also made it clear that they were themselves sufficient to the task ('"convenables"', as he put it, redoubling his point by the silent intervention of quotation marks (*CI*, 10; 1–2)) only to the extent that they were treated as being already under erasure: discredited and emptied of meaning as a result of their own past history, but for that very reason the site of an inescapable demand, one to which it is possible to respond only by what Blanchot calls their proper–improper abandonment (*CI*, 10; 2).

Bound as it is not only to the thought of the neutre but also to the absolute exteriority, beyond any world whatever, that Blanchot terms disaster, such a gesture of refusal yet submission, effacement yet re-inscription, gives a clear indication of the temporality and purpose of Blanchot's book. For while in *La Communauté inavouable* Blanchot was drawing lessons from the historical past, he did so by evoking, beyond presence, the very futurity that, perhaps surprisingly for some of his contemporaries, a certain, now distant past still contained. In that way, the suggestion on Blanchot's part was evidently also that those who hoped politically the future might prove to be different from the past might first have to relinquish any residual piety they might have in order to confront the radicality of what Blanchot invokes throughout *Le Pas au-delà*, in a sustained meditation on the lessons of May 1968, as a future without presence, self-identity, continuity, or *telos*; for only such a future, in Blanchot's view, founded on repetition, and intervening within time as infinite interruption rather than a manner of deferred presence, would paradoxically prevent the past from repeating itself, in time-honoured manner, as tragedy or farce: a verdict or injunction that in 1983 was not without its discreet relevance for a France already embarked, in conscious recollection of the lost opportunities of the Popular Front nearly a half-century earlier, on the first seven years of the socialist presidency of François Mitterrand.[1]

Like any testament, *La Communauté inavouable* has a prospective as well as retrospective dimension; and while on the one hand Blanchot takes the opportunity of recalling the pre-war political itinerary of Bataille and his own later experience of the campaign against the Algerian war and the *événements* of

May 1968, his more urgent concern is to respond in the book to a series of more recent writings, the most important of which, though in some ways the least visible, is arguably a paper by Derrida, first presented at the 1981 Cerisy conference on 'The Ends of Man', and itself addressed in part to Blanchot, entitled: 'D'un ton apocalyptique adopté naguère en philosophie' ('Of An Apocalyptic Tone Recently Adopted in Philosophy').[2] In that paper, at the end of a long discussion on the indissociability of enlightenment and eschatology, philosophical reason and apocalypse, Derrida concludes by evoking, as he had in an earlier text on Blanchot, the irreducible urgency and affirmative tone of a certain 'viens', meaning: come!, of which Derrida writes that, like some necessary but impossible pre-conceptual event that is precisely not an event, it resists appropriation by ontology, theology, rhetoric, grammar, even eschatology, precisely because it is the trace, or gesture, which gives rise to the conditions on which such determinations themselves depend. As such, writes Derrida, 'in this *affirmative* tone, "Come" marks in itself neither a desire, nor an order, nor a prayer, nor a request [ni un désir, ni un ordre, ni une prière, ni une demande]'.[3]

Blanchot immediately concurs, and glosses his accord by citing in modified form a passage from *Le Pas au-delà*, given three pages before the end of the book, that Derrida himself had cited in the course of his essay 'Pas' in 1976: 'Come, come, each and all, you for whom any injunction, prayer, or expectation is inappropriate' ('Viens, viens, venez, vous ou toi auquel ne saurait convenir l'injonction, la prière, l'attente') (*CI*, 26; 12).[4] Such closing words, Blanchot comments, and the writing of which they are the ruinous enactment, are intimately bound to the possibility of existence of community itself in that they address the unknown other; but if that is so, it is a necessary aspect of their address that they function as a disastrous or catastrophic invocation falling – coming – before the identification of any sender, or addressee, or language, or message, or judgement. Which is why, in a disastrous destruction of revealed truth, 'viens', in Derrida's terms, effects a kind of apocalypse without apocalypse, an apocalypse of apocalypse, so to speak, and why for Blanchot – 'perhaps', as the writer puts it – this apocalyptic voice also constitutes the condition of possibility – or impossibility – of community as such (*CI*, 26; 57).

Throughout *La Communauté inavouable*, with the sole exception of this particular – and particularly consonant – exchange, the reference to Derrida remains muted; elsewhere in the book, however, Blanchot makes a number of discreet gestures in the direction of this logic of redoubled apocalypse by

197

insisting on the irreducible – and self-questioning – excess of ethics or politics over ontology, and for instance by casting humankind as a whole at one stage, in its messianic dispersion and worklessness, in the role of the people of God failing even to leave Egypt in their quest for the promised land (*CI*, 57; 33). Turning aside from the debate with Derrida, Blanchot concerns himself instead with two more recent texts, Jean-Luc Nancy's essay 'La Communauté désœuvrée', and the story *La Maladie de la mort* by Marguerite Duras.[5] But, while ostensibly dealing with Nancy and Duras in turn, in the two halves of the book, namely 'La Communauté négative' ('The Negative Community') and 'La Communauté des amants' ('The Community of Lovers'), Blanchot's more urgent concern, in continuation of his earlier reading of Bataille and Levinas set out in *L'Entretien infini*, was to explore further the implications of the notion of double dissymmetry introduced there.

As a result of these various turns, *La Communauté inavouable* comes to be organised not as a philosophical treatise, but as an unavowable community of slippages between texts and between at times seemingly incompatible proper names. And as one name supplements or is substituted for another, what is described in Blanchot's text, between Derrida, Bataille, Levinas, Nancy, and Duras (not to mention Edgar Morin, Sade, Sartre, Lacoue-Labarthe, Heidegger, Leiris, Char, Kierkegaard, Plato, the Old Testament, Dante, Tsetaieva, Proust, Wittgenstein, Blanchot himself, and others too), is a kind of textual drift dramatising how the writer, far from adopting a philosophical position exclusive of all alterity, is instead, in writing, constantly being exposed to questioning by a proliferating number of different literary, philosophical, political discourses and events. In this, of course, Blanchot is doing nothing extraordinary, save perhaps to verify the plural, iterative structure of 'viens' itself. For as Derrida remarks at the end of his Cerisy paper:

> 'Come' is not addressed to an identity determinable in advance. It is a drifting [dérive] underivable from the identity of a determination. 'Come' is *only* derivable, absolutely derivable, but only from the other, from nothing that is an origin or a verifiable, decidable, presentable, appropriable identity, from nothing that is not already derivable and arrivable without demarcation [dérivable et arrivable sans rive].[6]

In addition to the exchange with Derrida, *La Communauté inavouable* was also written in response to a more localised occasion. This was the founding, at Derrida's suggestion, after the 1981 Cerisy conference, by Philippe Lacoue-

Labarthe and Jean-Luc Nancy, of a 'Centre de recherches philosophiques sur le politique', or Centre for Philosophical Research into the Political.[7] The purpose of the Centre, Lacoue-Labarthe and Nancy explained, was to engage in the specifically philosophical enterprise of questioning not politics in its epiphenomenality ('*la* politique'), but the logic of the political as such ('*le* politique'). Aside from political science or political philosophy, they argued, there was an urgent need to pose the more radical question of the very essence of the political. For Lacoue-Labarthe and Nancy, this meant ultimately attempting to think the question of relation outside of any concept of the subject and of subjective identification; and to this end they placed high on the agenda of their own work the project of examining the political itineraries of Heidegger and Bataille, who, within the general context of totalitarianism, were thought to have touched on the twin limits of the political not only by their reframing of community but also by their failure fully to dismantle their reliance on the concept of the subject.[8] Thus, according to Lacoue-Labarthe, Heidegger's reliance on the German Volk as a philosophical and political subject of destiny, which was what lay behind the endorsement of National-Socialism. Thus, too, according to Nancy, Bataille's forlorn search for sacrificial community, giving rise, he explains, to 'the paradox of a thinking drawn towards community, yet governed by the theme of the sovereignty of a *subject*'.[9]

Evidently, there was much in the analysis put forward by Lacoue-Labarthe and Nancy that could not fail to be of major interest to Blanchot. Given his own political itinerary since the early 1930s, and his own reading of Heidegger and Bataille since that period, it is not hard to see how Blanchot may have felt addressed by the work of the Centre.[10] Indeed, much of his own thinking of the question of the political, ever since the late 1950s, as the texts collected in *L'Entretien infini* show, was closely focused on the need to dismantle the concept of the subject in order to construe otherwise, with the help of Levinas, the very question of relation that Lacoue-Labarthe and Nancy sought to address in their work for the Centre. In this respect, *La Communauté inavouable* may best be read as constituting Blanchot's own contribution, presented so to speak in absentia, to the deliberations of the Centre. But while, by its very publication, the book was evidently supportive of the initiative of the Centre's foundation, it was also obliquely critical of at least some of the analysis put forward within the Centre; and while Blanchot entirely endorsed Lacoue-Labarthe's account of Heidegger's politics, as proposed in 1981 in the paper 'La Transcendance finit dans la

199

politique', his response to Nancy's work on Bataille, presented mainly in 'La Communauté désœuvrée', was much more nuanced.[11]

As always, evidence for this divergence of view is largely implicit within Blanchot's text. At first, in 'La Communauté négative' Blanchot closely follows Nancy's own exposition, even to the point of reproducing several of Nancy's quotations from Bataille from 'La Communauté désœuvrée', with the result that the opening ten or so pages of Blanchot's book read almost like an exact restatement of the corresponding sections of Nancy's original essay. In common with Nancy, for instance, Blanchot identifies hitherto existing communism as resting on a totalising conception of human immanence – what Nancy, followed by Blanchot, terms the immanence of man to man ('l'immanence de l'homme à l'homme') or the status of man as absolutely immanent being ('l'homme comme l'être absolument immanent') – and therefore on an understanding of man as constituted by the totality of his works, among which Blanchot counts humanity, nature, and God (and characteristically enough, in making this last point, Blanchot silently paraphrases the quotation from Herder provided by Nancy (*CI*, 11; 2)).[12] Similarly, Blanchot goes on to endorse Nancy's view of totalitarianism and individualism as representing the two sides of a single coin, with overarching unity on the one hand mimicking atomised closure on the other. And despite their responsiveness to the word communism, Nancy and Blanchot are agreed in their decisive rejection of any conception of community founded on the nostalgia for fusional, eucharistic communion and on the integrative, ultimately totalitarian power of nationalist or communitarian myth; community, instead, writes Blanchot, citing Nancy, is 'the presentation of finitude and of excess without return that founds finite-being [la présentation de la finitude et de l'excès sans retour qui fonde l'être-fini]' (*CI*, 24; 11).[13]

Rather than a choice between contending ideologies, such as liberalism or communism, the question of politics, for Blanchot, may perhaps best be described as the question of the alternative between the legacy of a society founded in totalising myth and in the image of its own self-identity and the futural prospect of a community exposed to exteriority and interrupted by alterity. In other words, between what in *La Communauté inavouable* Blanchot terms communion and substitution (*CI*, 24; 11), or between what he describes elsewhere, after Levinas, as the choice between the sacred and the saintly, or holy, that is, between effusion and election.[14] Up to a certain point, of course, much the same might be said of Nancy, were it not that Blanchot's slippage into the vocabulary of Levinas at this stage, within the community of thought constituted by Blanchot and Nancy, is evidence of a crucial but necessary divergence between them. For it is apparent that, by rephrasing Nancy's argument in Levinasian terms – with regard to the primacy or originality of which Nancy is clearly sceptical – Blanchot in his turn voices a degree of scepticism with regard to Nancy's endeavour to rethink 'community' on the basis of a re-articulation of Heideggerian 'Mitsein' (or 'l'être-avec', being-with, as Nancy phrases it) and thus within the framework of an ontology, albeit one that, as Nancy's subsequent work demonstrates, despite its Heideggerian starting point, it is difficult, if not impossible, to reconcile with Heidegger's own.[15]

Such at any rate is the implication behind Blanchot's insistence, expressed in 'La Communauté des amants', on the Levinasian principle of the priority of ethics over ontology (*CI*, 73; 43).[16] Nancy's scepticism towards Levinas is discreetly rebuffed, so to speak, by Blanchot's infinite scepticism towards Nancy. But infinite scepticism must not be confused here with dogmatic rejection; indeed, as Blanchot argues in his readings of Levinas, infinite scepticism is one of the chief characteristics of the movement of withdrawal and re-inscription traced by the thought of the neutre itself. And it is clear, as witnessed by the notion of abandonment used from the outset, that Blanchot's thinking of community is decisively oriented by the (non-)concept of the neutre. This explains Blanchot's strategy of acceptance and displacement, affirmation and transformation that governs his relation to Nancy's reading of Bataille. And this is also why Blanchot at one moment is able to adopt Nancy's vocabulary as his own, while at other times underlining his differences with Nancy and in the process changing much of the emphasis of Nancy's analysis. At the very moment Blanchot, unlike Nancy, affirms in 'La Communauté des amants' the excess of ethics over ontology, he provides the reader with an intriguing emblem of this double strategy by placing at the head of that essay, taken from an earlier paper by Nancy, 'L'Être abandonné', the following epigraph, which offers a kind of philosophical rejoinder on Nancy's part to Blanchot's earlier scepticism regarding the commitment to ontology, and provides a discreet clue to the divergence of view at stake in the exchange: 'The only law of abandonment, like that of love, is to be without return and without recourse [d'être sans retour et sans recours]' (*CI*, 51; 29).[17]

This epigraph functions as more than a decoration or homage. It highlights one of the most pervasive conceptual motifs running through *La Communauté inavouable*; at the same time, it marks both the accord and discord between

Blanchot and Nancy embodied in the book as a whole. Throughout, Blanchot's debate with Nancy is organised to a large extent by the different inflections of the word 'abandonner', taken in the first instance by Blanchot from Bataille, and doubled up in such a way as to signify both abandonment ('abandon') and gift ('don'), that is: gift as abandonment and abandonment as gift. ' "To sacrifice"', writes Blanchot, quoting Bataille, ' "is not to kill, but abandon and give [Sacrifier n'est pas tuer, mais abandonner et donner]." To be bound to Acéphale is to abandon oneself and to give oneself: *to give oneself without return to limitless abandonment [se donner sans retour à l'abandon sans limite]*' (*CI*, 30; 15).[18] As Blanchot explains:

> The gift or abandonment [le don ou l'abandon] is such that, at the limit, there is nothing to give or abandon and that time itself is only one of the ways in which this nothing to give is offered and withdrawn like the whim of the absolute which leaves itself behind by giving rise to other than itself, in the form of an absence.
>
> (*CI*, 30–1; 15)

The absence of community to which Bataille testifies in his writing, Blanchot concludes, is not the failure of community, but community's most extreme moment: of both possibility and impossibility.

According to Blanchot, this infinite movement of abandonment and giving is what makes the project of human sacrifice associated with Acéphale irreducible to the logic of sacrificial communion; and it is here, most visibly, that Blanchot in his reading of Bataille diverges from Nancy. For it was precisely, Nancy writes, Bataille's realisation of the 'total absurdity', not to say 'puerile character', of that project of sacrifice and the nostalgia for communion it represented that lay behind Bataille's abandonment of all communitarian endeavours after Acéphale.[19] Blanchot rejoins:

> Was it absurd? Yes, but not only that, for it meant breaking with the law of the group, the law that had constituted it by exposing it to that which transcended it, without that transcendence being other than that of the group, i.e. to the outside which was the intimacy of the group's singularity. In other words, the community, by organising and by taking on as a project the execution of a sacrificial death, may be said to have renounced its renunciation of creating a *work*, be it a work of death, or even the simulation of death. The impossibility of death in its most naked

possibility (the knife meant to cut the victim's throat and which, with the same movement, would cut off the head of the 'executioner'), suspended until the end of time the illicit action in which the exaltation of the most passive passivity would have asserted itself.

(CI, 29–30; 14)

On Nancy's reading, the project of Acéphale shows a Bataille imprisoned in a nostalgia for sacrificial communion deriving from the unthought legacy of a dialectic of the subject.[20] Blanchot for his part, though subscribing still to much of Nancy's general argument, at this point takes a very different view. At issue in this exchange is the question of the relationship between the community of Acéphale and death itself. In Blanchot's view, in its (self-)exposure to the impossibility of dying, Acéphale was already precisely not a community founded on the possibility and the subjective truth of death as a moment of dialectical closure. Indeed, the law of sacrifice Acéphale adopted as its apparently defining principle of identification or identity, Blanchot insists, was in fact scarcely a principle at all, to the extent that it was something Acéphale had already suspended in the very movement of its simultaneous constitution and dissolution.

Blanchot's claim, then, contrary to Nancy's assessment, is that Acéphale was not a community founded on immanence and on the work of death, but on the limitlessness of the alterity of dying. As such, it already belonged, he argues, to the impossibility of being and to that nameless exteriority Blanchot terms disaster, and in response to which community is instituted only for the duration of an apocalyptic 'viens'. For Blanchot, Bataille's thought of the community cannot be attributed to a logic of sacrificial subjectivity; rather, Blanchot maintains, the question of the death of the other, in Bataille, like friendship or love, is precisely not thought in relation to any concept of the subject, but rather what he calls 'the slippage beyond limits', 'le glissement hors des limites' (CI, 33; 16). ' "Inner experience" ', Blanchot adds,

> says the opposite of what it seems to say: it is a movement of contestation that, coming from the subject, ravages it, but has a deeper origin in that relation with the other which is community itself – community that would be nothing if it did not open whoever is exposed to it to the infinity of alterity – at the same time that it decides its inexorable finitude.

(CI, 33; 16–17)

Between Nancy and Blanchot the debate at this point turns on perhaps two differing interpretations of the term 'abandonment'. For Blanchot, according to the thought of disaster, abandonment necessarily implies all abandonment of being; while for Nancy abandonment is still thought by him as the being of the abandonment of being. The outcome, from Blanchot's perspective, is a fatal retention of thought within the orbit of ontology, which results in the fact, from Blanchot's perspective, that Nancy hypostatises Bataille's demand for community by situating his writing within the closure of sacrificial subjectivity and by analysing Acéphale exclusively as a moment of 'désœuvrement' within that closure (*CI*, 43; 23). To do so, however, is to be in some danger, in Blanchot's eyes, of disregarding the extent to which Bataille in his writing already exceeds the bounds of any received concept of the political; and this in turn would be to underestimate the suspensive, neutre force of the impossible alterity on which Bataille's search for community is in fact premised, and thereby miss the unavowable futurity – the unspeakable risk and chance – announced, albeit already in the historical past, by a project such as that of Bataille. It was at any rate to make that claim, in the name both of a politics of the future and of justice for the friend that was Bataille, that Blanchot addressed his text to Nancy (and others), appealing to their friendship, as Bataille once had it, as to that friendship which is 'friendship for the unknown without friends', and 'friendship for the exigency of writing that excludes all friendship' (*CI*, 44; 24).

'La Communauté négative' concludes with this oblique dedication or demand, to which it adds a closing reference to the heart (or law) of fraternity that for Bataille – and Blanchot – is proposed here as one of the fundamental secrets of community, thereby prompting at least one reader – Jacques Derrida – to question what is at stake in this final invocation of brotherhood in a text explicitly dedicated to community without communion.[21] But at this very point, as though in advance of that objection, Blanchot interrupts his account of Bataille and Nancy in order to supplement it, in a manner he claims was unforeseen and unplanned, with an essay devoted to Duras's *La Maladie de la mort*, in which at least two important further slippages beyond established limits take place: the shift to a literary (rather than philosophical) text and to a female-authored (rather than male-authored) work.

This twofold displacement does not however represent a retreat from the demand of community or from the question of the political. On the contrary, the name of Duras, like that of Bataille, is also that of a former political ally and personal friend, and Blanchot records as much by evoking their common past involvement in the campaign against the Algerian war and in the *événements* of May 1968 (*CI*, 51–8; 29–34). Moreover, on each of the three previous occasions when he had written about Duras's work, Blanchot had also shown himself to be one of the few readers to realise that her texts were all stories of the impossible reciprocity of love and of the incommensurability of sexual and social relations.[22] To introduce the name of Duras into the debate with Bataille and Nancy was thus not only to raise the issue of community and communication with regard to literature, but also to pose the question of the place of desire and sexual difference within community as such.

As he turns to *La Maladie de la mort*, Blanchot exposes his account of Bataille and thoughts on fraternity to a question of sexual difference. With respect to community, his text asks, is sexual difference primary or secondary? Is it internal or external to community? As Blanchot reminds the reader, the Biblical evidence on this point is confused, with Genesis providing two mutually incompatible strategies for configuring the origin of the sexes, one that posits duality before unity, the other that first posits unity, then duality (*CI*, 68; 40).[23] As many of Duras's own texts suggest, what this indicates is a deep-seated resistance to all narrative teleology or linearity on the part of sexuality, and it is as though the conundrum of sexual difference – separation within the One or infinite non-complementarity of the more than One? – throws into question the possibility of constructing any coherent narrative of community at all, and thus strikes, so to speak, at the very possibility of community as such. Sexual difference on this reading would seem to belong not to community as an entity present to itself, but to disaster, the outside, and irreducible and incommensurable alterity. During May 1968, on the other hand, Blanchot reports, in a rare convergence of presence and non-presence, differences of sex and gender, like distinctions of class or age, if not annulled, were nonetheless suspended; and the result was what Blanchot describes as explosive communication: 'that openness that allowed each and every one, without distinction of class, age, sex, or culture, to mix with the first comer, as if with a person already loved, precisely because they were the unknown-familiar [le familier-inconnu]' (*CI*, 52; 30–1). What such moments serve to illustrate, however, Blanchot argues, is not the precedence of community over social or sexual differences, but rather that a community such as that formed, briefly, during the *événements* of May 1968, was a necessary response to the dissymmetry between Same and Other and that, for that dissymmetry to be realised, community itself must be affirmed, even as, at the very same time, it must also be put under erasure, maintained as a suspended moment of non-presence rather than being absorbed once again within the closure of sacrificial subjectivity.

Sexual difference in Blanchot inscribes a twofold process: it exposes community to alterity and exposes alterity to community. It is thus a condition both of possibility and of impossibility. Indeed, without sexual difference it is difficult to see how any community is conceivable at all; but it is clearly also one of the fundamental properties of sexual difference at the same time to threaten the existence of any such possibility of community. The heterogeneity embodied in sexual difference effects what Bataille calls an insidious loosening of the social bond, and this is why for Blanchot, as for Duras's story, sexual difference is seen as corresponding to a logic that is not only an interruption of logic, but also an interruption of the possibility of narrative and of the homogeneity that threatens in all social organisations. Blanchot explains the point by contrasting here two relations to death that are also two logics of sexual relation and two sharply opposed types of social or political structure: the one, embodied in homogeneity, immanence, and the enforcement of law, finding expression for instance in the homosexual exclusion of the sexual Other by the group (the example given is the classically paradigmatic case of the Hitlerite SA); and the other dedicated to heterogeneity, alterity, and the suspension of law, in which, according to Blanchot, 'woman then becomes the "outsider" [l'"intruse"] who perturbs the untroubled continuity of the social bond and does not recognise prohibitions [l'interdit]. She is hand in glove with the unavowable [Elle a partie liée avec l'inavouable]' (*CI*, 70; 59).[24]

The logic of sexual relations in *La Maladie de la mort*, as Blanchot demonstrates, is a logic of disarticulation before it is one of articulation; it affirms disjunction, non-complementarity, and the impossibility of satisfaction as the groundless ground for the encounter – if any such word may be deemed adequate – between the book's two protagonists. The only relation between them is a relation founded on non-contemporaneity and dissymmetry, and thus on the very absence of relation. From the perspective of Duras's text, sexual difference belongs to no common, shared world, but rather to an absent horizon and an always already prior absence of world; as a result, the reputed worldliness of love relations gives way in her story to the radical worldlessness of desire itself. This possibility of speaking the absence of world in its very impossibility is the only scant privilege Blanchot confers here on literature, raising Duras's story – problematically, as Blanchot is the first to admit

(*CI*, 88; 54) – to the status of original or pre-original myth by giving to Duras's unnamed female protagonist the name of Eve, or Lilith – Adam's first wife, according to Rabbinical tradition, before the creation of Eve – or by casting her in the part of chthonian Aphrodite, whose pact is not with the world but the underworld, and whose relation is not with life but rather with death (*CI*, 77; 46). But what is precisely at stake here, in Blanchot's thinking of community, with respect not only to sexual difference, but literature too, is this question of death, that is, not the sacrificial sublation of death as work, project, or monument, but rather that relation of non-relation for which death is only ever a sign of the impossibility of dying and, beyond finitude, of the infinity that is desire, and the demand that is community.

It is for this reason, as Blanchot puts it, that Duras's lovers in *La Maladie de la mort* are not so much separated, or divided from each other, as infinitely inaccessible to one another. The other face of finitude, Blanchot insists, is the infinite relation with the Other that finitude necessarily implies. The worldlessness experienced by Duras's lovers is thus not a basis for romantic nostalgia, but a kind of violent contestation of the closure implied by any world as such. It is in this sense that love in Duras may be seen as an apocalyptic indictment of the finite character of the world; but if love is to be the source of catastrophic revelation, as far as Blanchot is concerned, it is not because love offers its derelict participants the hope of communion within some higher unity, but because inherent in finitude itself is the knowledge that any limit is necessarily accompanied, as by its invisible shadow, by the limitlessness that is both cause and effect of the limit, and that the absence of relation with the Other is therefore only another name for the infinity of that relation. Love here, for Blanchot, acts as a kind of reprise of the ethical relation. As such, it insists not on the necessity of obeying worldly laws, but on the need to contest all such laws; but if it chooses to defy these laws, it can only be in the name of the higher law that comes before all codes of law or morality, and which is the law of that from which law derives, which is responsibility towards the Other, and to which responsibility is owed not because it is the law but because, like passion, it is what precedes freedom, choice, deliberation as such.

In *La Communauté inavouable*, under the rubric of the ethical, what Blanchot endeavours to address, as in his readings of Levinas, is an alterity that is irreducible not only to immanence but, Blanchot puts it, any received form of transcendence also. Such alterity without name, transcending all transcendence, Blanchot in *La Communauté inavouable* calls disaster. Disaster here is another name for the infinite contestation or anonymity that in earlier texts Blanchot formulates as the neutre; at any event, as an inassimilable force of infinite withdrawal, separation, and displacement, it is that which requires community, if it is to be affirmed at all, to remain unavowable. The word is one Blanchot takes, like others in this context, from Bataille.[25] Twice before explicitly introducing the phrase: 'la communauté inavouable' in the book, Blanchot uses it by inverting subject and adjective as 'l'inavouable communauté'. This is no doubt done for stylistic effect, but it also leaves it uncertain whether it is community that gives rise to the unavowable secret or the secret to community. In either case, the secret itself is left unexplained, save that, like the allusion to an unspeakable pre-conceptual singularity, it is what, in language, nonetheless stands separate from language. The secret of community, like the secret to which the narrator of L'Arrêt de mort remains attached as to a compelling absence from words, is a secret that is beyond possibility; to the extent it is a secret to be revealed at all, it is a secret without secret, a revelation without revelation. An unthematisable interval separates community from itself as the ground without ground of the futurity of community and its openness to the Other.

As Blanchot writes elsewhere, apocalypse here disappoints (A, 118–27). The invocation of the end is a tribute necessarily paid to infinity, as Blanchot makes clear by pointing at the end to the self-defeating paradox of Wittgenstein's famous conclusion to the Tractatus. To speak of the end is always to defer the end; no sooner is it pronounced than the finality of an apocalyptic 'come!' in fact suspends the end as a moment of perpetual (re)beginning. Apocalypse in Blanchot is therefore not an apocalypse, for it is apocalypse without end, truth, or finality. It is, as Derrida had predicted, apocalypse without apocalypse. Blanchot says as much himself at the end of La Communauté inavouable, as he translates into something resembling a project the 'viens' that precedes and exceeds his text and which he addresses to his reader as a sign of the unavowability of community as that which in language is always other than language. This explains why perhaps, in La Communauté inavouable as a whole, beyond literature itself, the only moments of community which Blanchot is able to affirm – Acéphale, the events of May 1968, the demonstrations of 13 February 1962 in protest at the Charonne killings – are all so many (non-)events of uncertain status.[26] Like the love enacted in La Maladie de la mort, their main effect seems to have been to put the world into parentheses by virtue of the deconstructive force of the neutre, and in that interruption of world and power to have affirmed the infinity of responsibility to alterity and the Other. This is why Blanchot refuses, vigorously and incisively, all modes of political representation and all forms of politics premised on the pursuit of power. The politics to which Blanchot's writing gives voice instead is an eschatology – eschatology beyond eschatology – which addresses the future not as power but as judgement, not as imminent presence but as infinite promise. The hope is not for more, or better representation, but rather for the destruction of the present as such and thus for a revolution that would open time itself to the otherness that presence always excludes: what Blanchot in May 1968 invoked as

> a revolution ... destroying all without anything destructive, destroying, rather than the past, the very *present* in which it took place and not attempting to provide a future, extremely indifferent to any possible future (judged as success or failure), as though the time it sought to open up was already beyond these standard determinations.
>
> (Révolution ... détruisant tout sans rien de destructeur, détruisant, plutôt que le passé, le *présent* même où elle s'accomplissait et ne cherchant pas à donner un avenir, extrêmement indifférent à l'avenir possible (la réussite ou l'échec), comme si le temps qu'elle cherchait à ouvrir fut déjà au-delà de ces déterminations usuelles.)[27]

One might conclude that Blanchot's politics, like those of Duras, are to this extent a politics of disaster.[28] But this is not the same as a politics of despair. Quite the reverse.

The unexpected word

> The example of Marx helps us to understand that the language of writing [la parole d'écriture], which is a language of ceaseless contestation, must constantly be developed and interrupted in *multiple* ways. The language of communism is always *at one and the same time* tacit and violent, political and wise, direct, indirect, total and fragmentary, lengthy and nearly instantaneous. Marx does not live comfortably with this plurality of languages constantly colliding and being forced apart within him [qui toujours se heurtent et se disjoignent en lui]. Even if these languages seem to converge towards the same end, they remain untranslatable into one another, and their heterogeneity, and the distance and interval that decentre them, make them non-contemporaneous with each other [non contemporains], such that, giving rise to an effect of irreducible distortion, they oblige those who have to withstand the challenge of reading (or executing) them to submit to a process of ceaseless readjustment.
>
> 'Les Trois Paroles de Marx' (*A*, 117)

There are, Blanchot maintains, always at least two languages, two voices, two demands. Such multiplicity of tone, according to Derrida, is a trait common to all eschatology; but Blanchot raises it to the status of a philosophical, literary, and political strategy. Writing, he argues, falls subject to an injunction which by definition cannot be satisfied and is capable of supplying neither sanction nor recompense. But for every demand addressed to the act of writing by virtue of its own absence of worldly foundation or justification, there is always another demand requiring that justice be done without delay in the world. These two demands, the one requiring the obliqueness of infinite patience, the other demanding urgent and decisive action, function according to different rhythms, different temporalities, and different logics of possibility and of impossibility. While not necessarily opposed to one other, and not homogeneous even within themselves, they are nonetheless radically disjoined, and it is essential, in the nameless name of the neutre, Blanchot argues, that the dissymmetry arising from this disjunction be affirmed, respected and obeyed.[1]

The two demands, most crucially of all, must not therefore be mistaken the one for the other, or homogenised with each other, which is also why absolute dedication to the one does not constitute grounds for release from the urgency of the other. While the language of politics, as Blanchot argues in La Communauté inavouable, must allow itself to be interrupted by the alterity of writing, so the commitment to the dissymmetry and infinity of relation that writing introduces into community does not thereby dispense the writer – not as a citizen, but as writer – from the challenge of meeting politics on its own terms: indeed, this is, according to Blanchot, precisely what writing demands, even if the endeavour to respond to that demand may imply abandoning, provisionally, the indirect discourse of the literary in order to contend with the immediacy of the political as such. Commitment here depends not on the figure of the intellectual as superior consciousness or exemplary conscience, addressing the community at large with the authority of universal values, but rather on the solitude and alterity of writing itself, in whose name the writer is unavoidably bound to affirm freedom as an absolute, irreducible condition of language and community as such. Its emblem, therefore, for Blanchot, is not, say, the image of Sartre, whom even de Gaulle mistook for Voltaire, writing plays so as not to foment despair in the hearts of the Renault car workers of Billancourt, but the gesture of Hölderlin, in a letter to his brother on New Year's Day 1799, declaring himself ready to throw his pen under the table in order to go wherever the need was greatest to defend the cause of liberty against the threat of darkness.[2]

Blanchot's relationship as a writer with the political is, in this way, both singular and far-reaching; for that reason alone it is worth examining here that thinking and questioning of the political put to the test by Blanchot in a remarkably heterogeneous series of political writings – including statements of political principle, polemical texts, open letters, petitions, journalism, and responses to questionnaires – written, intermittently and irregularly, alone or in collaboration with others, during the period following his return to Paris in 1957 and in response to several important and challenging political events, each of which, Blanchot wrote in 1986, for one reason or another, was greater than its own actual meaning.[3] As Blanchot has indicated in various retrospective accounts of his own, these moments, so many turning points, so to speak, were essentially three in number: the resistance to the Algerian War from 1958 till 1962; the *événements* of May 1968; and the memory and witness to the Nazi death camps that came to dominate much of Blanchot's political thinking after 1971.

Blanchot's first explicitly political text to be published since before the Second World War appeared in October 1958 in *Le 14 Juillet*. Called 'Le Refus', ('Refusal') (*A*, 130–1), it was the first of two contributions by Blanchot to the campaign, launched earlier that year by Mascolo and Schuster, to challenge the legitimacy of de Gaulle's return to power in May. The title of the piece was no doubt symbolic. Importantly, however, it also mobilised, with undiminished virulence, but in the service of a different kind of political project, one of the few terms in Blanchot's political lexicon to have survived from his pre-war activist past.[4] This shows how far Blanchot's return to political commitment, whatever some have charged, was not premised on a culpable repudiation of his pre-war involvements, which in any case remained largely unknown to the majority of his new political associates. Equally, however, this return to politics can hardly be seen, on Blanchot's part, as constituting an uncritical continuation of his pre-war political endeavours, and it is indisputable that throughout the 1950s, 1960s and 1970s, though at times obliquely, Blanchot in all his political thinking was constantly reflecting on the events that had led up to 1938. This is demonstrated by the frequency with which questions of nationalism and internationalism, militarism and freedom of speech, anti-semitism and colonialism recur in his later political writings.

To refuse the present, as Blanchot wrote to Mascolo in 1958, also meant refusing the past; and in both cases what Blanchot had uppermost in his mind was the need to refuse – more radically still, as I have suggested, than he had

211

done during the 1930s – not only all complicity with the politics of representation, but also any reliance on the self-presence of the nation as subject of history. In 1958, then, refusal in Blanchot was not a simple posture of negation or revolt, and it would be wrong to see Blanchot's opposition to de Gaulle and to the Algerian War as relying on a simple gesture of protest. Refusal for Blanchot was not an isolated or token matter, but an act, as he put it in 'Le Refus', that was absolute and categorical in itself and as a result potent enough, albeit in negative terms, to call forth a community, a community founded, so to speak, on what Blanchot calls 'the friendship of this No, certain, unshakable, and exacting [l'amitié de ce Non, certain, inébranlable, rigoureux], which holds men united in solidarity' (A, 130).

The refusal to sanction de Gaulle's return to power was not on Blanchot's part a passing concession to the demands of the moment. It was a natural extension of much of Blanchot's thinking about literature during the previous decade; indeed what it evoked most clearly of all, on one level, was the same logic of all or nothing, without mediating concept, that Blanchot had explored in relation to writing in 'La Littérature et le droit à la mort', and which, in so far as it corresponded to an act of absolute refusal of the world and power, was also to be understood, implicitly, as an act of absolute affirmation of that which was radically other than world or power. And it was in much the same way, over and beyond a profound objection to de Gaulle's militarism and self-important nationalism, that what Blanchot's act of political refusal affirmed was the necessity of rupture: of a break in continuity in politics, so to speak, and one that put at the centre of political discourse an interval and a disjunction – beyond being and non-being, so to speak – that not only called into question de Gaulle's endeavour to substitute his own personalised pseudo-religious authority for democratic government, but also entirely discredited the opportunism of those who were content to accept the new ideological order in the name of so-called political realism and which did no more in fact than emphasise the esssential complicity between politics in the received sense and the established order itself.

This was not all. In 1958 Blanchot was clearly aware that it was not enough merely to attempt to create an interval in the process of political representation. It was equally important, if not indeed more so, within that interval to refuse the lure of the nation's demand for self-presence and self-identification, which would always risk reinforcing the rule of representation as such, and to respond instead to the demand of the Other. This is why, as the campaign developed, it

212

became a struggle whose prime goal was not to defend the constitutional, democratic traditions of the French republic, but rather to end the oppressive rule of French colonialism in Algeria (which during the 1950s democratically elected governments in France had struggled to defend as proper and legitimate). And this was one of the ways in which, in the specifically political domain, Blanchot endeavoured to avoid all the dangerous ambiguity of his revolutionary pronouncements of 1936 and 1937, and draw the necessary conclusions from that (for many) largely forgotten pre-war history.

As the struggle against de Gaulle turned into the campaign against the Algerian War, the logic of interruption inherent in the act of political refusal, as Blanchot saw it, underwent a further inflection. This was most clearly visible in the full title – devised, it seems, by Blanchot himself – adopted by Mascolo, Schuster, Blanchot, Nadeau, and the document's other co-authors, to head the text that, distributed clandestinely in September 1960, quickly came to be known by the more familiar name of the 'Manifeste des 121'. The document's full title was: 'Déclaration sur le droit à l'insoumission dans la guerre d'Algérie' ('Declaration on the Right to Insubordination in the Algerian War'). As Marguerite Duras, in whose flat in the rue Saint-Benoît the Declaration was first drafted, later commented, on the occasion of the twenty-fifth anniversary of the publication of the text, the document was not a pacifist one, did not amount to a refusal of war in general, if only because of the deep association of that position, in French eyes, with the appeasement of Hitler at Munich in 1938.[5] But nor did the Declaration appeal to any sense of obligation or duty on the part of its readers. What it did instead, Duras continued, was to place those to whom it was addressed before an essential and solitary responsibility, which was the responsibility to decide both for themselves and in relation to themselves; this was why the text of the Declaration, while referring to a set of specific circumstances, invoked not an obligation, but an absolute, fundamental, and inalienable right. The distinction was an important one. As Blanchot explained in his interview with Madeleine Chapsal:

> I believe that the whole force of the Declaration, its whole power of disturbance [tout son pouvoir d'ébranlement], comes from the authority with which it utters the single word insubordination, a solemn word, signifying utmost refusal: the Right to insubordination. I say Right and not Duty [Droit et non pas Devoir], as some, in an ill-considered way, would have liked the Declaration to say, no doubt in the belief that the

213

formulation of a duty goes further than that of a right. But not so: an obligation refers to a prior moral code that shields, guarantees, and justifies it; wherever there is duty, all that is necessary is to close one's eyes and carry it out blindly; everything then is quite straightforward. The right to do something, on the other hand, refers only to itself, to the exercise of that freedom of which it is the expression; a right is a free power for which each individual, for himself and with regard to himself, is responsible and which binds him completely and freely: nothing is stronger, nothing is more serious. That is why it is essential to say: the right to insubordination; each person takes their own sovereign decision [chacun en décide souverainement].[6]

In its opposition to the war, the Declaration did not invoke a moral duty, based on a universalising code of laws, principles, values, and obligations. As Blanchot points out, it was this that distinguished it from an act of commitment in the Sartrian sense; indeed it might be argued in this respect that the Declaration was one of the first texts, in France, to contest and rethink the figure of the intellectual as universal conscience, as Foucault and others were increasingly to do after May 1968.[7] Instead of appealing to morality, and thus necessarily to some institutionalised code that had disquieting similarities with the very authority of the state it sought to challenge, the Declaration reaffirmed each signatory's inalienable right of refusal, a right that was absolute to the extent that it logically preceded any form whatsoever of recognition of the power of the state and any complicity in its decisions.

In its own way, of course, the affirmation of the right to insubordination was an act of political violence, and Blanchot was well aware that, implicit though it was, such violence was liable to provoke a violent response from the state itself. But to acknowledge the violence of refusal arguably also made the Declaration politically more effective, for the signatories to the text found themselves not in the position of seeking to impose upon others the obligation to act in conformity with a given set of universalising values, but in the position of taking their own share of responsibility, with the modest means at their disposal, for the violence being committed in their name by the French Republic in its prosecution of the Algerian War, a war which, crucially, the French state even declined to acknowledge as such, claiming it to be a purely domestic matter of internal security.

The reaction of the state to the Declaration was immediate and uncompromising; the document was suppressed and each of its co-authors became the object of criminal proceedings. On one level this was hardly surprising; but it served to make clear, if clarity was needed, that the conflict between the state and the resistance to the war was itself a form of warfare, in which the state sought to defeat the actions undertaken against it by deploying against its opponents greater, or more effective, violence than they themselves were able to muster in their defence. The analogy here, already evoked in the text of the Declaration itself, was between the regime installed by the French military in May 1958 and that set up under the Occupation by Pétain in 1940. In both cases, the legal machine of government had lost democratic legitimacy and, though the state pretended otherwise, was in the hands of an oppressive, authoritarian regime. So much was evident from the Jeanson trial of September 1960, the smooth running of which it had been the initial purpose of the Declaration to disrupt. But what the trial in its turn demonstrated, and as the Declaration itself confirmed, was that, alongside the war of arms being waged between the state and the – illegal – opposition, another, equally important conflict was taking place; and that, as Blanchot was to discover during the court proceedings against him, this other war was a war of language and discourse.[8]

It is here that the logic of absolute, categorical refusal which Blanchot develops in his political texts of the late 1950s and 1960s demonstrates its particular originality and political significance. For if refusal was a right, as Blanchot maintained, it was in the first instance essentially always a right to refuse a certain kind of language: authoritarian, self-assured, peremptory, repetitive, oppressive. Such language, however, was at best only a hollow parody of the language of literature and writing, an attempt to escape rather than confront the emptiness at the heart of language; this at any rate was what Blanchot had argued in a 1955 essay entitled 'Mort du dernier écrivain' ('The Death of the Last Writer') (LV, 265–70; BR, 151–6), in which he puts forward a portrait of the dictator as a spectacular kind of failed writer. If the analogy was correct, it explained not only the liking for great art expressed by countless emperors and dictators down the ages and why the national-aestheticism of many of Blanchot's contemporaries had led them in the 1930s to endorse a host of authoritarian political systems, but also why, more importantly, for Blanchot the language of power was ultimately always vulnerable: vulnerable not to the challenge that might come from a rival code of values, equally authoritative in its own terms as that embodied in dictatorship, but vulnerable instead to the infinite scepticism affirmed by the language of writing itself.

In that case, it was, Blanchot argued, in its very refusal of the language of politics in the received sense that literature might be seen to be the most profoundly political mode of thinking of all. 'That is why', suggested Blanchot in 1955, referring to a writer not very different from himself, 'when speaking of politics, he is already speaking of something else: of ethics; when speaking of ethics, of ontology; when speaking of ontology, of poetry; when speaking, last of all, of literature, "his sole passion", it is to revert again to politics, "his sole passion"' (*LV*, 302; *GO*, 119). Here, what was most important of all about the right of refusal – like the right to death that it mirrored – was that, like literature itself, it placed at the centre of political discourse a disjunction of languages, an infinite gap or interval that was a space both of silence and endless contestation. In so doing, what it put at the top of the political agenda was the need not simply to bring about a change in the content of politics, but a radical transformation, too, in the very language of politics; and as the 'Entretien sur un changement d'époque' ('Conversation on a Change of Epoch') (*EI*, 394–404; 264–71) in April 1960 had testified, it was to the imminent possibility of such a radical transformation, affecting the way in which politics and community might henceforth be addressed, that Blanchot sought to contribute in his ill-fated efforts to realise the project of an International Review.

If all Blanchot's renewed political activities of the late 1950s and early 1960s may be placed under the rubric of what one might call a politics of refusal, the same is true – if not indeed more so – of his involvement in the events of May 1968. There was of course much that was new and unexpected about May; but most striking of all was that, for the vast majority of those who took part in the *événements*, it was politics itself that demanded an absolute rejection of the politics of representation embodied in the French parliamentary system and in all established political parties. The real political arena of the movement of May was in this sense the street. This corresponded suggestively to the whole question of the place – or non-place – of the outside that Blanchot had been articulating in relation to literature since the early 1950s; and indeed, in a text entitled 'Tracts, affiches, bulletin' ('Handbills, Posters, Bulletin'), which appeared unsigned in *Comité* in October 1968, Blanchot was suggesting that one of the most distinctive and far-reaching manifestations of May were the many different, evanescent modes of writing – named in Blanchot's title – to which the movement gave rise and that, like so many nomadic, anonymous inscriptions or graffiti, belonged to the infinite exteriority of a time that was the time of the absence of time and a place that was the place of the absence of place. Of such texts, Blanchot wrote:

> They do not say everything, but on the contrary ruin everything, are outside everything [hors de tout]. They act, reflect in fragmentary fashion. They leave no traces behind: traits without trace [Ils ne laissent pas de traces: trait sans trace]. Like the words on the walls, they are written in insecurity, received under threat, are themselves the bearers of danger, then pass with the passer-by who passes them on, loses or forgets them.[9]

Blanchot's particular involvement in the événements, as mentioned earlier, was largely as a member of the Comité d'action étudiants-écrivains (the Students-Writers Action Committee). As a mode of revolutionary organisation – or, rather, non-organisation – the action committee was a distinctive, intensely anti-authoritarian form of political activity and one that, in the course of the événements, quickly emerged as the key embodiment of the movement of May itself. Such committees all functioned on an ad hoc basis; they fulfilled no expressive or representative function; the purpose was not the pursuit of power, but the contestation of all power in whatever form, and this explains why, as Blanchot put it in 'Tracts, affiches, bulletin', as far as the action committees were concerned, all notions of success or failure were at best irrelevant, at worst pernicious. Meetings as a result would last as long as they lasted, and committees would exist beyond themselves only as what they were in themselves, during which time, so to speak, the revolution itself became like an immediate, if evanescent, presence (without present). 'This is why', Blanchot wrote to Mascolo on the subject of such committees in December 1968, 'they are nothing outside of the presence constituted by each meeting, a presence that is their whole existence, and in which it goes without saying that the Revolution, by that very fact, is present: in much the same way as in seances when a Spirit shows itself'.[10] As Blanchot's letter went on to suggest, the limitations of the action committee as a mode of political activity were self-evident; but in themselves these were not important, for what such committees created, by their very existence, was potentially much more subversive than it seemed; for what they effected was a radical hiatus in the political order itself.

As far as the Students-Writers Action Committee was concerned, what went on in meetings was that texts were proposed, contested, withdrawn, and rewritten, until by collective decision they were finally either affirmed or annulled. The political activity of the committee was essentially, therefore, a

217

linguistic or textual one; and what it placed highest on the political agenda, therefore, as *Le Très-Haut* had predicted twenty years before, beyond all economism, reformism, or concern with party political organisation, was the need to suspend the dialectical closure of representational politics, alongside the essential complicity of government and legal opposition deriving from it, in order to affirm a different kind of politics, no longer dependent on the law of possibility, and, as *La Communauté inavouable* suggests, beyond the reliance on received political concepts such as those of project or subject.[11] This was why the anonymous production of texts, literary as well as non-, extra- and anti-literary, by doing away with such concepts, was such a crucial political touchstone. Making an obvious comparison at one stage, in *Comité*, between May 1968 in France and the Prague Spring, Blanchot suggested that what was at stake in both movements was far more vital than a call for greater dialogue between government and governed:

> Something quite different is at issue: a movement beyond measure, irrepressible, incessant, the impetus of *outraged* speech [l'élan d'une parole d'*outrage*], speaking always beyond, transcending, overwhelming and thereby threatening all that confines and limits [parlant toujours au-delà, dépassant, débordant et ainsi menaçant tout ce qui borde et tout ce qui limite]; the transgressive act of speech itself.[12]

In the demand for greater freedom and plurality in speech, the community Blanchot sought to address and call into existence was a community beyond nationalism or patriotism, even beyond culture itself. It was a community that, being essentially beyond community, and in relation to itself always already under erasure, coincided only with a demand for community that was a demand for exteriority, and that demand put it beyond the self-presence or self-identity of any existing community whatever. This demand for alterity was what in 1968 Blanchot named as: communism, and which he went on to define – while refusing to define it – in *Comité*, in a celebrated text entitled 'Le Communisme sans héritage', as 'that which excludes (and excludes itself from) all already constituted community'.[13] Yet despite the radicality of this refusal of the past, Blanchot in May cannot be termed an anarchist. For while Blanchot insisted on the necessity for speech or writing to challenge all laws, he did so in the name of a rupture or break that, far from being a refusal of all constraint, is in the form of an absolute submission to the law of infinite contestation, which is also the law of infinite commitment to alterity. Such a law was necessarily opposed to the

218

established political and moral order, and to this extent May embodied for Blanchot a moment of necessary political violence. That violence, however, he wrote, was infinite; like the law it obeyed, it was both calm and terrible. The most violent moment of May, he suggests, was in this respect more a moment of extreme non-violence, and occurred when demonstrators – workers, students, and revolutionaries alike – responded to the deportation of Daniel Cohn-Bendit and to anti-semitic jibes by government ministers against him by launching the famous slogan: 'Nous sommes tous des juifs allemands' ('We are all German Jews'). This repudiation of anti-semitism, writes Blanchot, was an exemplary moment in the entire unfolding of May: 'Never', he claims, 'had this previously been said anywhere, never at any time: it was an inaugural moment of speech, opening and overturning borders, opening, overthrowing the future [ouvrant et renversant les frontières, ouvrant, bouleversant l'avenir]'.[14]

In another text from *Comité*, entitled 'Rupture du temps : révolution', Blanchot suggested, after Walter Benjamin, that the interruption of history effected by a revolution such as May necessarily ushered in a moment of innocence.[15] Such innocence, however, proved to be short-lived. For it was precisely such innocence, together with the redemption from history it blindly assumed to be already at hand, that, according to Blanchot, was the cause of the decision of those groups on the extreme left which had emerged from May, in the name of anti-imperialism and anti-Zionism, to formulate their explicit opposition to the existence of the State of Israel. Fearing this to be anti-semitism under another name, Blanchot withdrew at this point from all active involvement in the aftermath of May. This turning aside from politics obviously raises numerous issues. But perhaps most importantly of all it poses the question of the relationship between the interruption of history and of political discourse embodied in May and the question of ethics. Did transgression of the established order also suspend ethics, or, in the suspense of history, did the claim of the ethical become more compelling still? Was the end of the political also the end of ethics or, more radically perhaps, the possibility of its very beginning? And did the step beyond history take for granted the possibility of beginning anew, or was it not rather a sign of the impossibility of beginning, and of the return of all that history had hitherto excluded and sought to forget and still needed to be confronted again?

Such were the questions that the outcome of May bequeathed to Blanchot; and it is not difficult, reading Blanchot's texts of the 1970s and 1980s, to see how these political issues, though they may have rarely been named as such,

219

remained at the heart of all his writing as the fundamental interrogation with which those late texts are concerned. That this is so is shown by Blanchot's explicitly political actions of the period; for the aftermath of May left him, like many others in France at the time, writers of fiction and philosophers alike, returning obsessively, and far more explicitly than ever before, to the question that was to dominate all of Blanchot's thinking for the next twenty-five years, and which is the question of responsibility for the Nazi death camps. If anti-semitism, as Blanchot wrote to Levinas in 1969, was the limit he was not prepared to cross, what this suggested to him was that anti-semitism, to the extent it constituted what one might call the limit of the political as such, was the moment when political power, founded as it was on the self-identity of the national community and on the exclusion of all nomadic alterity, showed itself in its true identity. This is what confers on the name Auschwitz its potency as an emblematic event for Blanchot, albeit an emblematic event that is the result of a specific history, and an event to which grave disservice is done once it becomes merely a symbol, albeit a symbol only of itself. But despite the difficulty of naming Auschwitz, the question remains: for if Auschwitz represents the unthinkable, extreme point of the political in the West in the modern age, how is it possible to think politics after Auschwitz, and think a politics which follows that injunction of Adorno's which requires of us that we act in such a way that Auschwitz does not repeat itself?

Responding to Auschwitz, Blanchot writes, can only mean responding to the double bind – the aporia and impossibility – contained in two mutually exclusive injunctions: 'Know what happened, do not forget, and at the same time never will you know' (ED, 131; 82). Responding to Auschwitz is impossible, since Auschwitz outstrips all limits, of knowledge, understanding, experience, or empathy. But precisely because it is impossible to know, one must rejoin, so it is essential to remember, even if what is being remembered is the impossibility of remembering. To remember the impossibility of memory, though, is to acknowledge the limits of remembering and to respect the limitlessness of forgetting which alone makes memory possible. Auschwitz here becomes the name without name for an event with which no politics can ever be commensurate, and to which the only response, in the certain knowledge of its inadequacy, is one of infinite responsibility. The quest for a politics that would be adequate to the Holocaust can only be in the form of infinite memory and attention to alterity; and this has been what has motivated, since 1971, Blanchot's repeated commitment in his writing to the impossible necessity of bearing witness in the absence of all witness to the event of the camps, to the necessity for the survival of Israel, for human rights, for Salman Rushdie, against apartheid.

Like that of many other men and women of his generation, Blanchot's political thinking since 1971 is traversed by the sombre legacy of the camps; and to the extent that the memory of Auschwitz remains as a necessary burden to be confronted by each and every future political project, proposal, or venture, his own political legacy may seem to some readers pessimistic and despairing. On one level this may be true, and to pretend otherwise would be to ignore the fact that the political history of the twentieth century has largely been a tale of alienation, oppression, totalitarianism, and genocide committed in the name of this or that political code or dogma; but in remembering this, Blanchot enjoins us also not to forget that no invocation of the end is without also necessarily invoking the limitlessness of the end; and therefore the fact that the impossible demand of the Other leaves us always already without recourse is itself testimony to the infinite alterity of language itself.

5

Extreme contemporary

> No finality where finitude reigns.
> *La Communauté inavouable* (*CI*, 38; 20)

— You've left out rather a lot.

— But is it ever possible to avoid gaps and deficiencies in a work of this kind? I know some readers will think I've gone on about Blanchot for far too long as it is. Leaving things out is surely a condition of saying anything. You start out trying to speak of everything, then you find this can't be done, for reasons of fatigue, lack of time or space, ignorance, laziness, or plain stupidity; then you realise it's more serious than that, and that what's been left out is what makes it possible to say anything at all. The more you try to reach the end, the more the end becomes impossible to reach. I know this paradox has become dreadfully familiar. But like the one about the Cretan liar which Foucault recalls in his essay on Blanchot, it's rigorously inescapable. Blanchot shows how it ruins all attempts at closure or totalisation and implies that at the very outset of speech or writing there is an otherness at work, or, more accurately, not at work, beyond all thought of work, at the non-existent origin of work and non-work, which escapes the whole and is irreducible to it. In these circumstances, it is necessarily the case that there isn't a discourse which will frame Blanchot's texts and that all the discourses that attempt this turn out to be riddled with gaps. This is unavoidable. The only alternative is to say nothing, but, as Blanchot keeps reminding us, to say nothing is always already to have said something.

— I want to come to your fondness for pastiche in a moment. In the

222

meantime, I was hoping you might say something about the title. Isn't it another quotation?

– Yes, it's another quotation. Let me own up to an absurd hypothesis. What I had in mind was this. Take all the major French philosophers or literary critics that have become associated in Britain or America with the preposterous term of post-structuralism, thinkers like Foucault, Derrida, Deleuze, Bataille, Klossowski, Levinas, Lacoue-Labarthe, Lyotard, Nancy, Barthes, Kristeva, others I've forgotten. Then draw up a list of the most important or influential writers in French over the last fifty years: Beckett, Duras, Perec, Laporte, Antelme, Des Forêts, Char, Paulhan, Leiris, Robbe-Grillet, Jabès, who else? Finally, make up a third list including all the key figures of our modernity: Sade, Kafka, Sartre, Musil, Heidegger, Nietzsche, Mallarmé, Broch, Ponge, Hegel, Woolf, Hölderlin, Rilke, Freud, Henry James, Breton, Marx, Artaud, Celan. You're allowed to add other names too if you wish. But if you then look at where these different lists connect up or intersect, you will find that they all do in the place – but can it be called a place? – occupied by the name of Blanchot. This tells us, I think, two things: that the name Blanchot is not a stable identity consistently present to itself, but more like a field of forces, an empty name that coincides with its own multiplicity and endless fragmentation; but also that, wherever you look across the vast network of texts that go to make up what might be described as contemporary thought or the thought of the present in general, what is most striking of all is this insistent reference to the text of Blanchot.

– I'd like to pause here. I appreciate what you're saying, but isn't it more important to challenge this kind of foolish totalisation? And shouldn't we be infinitely sceptical about this idea of contemporaneity? I'm sure we all remember those passages where Blanchot specifically throws into doubt the very concept of contemporaneity, invoking instead, alongside Levinas, the inescapable diachrony of the relation of non-relation I entertain with the Other. This surely disqualifies the notion that the present is somehow contemporary with itself. In any case, to think of yourself as your own contemporary would be to think of the future in metaphysical terms as a kind of deferred present. And, even then.

– Allow me to interrupt. I think it was Mallarmé who pointed out how uninformed one would have to be to believe oneself one's own contemporary. But isn't it possible that we can take extreme contemporary in a slightly different sense? One might say that the contemporary, to be contemporary at all, has also to be that which is beyond the contemporary, and which addresses

223

the present only to the extent that the present is understood, here and now, as that which is without presence and offers – Mallarmé again! – only a false appearance of the present. In that sense, the present would be more like the future, the future not as deferred presence but as the outside, that absolute alterity which is chance, which we cannot address precisely because it is what addresses us.

– In that sense, if I follow what you're proposing, extreme contemporary would be both what addresses us in the present most radically, and in that very gesture addresses us from some other place or time which does not belong to the contemporary, but creates a fissure or caesura in temporality itself. That would seem to imply that the extreme contemporary is neither extreme nor contemporary at all; but that the two words, being vacated by their own meaning, are given to the reader as a kind of infinite absence.

– Wouldn't that also suggest that to be contemporary would mean to have exhausted all the discourses it is possible today for a writer to employ, and thus to have reached a point of absolute unreadability? Is that why people find Blanchot so hard to read?

– Reading is never easy. But it's perhaps more that Blanchot's texts demand infinitely close attention. But there is another point here, too. I'm aware that to say anything of the change of epoch Blanchot promises is to pre-empt the future by reducing it to the horizon of the already known. But what future do you see for Blanchot's texts?

– The future of Blanchot's texts depends on the future within those texts, and in writing this book that future has really been my sole preoccupation. I certainly haven't wanted to imply there is only one possible way of reading Blanchot. There are obviously an infinite number and this particular book has only had space for one or two. In any case, the future is not down to me, but Blanchot's texts and their readers. Other than that, the future is surely incalculable.

– I wonder if you don't somehow still think it possible to say everything there is about Blanchot? Wouldn't that miss the point and turn reading Blanchot into a sterile academic exercise, whose fidelity to what is at stake in Blanchot's writing would be seriously in jeopardy?

– Blanchot shows that all commentary is necessarily unfaithful. It's one of the things that distinguish him from Heidegger. I'm sure we agree that each one of us has a duty to justice and that we're all obliged to avoid misrepresentation, distortion, and falsehood wherever possible. But one is also required, it seems, to respond to Blanchot's writing according to the singularity of one's own proper name, in the knowledge that any response will necessarily be inadequate. The other condition – in fact it's the only condition – is that one takes responsibility for what one has written by pursuing it to the limit, which is where the approach adopted breaks down of its own accord anyway.

– As here.

– Yes.

– My turn, then?

– Yes.

– Yes.

Notes

Chapter 1 An intellectual itinerary

Why Blanchot?

1 See Bataille's two reviews of Blanchot's *récits*, *Au moment voulu* and *Le Dernier Homme*, in: *Œuvres complètes*, 12 vols (Paris, Gallimard, 1970–88), XII (1988), 173–8 and 457–66; and Jacques Derrida, *Parages* (Paris, Galilée, 1986).

2 On the importance of literary journalism in France during the period 1930 to 1960, see Régis Debray, *Le Pouvoir intellectuel en France* (Paris, Ramsay, 1979).

3 I am drawing here on Derrida's (oral) contribution to Didier Cahen and Jean-Claude Loiseau, *Sur les traces de Maurice Blanchot*, broadcast by France-Culture, 17 September 1994.

4 Jacques Derrida, *Parages*, 55. In his turn, Blanchot has offered his own thanks to Derrida in: 'Grâce (soit rendue) à Jacques Derrida', *Revue philosophique*, 2, April–June 1990, 167–73 ('Thanks [Be Given] to Jacques Derrida', *BR*, 317–23).

5 See Pierre Madaule, *Une tâche sérieuse?* (Paris, Gallimard, 1973). Madaule's title is itself, of course, a reprise of the closing words of the now deleted final paragraph of Blanchot's *L'Arrêt de mort* (*Death Sentence*) of 1948.

An ethics of discretion

1 Maurice Blanchot, 'Les Intellectuels en question', *Le Débat*, 29, March 1984, 3–28 (17) (*BR*, 206–27 [217]).

2 Maurice Blanchot, 'Sur Edmond Jabès', *Les Nouveaux Cahiers*, 31, Winter 1972–73, 51–2. One of these fragments had in fact appeared even earlier in: 'Fragmentaires', *L'Ephémère*, 16, January 1971, 376–99 (388–9).

3 Paul Auster, in his English translation of this text, renders this first clause as: 'History does not withhold meaning'. Unfortunately, as the context will confirm, this is almost

exactly the opposite of what Blanchot originally wrote. Readers of Blanchot in English need sometimes to note: Caveat lector!

4 Maurice Blanchot, 'Les Intellectuels en question', *Le Débat*, 29, March 1984, 3–24 (*BR*, 206–27).

5 Maurice Blanchot, 'Les Intellectuels en question', 13 (*BR*, 213).

6 The phrase is used again by Blanchot as the title of the two following pieces: 'N'oubliez pas!', *La Quinzaine littéraire*, 459, 16–31 March 1986, 11–12; and ' "N'oubliez pas" ', *L'Arche*, May 1988, 68–71 (*BR*, 244–9). For a detailed assessment of Blanchot's references to Auschwitz during the 1970s and 1980s, see Michel Lisse, 'Écrire "après Auschwitz"? Maurice Blanchot et les camps de la mort', La Littérature des camps, Vincent Engel (ed.), *Les Lettres romanes*, special issue, 1995, 121–38.

A share of biography

1 Maurice Blanchot, 'Les Rencontres', *Le Nouvel Observateur*, 1045, special issue, November 1984, 84.

2 Maurice Blanchot, 'Pour l'amitié', in: Dionys Mascolo, *A la recherche d'un communisme de pensée, entêtements* (Paris, Éditions Fourbis), 1993, 5–16 (16). Among Blanchot's other memories of their encounter, see the letter reproduced in *Exercices de la patience*, 1, 1980, 67; 'Notre compagne clandestine', in *Textes pour Emmanuel Lévinas*, François Laruelle (ed.) (Paris, Jean-Michel Place, 1980), 79–87; and ' "N'oubliez pas" ', *L'Arche*, May 1988, 68–71 (*BR*, 244–9). Levinas, for his part, recalls their relationship in: François Poirié, *Emmanuel Lévinas : Qui êtes-vous?* (Lyon, La Manufacture, 1987), 70–1.

3 See Maurice Blanchot, 'Penser l'apocalypse', *Le Nouvel Observateur*, 22–8 January 1988, 77–9.

4 On Aminadab Levinas (whose name, in Hebrew, is said to signify 'my people is generous'), see Marie-Anne Lescourret's otherwise disappointingly unreliable biography of Levinas, *Emmanuel Levinas* (Paris, Flammarion, 1994); for an account of Blanchot's action on behalf of Levinas's family, see 121–2. More recently, Levinas's daughter, Simone, has added her own personal testimony regarding Blanchot's actions on her behalf and that of her mother and grandmother during the Occupation; see Simone Hansel, née Levinas, 'Pour Maurice Blanchot', *Le Monde*, 1–2 December 1996, 10.

5 See Michel Surya, *Georges Bataille, la mort à l'œuvre*, 2nd edn (Paris, Gallimard, 1992), 378–84; and Pierre Prévost, *Pierre Prévost rencontre Georges Bataille* (Paris, Jean-Michel Place, 1987), 86. Drawing up a curriculum vitae of his own in 1958, Bataille, referring to himself in the third person, wrote as follows: 'By the end of 1940, he meets Maurice Blanchot with whom in admiration and agreement he forms an immediate bond of friendship', *Œuvres complètes*, VII (1976), 462.

6 This is the view proposed by Pierre Klossowski in a fragmentary memoir of his own entitled: 'De "Contre-Attaque" à "Acéphale" ', *Change*, 7, July 1970, 103–7 (107).

7 Beyond the unpredictability of what was necessarily a chance event, the name and text of Nietzsche provide perhaps a clue to the reason for the immediate friendship between

Blanchot and Bataille. Although Blanchot is unlikely to have been aware of it at the time, in January 1937 Bataille brought out an issue of *Acéphale* devoted to the theme: 'Nietzsche et les fascistes'. In the first of his contributions to the issue (now reproduced in his *Œuvres complètes*, I (1970), 447–65), Bataille cites a press cutting, taken from the front page of the daily paper *Le Temps* for Saturday, 4 November 1933, which recounts the gift to Hitler by Elisabeth Foerster-Nietzsche of a sword-stick having previously belonged to her brother (448). Bataille adds a reference to a photograph showing Hitler in Weimar standing alongside Nietzsche's bust, a photograph which was used by Nietzsche's cousin Richard Oehler as the frontispiece for his 1935 book *Friedrich Nietzsche und die deutsche Zukunft*, a book in which Oehler attempted to portray the author of *Mein Kampf* as Nietzsche's direct philosophical heir. Bataille's point, in 1937, was to underline the unscrupulous 'treachery' of Nietzsche's immediate family and their willingness to falsify Nietzsche's work for their own crude anti-semitic and fascist ends. Thirty-two years later, in 1969, in a long footnote to his essay, 'Nietzsche, aujourd'hui' (*EI*, 204–5; 449), wishing to make a similar point about the Nazi appropriation of Nietzsche, though without mentioning the name of Bataille, Blanchot included a reference to the same photograph and the same book by Oehler, and even went as far as to cite the self-same press cutting from 4 November 1933. Oddly enough, while Bataille reproduces the cutting from *Le Temps* accurately, Blanchot modifies the text slightly, though without altering its sense in any way. Nevertheless, it is somehow as though what is being recalled here, despite or even because of these minor stylistic changes, discreetly and obliquely, in belated homage to his late friend, is an encounter between Blanchot and Bataille around the name of Nietzsche, and around the affirmation of the irreducibility of Nietzsche's texts to fascism. (Throughout the period of their first meeting, Bataille was still actively reading Nietzsche, and from February to August 1944 was busy working at his *Sur Nietzsche*, which appeared the following year; see *Œuvres complètes*, VI (1973).)

8 On the dating of Blanchot's various manuscripts during that period, see the letter from Blanchot to Bataille, dated 13 January [1948], BN, Mss, N. a. fr. 15853/295. The sluggishness of Gaston Gallimard in publishing some of these texts – as was notably the case with *Le Très-Haut* – seems to have given Blanchot some grounds for complaint; as a result, his contractual obligations to Gallimard were the source of some friction at the time (and at one point, for instance, Blanchot even explored the possibility of having the Editions de Minuit, which had recently taken over responsibility for publishing *Critique*, buy back the rights for his books from Gallimard).

9 The text was reissued in 1973 under the now more familiar title of *La Folie du jour*. On the problematic character of the title, see Derrida, *Parages*, 131–5.

10 See the letter from Blanchot to Bataille, undated, BN, Mss, N. a. fr. 15835/252. Something of this tension is apparent in the fact that when the second part of Blanchot's essay 'Rilke et l'exigence de la mort' ('Rilke and Death's Demand') appeared in *Critique* for May 1953, the editors felt obliged to append a postscript offering the reader some account of the volume purported to be under review! The article was to be Blanchot's last regular contribution to the journal.

11 For the quotation from Mallarmé, see Stéphane Mallarmé, *Œuvres complètes*, Henri Mondor and G.Jean-Aubry (eds) (Paris, Gallimard, 1945), 645–6.

12 'Un itinéraire politique', interview with Dionys Mascolo by Aliette Armel, *Le Magazine littéraire*, 278, June 1990, 36–40 (40). The three issues of *Le 14 Juillet* are now available in a facsimile reprint as: *Le 14 Juillet* (Paris, Séguier-Lignes, 1990).

13 On the campaign of intellectuals against the war, see Hervé Hamon and Patrick Rotman, *Les Porteurs de valise : la résistance française à la guerre d'Algérie* (Paris, Seuil, revised edn, 1982), where the text of the Manifesto is reproduced (393–6). Attempts at wider dissemination of the document led to Blanchot's only ever recorded interview, with Madeleine Chapsal, for *L'Express*, which, however, refused to carry it; the text appeared some time later in: *Le Droit à l'insoumission : 'le dossier des 121'* (Paris, François Maspero: Cahiers libres, 14, 1961), 90–3 (*BR*, 196–9).

14 On the history and background of the project, see the collection of preparatory texts and editorial correspondence in: *Lignes*, 11, September 1990, 179–301. Only one issue of the 'revue internationale' in fact ever appeared, which it did in 1964 under the auspices of the Italian journal *Il Menabò*. As Blanchot commented in 1991: 'The failure of our project did not show it to be a utopian one. What does not succeed remains necessary. This is still my concern.' ('L'échec de notre projet n'a pas démontré que c'était une utopie. Ce qui ne réussit pas reste nécessaire. C'est toujours notre souci.') See Maurice Blanchot, 'Sur le nationalisme', *La Règle du jeu*, 3, January 1991, 221–2.

15 Robert Antelme, *L'Espèce humaine* (Paris, Gallimard, [1947] 1957). From 1939 to 1945 Antelme was also married to Marguerite Duras, who recounts her experience of Antelme's deportation in *La Douleur* (Paris, POL, 1985), translated by Barbara Bray as *La Douleur* (London, Collins, 1986). Dionys Mascolo, a close friend of both Antelme and Duras at the time, records his own version of those events in his homage to Antelme, *Autour d'un effort de mémoire : sur une lettre de Robert Antelme* (Paris, Maurice Nadeau, 1986). Antelme left an indelible impression on all who knew him; see for instance the description by Claude Roy in: *Nous* (Paris, Gallimard, 1972), 102–9, and the obituary of Antelme written by Edgar Morin in *Le Monde*, 2 November 1990. Blanchot himself writes further of Antelme in a brief contribution to the special issue of *Lignes*, 21, January 1994, devoted to Antelme's memory, now republished, with additional material, as Robert Antelme, *Textes inédits, sur 'L'Espèce humaines', essais et témoignages* (Paris, Gallimard, 1996).

16 On Blanchot's experience of May 1968, see his remarks in *La Communauté inavouable* (*CI*, 52–6; 29–33) and in *Michel Foucault tel que je l'imagine* (*MF*, 9–10; 63–4). Of the thirty or so original texts included in this first (and only) issue of *Comité*, Dionys Mascolo attributes as many as eighteen to Blanchot (personal communication, 18 April 1994). Of these only one, entitled 'Lire Marx', has ever been claimed explicitly by Blanchot and is reproduced as 'Les Trois Paroles de Marx' in: *L'Amitié* (*A*, 115–17); two more were attributed to Blanchot by *Gramma* in 1976; and in 1984 Mascolo reproduced a selection of material from the issue under the title: 'Mots de désordre', *Libération*, ·28–9 January 1984, 23, now available in a translation by Michael Holland in *The Blanchot Reader* (*BR*, 200–5).

17 Blanchot's letter is cited by Levinas in: *Du sacré au saint* (Paris, Minuit, 1977), 48–9. Blanchot makes a similar point about the extreme left's commitment to the Palestinian cause in: 'N'oubliez pas!', *La Quinzaine littéraire*, 459, 16–31 March 1986, 11–12. On Blanchot's continuing support for Israel (and for Shimon Peres rather than Menachem Begin), see 'Ce qui m'est le plus proche . . .', *Globe*, 30, July–August 1988, 56.

Pas de récit?

1 See the bibliography by Peter Hoy and Michael Holland in *Gramma*, 3–4 (1976), 224–45, and 5 (1976), 125–32. For an influential (though not always reliable) account of Blanchot's involvement with the Jeune Droite in the 1930s, see Jean-Louis Loubet del Bayle, *Les Non-conformistes des années 30, une tentative de renouvellement de la pensée politique française* (Paris, Seuil, 1969).

2 See for instance his response to Jeffrey Mehlman, reproduced in Mehlman's essay, 'Blanchot at *Combat*: Of Literature and Terror', *Modern Language Notes*, 95, 1980, 808–29 (819); to Diane Rubenstein, reproduced in her *What's Left: the Ecole Normale Supérieure and the Right* (Madison, University of Wisconsin Press, 1990), 187; and to Roger Laporte, in *Blanchot: the Demand of Writing*, Carolyn Bailey Gill (ed.) (London, Routledge, 1996), 209–11.

3 For the charge of historical evasiveness, see Jeffrey Mehlman, *Genealogies of the Text: Literature, Psychoanalysis, and Politics in Modern France* (Cambridge, Cambridge University Press, 1995), 194; and, more generally, Steven Ungar, *Scandal and Aftereffect: Blanchot and France since 1930* (Minneapolis and London, University of Minnesota Press, 1995). For a vigorously argued counterview, based on a reading of Blanchot's *L'Instant de ma mort*, see Jacques Derrida, 'Demeure : fiction et témoignage', in *Passions de la littérature: avec Jacques Derrida*, Michael Lisse (ed.) (Paris, Galilée, 1996). Often, while claiming to react against an excessive mythologisation of Blanchot as literary recluse and arch-proponent of the self-deconstructing, minimalist modern text, critics such as Mehlman or Ungar have in fact done litttle more than propose an alternative mythology, which privileges above all else one part of Blanchot's early journalism and, detaching it from its proper philosophical or historical context, construes the writer's subsequent intellectual itinerary solely in terms of the supposed psychological or moral legacy of these early political involvements. The historical and other distortions produced by this strangely reductive approach are many, and are perhaps best illustrated, in the wake of Mehlman and Ungar, by the unconvincing and at times almost wilfully extravagant attempt at remythologising Blanchot's intellectual and political career provided by Philippe Mesnard in his *Maurice Blanchot: Le Sujet de l'engagement* (Paris, L'Harmattan, 1996).

4 One of the most striking examples of Blanchot's determination to draw a discreet veil over the detail of his political past is the reference, in *La Communauté inavouable*, while discussing Bataille's pre-war involvement in groups such as Contre-Attaque and Acéphale, to what Blanchot calls 'our history' ('notre histoire', *CI*, 14; 5), meaning by that the parallel lives followed during the 1930s by Bataille and himself, even though

the pair only in fact met in 1940. In so doing, Blanchot boldly side-steps the explicit record of his own pre-war nationalist political affiliations, which were very different from those of Bataille; indeed, despite some surface similarities with those of Blanchot, Bataille's political activities during the 1930s all expressed his implacable opposition to nationalism; see, for instance, the texts for 'Contre-Attaque' written by Bataille in 1935 and 1936, in: Œuvres complètes, I (1970), 379–428.

5 Letter from Maurice Blanchot to Roger Laporte, 9 December 1984, in: *Blanchot: the Demand of Writing*, Carolyn Bailey Gill (ed.), 9.

The acts of the day (1)

1 By the end of the decade, in 1939, circulation of the *Journal des débats* had fallen to a modest 25,000 copies. This compares, in the same year, with 1,800,000 for the popular Paris evening paper, *Paris-Soir*, and 320,000 for *L'Humanité*, the Communist Party daily; *Le Temps*, one of the main rivals to the *Journal des débats*, was by then selling 90,000 copies; these sales figures and those of the other newspapers of the time are provided in: Raymond Manévy, *La Presse de la IIIᵉ République* (Paris, Joseph Foret, 1955), 243–4.

2 Georges Bataille, Œuvres complètes, V (1973), 256.

3 'Ses discours étaient toujours des triomphes et ses actes des échecs', wrote Blanchot in the piece, which is entitled simply 'M. Briand', *Journal des débats*, 9 March 1932, 1. The article is attributed to Blanchot by Levinas (who slightly misquotes the phrase); see Marie-Anne Lescourret, *Emmanuel Levinas*, 112.

4 For the review of Malaparte, see Blanchot, 'Comment s'emparer du pouvoir?', *Journal des débats*, 18 August 1931.

5 On the Jeune Droite and the various journals and other groups it spawned, see Jean-Louis Loubet del Bayle, *Les Non-conformistes des années 30*.

6 See Maurice Blanchot, 'Les Années tournantes', *Journal des débats*, 21 March 1933, and 'Le Monde sans âme', *La Revue française*, 27ᵉ année, 3, 25 August 1932, 460–70.

7 See Maurice Blanchot, 'Le Marxisme contre la révolution', *La Revue française*, 28ᵉ année, 4, 25 April 1933, 506–17.

8 On the political career of Georges Mandel (born Louis Rothschild), see John M. Sherwood, *Georges Mandel and the Third Republic* (Stanford, Stanford University Press, 1970) and Bertrand Favreau, *Georges Mandel ou la passion de la République 1885–1944* (Paris, Fayard, 1996). Lévy himself had formerly worked with Mandel, some thirty years before, as theatre correspondent on the newspaper *L'Aurore*. After the war, Lévy assembled the copious evidence for his own consistently anti-German and anti-Nazi stance in a volume of collected journalism entitled *Au temps des grimaces* (Paris, Nagel, 1948).

9 See, respectively, 'La Démocratie et les relations franco–allemandes', *La Revue du XXᵉ siècle*, 4, February 1935, 56–9 (58); 'La Vraie Menace du Troisième Reich', *Le Rempart*, 69, 29 June 1933, 3; 'M. de Monzie, émule de Mussolini et de Hitler', *Le Rempart*, 32, 23 May 1933, 1–2; and 'Des violences antisémites à l'apothéose du travail', *Le Rempart*,

10, 1 May 1933, 3. The paper's prescient and consistent condemnation of Hitler is clear and unambiguous in every issue of *Le Rempart* I have been able to trace; indeed it was claimed later, by Paul Lévy, at the time of Munich, that the very purpose behind setting up the paper in 1933 was to alert French opinion to the Nazi threat (see Paul Lévy, 'Le Sedan diplomatique', *Aux écoutes*, 24 September 1938, 19). All the more puzzling therefore is Steven Ungar's claim in his *Scandal and Aftereffect* that Blanchot's articles manifest 'a certain degree of admiration' for Hitler (97). Ungar misreads as advocacy for Hitler the endeavour on Blanchot's part, as early as 1933, to understand the reasons for Hitler's successful rise to power. Though Blanchot at the time was unconvinced that the Western parliamentary democracies had the will or strength to dispose of the threat to peace that Hitler represented (and events were of course unfortunately to prove Blanchot right), there is not the slightest evidence that Blanchot ever expressed a desire to see Nazism emulated in France either in its German form or in any corresponding French incarnation; it is difficult to resist the conclusion that Ungar's analysis is both superficial and tendentious.

10 See Maurice Blanchot, 'La Révolution nécessaire', *Le Rempart*, 62, 22 June 1933, 2. Reading these words, it is important to give due weight to the date when they were written. Ideological and political debate in the 1930s rarely stood still; all too often, perhaps, commentators of these texts have failed to see them in their proper historical context.

11 Maurice Blanchot, 'M. de Monzie, émule de Mussolini et de Hitler', *Le Rempart*, 32, 23 May 1933, 1–2.

12 De Fabrègues, though much the older, was perhaps the less important of the two editors, and it is the name of Thierry Maulnier that, throughout the 1930s, most often recurs in relation to that of Blanchot. A prolific literary critic and political journalist, Maulnier was the author of books such as *La Crise est dans l'homme* (1932), *Nietzsche* (1933), *Racine* (1935), *Le Nationalisme au-delà du nationalisme* (1938), *Lecture de Phèdre* (1943), and many others. Originally viewed as the natural successor to Maurras at the head of *Action française*, Maulnier, to Maurras's dismay, adopted during the 1930s a more radical, anti-capitalist stance; during 1936–39, he was the driving force behind *Combat*, and in 1937 became one of the founder editors of *L'Insurgé*. During the early years of the Occupation, he wrote regularly for *Action française* and other nationalist papers. After the war, Maulnier reverted to a more traditional conservatism and was eventually elected to the Académie française in 1964. On Maulnier's career, see Paul Sérant, *Les Dissidents de l'Action française* (Paris, Éditions Copernic, 1978), 211–44, and, for an account of his political and literary writings, David Carroll, *French Literary Fascism: Nationalism, Anti-Semitism, and the Ideology of Culture* (Princeton, Princeton University Press, 1995), 222–47. For an authorised (Action Française) view of Maurras's disagreements with Maulnier in 1937, at the time of the launch of *L'Insurgé* (which took place while Maurras was in prison), see Henri Massis, *Maurras et notre temps*, 2 vols (Paris-Geneva, La Palatine, 1951), II, 88–91.

13 See, for instance, Zeev Sternhell, *Ni droite ni gauche: l'idéologie fasciste en France*, new edn (Brussels, Éditions Complexe, 1987), 263–85.

14 See Robert Brasillach, *Notre avant-guerre* (Paris, Plon, 1941), 185–6. There is little doubt that one of the contributors Brasillach had in mind here was Blanchot; indeed the antagonism between the two men was mutual. Nevertheless, during the first year of *Combat*'s existence, Blanchot and Brasillach often found themselves contributing to the same issues (between February and December 1936 this occurred on six separate occasions). Eccentrically enough, according to Claude Roy, Brasillach thought Maulnier at *Combat* to be 'too much of a Marxist' (see Claude Roy, *Moi je* (Paris, Gallimard: folio, 1969), 244–6). On the disagreements between *Combat* and *Je Suis Partout* (which Brasillach edited from 1937), which stemmed mainly from the latter's virulent anti-semitism and enthusiasm for Hitler, see Pierre-Marie Dioudonnat, *Je suis partout 1930–44, les maurrassiens devant la tentation fasciste* (Paris, La Table ronde, 1973), 190. It is worth noting that when *Thomas l'Obscur* appeared in 1941, it was reviewed in *Je suis partout* by an unnamed critic (Lucien Rebatet?), whose verdict was brutally simple: here was a book, he wrote, 'as outdated as the Jewish art from which it takes its inspiration' ('aussi démodé que l'art juif dont il se réclame', *Je suis partout*, 18 October 1941, 8).

15 See Pierre-Marie Dioudonnat, *Je suis partout 1930–44, les maurrassiens devant la tentation fasciste*, 89.

16 Anti-semitism was not a consistent or even dominant feature of *L'Insurgé*; but in the work of several of its collaborators, including both writers and cartoonists, it was nevertheless quite explicit. Witness for instance the following remark which arises in the course of an attack on Blum's Jewishness: 'The invasion gets bigger day by day; one after the other the public services are jewified; in every ministry all you see are hook noses and frizzy hair' ('L'invasion va chaque jour en augmentant; tous les services publics l'un après l'autre sont enjuivés; dans tous les ministères, on ne rencontre que nez busqués et cheveux crépus'); see Robert Castille, ' "Nous sommes les fils du peuple de ce pays . . ." (Léon Blum)', *L'Insurgé*, 7, 24 February 1937.

A question of responsibility

1 See Tzvetan Todorov, *Critique de la critique* (Paris, Seuil, 1984), 73 (*Literature and its Theorists*, translated by Catherine Porter (London, Routledge and Kegan Paul, 1987), 61). In an equally expeditious move, Todorov extends his criticism to refer more widely to what he describes, bizarrely enough, as Blanchot's 'nihilism' (72); this appears to be directed at Blanchot's refusal to subordinate literature to what, with disarming naivety, Todorov calls 'truth and values'.

2 These are the texts whose genesis Blanchot describes in his letter to Roger Laporte of 9 December 1984 in the following terms:

It must be said that the émigré community which found in Paul Lévy a constant source of support constituted at the time almost my natural environment; the truth about the extreme danger represented by Hitler was plain to see there, but amidst other, fanciful rumours (that Hitler was seriously ill, or mad – and how could one avoid thinking that some kind of madness was behind his horrifying political projects: the Reichstag fire, *Kristallnacht*, or the annihilation of his close companions). Others, who were the most numerous, kept saying on the other hand: let's not exaggerate, it's essential to be careful, reserved, and to warn the Jews against themselves. This is how those texts came about for which I am reproached today, and rightly so. But it would be odious to displace on to others the responsibility which is mine alone. In addition, there was the distrust felt by assimilated French Jews towards Zionism. Levinas had taught me the importance and the meaning of the Diaspora, that unfortunate wandering which had as its counterpart the 'dissemination' of Jewish singularity, its exclusion from any form of nationalism as final truth, its participation in history in an entirely other manner. This is what caused me to say something – too much – about the 'new doctrine' of Israel.

('Il faut dire que l'émigration qui trouvait auprès de Paul Lévy un appui constant, constituait alors presque mon milieu naturel; la vérité sur l'extrême danger que représentait Hitler se faisait jour là clairement, mais parmi aussi des rumeurs fantaisistes (que Hitler était gravement malade, qu'il était fou – et comment ne pas assimiler à une sorte de folie ses desseins politiques horrifiants : l'incendie du Reichstag, la Nuit de Cristal, l'annihilation de ses proches compagnons). D'autres, les plus nombreux, disaient au contraire : n'exagérons rien, il faut être prudent, réservé, mettre en garde les Juifs contre eux-mêmes. C'est de là que sont venus les textes que, avec raison, on me reproche. Mais il serait odieux de rejeter sur d'autres une responsabilité qui est la mienne. A cela s'ajoutait la méfiance des Juifs français assimilés à l'égard du sionisme. Levinas m'avait appris l'importance et la signification de la Diaspora, l'errance malheureuse qui avait comme contrepartie la 'dissémination' de la singularité juive, son exclusion de tout nationalisme comme vérité dernière, sa participation à l'histoire sous une forme tout à fait autre. C'est pourquoi j'ai été amené à dire un mot (un mot de trop) sur la 'doctrine nouvelle' d'Israël'.)

See my 'Introduction', in *Blanchot: the Demand of Writing*, Carolyn Bailey Gill (ed.), 9–10. It is perhaps also worth adding at this stage that to write at all in *Combat* was to submit, willy-nilly, to certain constraints, and it is not out of the question, as Blanchot has been known to reveal on at least one occasion, that his texts in the paper were also the subject to editorial interference from those in control of its political line.

3 Maurice Blanchot, 'Blum, notre chance de salut . . .', *L'Insurgé*, 3, 27 January 1937, 4.

4 See Diane Rubenstein, *What's Left: the Ecole Normale Supérieure and the Right*, 187. It is impossible to say of course what form this assurance took; evidently, if Blanchot's condition was ever enforced, this did not happen until at least fifteen months after *Combat* began publishing, in March 1937, the date of Brasillach's last contribution to the magazine; interestingly, after Brasillach's own last piece in *Combat*, Blanchot himself was to contribute only two more articles of his own.

5 See Charles Deleuze, 'La Santé de nos enfants est en de bonnes mains . . .',*L'Insurgé*, 42, 27 October 1937, 5. Some months earlier, in an article published alongside a piece by Blanchot on the coronation of George VI, Deleuze had launched a bitter attack on the two teams playing in the French Cup Final for fielding between them eleven players who were not 'of pure French origin', a fact that, for the journalist, was proof that French football too had fallen victim to what he called 'a gang of Jews and wogs' ('une bande de juifs et de métèques'); see Charles Deleuze, ' . . . et les métèques l'envahissent', *L'Insurgé*, 19, 19 May 1937, 4.

6 *Aux écoutes* was founded by Lévy in 1922; but apart from his own regular column, the vast majority of articles in the magazine were left unsigned. It therefore cannot be said with any certainty when Blanchot became its *rédacteur en chef*; internal evidence suggests, however, he was playing a full part in the paper by June 1937 at the latest. In subsequent years, Blanchot's association with Lévy was to be one of the reasons for the violent hostility of the anti-semitic, collaborationist press towards Blanchot. This is explicit in the review of *Thomas l'Obscur* in *Je suis partout* mentioned earlier; and also, for instance, in a brief item reacting to the (unfounded) rumour that Blanchot was about to take over the *Nouvelle Revue française* from Drieu, under the title 'Videz Thomas', that appeared in *L'Appel*, 28 May 1942, 4.

7 See for example Maurice Blanchot, 'Le Caravansérail', *Combat*, 10, December 1936. One of the readers of Blanchot most troubled by what he sees as the writer's 'doctrine of violence' in these early texts is Michael Holland; see his 'A Wound to Thought', in *Blanchot: the Demand of Writing*, Carolyn Bailey Gill (ed.), 174–89. That Blanchot was aware of the explicit and violent language used by some contributors to *L'Insurgé*, and also prepared to go to some lengths to endorse that violence, is plain from the various court cases in which, as one of the founding editors of the paper, he became involved. The most notorious of these occurred in reaction to a vitriolic attack made in the paper on Léon Blum on grounds of his alleged responsibility for the deaths of two right-wing political activists, the one a member of the fascist Parti Populaire Français (PPF) and the other a member of the rival Parti Social Français (PSF). The offending article, 'Communistes assassins', signed 'L'Insurgé' and published in *L'Insurgé*, 8, 3 March 1937, led to the paper's seizure by the authorities and to a charge of provocation to murder and incitement to violence against Guy Richelet, the managing editor of the paper who, under French law, was legally responsible for it. In a letter of 4 March 1937, printed the following week, the five other founding editors (Thierry Maulnier, Jean-Pierre Maxence, Ralph Soupault, Kléber Haedens, and Maurice Blanchot) wrote to the examining magistrate in the case to claim collective responsibility for the article, a ploy that led to considerable procedural delays, and in due course, when the paper reiterated its attack on Blum, to further charges. The tactic was employed again by *L'Insurgé* later in the year. (It was of course also used twenty-three years later, in 1960, by the various co-signatories to the 'Manifeste des 121', who similarly claimed, before the examining magistrate, that they were each responsible for drafting the declaration.)

8 Maurice Blanchot, 'On demande des dissidents', *Combat*, 20, December 1937, [155].

9 Zeev Sternhell, *Ni droite ni gauche*, 257; and Jeffrey Mehlman, *Genealogies of the Text*, 87–8.

10 Maurice Blanchot, 'Le Marxisme contre la révolution', *La Revue française*, 28e année, 4, 25 April 1933, 506–17 (516).

11 See Jacques Derrida, *Force de loi* (Paris, Galilée, 1994).

12 This is clear for instance from the various articles published in *Le Rempart* throughout May 1933, recommending a taxpayers' strike as a means of protesting against what Blanchot saw as the financial incompetence of the government of the day.

The acts of the day (2)

1 See Thierry Maulnier, 'Il ne fallait pas faire cette guerre', *Combat*, 28, October 1938, [3–4], and 'Les Nouvelles Conditions imposées à l'action politique en France', *Combat*, 29, November 1938, [3–4]. Writing some months earlier, Louis Salleron, another regular contributor, had struck a more strident isolationist note in an article entitled 'La France doit-elle se battre pour la Tchécoslovaquie?', in *Combat*, 27, July 1938, [8–9], which concluded thus: 'Let us not carry at arm's length this stupid Europe that hates us. Let us go back into our own back yard and barricade ourselves inside it. It's at home we need to do some cleaning up. Not anywhere else.'

2 *Aux écoutes*, 24 September 1938, 19 and 9. Churchill's phrase is reported also in Hugh Dalton, *The Fateful Years* (London, Frederick Muller, 1957), 198.

3 On the paper's withdrawal to Clermont-Ferrand, see Jean-Noël Jeanneney, *François de Wendel en république : l'argent et le pouvoir 1914–1940*, 3 vols, thèse Université Paris X, 1976, II, 846–7 and III, 1374; according to a note in his diary, de Wendel met Nalèche for the last time in Vichy in May 1941, and attempted, in vain, to convince Nalèche 'how ignominious it is for the hired rag the *Journal des débats* has become to worship, every day, everything that, for ten years, it strove to destroy' (II, 847).

4 On Lévy's activities during the Occupation, see his *Journal d'un exilé* (Paris, Grasset, 1949), which recounts, in particular, how in November 1940 Lévy was warned by Blanchot's sister of his imminent arrest and was thus able to make good his escape (29–30).

5 *Aux écoutes*, 15 June–13 July 1940, 10.

6 For Blanchot's own account of his involvement in Jeune France, and in the negotiations with Paulhan and Drieu, see Maurice Blanchot, 'Pour l'amitié', in Dionys Mascolo, *A la recherche d'un communisme de pensée, entêtements* (Paris, Éditions fourbis, 1993), 5–16. The association Jeune France was set up at the end of 1940, with the financial support of the Vichy government, in order to promote various cultural initiatives across the country. As its president, Pierre Schaeffer, recounts in his autobiography, *Les Antennes de Jéricho* (Paris, Stock, 1978), the association was largely split between those who, in a populist, humanistic perspective, were in favour of providing leisure activities for the community at large, and those who, like Blanchot, insisted on the prime importance of creative autonomy and artistic integrity (276–7). Blanchot and those of his friends who shared this view soon left the organisation, which, in any case, was itself dissolved by

March 1942 as a result of its unpopularity with the Vichy government. In these early years of the Occupation there was obviously some debate among opposition intellectuals in Paris as to whether it was better to be active politically in some way and run the risk of being compromised, or preferable to stand aloof and demonstrate total rejection of the situation; some echo of the debate may be found in an entry in Michel Leiris's recently published diary of the period: see, for instance, the entry for 16 February 1941 in his *Journal 1922–1989*, Jean Jamin (ed.) (Paris, Gallimard, 1992), 336–8. In 1941 Leiris was a proponent of the second of these courses of action, and had little patience with those friends – like Bataille and Blanchot – who initially favoured the opposite; though Leiris in later years was to be a signatory to the Déclaration of the 121, his annoyance at Blanchot's politics extended to the latter's actions during May 1968, which he found overblown and, as he puts it in his diary, 'ridiculous' (628).

7 Maurice Blanchot, 'Pour l'amitié', in Dionys Mascolo, *A la recherche d'un communisme de pensée, entêtements*, 6.

A temptation?

1 Maurice Blanchot, 'De la révolution à la littérature', *L'Insurgé*, 1, 13 January 1937, 3.

2 See Maurice Blanchot, 'Nietzsche, aujourd'hui', *La Nouvelle Revue française*, 68, August 1958, 284–95 (*EI*, 201–15; 136–43). As Michael Holland has pointed out, Blanchot's text underwent considerable revision before being republished in *L'Entretien infini*; see his paper, 'A Wound to Thought', *Blanchot: the Demand of Writing*, Carolyn Bailey Gill (ed.), 174–89. Holland also draws attention to the fact that, in a quite unusual gesture, Blanchot the following month added a postscript to the article 'Passage de la ligne' (*EI*, 215–27; 143–51), explicitly stating his opposition to de Gaulle (and to the support for de Gaulle shown by Paulhan).

3 In a note to her translation of Blanchot's essay in *The Infinite Conversation* (451), Susan Hanson unfortunately mis-identifies the text by Heidegger to which Blanchot is referring here: it is in fact *not* the notorious Rectorship Address of 27 May 1933, 'Die Selbstbehauptung der deutschen Universität', which Hanson cites, but the far more explicit address Heidegger gave in Leipzig, on the anniversary of the armistice, 11 November 1933, in which, using much of the same language as he had in his properly philosophical writings, he publicly committed himself to Hitler and to the National-Socialist state; see Guido Schneeberger, *Nachlese zu Heidegger* (Bern, Suhr, 1962), 148–50, and *The Heidegger Controversy: a Critical Reader*, Richard Wolin (ed.) (Cambridge, Mass., MIT Press, 1993), 49–52.

Chapter 2 The (im)possibility of literature

Founding fictions

1 This is not to say there are not a number of useful studies of these early novels available for consultation. See, in particular, Jean-Paul Sartre, '*Aminadab* ou du fantastique considéré comme un langage', in *Situations*, I (Paris, Gallimard, 1947), 148–73 (*Literary and Philosophical Essays*, translated by Annette Michelson (London, Hutchinson, 1955), 56–72); Jean Starobinski, '*Thomas l'obscur*: chapitre premier', *Critique*, 229, June 1966, 498–513; Michel Foucault, 'La Pensée du dehors', *Critique*, 229, June 1965, 523–46 ('The Thought from Outside', translated by Brian Massumi in *Foucault–Blanchot* (New York, Zone Books, 1987), 9–58); Daniel Wilhem, *Maurice Blanchot: la voix narrative* (Paris, Union générale d'éditions, 1974); and Ann Smock, ' "Où est la loi?": Law and Sovereignty in *Aminadab* and *Le Très-Haut*', *Sub-stance*, 14, 1976, 99–116. In this section, I refer primarily to the 1941 version of *Thomas l'Obscur*, using the abbreviation *TO1*; wherever possible, I have also indicated the corresponding passages in the far shorter 1950 text (*TO2*) on which Robert Lamberton's 1973 English translation is based. On the two versions of the novel, see Rainer Stillers, *Maurice Blanchot: Thomas l'Obscur: Erst- und Zweitfassung als Paradigmen des Gesamtwerks* (Frankfurt a. M., Peter Lang, 1979).

2 The paradox is one Blanchot himself formulates elsewhere. Witness for instance, in a review of *Le Voyeur* by Alain Robbe-Grillet, the reference to the peculiarly uniform light characterising events in that novel, which Blanchot describes as: 'a brightness that makes all clear, and since it reveals all, except for itself, is the most secret thing of all' (*LV*, 195; *SS*, 207).

3 Emmanuel Levinas, *De l'évasion* (Montpellier, Fata morgana, 1982), 87. In the essay, first published in 1935, Levinas gives himself the task of drawing out the philosophical consequences of what he describes as contemporary literature's radical condemnation of the philosophy of being (69–70). As Blanchot was to remark some forty years later, referring to the similarly abrupt invocation of shame that occurs at the end of Kafka's *Trial*, 'one might think the death scene represents forgiveness, the termination of the interminable; only there is no end, since Kafka makes it clear that shame survives, which is to say, infinity itself, the mockery of life as life's beyond' (*ED*, 89; 53).

4 On the compelling figure of the *other* night in Blanchot, see *L'Espace littéraire* (*EL*, 169–84; 163–76).

5 See Martin Heidegger, 'Vom Wesen des Grundes' (1929) in *Wegmarken, Gesamtausgabe*, vol. 9 (Frankfurt a. M., Klostermann, 1976), 123–75. As Heidegger explains in his 1949 preface to the paper, 'The Nothing is the Not of that which is and is thus Being experienced from the standpoint of that which is' ('Das Nichts ist das Nicht des Seienden und so das vom Seienden her erfahrene Sein') (123).

6 Maurice Blanchot, 'L'Ébauche d'un roman', *Aux écoutes*, 30 July 1938, 31 (*BR*, 33–4); the recently translated volume of texts by Heidegger to which Blanchot is referring was

Qu'est-ce que la métaphysique?, translated by Henry Corbin (Paris, Gallimard, 1938). In addition to the title essay, the volume also contained complete versions of 'Vom Wesen des Grundes' and Heidegger's 1936 Rome lecture, 'Hölderlin und das Wesen der Dichtung', as well as §§ 46–3 and 72–6 of *Sein und Zeit*, and §§ 42–5 of *Kant und das Problem der Metaphysik*. See Tom Rockmore, *Heidegger and French Philosophy: Humanism, antihumanism and being* (London, Routledge, 1995), 217.

7 For Levinas's own early thinking on the topic, see *De l'évasion*, 70; and *De l'existence à l'existant* (Paris, Vrin [1947] 1990), 83–105 (*Existence and Existents*, translated by Alphonso Lingis (Dordrecht, Kluwer, 1978), 52–64). Levinas refers explicitly to *Thomas l'Obscur* in the discussion (*De l'existence à l'existant*, 103; *Existence and Existents*, 63). On the relationship between *es gibt* and *il y a*, see Levinas' preface to the second edition of the book, *De l'existence à l'existant*, 10–13; Heidegger himself comments on the difference in the 'Brief über den Humanismus' (1946), *Wegmarken*, 334–7 (Martin Heidegger, *Basic Writings*, David Farrell Krell (ed.) (London, Routledge, 1993), 237–40).

8 Levinas, *De l'existence à l'existant*, 100; *Existence and Existents*, 61.

9 Paul de Man, *Allegories of Reading* (New Haven and London, Yale University Press, 1979), 205.

How is literature possible?

1 See Philippe Lacoue-Labarthe, *L'Imitation des modernes* (Paris, Galilée, 1986), 175–200; and *La Fiction du politique* (Paris, Bourgois, 1987) (*Heidegger, Art and Politics*, translated by Chris Turner (Oxford, Blackwell, 1990)). On 'national-aestheticism' among the ideologues of the pre-war nationalist right in general, see David Carroll, *French Literary Fascism: Nationalism, Anti-Semitism, and the Ideology of Culture* (Princeton, Princeton University Press, 1995).

2 Maurice Blanchot, 'De la révolution à la littérature', *L'Insurgé*, 1, 13 January 1937, 3.

3 See, for instance, Maurice Blanchot, 'Le Silence des écrivains', *Journal des débats*, 19 April 1941, 3 (*BR*, 25–8), and 'Recherche de la tradition', *Journal des débats*, 16–17 June 1941, 3 (*BR*, 29–32).

4 Charles Maurras, *Romantisme et révolution* (Paris, Nouvelle Librairie Nationale, 1922), 272; Robert Brasillach, 'A propos de Mallarmé', *Je suis partout*, 7 June 1940, 3; Pierre Drieu La Rochelle, *Notes pour comprendre le siècle* (Paris, Gallimard, 1941), 100. On the reception of Mallarmé by the extreme right in general, see David Carroll, *French Literary Fascism: Nationalism, Anti-Semitism, and the Ideology of Culture*.

5 See Albert Thibaudet, *La Poésie de Stéphane Mallarmé* (Paris, Gallimard, 1926), 454–68; and Thierry Maulnier, *Introduction à la poésie française* (Paris, Gallimard, 1939), 100–1.

6 See for instance Paul Valéry, 'Je disais quelquefois à Stéphane Mallarmé', *Œuvres*, 2 vols, Jean Hytier (ed.) (Paris, Gallimard, 1957), I, 644–60. In numerous later texts, Blanchot is significantly more critical of Valéry's intellectualism, and writes for instance in December 1942 that 'The mind of Mallarmé worked with absolute rigour towards the poem he wanted to produce. The mind of Valéry works with equal rigour towards

the work of which the poem is the effect'; see 'Les *Mauvaises Pensées* de Paul Valéry', *Journal des débats*, 16 December 1942, 3. I have examined Blanchot's reading of Mallarmé at greater length elsewhere; see my 'Blanchot and Mallarmé', *MLN*, 105, 5, December 1990, 889–913.

7 In Blanchot's literary criticism for the *Journal des débats*, there is surprisingly little explicit evidence of the writer's pre-war nationalism; this is probably explained by Blanchot's distaste at the possibility of being too closely associated by his readership with Vichy ideology. However, at critical moments, the question of French national literary tradition does arise and, with it, if only indirectly, the question of the current state of France. Often, as in a piece like 'Le Jeune Roman', *Journal des débats*, 14 May 1941, 3 (*FP*, 209–12), the literary analysis offers a transposed version of current political debate, with Blanchot, in this instance, upbraiding contemporary French novelists for their complacent and mistaken reliance on a dubious tradition of literary realism; elsewhere, Blanchot – with discreet provocation – elects as the embodiment of all that is most essential in the French literary tradition a lineage of writers running from Scève to Éluard via Mallarmé. See 'La France et la civilisation contemporaine', *Journal des débats*, 26–27 May 1941, 3.

8 See Jean Paulhan, *Les Fleurs de Tarbes, ou la terreur dans les lettres*, Jean-Claude Zylberstein (ed.) (Paris, Gallimard: idéés, [1941] 1973). Blanchot wrote three pieces in all in response to Paulhan's book: 'La Terreur dans les lettres', *Journal des débats*, 21 October 1941, 3; 'Comment la littérature est-elle possible?' (I), *Journal des débats*, 25 November 1941, 3; and 'Comment la littérature est-elle possible?' (II), *Journal des débats*, 2 December 1941, 3. All three articles were collected in 1942 in a slim volume entitled *Comment la littérature est-elle possible?* (*BR*, 49–60); the second two were reproduced again in *Faux Pas* (*FP*, 92–101). Blanchot returns to his reading of Paulhan in three other essays: 'Le Mystère dans les lettres' and 'Le Paradoxe d'Aytré' (*PF*, 49–78; 43–73), and 'La Facilité de mourir' (*A*, 172–91; *BR*, 301–16). For a succinct summary of the early debate between the two, see Michael Syrotinski, 'How Is Literature Possible?', *A New History of French Literature*, Denis Hollier (ed.) (Cambridge, Mass., Harvard University Press, 1989), 953–8.

9 Michael Syrotinski, 'How Is Literature Possible?', 955.

10 This circular conclusion is not present as such in the 1941 version of Paulhan's book, to which he planned to add a second volume; though this never in fact appeared, there is good evidence, based on the earlier, 1936 version of Paulhan's text (which Blanchot may have read when it was serialised in *La Nouvelle Revue française*), that this was the ending Paulhan originally intended. See *Les Fleurs de Tarbes*, 217–49.

11 On Hölderlin's theory of tragedy in this context, see Philippe Lacoue-Labarthe, 'La Césure du spéculatif', *L'Imitation des modernes*, 39–69 ('The Caesura of the Speculative', translated by Robert Eisenhauer, in Philippe Lacoue-Labarthe, *Typography: Mimesis, Philosophy, Politics* (Cambridge, Mass., Harvard University Press, 1989), 208–35). It falls to Blanchot, in a later essay on Paulhan, to make the important point that, whatever Paulhan's commitment to unity in *Les Fleurs de Tarbes* and elsewhere, his

account of paradox, inversion, and logical circularity was far removed from the duplicities of speculative dialectics (*A*, 175; *BR*, 303).

12 This is the view presented by Jeffrey Mehlman in his *Legacies of Anti-Semitism in France*, 13, and by Steven Ungar in *Scandal and Aftereffect*, 120–1. But while Mehlman reads Blanchot's essay on Paulhan as a 'coded farewell to plans for a French fascism', Ungar claims the very opposite, admittedly with slightly more justification, suggesting that in 1941 Blanchot was 'displacing the violence and radicality of political revolution onto the concept of literature itself'.

'Naming the gods': from Heidegger to Hölderlin

1 Corbin's preface justifying this term is reproduced in Martin Heidegger, *Questions I* (Paris, Gallimard, 1968), 13–20. Jacques Derrida comments on the philosophical consequences of this – now abandoned – translation of 'Dasein' in 'Les Fins de l'homme', *Marges de la philosophie* (Paris, Minuit, 1972), 135–9 ('The Ends of Man', *Margins of Philosophy*, translated by Alan Bass (Brighton, Harvester, 1982), 114–17).

2 Martin Heidegger, 'Hölderlin und das Wesen der Dichtung', in *Erläuterungen zu Hölderlins Dichtung, Gesamtausgabe*, vol. 4 (Frankfurt a. M., Klostermann, 1981), 33–48. All further references to Heidegger's texts on Hölderlin will be to this edition and given in the text, preceded by the abbreviation *E*; unless otherwise indicated, all translations from Heidegger's German are my own. (A version of Heidegger's 1936 lecture, translated by Douglas Scott, is available in English as 'Hölderlin and the Essence of Poetry', in *Existence and Being* (London, Vision Press, 1949), 293–315.)

3 See Friedrich Hölderlin, *Werke und Briefe*, Friedrich Beißner and Jochen Schmidt (eds), 3 vols (Frankfurt a. M., Insel Verlag, 1969), I, 163; and Friedrich Hölderlin, *Poems and Fragments*, translated by Michael Hamburger (London, Routledge and Kegan Paul, 1966), 428–9.

4 There are a number of other echoes, both implicit and explicit, of Heidegger elsewhere in Blanchot's critical essays of the time; an almost identical passage to the one cited here, for instance, appears in 'La Poésie de Mallarmé est-elle obscure?', *Journal des débats*, 24 February 1942, 3 (*FP*, 128–9); on that occasion, interestingly, Blanchot deleted his original reference to phenomenology ('les phénoménologues') when revising the paper for inclusion in *Faux Pas*; he similarly also removed Heidegger's name from the essay on Meister Eckhart first published in *Journal des débats* for 4 November 1942, 3 (*FP*, 31–6).

5 In a fascinating account of the relation between Blanchot, Heidegger and Levinas, Paul Davies reads the phrase *à peu près* (meaning 'more or less', but which Davies, like Charlotte Mandell in *The Work of Fire*, renders, somewhat inaccurately in the circumstances, as 'almost') as constituting the exact measure of the distance that separates and joins the thinking of Blanchot and Heidegger on the topic of poetry; see Paul Davies, 'A Linear Narrative? Blanchot with Heidegger in the Work of Levinas', in *Philosophers' Poets*, David Wood (ed.) (London, Routledge, 1990), 37–69 (59). In what follows, I want to suggest that in Blanchot's account of Heidegger there is clear

evidence of a more decisive break than is allowed by Davies's argument, a break which is not just poetological but philosophical and political, too.

6 On Heidegger's political involvement with Nazism, see Hugo Ott's now authoritative *Martin Heidegger: A Political Life*, translated by Allan Blunden (London, HarperCollins, 1993). Heidegger's first seminar course on Hölderlin (for 1934–5) appears in vol. 39 of the *Gesamtausgabe* (Frankfurt a. M., Klostermann, 1980); a number of elements from that course are incorporated into 'Hölderlin und das Wesen der Dichtung'.

7 Blanchot's rejection of Heidegger's Nazism is perhaps the most likely motive behind the unexpectedly disparaging reference to 'the dross produced by German philosophy, particularly that of Heidegger' ('les produits de rebut de la philosophie allemande, en particulier celle de Heidegger') that appears in Blanchot's review of Denis de Rougemont's *Penser avec les mains* in *L'Insurgé*, 3, 27 January 1937, 5. The remark is all the more curious in that nowhere in Rougemont's book is the name of Heidegger in fact ever mentioned! In later texts, Blanchot lingers at much greater length on the implications of Heidegger's politics; see, for instance, the long note in *L'Entretien infini* to which I have already referred (*EI*, 208–10; 449–51), and Blanchot's contributions to the so-called Heidegger affair of 1988: 'Penser l'apocalypse', *Le Nouvel Observateur*, 22–8 January 1988, 77–9; and ' "N'oubliez pas" ', *L'Arche*, May 1988, 68–71.

8 Geert Lernout, *The Poet as Thinker: Hölderlin in France* (Columbia, Camden House, 1994), 10.

9 Friedrich Hölderlin, *Werke und Briefe*, I, 135–7; *Poems and Fragments*, 372–7. Heidegger's paper, entitled: ' "Wie wenn am Feiertage..." ', is collected in: *Erläuterungen zu Hölderlins Dichtung*, 49–77; the piece was given as a lecture in 1939 and 1940 and first published in 1941. The secondary literature devoted to Heidegger's readings of Hölderlin is of course huge; for a discussion of some of the issues, see Beda Allemann, *Hölderlin und Heidegger* (Zurich and Freiburg i. Br, Atlantis Verlag, 1954); Paul de Man, *Blindness and Insight*, second edn (London, Routledge, 1983); Philippe Lacoue-Labarthe, *L'Imitation des modernes* and *La Fiction du politique*; Andrzej Warminski, *Readings in Interpretation: Hölderlin, Hegel, Heidegger* (Minneapolis, University of Minnesota Press, 1987); Véronique M. Fóti, *Heidegger and the Poets: Poésis/Sophia/Techné* (New Jersey and London, Humanities Press, 1992); Christopher Fynsk, *Heidegger: Thought and Historicity*, expanded Ithaca, NY (Ithhaca, NY, Cornell University Press, 1993); and Marc Froment-Meurice, *C'est à dire* (Paris, Galilée, 1996).

10 On the dating of the article, see Blanchot's letter to Bataille of 17 October [1946], BN, Mss, N. a. fr. 15853/232, in which Blanchot writes: 'At any event, I would be tempted by your proposal about Hölderlin, although I've not seen the *Fontaine* special issue, despite the fact that poetry is beginning to whisper discreetly in my ear that I'm wearing it out.' ('De toute manière, je serais tenté par votre proposition sur Hölderlin, bien que je n'aie pas vu l'ensemble de *Fontaine* et que la poésie commence à me dire discrètement, à l'oreille, que je la fatigue.') In a very different way, the years immediately following the end of the war were crucial ones for Heidegger as well. As Hugo Ott describes, Heidegger was able to achieve a degree of philosophical rehabilitation at the time only as a result of the interest shown in his work by the

French; indeed in the very month that Blanchot's essay appeared, Heidegger was finally relieved of his post at Freiburg and banned from all further university teaching. In France itself, the appearance of Blanchot's article also coincided with some vigorous discussion of Heidegger's politics, with the attempt being made, by some, to disengage Heidegger's thought from the political choices with which it was identified before 1945, a move that, perhaps surprisingly, found a willing audience on the intellectual left, notably in Sartre's *Les Temps modernes*. See Maurice de Gandillac, 'Entretien avec Martin Heidegger' and Alfred de Towarnicki, 'Visite à Martin Heidegger', *Les Temps modernes*, January 1946, 713–24; an informed rebuttal of these attempts to defend Heidegger against the charge of Nazism followed later the same year in the form of Karl Löwith's 'Les Implications politiques de la philosophie de l'existence chez Heidegger', *Les Temps modernes*, November 1946, 343–60 (the article is reproduced in *The Heidegger Controversy*, Richard Wolin (ed.), 167–85).

11 Herman Rapaport, *Heidegger and Derrida, Reflections on Time and Language* (Lincoln, University of Nebraska Press, 1989), 112. In fact, the motifs in Blanchot's essay that Rapaport claims to be the result of Blanchot's intuitive anticipation of later work by Heidegger are already to be found in Heidegger's two Hölderlin papers of 1936 and 1941.

12 Blanchot returns to the debate, albeit obliquely, on a number of later occasions; see, for instance, 'La Folie par excellence', *Critique*, 45, February 1951, 99–118 (*BR*, 110–28); 'L'Itinéraire de Hölderlin' (*EL*, 283–92; 269–76); 'Le Livre à venir' (*LV*, 271–97); and 'Le Grand Refus' (*EI*, 46–69; 33–48).

13 Friedrich Hölderlin, *Werke und Briefe*, I, 143; *Poems and Fragments*, 389.

14 The gesture is of course crucial to Heidegger's account of the work of art as such; compare for instance the remarks on the translation of Greek into Latin in the opening section of 'Der Ursprung des Kunstwerks', *Holzwege* (Frankfurt a. M., Klostermann, 1950), 7–8 ('The Origin of the Work of Art', *Basic Writings*, 149).

15 'The thinker speaks Being. The poet names the sacred' ('Der Denker sagt das Sein. Der Dichter nennt das Heilige'), Heidegger puts it; see Martin Heidegger, *Wegmarken*, *Gesamtausgabe*, 9 (Frankfurt a. M., Klostermann, 1976), 312.

16 Friedrich Hölderlin, *Werke und Briefe*, II, 671.

17 See Martin Heidegger, *Sein und Zeit* (Tübingen, Niemeyer, 1986), §§ 50–3, 249–67.

18 I am quoting here from the revised version of the essay given in *La Part du feu*; in the original 1946 text, instead of 'il se laisserait apaiser', Blanchot had written: 'il se *laisse* apaiser' (see 'La Parole "sacrée" de Hölderlin', *Critique*, 7, December 1946, 579–96 (592), emphasis mine). This shift from indicative to conditional, from the constative to the alleged, which is echoed elsewhere in the text, denotes an unmistakable hardening of Blanchot's critical stance towards Heidegger. Sad to say, like much else in the text, the nuance receives no acknowledgement from Blanchot's translator on this occasion, Charlotte Mandell.

19 Interestingly enough, Blanchot treats Heidegger's sentence in this way on each occasion he cites it, which he does at least twice more in his work. See 'La Folie par excellence', *Critique*, 45, February 1951, 106 (*BR*, 115–16); and 'Le Grand Refus' (*EI*, 51–2; 37).

In this last instance, Blanchot is evidently quoting from memory or from his own previous text.

20 Martin Heidegger, *Holzwege*, 48, *Basic Writings*, 186–7.

21 Blanchot, most likely quoting from his own earlier work, attributes the lines to Hölderlin for a second time in 'Énigme', *Yale French Studies*, 79, 1991, 5–7 (7).

22 Friedrich Hölderlin, *Werke und Briefe*, I, 148; Michael Hamburger translates the line somewhat differently as: 'A mystery are those of pure origin', *Poems and Fragments*, 411.

23 The gesture is the same as in 1959 when Blanchot, invited to contribute to a Festschrift for Heidegger, supplied a fragment of what was later to become *L'Attente L'Oubli*; see 'L'Attente', *Martin Heidegger zum siebzigsten Geburtstag* (Pfullingen, Verlag Günter Neske, 1959), 217–24 (*BR*, 272–8).

The limitlessness of the limit

1 For a later formulation of the structure of the limitless of the limit, see Maurice Blanchot, 'La Voix narrative (le "il", le neutre)' ('The Narrative Voice (the "he", the neutral)'), *EI*, 556–67; 379–87.

2 On the title(s) of Blanchot's *récit*, see Jacques Derrida, *Parages* (Paris, Galilée, 1986) ('Living On', translated by James Hulbert, in Harold Bloom *et al.*, *Deconstruction and Criticism* (London, Routledge and Kegan Paul, 1979), 75–176). Derrida reproduces the original cover, table of contents, and first page of the story in *Parages*, 132–4.

3 Jacques Derrida, *Parages*, 143; *Deconstruction and Criticism*, 97–8.

4 Philippe Lacoue-Labarthe, *L'Imitation des modernes*, 64–5; *Typography: Mimesis, Philosophy, Politics*, 231–2.

5 It is now known, of course, from the account given in *L'Instant de ma mort*, that the scene of confrontation with death that features in *La Folie du jour* had a particular autobiographical relevance for Blanchot. Interestingly, the same word – 'allégresse', joy or gaiety – is used in both texts to describe the experience (*FJ*, 12; 7; and *IM*, 10).

6 See Friedrich Hölderlin, 'Anmerkungen zum Oedipus', *Werke und Briefe*, II, 736 ('Remarks on *Oedipus*', *Essays and Letters on Theory*, translated by Thomas Pfau (Albany, NY, State University of New York Press, 1988), 108). Hölderlin describes the principle of this idea of return in a famous letter to Böhlendorff (4 December 1801) in *Werke und Briefe*, II, 940–2; *Essays and Letters on Theory*, 149–51. Blanchot's own commentary, which draws extensively on the work of Beda Allemann, appears in *L'Espace littéraire* (*EL*, 284–7; 270–2).

7 On the Hölderlinian 'caesura', see Philippe Lacoue-Labarthe, *L'Imitation des modernes*, 39–69, *Typography: Mimesis, Philosophy, Politics*, 208–35. As Hölderlin writes in explanation, in the 'Remarks on *Oedipus*', in a passage that is already almost a reading of *La Folie du jour*:

Indeed, tragic *transport* is properly empty, and it is the most unbound. As a result, in the rhythmic sequence of representations in which *transport* presents itself, there becomes necessary *what in prosody is called a caesura*, the pure word, the counter-rhythmic interruption [das reine Wort, die gegenrhythmische Unterbrechung], so as to meet the surging alternation of representations at their apogee, with the result that what then appears is not the alternation of representation, but representation itself [nicht mehr der Wechsel der Vorstellung, sondern die Vorstellung selber].

(*Werke und Briefe*, II, 730; *Essays and Letters on Theory*, 101–2, translation modified)

Chapter 3 Writing the neuter

From work to worklessness

1 In his opening speech in the first scene of the fragmentary third version of the play, Empedocles affirms: 'For death is what I seek. It is my right' ('Denn sterben will ja ich. Mein Recht ist dies'). See Friedrich Hölderlin, *Werke und Briefe*, II, 551; *Poems and Fragments*, 327.

2 See G. W. F. Hegel, *Werke*, Eva Moldenhauer and Karl Markus Michel (eds), 20 vols (Frankfurt a. M., Suhrkamp, 1970), III, 294–311; *Phenomenology of Spirit*, translated by A. V. Miller (Oxford, Clarendon Press, 1977), 237–52.

3 See Alexandre Kojève, *Introduction à la lecture de Hegel*, Raymond Queneau (ed.) (Paris, Gallimard, 1947). Kojève writes that 'Hegel's "dialectical" or anthropological philosophy is, in the last analysis, *a philosophy of death* (or what amounts to the same thing: of atheism)' (539). For a detailed account of Blanchot's use of Kojève, see Anne-Lise Schulte Nordholt, *Maurice Blanchot: l'écriture comme expérience du dehors* (Geneva, Droz, 1995), 31–57. Like several other commentators, however, Schulte Nordholt falls into the trap of attempting to systematise Blanchot's text. This leads to some distortion; despite claims to the contrary, for instance, Blanchot in 'La Littérature et le droit à la mort', does *not* hold to the view that language may be divided into two modes, functional and essential; indeed, no sooner is the dichotomy introduced than Blanchot demonstrates its profound chiasmic instability.

4 For Kojève's commentary on the 'spiritual animal kingdom', see Alexandre Kojève, *Introduction à la lecture de Hegel*, 90–4; Bataille's letter to Kojève, including further unpublished material is in Georges Bataille, *Œuvres complètes* V (1973), 369–71 and 562–5. Bataille refers explicitly to the concept of the Tierreich in a passage from the letter omitted from the published version (see 564).

5 Alexandre Kojève, *Introduction à la lecture de Hegel*, 91.

6 Alexandre Kojève, *Introduction à la lecture de Hegel*, 93–4.

7 Georges Bataille, *Œuvres complètes*, VI (1973), 416.

8 See Georges Bataille, *Œuvres complètes*, V, 289, 369–71, 562–3. Blanchot returns to the concept of 'négativité sans emploi' in a later essay on Bataille. See his 'L'Affirmation et la passion de la pensée négative' (*EI*, 300–13; 202–11).

9 Jean-Paul Sartre, *Qu'est-ce que la littérature?* (Paris, Gallimard: folio, 1948); *What is Literature?*, translated by Bernard Frechtman (London, Methuen, 1950). The essays

collected in the volume were first published in *Les Temps modernes* between February and July 1947.

10 Jean-Paul Sartre, *Qu'est-ce que la littérature?*, 27; *What is Literature?*, 12.

11 It was largely in these terms, of course, that Sartre had attacked Bataille in his 1943 review of *L'Expérience intérieure*. See Jean-Paul Sartre, 'Un nouveau mystique', *Situations*, I, 174–229.

12 See G. W. F. Hegel, *Werke*, III, 296–8; *Phenomenology of Spirit*, 239–40. The passage, to which Blanchot returns on a number of other occasions, is paraphrased towards the beginning of 'La Littérature et le droit à la mort' (*PF*, 295–7; 302–5).

13 See Rodolphe Gasché, 'The Felicities of Paradox. Blanchot on the Null-Space of Literature', in *Blanchot: the Demand of Writing*, 34–69. Blanchot gives his own explanation of the strategy behind his deconstructive exacerbation of the Hegelian dialectic in a series of fragments published in *L'Écriture du désastre* (*ED*, 100–1, 118–20; 61, 72–4). On Blanchot's reading of the *Phenomenology*, see also Andzej Warminski, *Readings in Interpretation: Hölderlin, Hegel, Heidegger*, 183–91. As Blanchot observes in *L'Écriture du désastre*, in a discussion of Hegel's two deaths, conceptual and natural:

> Indeed, let us recall Hegel's earliest work. He too, even before what is termed his early philosophy, considered that the two deaths could not be dissociated, and that only the fact of confronting death, not merely facing it or exposing oneself to its danger (which is what characterises heroic courage), but of entering into its space, of undergoing it as an infinite death and, also, mere death, 'natural death', could found sovereignty and mastery: spirit and its prerogatives. The result was perhaps absurdly that what set the dialectic in motion, the inexperienceable experience of death, was what immediately brought it to a halt, a halt of which the entire subsequent process retained a sort of memory, as of an aporia that was necessarily always part of the equation.
>
> (*ED*, 111–12; 68)

14 The gesture is not without recalling Blanchot's robust rebuttal of Hegel's anti-Judaism, even anti-semitism, in *L'Écriture du désastre* (*ED*, 104; 63).

15 Interestingly, while Blanchot in his footnote attributes the description of the *il y a* to Levinas and refers the reader to *De l'existence à l'existant*, Levinas, for his part, in a footnote in that self-same book (103; *Existence and Existents*, 63), attributes the description of the *il y a* to Blanchot and refers the reader to the second chapter of *Thomas l'Obscur*. To speak of the *il y a* at all, it seems, is always already to subscribe to a principle not of priority, originality, or propriety, but of repetition, endebtedness, alterity, and return.

16 For a wide-ranging account of some of the implications of Blanchot's use of the *il y a*, see Simon Critchley, '*Il y a* – A Dying Stronger than Death (Blanchot with Levinas)', *Oxford Literary Review*, 15, 1–2, 1993, 81–131.

17 It is true that later accounts by both Levinas and Blanchot claim that the thought of the *il y a* arose entirely independently of their reading of Heidegger. My claim here is not a

historical one; it is simply to emphasise, whatever its origins, to what extent the *il y a* necessarily comes to function as a reworking and displacement of Heideggerian Being.

18 The passage from the Preface to the *Phenomenology* to which Blanchot refers here is as follows:

> Death, if that is what we want to call this non-actuality [jene Unwirklichkeit], is of all things the most dreadful [das Furchtbarste], and to hold fast what is dead requires the greatest strength. Lacking strength, Beauty hates the Understanding for asking of her what it cannot do. But the life of Spirit is not the life that shrinks from death and keeps itself untouched by devastation, but rather the life that endures and maintains itself in it [Aber nicht das Leben, das sich vor dem Tode scheut und vor der Verwüstung rein bewahrt, sondern das ihn erträgt und in ihm sich erhält, ist das Leben des Geistes]. It wins its truth only when, in utter dismemberment [in der absoluten Zerrissenheit, what Blanchot translates as 'la déchirure de l'homme'], it finds itself. It is this power [Macht], not as something positive, which closes its eyes to the negative, as when we say of something that it is nothing or is false, and then, having done with it, turn away and pass on to something else; on the contrary, spirit is this power only by looking the negative in the face, and tarrying with it. This tarrying with the negative is the magic power [die Zauberkraft] that converts it into being [in das Sein]. This power is identical with what we earlier called the Subject [das Subjekt], which by giving determinateness an existence in its own element supersedes [aufhebt] abstract immediacy, i.e. the immediacy which barely is, and thus is authentic substance: that being or immediacy whose mediation is not outside of it but which is this mediation itself.

> (G. W. F. Hegel, *Werke*, III, 36; *Phenomenology of Spirit*, 19)

19 In this respect, dying in Blanchot has many similarities – as well as important differences – with ecstasy as articulated by Bataille: i.e. not a fusion of subject with object, but rather an interval or interruption in subjectivity, language, time itself; as Blanchot observes:

> One can write the word (ecstasy) only by putting it carefully between quotation marks, because nobody can know what this is, and first whether it ever took place: going beyond knowledge, implying non-knowledge, it refuses to be affirmed other than through chance words that cannot in any way guarantee it. Its decisive trait is that the one who experiences it is no longer there when he experiences it, is thus no longer there to experience it.

> (*CI*, 36–7; 19)

I examine the question of quotation marks and their relationship with the neutre in Blanchot later in this chapter.

The worklessness of being

1 On the relation between the *il y a* and hypostasis, see Levinas, *De l'existence à l'existant*, 107–45 (*Existence and Existants*, 65–85); and *Le Temps et l'autre* (Paris, Presses universitaires de France [1948], 1983), 31–4; also John Llewelyn, *Emmanuel Levinas, the Genealogy of Ethics* (London, Routledge, 1995), 21–30.

Outside

1 G. W. F. Hegel, *Werke*, XIII, 25.

2 See Heidegger, 'Der Ursprung des Kunstwerks', in *Holzwege*, 1–72 (the Afterword appears on 65–7), *Basic Writings*, 143–212 (204–12). Heidegger's essay, though first published in 1950, was completed in 1936, making it exactly contemporary with the first of Heidegger's published essays on Hölderlin discussed earlier. Also worth mentioning here, and contained in the same volume (*Holzwege*, 265–316), is Heidegger's essay of 1946 on Rilke, 'Wozu Dichter?' ('What are Poets For?') in *Poetry, Language, Thought*, translated by Albert Hofstadter (London, Harper and Row, 1971), 91–142, which takes its title from Hölderlin's famous line in the elegy 'Brot und Wein': 'wozu Dichter in dürftiger Zeit?' ('Wherefore poets in time of distress?') which Heidegger had already cited, in 1936, in conclusion to 'Hölderlin und das Wesen der Dichtung' (*Erläuterungen zu Hölderlins Dichtung*, 47–8; *Existence and Being*, 315). For convenience, I follow Blanchot (and Ann Smock in *The Space of Literature*) in translating Hölderlin's 'in dürftiger Zeit' as 'in time of distress'. There are many other possible translations of 'dürftig', including: destitute, needy, wretched, miserable, meagre, etc.

3 Reliance on the earth is of course a central theme in 'Der Ursprung des Kunstwerks', and it is one that, as Derrida has shown, has some surprising implications for Heidegger's treatment of van Gogh's paintings of 'a pair of peasant shoes'. See Jacques Derrida, *La Vérité en peinture* (Paris, Flammarion, 1977), 291–436 (*The Truth in Painting*, translated by Geoffrey Bennington and Ian McLeod (Chicago, University of Chicago Press, 1987), 255–382). As long ago as 1940, if not indeed before, disquiet at the political implications of Heidegger's peasant reliance on the earth was one major reason why Levinas's thinking was governed, as he puts it, by 'a profound need to leave the climate of that philosophy' (*De l'existence à l'existant*, 19; *Existence and Existents*, 19); and it is arguably to a similarly disturbing valorisation of motifs such as that of the earth that Blanchot is alluding here.

4 See 'Hölderlin und das Wesen der Dichtung', *Erläuterungen zu Hölderlins Dichtung*, 47, *Existence and Being*, 313.

5 'Der Ursprung des Kunstwerks', *Holzwege*, 66, *Basic Writings*, 205.

6 See ' "Wie wenn am Feiertage..." ', *Erläuterungen zu Hölderlins Dichtung*, 51.

7 As Heidegger puts it in his opening remarks in the essay 'Wozu Dichter?':

> The nearer it reaches midnight in the night of the world, the more exclusively that which is distressing [das Dürftige] prevails in that it withdraws its essence. Not only does the sacred as the trace [die Spur] of divinity go missing, but even the

traces of this lost trace [die Spuren zu dieser verlorenen Spur] have become virtually extinguished [ausgelöscht].

(*Holzwege*, 268; *Poetry, Language, Thought*, 94–5).

As Blanchot would rejoin, a quarter of a century later: 'All must be effaced, all will be effaced. Writing takes place and takes its place in accordance with the infinite demand of effacement' ('Tout doit s'effacer, tout s'effacera. C'est en accord avec l'exigence infinie de l'effacement qu'écrire a lieu et a son lieu') (*PA*, 76; 53).

8 Compare Heidegger's assertion that: 'Each answer remains in force as an answer only so long as it is rooted in questioning' ('Jede Antwort bleibt nur als Antwort in Kraft, solange sie im Fragen verwurzelt ist') (*Holzwege*, 57; *Basic Writings*, 195).

9 As Blanchot puts it in a paper belonging to the same period, which retraces much of the same argument:

Whoever affirms literature in itself affirms nothing. Whoever seeks it seeks only that which slips away; whoever finds it finds only what falls short of literature or, even worse, what lies beyond it. This is why, in the end, it is non-literature that each book pursues as the essence of what it loves and yearns passionately to discover.

('La Disparition de la littérature', *LV*, 244; *BR*, 142).

10 'Die Wahrheit ist in ihrem Wesen Un-wahrheit' ('Truth, in its essence, is un-truth'), (*Holzwege*, 40, *Basic Writings*, 179).

11 'Der Ursprung des Kunstwerks', *Holzwege*, 61, *Basic Writings*, 200. Heidegger's word 'das Un-geheure', which Albert Hofstadter translates here as 'awesome', is the term lying hidden in Blanchot's 'monstrueux' (monstrous) in the passage that follows.

12 Levinas's account of the differences between Heidegger and Blanchot is characteristically astute: 'the move that dominates the later philosophy of Heidegger', he writes in a 1956 review of *L'Espace littéraire*:

consists in interpreting the essential forms of human activity – art, technology, science, economy – as modes of truth (or its forgetting). That the march towards the truth, the response to the call, involves for Heidegger taking paths that lead one astray, and that error is contemporary with truth, and that the revelation of being is also its concealment, all points to the existence of a very close relationship between the Heideggerian notion of being and the making real of the unreal, the presence of absence, the existence of nothingness that is what, in Blanchot's view, the work of art or the poem voices. But for Heidegger the truth – a primordial unveiling – is the condition of all wandering, which is why the whole of the human can be finally spoken of in terms of truth and be described as an 'unveiling of being'. In Blanchot, *the work discloses, in a disclosure that is not truth*, a darkness. A disclosure that is not truth! What a strange way of disclosing and seeing the 'content' which its formal structure determines: a darkness that is absolutely exterior, on which no purchase is possible. Like in a desert one finds no residence. From the depths of sedentary existence a nomadic memory arises. Nomadism is not an approach of the sedentary state. It is an irreducible relationship with the earth: a residence without *place*. Faced with the night to which art calls it back, as in the face of death, the 'I', as support of power, dissolves into the anonymous 'one', across a land of pilgrimage. The Self of a timeless Nomad, grasping itself in its displacement and not its place, on the borders of non-truth, the realm that spreads further than the true.

(Emmanuel Levinas, *Sur Maurice Blanchot* (Montpellier, Fata morgana, 1975), 21–2)

13 Blanchot develops his criticism of Heidegger's negative view of anonymity and impersonality in a remarkable reading of Louis-René Des Forêts's novel, *Le Bavard*, 'La Parole vaine', in *L'Amitié* (*A*, 137–49, esp. 145–6).

14 'Philosophy', claimed Heidegger in 1966,

will not be able to effect an immediate transformation of the present condition of the world. This is not only true of philosophy, but of all merely human thought and endeavour. Only a god can still save us. The sole possibility of salvation that is left to us is to propose a sort of readiness, through thinking and poeticizing, for the appearance of the god or for the absence of the god in the time of decline; so that, crudely put, we do not simply rot away [daß wir nicht, grob gesagt, 'verrecken'] but, if we do perish, do so in the face of the absent god [im Angesicht des abwesenden Gottes].

(*Antwort. Martin Heidegger im Gespräch*, Günther Neske and Emil Kettering (eds) (Neske, Pfullingen, 1988), 99–100; *The Heidegger Controversy: a Critical Reader*, Richard Wolin (ed.), 107, translation modified)

Some pages later, Heidegger glosses the readiness to which he refers here, as ever, with an invocation of Hölderlin as 'the poet who points into the future, expects god and thus ought not to remain solely an object of Hölderlin Studies in the literary historical sense' (106; 112). Though Blanchot might plausibly concur with this last sentiment, it is clear from these lines that in every other respect he develops a radically different understanding of the future to that proposed by Heidegger.

Neutre

1 'René Char et la pensée du neutre', *L'Arc*, 22, Summer 1963, 9–14 (11–12). The covert citation contained in the last sentence of this passage, as readers of the chapter 'Parler, ce n'est pas voir' will recall (*EI*, 44; 31), is from Heraclitus, Fr. 93: 'The lord whose oracle is in Delphi neither speaks out nor conceals, but gives a sign', according to the translation proposed by G. S. Kirk, J. E. Raven, and M. Schofield, *The Presocratic Philosophers*, second edn (Cambridge, Cambridge University Press, 1983), 209.

2 These particular changes were first brought to attention in 1973 by Roger Laporte in his essay 'Une Passion', in Roger Laporte and Bernard Noël, *Deux lectures de Maurice Blanchot*, 142–3. Prefacing a later, revised version of the essay, Laporte tells how he came to regret the tone of his earlier remarks on Blanchot's rewriting and has since

refused to allow the 1973 version of the essay to be reprinted. It was at Blanchot's suggestion, however, Laporte states, that in 1983, in his turn, like Blanchot with *Thomas l'Obscur*, he came to rewrite the essay under the title: 'Une Passion (nouvelle version)'; see Roger Laporte, *A l'extrême pointe: Bataille et Blanchot* (Montpellier, Fata morgana, 1994), 34–53. To write at all, it seems, for both Blanchot and Laporte, is to be condemned to the inescapable necessity of rewriting; which is simply to say, of course, that writing itself is always already a rewriting, a perpetual redrafting of what is necessarily without beginning or end. As Blanchot writes in *Le Pas au-delà*, 'to write, in this sense, is first always to rewrite, and to rewrite does not refer to any previous writing, any more than to an anteriority of speech or of presence or of signification' (*PA*, 48; 32).

3   See Roger Laporte, *A l'extrême pointe: Bataille et Blanchot*, 41. As far as the early work of Derrida is concerned, the key date is 1967, which saw the original publication of *Grammatology, Speech and Phenomena*, and *Writing and Difference*. Blanchot himself writes of his debt to Derrida in the essay 'Grâce (soit rendue) à Jacques Derrida', *Revue philosophique*, 2, April–June 1990, 167–73 (*BR*, 317–23). Derrida's influence on (at least) Blanchot's vocabulary is evident from the changes made to some of the articles of the late 1950s or early to mid-1960s in the versions published in *L'Entretien infini* and *L'Amitié*; alongside the withdrawal of terms like 'présence', for instance, Blanchot also has more extensive recourse to words such as 'écriture' or 'différence', using them in their largely Derridean sense. One example may suffice: in the initial version of 'La Voix narrative' (first published October 1964) the following sentence appeared: 'And narrative may be said to be nothing other than an allusion to the initial detour that is borne by speech, that carries it away and causes us, in speaking, to yield to a sort of perpetual turning aside'; but when the passage reappeared in *L'Entretien infini*, the two references to speech and speaking, 'la parole' and 'parlant', had been deleted, replaced, respectively, by 'l'écriture' and 'écrivant' (*EI*, 564; 385). Admittedly, as Derrida points out, the phenomenon was a general one in France at the time, and Blanchot was far from the only writer to revise his texts in this way; see Jacques Derrida, *Résistances de la psychanalyse* (Paris, Galilée, 1996), 80. While the responsiveness of Blanchot to Derrida is beyond question, Derrida's own debt to Blanchot, as Derrida has been the first to make clear, is difficult to underestimate; indeed, much of the principle – if not the detail – of Derrida's account of phonocentrism in *De la grammatologie* in 1967 is already contained in the opening pages of Blanchot's essay on Char, 'La Bête de Lascaux', first published in 1953.

4   Elsewhere in Blanchot's writing there is ample evidence of a similar endeavour to re-invent the implications of the term 'presence'. Witness for instance in *Le Dernier Homme* of 1957 the following description of the narrator's friend and associate:

He was present in such a strange manner: so completely and so incompletely. When he was there, I could not help coming up against his self-effacement, which made his approach even more clumsy, cruelly disproportionate: maybe insignificant, maybe dominating. As though his presence was all there was of

251

him and did not allow him to be present: it was an immense presence, and even he did not seem able to fill it, as though he had disappeared into it and had been absorbed by it slowly, endlessly – a presence without anyone there perhaps [une présence sans personne peut-être]? . . . His presence and not the idea of his presence. It seemed to me this presence destroyed all idea of itself, that I couldn't even have a false idea of it.

(*DH*, 50–1; 28)

5 'Neutre' in Blanchot's text is not an easy word to translate. Of the possibilities available in English, the term 'neuter' is normally taken to mean: neither masculine nor feminine; as for the word 'neutral' (the translation preferred by Susan Hanson in *The Infinite Conversation*), this is mainly used to refer to impartiality or the refusal to engage in conflict (neutrality, in addition, has the disadvantage of being a traditional Latinate concept). The difficulty with Blanchot's 'neutre' is that while it may encounter some of these meanings, it is irreducible to them all; it is a term that, while not single in itself, nevertheless resists generality, which is why, for my part, in this discussion and subsequently in this book, as though using a strange proper name, I have preferred to call it: the neutre.

6 See Emmanuel Levinas, *Totalité et infini* (Paris, Le Livre de poche, 1990), 332 (*Totality and Infinity*, translated by Alphonso Lingis (Dordrecht, Kluwer, 1991), 298). On Levinas's (mis)reading of Heideggerian *Sein* as neutrality, see Jacques Derrida, 'Violence et métaphysique' in *L'Écriture et la différence* (Paris, Seuil, 1967), 200–6 (*Writing and Difference*, 136–40).

7 See Maurice Blanchot, 'L'Étrange et l'étranger', *La Nouvelle Revue française*, 70, October 1958, 673–83 (681). Unusually, this article by Blanchot is one of the few not to have been incorporated by him in a subsequent collection. First published in *Revue de métaphysique et de morale*, 3, 1957, 241–53, 'La Philosophie et l'idée de l'infini' is reproduced in Emmanuel Levinas, *En découvrant l'existence avec Husserl et Heidegger*, third edn (Paris, Vrin, 1974), 165–78 (*Collected Philosophical Papers*, translated by Alphonso Lingis (Dordrecht, Martinus Nijhoff, 1987), 47–59).

8 As Levinas himself concedes in 1971, in an interview with André Dalmas, in answer to a question about the difference between Heidegger and Blanchot on the subject of the neuter:

As the distance of After death 'with respect to being', which cannot be arrived at by simple negation, Blanchot's Neutre is foreign to the world – with a foreignness beyond all foreignness, with an 'exponent', so to speak. Further than any God. Quite different to Heidegger's *Sein* – which is anonymous, too – which (different from beings, as you rightly point out) is the very luminosity of the world, place, landscape, peace.

(Emmanuel Levinas, *Sur Maurice Blanchot*, 49)

9 Emmanuel Levinas, *Sur Maurice Blanchot*, 52.

10 'Comment découvrir l'obscur?', *La Nouvelle Revue française*, 83, November 1959, 867–79 (876).

11 Martin Heidegger, 'Moira (Parmenides VIII, 34–41)', in: *Vorträge und Aufsätze* (Pfullingen, Neske, 1954), 243–4.

12 The question arises here as to the relationship between the *il y a* and the *neutre* in Blanchot, and whether this is best portrayed as one of surreptitious continuity or decisive opposition. It is true, on the one hand, that the *il y a* is formulated primarily by Blanchot (and Levinas) as the thought of the presence of the absence of being and of the inescapability of being or its irreducibility to negation, all of which would seem to put the *il y a* decidedly within the realm of ontology and at some distance from the *neutre*. But, on the other hand, to the extent that the *il y a* ultimately deprives being of all proper foundation and undermines the distinction between being and non-being, it would seem that the *il y a* is in fact already pointing beyond being, and thus not only towards the thought of the Other, but towards the thought of literature as well, and in that case it may be argued that the *il y a*, as an instantiation of the *neutre*, has already begun to suspend the whole question of being or non-being. It is at any rate in terms such as these that Blanchot, in a number of later retrospective texts, tends to describe the *il y a*. 'Above all', he writes for instance in *L'Écriture du désastre*, 'the *there is* [l'*il y a*], as neuter [en tant que neutre], eludes the question that relates to it: if asked, it ironically absorbs the asking, which has no priority over it' (*ED*, 108; 65).

13 Much the same emphasis is of course found in Levinas; compare for instance, *Totalité et infini*, 13 (*Totality and Infinity*, 28). It might be argued that Blanchot's criticism of the optical metaphor can find an easy target in much of Blanchot's own earlier work, where, as we have seen, the figure of the light of day in particular plays a major role. The question is one Blanchot raises himself, albeit obliquely, in an inconclusive exchange between two of the interlocutors in 'Parler, ce n'est pas voir', when one speaker voices his faith in the idea that 'in the speaking that responds to waiting, there is a manifest presence that does not belong to the day, a disclosure that discloses before any *fiat lux*, disclosing the darkness by the detour that is the essence of darkness'. To which his partner replies: 'In spite of all your efforts, when speaking of the darkness, to avoid us having to refer to the light, I cannot help but relate everything you say back to the day as the sole measure' (*EI*, 43; 31).

14 In the version of this sentence given by Susan Hanson in *The Infinite Conversation*, the translator unfortunately misconstrues this last clause which she renders as: 'a possibility of saying that would say being without saying it, and yet without denying it either'. This is to have the phrase say the reverse of what it means; oddly, when faced with an identical statement elsewhere in *L'Entretien infini* (*EI*, 104; 73), Hanson translates it accurately!

July 1948: writing, dying; dying, writing

1 The appearance of the two volumes was accompanied by two notices in Gallimard's NRF Bulletin for July 1948 (No. 13, 1–2); the second of these, devoted to *Le Très-Haut*, began as follows:

> 'These two books,' writes Maurice Blanchot, '*Le Très-Haut* and *L'Arrêt de mort*, that have appeared simultaneously have no doubt nothing in common. But it seems to me, having written them, that one is present so to speak behind the other, not like two texts implicated within each other, but like two divergent and yet concordant versions of a same reality that is equally absent from both.'

> ('Il n'y a,' écrit Maurice Blanchot, 'sans doute rien de commun entre ces deux livres, *Le Très-Haut*, *L'Arrêt de mort*, qui paraissent en même temps. Mais, à moi qui les ai écrits, il me semble que l'un est comme présent derrière l'autre, non comme deux textes impliqués, mais comme les deux versions inconciliables et cependant concordantes d'une même réalité, également absente de toutes deux.')

2 Maurice Blanchot, 'Le Chant des sirènes', *La Nouvelle Revue française*, 19, July 1954, 95–104. Among the most influential earlier proponents of this distinction between *roman* and *récit* in France was André Gide, for whom a *roman* required a large cast of characters, a wealth of incident, a multiplicity of different narrative viewpoints, and a third-person narrative voice, while a *récit* entailed instead a limited number of characters, few events, restricted narrative point of view, and narration in the first person.

3 This is by way of the phrase, 'la reine-mère' ('the Queen Mother'), used in *Le Très-Haut* by the narrator's sister, Louise, to refer to their mother (*TH*, 59; 55), and repeated in *L'Arrêt de mort* by J.'s sister, also called Louise, to refer also to their mother (*AM*, 12; 4). It may be remembered that the main female character of 'L'Idylle' is also named Louise.

4 The phrase, used in *Le Très-Haut* to describe the image in the dilapidated tapestry in Louise's room, is not without recalling the phrase, 'l'ancien, l'effroyablement ancien', referring to the temporality of narrative and myth as such, that, as Roger Laporte has recorded, recurs no less than seven times in Blanchot's essays and *récits*; see Roger Laporte, *Études* (Paris, POL, 1990), 11–50. It is worth noting perhaps that the scene with Louise ends with the narrator saying to her: 'Viens donc. . . . Viens!' (*TH*, 56; 53).

5 Among the more striking or controversial contributions to the debate, see Pierre Madaule, *Une tâche sérieuse?* (Paris, Gallimard, 1973) and *Véronique et les chastes* (Dijon, Ulysse fin de siècle, 1988); Bernard Noël, 'D'une main obscure', in *Deux lectures de Maurice Blanchot* (Montpellier, Fata morgana, 1973), 9–47; Jacques Derrida, 'Living On', in: *Deconstruction and Criticism*, 75–176, and in *Parages*, 119–218; Jeffrey Mehlman, *Genealogies of the Text*, 82–96; Edmond Jabès, *Dans la double dépendance du dit* (Montpellier, Fata morgana, 1984), 65–6; J. Hillis Miller, *Versions of Pygmalion* (London, Harvard University Press, 1990), 179–210; Marie-Claire Ropars-Wuilleumier, *Écraniques : le film du texte* (Paris, Presses universitaires de Lille, 1990), 33–55; and

Michael Holland, 'Rencontre piégée : "Nadja" dans *L'Arrêt de mort*', in *Violence, théorie, surréalisme*, Jacqueline Chénieux-Gendron and Timothy Mathews (eds) (Pleine marge, 3, Paris, Lachenal & Ritter, 1994), 117–38. It is worth noting that in 1971 *L'Arrêt de mort*, like many other titles by Blanchot, was reissued by Gallimard; as well as adopting a new format and different pagination, this reprint also deleted the appellation *récit* and the short third section of the narrative (which is retained in Lydia Davis's 1978 English translation). Unless otherwise indicated, all references to the French text will be to this 1971 edition.

6 The ellipses regarding proper names in *L'Arrêt de mort* are perhaps what are most reminiscent of Constant's *Adolphe*, to which Blanchot had devoted an essay in October 1946, in which one also reads:

> The key element in Constant's tragedy is that he is exposed, in its pure state, with all the acuteness of a singular sensitivity, to the following paradox: that we have relations with others only if we are not as one with others, and communicate fully with someone only by possessing not what they are but what separates us from them, their absence rather than their presence, in other words, the infinite movement towards overcoming and thus regenerating this absence.
>
> (*PF*, 229; 234–5)

The words, of course, clearly have some bearing on not only *L'Arrêt de mort* but Blanchot's later *récits* as well.

7 The references to Munich are of course what has prompted Jeffrey Mehlman, in *Genealogies of the Text* (82–96), to jump to the conclusion that *L'Arrêt de mort* is an allegorical portrayal of Blanchot's renunciation of his alleged commitment to French fascism. Mehlman supports this contention by reminding the reader that Munich represented an important turning point for the French extreme right, which was now forced to choose between its commitment to French nationalism and its enthusiasm for German fascism. It is indeed true that for Blanchot, as for many of his contemporaries, the year 1938 was a crucial moment, and in Blanchot's case it does seem to have marked the moment of his abandonment of revolutionary nationalism, and his decision, in spite of all, to rally to the cause of the Republic. That particular shift, however, to judge from the evidence of Blanchot's published texts, took place much earlier in the year, well before the Autumn of 1938; in any case, Blanchot had long been a fierce opponent of the policy of appeasement that culminated in Munich, and his own opposition to Munich, when it came, was robustly unambiguous. As for the temptation of fascism, it is clear that on this score, too, Blanchot's mind had been made up for several years, since at least 1933; but, regrettably, this is a feature of the historical record Jeffrey Mehlman in his reading of *L'Arrêt de mort* is plainly unwilling to acknowledge.

8 On the dating of this scene, see Pierre Madaule, *Véronique et les chastes*, 119.

9 Michael Holland, 'Rencontre piégée: "Nadja" dans *L'Arrêt de mort*', 137.

10 On Laure's dying words, see Georges Bataille, *Œuvres complètes*, V, 512. Bataille's account of Laure's death was originally intended to be part of *Le Coupable*, but was

deleted by Bataille shortly before publication; Colette Peignot's own writings are now collected in Laure, *Écrits, fragments, lettres*, Jérôme Peignot (ed.) (Paris, Pauvert, 1977). The recurrence of the 12 October in *L'Arrêt de mort* and Bataille's account of Laure's death, together with the repeated motif of the rose, are among the elements discussed by Derrida in his reading of *L'Arrêt de mort*; see *Parages*, 192–208, *Deconstruction and Criticism*, 148–64.

11 See Pierre Madaule, *Véronique et les chastes*, 119. The narrator comments: 'These comings and goings [ces péripéties], at a time like this, seem to me like the last grimace of the world' (*AM*, 118; 74). The words are significant ones; what they suggest is that personal actions are not reducible to world historical ones, and that if *L'Arrêt de mort* does have a historical or political message, it is that in spite of history men and women can still perform honourable acts, and that in the face of a catastrophe such as Munich and the events that followed, the only viable response is to invoke the impossible, to refuse history, and affirm the limitlessness of life itself even into death. Witness the closing homage, paid to J., after her death, by the narrator: 'For myself,' he concludes, 'I see nothing important in the fact that this young woman, who was dead, returned to the living in response to my call, but I see an astounding miracle in her fortitude, and in her energy, which was great enough to make death impotent as long as she wanted' (*AM*, 52–3; 30).

12 The publisher's blurb for *L'Arrêt de mort* given in Gallimard's NRF Bulletin for July 1948 (1–2), which Blanchot is more than likely to have written himself, confirms this date as follows: 'This [hi]story isn't a dream, and doesn't take place in any dream world; it began some years ago, on Wednesday 13 October; it happened amongst us, and it is possible it is still not over.' ('Cette histoire n'est pas un rêve, elle n'a pas lieu dans un monde de rêve; elle a commencé il y a peu d'années, le mercredi 13 octobre; elle s'est déroulée parmi nous, et il se peut qu'elle ne soit pas encore finie.')

13 Interestingly enough, perhaps, on 13 October 1943, Blanchot published in the *Journal des débats* a book review, devoted mainly to Roger Caillois's *Puissances du roman* and entitled 'Récits autobiographiques' ('Autobiographical Narratives'), the main contention of which was the uncertain character of the borderline between autobiography and fiction, indeed the merging of the two in many cases. 'Why', asks Blanchot, 'does one generally hesitate in considering autobiographical works as novels . . . ?'

14 Referring to this unspecified living proof of the events in the story, Blanchot's narrator first writes: 'preuve "vivante" ' (*AM*, 9; 3), then, on the following page: 'cette "preuve" ' (*AM*, 10; 3), and it is as though the use of quotation marks, like a silent intervention of the neutre, applied now to one word, then to the next, functions to dissipate the enigma by making it more enigmatic still: for here is 'living' 'proof' that is not living, nor is it proof of anything at all.

15 In this respect, the irremediable is perhaps simply another name for finitude (or death itself); this, at any rate, is what is implied by the story of the squirrel Blanchot's narrator uses to explain the word; he writes:

I once saw a squirrel caught in a cage hanging from a tree: he was about to cross

256

the threshold with all the enthusiasm of his happiest of lives, but hardly had he landed on the board inside when the trigger clapped the door shut, and though he had not been hurt, and was still free, since the cage was huge, with a small pile of nuts inside, his jump froze at a stroke, and he stood there paralysed, struck in the back by the certainty that the trap had closed upon him.

(AM, 65–6; 38–9)

A threshold, a confined space, leading to immobility, paralysis, and a sense of entrapment, together with a boundless appetite for freedom: these are the motifs with which one might perhaps begin to articulate a poetics of Blanchot's *récits*; such a poetics, however, would be impossible, for there is no place from which to construe it: the reader, too, like the narrator of *Celui qui ne m'accompagnait pas*, is condemned to remain perpetually 'nailed to the spot', 'cloué sur place' (*CQ*, 46; 23).

16 Blanchot makes use of this figure of the window pane, which is like the figure (without figure) of figurality itself, both in *Au moment voulu* and in *Celui qui ne m'accompagnait pas*, where it features as a way of suspending narrative and problematising questions of space and time, identity and alterity, repetition and singularity. The topos of the 'vitre' also recurs in a semi-autobiographical context in *L'Écriture du désastre* (*ED*, 117; 72). On Blanchot's use of the motif in *L'Arrêt de mort*, see Jacques Derrida, *Parages*, 183–7, *Deconstruction and Criticism*, 139–44; and J. Hillis Miller, *Versions of Pygmalion*, 179–210.

Chapter 4 The absence of the book

Beyond philosophy?

1 Blanchot addresses *Totalité et infini* explicitly in three consecutive chapters in *L'Entretien infini*: 'Connaissance de l'inconnu' ('Knowledge of the Unknown'), 'Tenir parole' ('Keeping to Words') and 'Le Rapport du troisième genre' ('The Relation of the Third Kind') (*EI*, 70–105; 49–74). Of these, the first two essays originally appeared in the *Nouvelle Revue française* for December 1961 and February 1962 respectively; albeit with numerous minor changes, both are reproduced in *L'Entretien infini* in essentially the same form in which they were first published. In April 1962, Blanchot brought out a third, related essay, 'L'Indestructible', devoted in part to *L'Espèce humaine* by Robert Antelme, most of the matter which now appears under the title 'L'Espèce humaine' ('Humankind') in a later section of *L'Entretien infini* (*EI*, 191–200; 130–5). In place of the original third article on Levinas from April 1962, Blanchot incorporated into *L'Entretien infini*, under the title 'Le Rapport du troisième genre', a chapter made up of two passages retained from 'L'Indestructible' and a significant amount of new material, presumably written shortly before publication in 1969 (*EI*, 94–9, 100–2, 103–5; 66–70, 70–1, 72–4). Six years later, following the publication of Levinas's *Humanisme de l'autre homme* (1972) and *Autrement qu'être, ou au-delà de l'essence* (*Otherwise Than Being*, 1974), Blanchot also published a series of fragments on Levinas, under the title 'Discours sur la patience', in *Le Nouveau Commerce*, 30–1, 1975, 19–44; these were

later incorporated, with modifications, into *L'Écriture du désastre*. Blanchot's last essay, 'Notre compagne clandestine', appeared in a Festschrift for Levinas, *Textes pour Emmanuel Lévinas*, François Laruelle (ed.) (Paris, Jean-Michel Place, 1980), 79–87 (translated by David B. Allison as 'Our Clandestine Companion', in *Face to Face with Levinas*, Richard A. Cohen (ed.) (Albany, NY, State University of New York Press, 1986), 41–50). There are numerous other references to Levinas in Blanchot's texts of the 1970s and 1980s that are too extensive to list here.

2 See, for instance, Blanchot's personal tribute published in the special Levinas issue of *Exercices de la patience*, 1, 1980, 67. On the philosophical relationship between the two, see Françoise Collin, *Maurice Blanchot et la question de l'écriture* (Paris, Gallimard, 1971), and 'La Peur : Emmanuel Lévinas et Maurice Blanchot', *Cahiers de l'Herne: Emmanuel Levinas*, Catherine Chalier and Miguel Abensour (eds) (Paris, L'Herne, 1991), 313–27; Joseph Libertson, *Proximity: Levinas, Blanchot, Bataille and Communication* (The Hague, Martinus Nijhoff, 1982); Paul Davies, 'Difficult Friendship', *Research in Phenomenology*, XVIII, 1988, 149–72; and 'A Fine Risk: Reading Blanchot Reading Levinas', in *Re-Reading Levinas*, Robert Bernasconi and Simon Critchley (eds) (Bloomington and Indianapolis, Indiana University Press, 1991), 201–26; and Simon Critchley, '*Il y a* – Holding Levinas's Hand to Blanchot's Fire', in *Maurice Blanchot: the Demand of Writing*, Carolyn Bailey Gill (ed.), 108–22.

3 But if proximity is derived from distance in this way, Blanchot writes in *Le Pas au-delà*, it still risks being thought within being as deferred presence; this is why, Blanchot contends, proximity is in fact perhaps the greatest distance of all, the true infinity beyond both presence and absence. If so, proximity and distance both need to be thought outside of being or non-being; Blanchot writes: 'Far and near are dimensions of what escapes presence as well as absence under the attraction of the [impersonal] "it" [sous l'attrait du "il"]. It draws away, draws close, the same ghostly affirmation, the same premises of non-presence' (*PA*, 100; 71).

4 Emmanuel Levinas, *Sur Maurice Blanchot*, 9–10.

5 For the allusion to Amalek, see Emmanuel Levinas, *Sur Maurice Blanchot*, 26. Amalek, in the Bible, is eventually defeated by the Jews; however, as God says to Moses: 'Write this for a memorial in a book, and rehearse it in the ears of Joshua' (Exodus, 17: 14). Or, as Blanchot phrases it many years later, 'N'oubliez pas!', 'Do not forget'. Blanchot provides his own pertinent gloss on the figure of Amalek in two subsequent texts: 'L'Écriture consacrée au silence', *Instants*, 1, 1989, 239–41; and 'Grâce (soit rendue) à Jacques Derrida', *Revue philosophique*, 2, April–June 1990, 167–73 (*BR*, 317–23 [322]).

6 Emmanuel Levinas, *Sur Maurice Blanchot*, 23. On Heidegger's refusal of 'ethics', see the famous passage in the 'Brief über den Humanismus', in *Wegmarken*, 352–7, *Basic Writings*, 254–9. Heidegger's position on ethics is still of course the subject of some controversy, as Joanna Hodge has shown; see her *Heidegger and Ethics* (London, Routledge, 1995). By way of explanation in his own case, Blanchot in 1962, in a dialogue on Levinas collected in *L'Entretien infini*, has both his interlocutors each announce their distrust of the term 'ethics': 'I find in this word', says one, 'only secondary meanings [que des sens derivés]' (*EI*, 89; 63).

7 Emmanuel Levinas, *Sur Maurice Blanchot*, 24.

8 See Maurice Blanchot, 'Notre compagne clandestine', 79, 'Our Clandestine Companion', 41.

9 Maurice Blanchot, 'Notre compagne clandestine', 80, 'Our Clandestine Companion', 42. As readers of Levinas will be aware, the motif of wakefulness – and insomnia – is another borrowing from Levinas; it is also worth noting at this stage to what extent the relation with philosophy for Blanchot, like that with the (other) law in *La Folie du jour*, is dramatised in relation to the question of sexual difference.

10 See Maurice Blanchot, 'Notre compagne clandestine', 83, 'Our Clandestine Companion', 45. Blanchot makes a similar point in relation to Georges Bataille in *L'Amitié* (*A*, 328).

11 See Maurice Blanchot, 'Pour l'amitié', in Dionys Mascolo, *A la recherche d'un communisme de pensée*, 16.

12 Maurice Blanchot, 'Notre compagne clandestine', 84, 'Our Clandestine Companion', 47. The phrase from Levinas given just before – that Blanchot slightly misquotes in 'Notre compagne clandestine' – comes from: *Autrement qu'être ou au-delà de l'essence* (The Hague, Martinus Nijhoff, [1974] 1978), 8 (*Otherwise Than Being or Beyond Essence*, translated by Alphonso Lingis (The Hague, Martinus Nijhoff, 1981), p. 7). Blanchot provides further commentary on the phrase in *L'Écriture du désastre* (*ED*, 176; 114).

Transcendence and the Other

1 Blanchot's growing reservations regarding the term 'dialogue' – on the grounds that it subordinates the multiple to the One – are clearly visible if one compares the two versions of an essay on psychoanalysis first published in September 1956 and republished in 1969, with extensive revisions, as 'La Parole analytique' ('The Speech of Analysis') (*EI*, 343–54; 230–7). In the first version, Blanchot, following Lacan's celebrated 'Rome Discourse' of 1953, had grudgingly accepted that the analytic encounter might be described in terms of a dialectical relation between analyst and analysand. Thirteen years later, this reference to dialectics is the occasion for a series of trenchant and detailed qualifications. Blanchot accordingly withdraws the word dialogue by surrounding it with quotation marks, much as he does with 'présence' elsewhere; these diacritical marks serve, as it were, both to interrupt the text and to displace the whole concept of dialogue by silently invoking the infinity of language and the otherness of the neutre.

2 In the essay '"Il ne saurait être question de bien finir"' ('A happy end is out of the question'), published under the title 'Quand la morale se tait' as early as January 1954, Blanchot writes for instance of art's demand as follows:

> What kind of demand is being announced here, of a sort that may not be assimilated to any current morality, does not make whoever transgresses it guilty, nor innocent whoever believes they are carrying it out, that releases us from all the injunctions of 'I must', all the pretentions of 'I want' and all the resources of 'I

can', in order to leave us free? yet not free, not deprived of freedom either, as though it were drawing us forward to a point where, the air of the possible having been exhausted, what is held out to us is the bare relation that is not power, which precedes even all possibility of relation.

(*LV*, 38; *SS*, 46)

3 Compare for instance Emmanuel Levinas, *Totalité et infini*, 69–75 (*Totality and Infinity*, 72–7).

4 Witness for instance in the following passage from Levinas's conclusion:

Man as Other comes to us from the outside, a separated – or holy – face. His exteriority, that is, his appeal to me, is his truth. My response is not added as an accident to a 'nucleus' of his objectivity, but first *produces* his truth (which his 'point of view' upon me cannot nullify). This surplus of truth over being and over its idea, which we suggest by the metaphor of the 'curvature of intersubjective space', signifies the divine intention of all truth. This 'curvature of space' is, perhaps, the very presence of God.

(*Totalité et infini*, 324; *Totality and Infinity*, 291)

5 Both statements are in fact loose quotations: the first paraphrases Levinas's comment, based on Plato's *Phaedrus*, that 'Le Discours est discours avec Dieu et non pas avec les égaux' (*Totalité et infini*, 330; 'Discourse is discourse with God and not with equals', *Totality and Infinity*, 297); while the second (which Blanchot also cites in *La Communauté inavouable* (*CI*, 67–8; 40)) is based on a sentence from 'La Philosophie et l'idée de l'Infini' of 1957, which reads: 'Il faut qu'Autrui soit plus près de Dieu que Moi' (*En découvrant l'existence avec Husserl et Heidegger*, 174; 'The other must be closer to God than I', *Collected Philosophical Papers*, 56).

6 See for instance the 1967 essay, 'L'Athéisme et l'écriture. L'Humanisme et le cri' ('Atheism and Writing. Humanism and the Cry') (*EI*, 367–93; 246–63).

7 See Emmanuel Levinas, *Humanisme de l'autre homme* (Paris, Le Livre de poche, [1972] 1990), 89.

8 Maurice Blanchot, 'Parole de fragment', in *L'Endurance de la pensée*, (Paris, Plon, 1968), 103–8 (103); a modified version of the essay, without the dedication, is reprinted in *EI*, 451–5; 307–10. On the fraught circumstances surrounding the dedication, see Geert Lernout, *The Poet as Thinker: Hölderlin in France*, 38.

9 See Emmanuel Levinas, *Du sacré au saint*, 46–9. Describing the philosophical singularity of Judaism himself in 1962, Blanchot, for his part, did so in largely secular, linguistic terms:

let me say, brutally, that what we owe to Jewish monotheism is not the revelation of the one God, but the revelation of speech as the place where men hold themselves in relation with what excludes all relation: the infinitely Distant, the absolutely Foreign. God speaks, and man speaks to him. This is the great achievement of Israel.

(*EI*, 187; 127–8)

Blanchot re-emphasises the view expressed in his 1969 letter in a number of later texts; as well as the footnote added to the text of *L'Écriture du désastre* in 1980 (*ED*, 45; 148–9), see for instance 'Le Bienfait le plus lourd', *Le Nouvel Observateur*, 31 May–6 June 1985, 79; and ' "N'oubliez pas" ', *L'Arche*, May 1988, 68–71.

10 The move is a problematic one for many reasons, not least of which is the irreducibility, as Levinas himself construes it, of the ethical to the socio-political. Already in 1964, in 'Violence et métaphysique' in *L'Écriture et la différence* (152), Derrida, by querying its very possibility, took issue with Blanchot's contention, expressed a few pages later, to the effect that Levinas's account of language as constituting the transcendent relation as such must be maintained independently of the 'theological context' in which it appears (*EI*, 80; 56). Blanchot, in a subsequent note, accepts the objection; at the same time he also reaffirms his original point by adding elsewhere to the 1969 version of 'Connaissance de l'inconnu' the qualification: 'for my part exclusively', that now appears within parentheses in the passage cited. The more general question arises here: can there be a politics that is faithful to Levinas's thinking? In *The Ethics of Deconstruction* (Oxford, Blackwell, 1992), Simon Critchley for instance claims that for Levinas 'ethics is ethical for the sake of politics' (223), but this subordination of the ethical to the political raises perhaps more questions than it answers. Levinas, for his part, consigns the properly political to the realm of history and thus to the province of being; as he puts it in the title given to one of the pieces collected in *L'Au-delà du verset* (Paris, Minuit, 1982, 221–8; *Beyond the Verse*, translated by Gary D. Mole (London, Athlone, 1994), 188–95), 'Politique après!' ('Politics Last!'). Ethics, on the other hand, as addressed by Levinas, is what disrupts being and history, and by effacing the present opens it to the infinite claims of eschatology. The issue then is this: how to maintain together – but without joining or articulating them by recourse to any prior conceptuality – the 'ethical' and the 'political'? The question sets the scene, one might argue, for Blanchot's own later political writings, the very motto of which, in their refusal to embrace any single totalising political discourse or strategy, and in their endeavours always to contest the possibility of power in the name of the impossibility beyond power, might be: politics or eschatology? or even: politics *and* eschatology?

11 See Emmanuel Levinas, *L'Au-delà du verset*, 148, *Beyond the Verse*, 120. If less explicitly or vigorously than in many later texts, Levinas is nonetheless already arguing in favour of a non-theological and non-ontological understanding of God in *Totalité et infini*; see for example, 325–6 (*Totality and Infinity*, 293–4). As far as Blanchot's own later texts are concerned, the key issue remains the need rigorously to divorce the transcendence of the Other from all ontology, in which requirement Blanchot is of course still following Levinas. As Blanchot enjoins in *L'Écriture du désastre*:

Abandon the futile hope of finding in being support for the separation, the rupture, the revolt that could be achieved, and thus *verified*. For this would mean you still need the truth and still need to raise it above 'error', just as you want to distinguish death from life and death from death, remaining loyal to the absoluteness of a faith which dares not acknowledge its own emptiness and is content with a transcendence of which *being would still be the measure*.

(*ED*, 140; 88–9)

12 See Emmanuel Levinas, *De Dieu qui vient à l'idée* (Paris, Vrin, 1986), 115 (*Collected Philosophical Papers*, 165–6). Interestingly, this particular paper by Levinas appeared for the first time alongside Blanchot's 'Discours sur la patience' in 1975; and the passage cited is one Blanchot himself paraphrases at length in the quotation from 'Une compagne clandestine' that is given as an epigraph for this section.

13 On asymmetry in Levinas, see, for instance, the section 'Asymétrie de l'interpersonnel' ('The Asymmetry of the Interpersonal'), *Totalité et infini*, 236–8 (*Totality and Infinity*, 215–16). It is worth noting that the passage in 'Le Rapport du troisième genre' which develops this notion of double dissymmetry is a later addition from 1969. A fuller account of the exchanges between Blanchot and Levinas would of course have to take into consideration Levinas's later texts of the 1960s, written while on the way to *Autrement qu'être*, and examine the impact of Blanchot's work on that of Levinas during that whole period. For reasons of space, the task is unfortunately one that cannot be undertaken here.

14 This is the charge levelled at Blanchot's reading of Levinas in *L'Entretien infini* by Joseph Libertson, in his *Proximity: Levinas, Blanchot, Bataille and Communication*, 274–88. Libertson's main contention, already in fact pre-empted by Blanchot, is that, in appealing to the notion of double dissymmetry, Blanchot lapses into an uncritical and ultimately Hegelian concept of intersubjectivity.

15 Blanchot's use of ' "l'homme" ', in this context, albeit within the displacement effected by quotation marks, and though clearly intended to be taken not as *vir*, but as *homo*, raises nevertheless a question about sexual difference in Blanchot's writing. Does ' "l'homme" ' include or exclude 'la femme'? And, assuming it might be possible to answer this question satisfactorily in either one way or the other, what then would be the implications? The issue of sexual difference is not one Blanchot addresses at all explicitly in his critical or philosophical work; it remains nonetheless crucial in many of his fictional texts, notably, as we have seen, *Le Très-Haut*, *L'Arrêt de mort*, and *La Folie du jour*, not to mention such later narratives as *Au moment voulu* and *L'Attente L'Oubli*.

16 Emmanuel Levinas, *Sur Maurice Blanchot*, 52. While he acknowledges that Blanchot never in fact uses the term, Levinas may nevertheless regularly be found reading Blanchot as a thinker of transcendence; see, for instance, *Sur Maurice Blanchot*, 13.

17 It is of course consistently in these terms that the neutre is presented by Blanchot. Using it at one point as the basis for a reading of Kafka's *Castle*, in the essay 'Le Pont de bois' ('The Wooden Bridge'), Blanchot comments:

What then is above Transcendence, what is below Transdescendence? . . . Let me choose momentarily to call it by the most modest, effaced, and neutral of names: precisely by calling it the neuter – because to name the neuter is perhaps, is surely to dissipate it, but necessarily still in favour of the neuter.

(*EI*, 580; 395)

The neutre, one might say, not only designates the neutre, but is itself neutre, which is why it names only namelessness and the infinity of its own withdrawal.

18 See for instance Blanchot's remark in *Après coup*, in the course of which he translates the Levinasian concept of Saying precisely into the neutre of the 'narrative voice', which, chronologically, at any rate, predates Levinas's own expression, first introduced in 1968; as Blanchot writes:

> prior to all distinction between form and content, signifier and signified, even before the separation between the act of speaking and the utterance, there is the unqualifiable Saying, the glory of a 'narrative voice' which speaks clearly, without it being possible for it to be obscured by the opaqueness or enigma or terrible horror of what is communicated.
>
> (*AC*, 97–8; 68)

19 See for instance the two biblical commentaries cited in the preceding section, 'L'Écriture consacrée au silence', in which Blanchot writes, for instance, of ' "Dieu" (le nom innommable)' [' "God" (the unnamable name)'], and 'Grâce (soit rendue) à Jacques Derrida', where, similarly, Blanchot writes: ' "God" (we name him thus by our incapacity to name him)'. Later in the same piece, Blanchot describes ' "God" ', as 'the first and last writer', and it is this, finally, that is perhaps Blanchot's clearest response to the challenge of Amalek.

The demand of writing

1 This (improper) property is one that the word 'absence' in Blanchot's later texts shares increasingly with terms such as: 'fragment' or 'désastre'; as in Derridean 'différance', what comes to be at stake in such words is the necessity to suspend such philosophical distinctions as between passive and active, presence and absence in order to affirm instead the infinity of the relation between any name and its Other. Blanchot offers his own account of this process in a fragment from *L'Écriture du désastre* (*ED*, 120–1; 74–5).

2 This position derives from the essential non-essentiality of writing formulated by Blanchot in *L'Espace littéraire*. But it is also possible to find here an echo of Blanchot's dialogue with Bataille during the early 1940s. Bataille, it will be remembered, when formulating the rules of the inner experience, credits Blanchot with advancing the fundamental principle that the inner experience is its own authority, but that this authority must be expiated. In much the same way, writing for Blanchot is its own only authority; but that authority, too, must be challenged, and the price paid.

3 Maurice Blanchot, 'Nous travaillons dans les ténèbres', *Le Monde*, 22 July 1983. What this implies too, of course, is that the ethical demand of writing is always multiple, never single, always in the form of an astringent double bind. As Blanchot writes in *L'Écriture du désastre*:

> To write is to distrust writing absolutely by trusting in it absolutely [Écrire, c'est se méfier absolument, en s'y confiant absolument, de l'écriture]. Whatever

foundation one gives to this double movement, which is not as contradictory as this compressed formulation gives to understand, it remains the rule of every writing practice: 'giving withdrawing' [le 'se donner se retirer'] finds here, not its application or illustration, for these are inadequate terms, but that which, by means of dialectics and outside dialectics, justifies itself by letting itself be said, once there is saying and by which there is saying.

(ED, 170–1; 110–11)

'Giving withdrawing', 'se donner se retirer': one might devise no better way of translating the neutre.

4 As Michael Holland points out in The Blanchot Reader (BR, 256–60), though Blanchot showed considerable interest in the literary fragment throughout the 1950s, it was not until after 1958, when the first versions of material belonging to L'Attente L'Oubli began to be published, and in the context of a rereading of Nietzsche, that Blanchot began reconsidering the possibilities of fragmentary writing as such, and which were a crucial part of his plans in connection with the project for the International Review in the early 1960s.

5 Referring to relations between his two protagonists, in what is also a metatextual gloss on both L'Attente L'Oubli and his own earlier text, Blanchot writes as follows:

From the outside, he would have liked it to be seen more clearly how matters stood: in place of the beginning, a kind of initial void, an energetic refusal to let the story [l'histoire] commence. Story, what does she mean by that? He recalls the words which had one day exploded into his life: 'Nobody here desires to bind themselves to a story.' The memory is almost extinct yet still makes him shudder.

(AO, 22)

6 See 'Le Retour', Botteghe Oscure, VII, 1951, 416–24.
7 On the status of the récit as an event in its own right, even in the absence of any recounted events, see 'La Rencontre de l'imaginaire' (LV, 9–17; SS, 59–65) to which reference was made in the previous chapter.
8 Two further occurrences of 'à nouveau, à nouveau' are worth noting. First, in Celui qui ne m'accompagnait pas, interwoven with the motif of the window-pane:

While searching for it almost at random, I saw in a flash – a flash that was the brilliant, tranquil light of summer – that the figure [cette figure, figure or face] was before my very eyes, a few steps away from me [à quelques pas], the few steps which probably stood between me and the bay-window, and the impression was so deep that it was like a spasm of illumination, a shudder of cold light. I was so struck by this that I could not prevent myself from murmuring: 'Don't move, I believe there is somebody there.' 'Somebody? Here?' 'Somebody is looking at us through the window-pane.' 'Through the window-pane?' The words immediately gave me a sense of terror, of horror, as though the emptiness of the window-pane were itself reflected in them, and as though all that had already taken place, and was doing so again, and again [à nouveau, à nouveau]. I think I cried out, and slipped or fell against what seemed to me to be the table. Yet I could still hear him saying: 'You know, there's nobody there [il n'y a personne].'

(*CQ*, 36–7; 17–18)

The phrase: 'again, again' evidently here has to do with the transformation of something into nothing, presence into absence, a singular event into empty reflection. For a much later occurrence of the phrase, which imples a similar absence of foundation at the very origin of meaning, see Maurice Blanchot, 'Énigme', *Yale French Studies*, 79, 1991, 5–10 (5). Of the proposed title for the issue to which he was invited to contribute, 'Literature and the Ethical Question', Blanchot writes: ' "Again, again" ["A nouveau, à nouveau"], I kept saying to myself. Not that I have any claim to have exhausted an inexhaustible subject, but on the contrary with the certainty that a subject such as this returns to me [qu'un tel sujet me revient] because it is intractable.' Return, here, in its urgency as an ethical demand, becomes inseparable from literature's refusal of all foundation, its contestation of all morality, its submission to the emptiness and the alterity of the outside.

9 See Pierre Klossowski, *Nietzsche et le cercle vicieux* (Paris, Mercure de France, 1969). Blanchot comments at length, albeit obliquely, on Klossowski's book (and on the notion of return implied in it) in 'L'Exigence du retour', first published in *L'Arc* in 1970 (and given in translation in that original form in *BR*, 290–7); the essay was subsequently incorporated into the opening sections of *Le Pas au-delà*.

An uninterrupted questioning

1 As Blanchot puts it in *Le Pas au-delà*, in lines written, it is worth remembering, shortly after the *événements* of May 1968:

Know only – in an injunction that does not present itself – that the law of return, valid for the whole of the past and the whole of the future, will never allow you, except by a misunderstanding, to leave a place for yourself in a possible present, nor let any presence reach as far as you.

(*PA*, 20–1; 11)

2 See Jacques Derrida, *D'un ton apocalyptique adopté naguère en philosophie* (Paris, Galilée, 1983); 'Of an Apocalyptic Tone Recently Adopted in Philosophy', translated by John P. Leavey, Jnr, *The Oxford Literary Review*, 6, 2 (1984), 3–37.
3 Jacques Derrida, *D'un ton apocalyptique*, 93, 'Of an Apocalyptic Tone', 34.
4 See *Le Pas au-delà* (*PA*, 185; 135). In his essay 'Pas' as a whole Derrida makes great play of all the many 'instances' of this 'viens' in numerous texts by Blanchot, including notably *L'Arrêt de mort* and *L'Attente L'Oubli*; see Jacques Derrida, *Parages*, 20–116 (the quotation from *Le Pas au-delà* appears on 50).
5 See Jean-Luc Nancy, 'La Communauté désœuvrée', *Alea*, 4, February 1983, 11–49. The essay appeared simultaneously with Nancy's *L'Impératif catégorique* (Paris, Flammarion, 1983), to which Blanchot also makes reference; it was later republished,

in an extended version, as the first chapter of the book *La Communauté désœuvrée* (Paris, Bourgois, [1986] 1990), translated by Peter Connor *et al.* as *The Inoperative Community* (Minneapolis, University of Minnesota Press, 1991). The differences between the two texts are significant; for convenience, therefore, I shall be referring here to the 1983 *Alea* version, to which Blanchot's remarks were originally addressed. Written like Nancy's essay in the latter part of 1982, Duras's *La Maladie de la mort* (Paris, Minuit, 1983), translated by Barbara Bray as *The Malady of Death* (New York, Grove Press, 1986), also appeared at almost exactly the same time, prompting from Blanchot a review in *Le Nouveau Commerce* that was incorporated into *La Communauté inavouable* later that year. Interestingly, alongside Blanchot, Heidegger, Levinas, and Genet, Duras is one of the few other contemporary names invoked by Derrida in his *D'un ton apocalyptique*. For an account of Duras's work in general and its relationship to that of Blanchot, see my *Marguerite Duras: Apocalyptic Desires* (London, Routledge, 1993).

6 Jacques Derrida, *D'un ton apocalyptique*, 94–5, 'Of an Apocalyptic Tone', 34.

7 The 'Centre de recherches philosophiques sur le politique' was founded in November 1980; by the time of its dissolution in November 1984, it had given rise to two published volumes of collected papers, *Rejouer le politique* (Paris, Galilée, 1981), and *Le Retrait du politique* (Paris, Galilée, 1983).

8 See Philippe Lacoue-Labarthe and Jean-Luc Nancy, 'Ouverture', *Rejouer le politique*, 22–3. On the question of relation, see Philippe Lacoue-Labarthe and Jean-Luc Nancy, 'Le "Retrait" du politique', *Le Retrait du politique*, 196–8.

9 Jean-Luc Nancy, 'La Communauté désœuvrée', 32; *The Inoperative Community*, 23.

10 It is from this period, too, that dates the project by Lacoue-Labarthe and Nancy of a sustained analysis of Blanchot's own political itinerary during the 1930s, a project that, at the time of writing, is regrettably far from reaching completion.

11 See Philippe Lacoue-Labarthe, 'La Transcendance finit dans la politique', *Rejouer le politique*, 171–214; the essay is collected, alongside other papers on Heidegger and Hölderlin, in *L'Imitation des modernes*, 135–73 (*Typography: Mimesis, Philosophy, Politics*, 267–300) and is probably the most immediate source for Blanchot's remark that Heidegger's 'mimetological' formulation of Germany's Hellenic destiny was what lay behind his commitment to National-Socialism (*CI*, 27; 13). Lacoue-Labarthe subsequently developed his analysis at greater length in 1987 in *La Fiction du politique* (*Heidegger, Art and Politics*), a book he dedicated to Blanchot; for Blanchot's own response to the book, see his 'Penser l'apocalypse', *Le Nouvel Observateur*, 22–28 January 1988, 77–9.

12 See Jean-Luc Nancy, 'La Communauté désœuvrée', 13; *The Inoperative Community*, 3.

13 Compare Jean-Luc Nancy, 'La Communauté désœuvrée', 24; *The Inoperative Community*, 15. In fact, this is a double misquotation on Blanchot's part; Nancy's original text reads: 'la présentation de la finitude et de l'excès sans *recours* qui *font* l'être-fini' ('the presentation of finitude and of excess without *recourse* that *constitute* finite-being', emphasis mine). While for Blanchot it is (infinite) excess that founds the (finite) being that is community, for Nancy it seems that it is irreparable excess that, together with finitude, constitutes finite being. What weight do Blanchot's two unavowed

interventions carry? One might answer: none, were it not that the difference between these two versions seems to inscribe a parting (or 'partage'), on either side of which one finds, in the form of either infinite giving or finite dereliction, two discreetly divergent readings of Bataille's phrase: 'sacrifier, ce n'est pas tuer, mais donner et abandonner', on which the relation between Blanchot and Nancy in these texts arguably turns.

14 Compare for instance *L'Écriture du désastre*, ED, 217–18; 143–4.

15 See Jean-Luc Nancy, *Être singulier pluriel* (Paris, Galilée, 1996).

16 For Nancy's reservations about Levinas, which are not without evoking in part some of the hesitations voiced by Blanchot in *L'Entretien infini*, see Jean-Luc Nancy, *Une pensée finie* (Paris, Galilée, 1990), 260–1 (*The Inoperative Community*, 104–5), and *Être singulier pluriel*, 52. In an abruptly polemical account of the debate between Nancy and Blanchot, Robert Bernasconi has argued that Blanchot's text demands in fact to be read as an implicit rejection, from a Levinasian standpoint, of Nancy's whole analysis of community. This is a simplification; indeed to reach this conclusion, Bernasconi is forced into a doubly reductive argument, which by aligning Nancy with Bataille and Blanchot with Levinas, seriously understates the complexity of Blanchot's text and, misleadingly, construes it in terms of a false opposition between the absence of community and the dissymmetry between Same and Other. See Robert Bernasconi, 'On Deconstructing Nostalgia for Community within the West: the Debate between Nancy and Blanchot', *Research in Phenomenology*, XXIII, 1993, 3–21. Incidentally, in *La Communauté inavouable* Blanchot for once uses Levinas's own term asymmetry ('asymétrie') to refer to the (non-)relation between Same and Other, rather than his customary dissymmetry ('dissymétrie'); in so doing, as though to concede its impropriety, he conspires to misspell the word as: 'assymétrie' (*CI*, 22; 9)!

17 Jean-Luc Nancy, *L'Impératif catégorique*, 153.

18 For the quotation from Bataille, see Georges Bataille, *Œuvres complètes*, VII (1976), 310. Bataille continues, some pages later:

> The sacred is that prodigal ebullience of life which, to endure at all, the order of things domesticates and which domestication turns into an unleashing, in other words, into violence. Without pause it threatens to break down dams, and set against productive activity the precipitate and contagious movement of the pure glory of consumption. The sacred is precisely comparable to the flame that destroys wood by consuming it.
>
> (ibid, 312–13)

In 1959, in a series of notes on 'Le Coupable', Bataille famously declared, with explicit reference to Acéphale: 'I was determined, if not to found a religion, at least to head in that direction' ('j'étais résolu, sinon à fonder une religion, du moins à me diriger dans ce sens') (*Œuvres complètes*, VI [1973], 369). Reading lines such as these, it is easy to understand how for so many readers, as Blanchot concedes, Bataille's name is identified with the mystical quest for ecstatic experience (*CI*, 18; 7); and how Nancy can find in Bataille much evidence of nostalgia for the sovereign subject. But which of these two readings of Bataille, that of Blanchot or that of Nancy, may be said to be more faithful? The question, no doubt, can be answered in many different ways; what it raises is the whole question of the status or meaning of community itself, starting with the interpretative community made up of the readers of Bataille. For an account of the important issues at stake here, see Geoffrey Bennington, 'Lecture : de Georges Bataille', *Georges Bataille après tout*, Denis Hollier (ed.) (Paris, Belin, 1995), 11–34.

19 See Jean-Luc Nancy, 'La Communauté désœuvrée', 26, *The Inoperative Community*, 17.

20 Nancy gives a slightly different emphasis to the point in his 1989 text 'L'Insacrifiable' when he writes: 'the thinking of Bataille was, ultimately, less a thinking of sacrifice than a thinking unremittingly strained and riven by the impossibility of renouncing sacrifice'; see Jean-Luc Nancy, *Une pensée finie*, 65–106 (86). It is worth noting at this point that, already twenty-one years earlier, Blanchot himself had recorded a rather different view of Acéphale than that given in *La Communauté inavouable*, more consistent with the criticisms voiced here by Nancy. Indeed, in an article on Bataille first published in 1962, and collected in *L'Entretien infini*, Blanchot wrote:

> the fact is that this act of supreme negation which we have just supposed, and that for a time the enterprise of *Acéphale* represented for Georges Bataille, still belongs to the possible. Power can do this, it can do everything, even do away with itself as power (the explosion of the atom itself, one of the furthest examples of nihilism). Such an act would not in any way make us accomplish the decisive step, the step that delivers us – in some way in our absence – into the surprise of impossibility, by allowing us to belong to *the non-power that is not simply the negation of power*.
>
> (*EI*, 309–10; 208)

The question again arises: which of these accounts is the more faithful? and more faithful to what? to the possibilities or impossibilities inherent in Bataille's endeavour?

21 See Jacques Derrida, *Politiques de l'amitié* (Paris, Galilée, 1994), 56–7, note.

22 For Blanchot's earlier discussions of Duras, see: 'La Douleur du dialogue' ('The Painfulness of Dialogue') (*LV*, 185–94; *SS*, 199–206); 'La Voix narrative (le "il", le neutre)' ('The Narrative Voice (the "he", the neutral)') (*EI*, 556–67; 379–87); and 'Détruire' (*A*, 132–6).

23 In Genesis, I: 27, it is written of man that God created them both male and female; by Genesis, II: 22, however, God is forming Eve from Adam's rib; according to whichever version is believed, it would seem that sexual difference is *both* primary *and* secondary as far as humanity as a whole is concerned.

24 It is worth adding here that this distinction between the homosexual group and the heterosexual community in itself implies no condemnation of homosexuality as such, but rather of the institutionalised and oppressive cohesiveness of certain same-sex social groups, in which commitment to the reproduction of authority or power outweighs responsiveness to the Other, irrespective of whether such groups are made up of individuals who identify themselves as homosexual or heterosexual. (In fact, in May 1996, Blanchot added his name to that of 232 other influential intellectuals in calling on

the French government to implement a recommendation from the European Parliament that 'all forms of legal, administrative and social discrimination towards homosexuals' be abolished, and urging it in particular to grant legal recognition in France to all gay and lesbian couples; see 'Pour une reconnaissance légale du couple homosexuel', *Le Nouvel Observateur*, 9–15 May 1996, 44–5.)

It is worth noting also that, in reading *La Maladie de la mort*, Blanchot refuses to attribute the incommensurability of relation that is the crux of the story to the non-coincidence of desire between a heterosexual woman and a homosexual man; to do so, in Blanchot's view, by naming or thematising it, would necessarily result in a reduction of the fundamental dissymmetry between Same and Other, and trivialise that relation of non-relation by casting it exclusively in terms of sexual preference; this is not to say, of course, that sexual orientation is unimportant, only that the prior affirmation has to do with the precedence of the Other over the Same. Surprisingly perhaps, in this respect, Duras herself was one of the first to take issue with Blanchot's alleged disregard of the question of homosexuality in *La Maladie de la mort*; see Marguerite Duras, 'Dans les jardins d'Israël il ne faisait jamais nuit', interview by Pascal Bonitzer, Charles Tesson and Serge Toubiana, *Les Cahiers du cinéma*, 374, July–August 1985, 5–12.

25 See Georges Bataille, *Œuvres complètes*, V, 196, where Bataille writes, in 'Méthode de méditation', under the heading 'L'Essentiel est inavouable' ('The Essential is unavowable'), as follows:

> What is not servile is unavowable [inavouable]: a reason to laugh, to . . . : the same is true of ecstacy. What isn't useful must be hidden (beneath a mask). A criminal in his final throes was the first to formulate this commandment, shouting to the crowd: 'Never confess' ['N'avouez jamais'].

26 On the Charonne killings, see Hervé Hamon and Patrick Rotman, *Les Porteurs de valises*, 379. On 8 February 1962, during a demonstration in Paris against the OAS, the right-wing terrorist organisation whose aim was to prevent Algerian independence at any cost, eight deaths occurred in the crush at Charonne metro station that was provoked by the intervention of French riot police. Five days later, 500,000 Parisians marched in silent protest at the deaths. On 18 March 1962, the Evian accords were finally signed, giving independence to Algeria.

27 Maurice Blanchot, 'N'oubliez pas!', *La Quinzaine littéraire*, 459, 16–31 March 1986, 11–12.

28 On Duras's own politics in the wake of May 1968, see the first of her projects for the film *Le Camion* (*The Truck*) in *Le Camion* (Paris, Minuit, 1977), 73–4. As Duras writes: 'Let the world go to rack and ruin, let it go to rack and ruin, that is the only politics' ('Que le monde aille à sa perte, qu'il aille à sa perte, c'est la seule politique'). On Duras's politics more generally, see my *Marguerite Duras: Apocalyptic Desires*, 1–39.

The unexpected word

1 On the relation between disjunction and injunction in Blanchot, see Jacques Derrida, *Spectres de Marx* (Paris, Galilée, 1993), 21–85.

2 Friedrich Hölderlin, *Werke*, II, 893; Blanchot refers to the letter on a number of other occasions (*EL*, 221; 213; *ED*, 191; 124).

3 See Maurice Blanchot, 'N'oubliez pas!', *La Quinzaine littéraire*, 459, 16–31 March 1986, 11–12.

4 As a way of gauging the degree of continuity or discontinuity in at least some of Blanchot's political thinking from the early 1930s to the late 1960s, it is perhaps worth comparing here a piece such as 'Le Marxisme contre la révolution', published in the right-wing *Revue française* for 25 April 1933, with an unsigned article, subsequently attributed to Blanchot, such as 'Affirmer la rupture' from *Comité* in October 1968. In the first, at one point, Blanchot supports the call for radical (spiritual) revolution by arguing:

> Refusal is absolutely foreign to all true negation, all absence, all *nothing*. The act of opposition and destruction that represents it, represents also, at the highest point of its force, some desperate affirmation. Rejecting all the negations of consent and the constraints of acceptance, casting aside what abolishes it including even a part of itself, the rebellious spirit searches obstinately, amidst these defeats and deaths, for something proper to him and expressive of him. . . . His act of refusal rids him of everything that is not his own *person* [tout ce qui n'est pas sa *personne*], manifests him as a personal existence whose realisation is the final object and the safeguard of refusal itself.
>
> ('Le Marxisme contre la révolution', 516)

Thirty-five years later, in the second text, one reads:

> To carry the break [porter la rupture] is not only to disengage or attempt to disengage from their integration within established society those forces straining towards the break, it is to act in such a way that in reality and each time it takes place, without ceasing to be active refusal, refusal is not a *solely negative moment*. Politically and philosophically, that is one of the most powerful characteristics [traits] of the movement. In that sense, radical refusal, as borne by the movement and as we are enjoined to bear it too, far exceeds simple negativity, to the extent that it is the very negation of what has yet to be posited and affirmed. To clarify the singular character [le trait singulier] of this refusal is one of the theoretical tasks of the new political thinking.
>
> ('Affirmer la rupture', 4–5)

From one piece to the other, one movement to the other, there is evidently in Blanchot's thinking something of the same logic of absolute refusal and radical contestation; but, at the same time, there are several marked and essential differences, which affect in particular not only the agent of refusal as such – impersonal and anonymous here, personal and self-present there – but, as a result, the logic of refusal itself, which in 1933 is retained within the orbit of a purely self-identical subject and an essentially autonomous person, but which in 1968 is described as corresponding to a far more radical movement of affirmation and rupture, irreducible to any subjective dialectic. To differentiate more fully between these two political moments in Blanchot's itinerary would require, of course, a more detailed analysis than can be attempted here. At any event, there seems little foundation to the view, put forward among others by Steven Ungar in his *Scandal and Aftereffect* (124–36), that Blanchot's post-war political activities were at best an uncritical reprise of the so-called 'abject dissidence' of his pre-war nationalism.

5 See Marguerite Duras, 'Écrit pour tous les temps, tous les carêmes', *L'Autre Journal*, 9, November 1985, 73; the piece is now collected in *Le Monde extérieur* (Paris, POL, 1993), 78–80. Incidentally, with respect to the memory of Munich among post-war French intellectuals, it is worth recalling here that Duras in the latter years of the 1930s found herself working as an archivist at the French Colonial Office during the period Georges Mandel spent as minister of that government department; indeed, it was in collaboration with a close associate of Mandel, Philippe Roques, who was killed soon after while on a mission to London, that Duras, shortly before the outbreak of war, published under her own family name, Marguerite Donnadieu, her first book, which was a volume of nationalist propaganda largely inspired by the anti-German policies of Mandel and entitled *L'Empire français* (Paris, Gallimard, 1940).

6 'Interview de certains signataires', interview with Maurice Blanchot by Madeleine Chapsal, in *Le Droit à l'insoumission: 'le dossier des 121'*, 90–3 (90–1) (*BR*, 196–99 (196–7)). Blanchot's distinction between duty and right in this context echoes a similiar point made in relation to Kafka in *L'Espace littéraire*, where Blanchot describes suicide (and writing) as resting on

> an absolute right [un droit absolu], the only one that is not the corollary of a duty [le seul qui ne soit pas l'envers d'un devoir], and yet a right which no real power doubles or reinforces, which arches over like an endless footbridge [une passerelle infinie] that at the decisive moment simply stops, and becomes as unreal as a dream, but over which in reality one still has to pass – a right, then, without power and without duty [un droit donc sans pouvoir et sans devoir], a folly necessary to the integrity of reason, which, moreover, quite often seems to succeed: what is striking about all these traits is that they apply equally well to another experience, apparently less dangerous, but perhaps no less mad, which is that of the artist.
>
> (*EL*, 106; 105)

The experience of art that allows Blanchot to write these lines explains how, as Blanchot points out in the interview with Chapsal, the decision to put his signature to the Declaration was the act not of a political writer nor a politically active citizen, but of 'a non-political writer impelled to state publicly his position regarding problems that concern him in an essential way' (90).

271

7 As Blanchot noted of 'the 121' in 1984:

> those who signed the Declaration made no claim to be announcing a universal truth (insubordination for its own sake and in all circumstances), but were doing no more than support decisions they had not taken, acknowledging themselves to be responsible for these decisions and, in so doing, *identifying* with those who had been forced to take them.
>
> ('Les Intellectuels en question', *Le Débat*, 29, March 1984, 3–24 (27), *BR*, 206–27 (225))

8 In his account of the events surrounding the Declaration in 'Pour l'amitié', Blanchot recounts how at one stage he was summoned by the examining magistrate in the case to make a formal statement; once Blanchot had finished speaking, the magistrate, according to legal convention – the practice is one that has its counterpart in many other European countries – began dictating Blanchot's statement to the clerk of the court. Blanchot however protested, insisting that his own words be recorded, not those of the examining magistrate. As Blanchot comments:

> There is a seriously deficient point in this affair, which is the debate between a man with a wealth of legal expertise at his fingertips and another who has perhaps few words and does not even know the sovereign value of speech, of *his* speech. Why is it that the judge has the right to be sole master of language, dictating (in what is already a *diktat*) the words of another, as seems appropriate to him, reproducing them not as they were said, stuttering, meagre and unsure, but made worse, because finer, more consistent with the classical ideal, and, most of all, more definitive.
>
> (Maurice Blanchot, 'Pour l'amitié', in Dionys Mascolo, *A la recherche d'un communisme de pensée, entêtements*, 5–16 (11))

9 [Maurice Blanchot], 'Tracts, affiches, bulletin', *Comité*, 1, October 1968, 16 (*BR*, 205).

10 See [Maurice Blanchot], 'Sur les Comités d'action', *Les Lettres nouvelles*, June–July 1969, 184–5 (184). First published anonymously, the letter is attributed to Blanchot and reproduced by Dionys Mascolo in: *A la recherche d'un communisme de pensée*, 359–60. It implies much the same view of May as that given in *La Communauté inavouable* (*CI*, 52–6; 29–33). For a less flattering and, by some, contested account of what actually went on in the Students–Writers Action Committee, see [Marguerite Duras], 'Naissance d'un Comité', *Les Lettres nouvelles*, June–July 1969, 144–50, attributed to Duras and reproduced in *A la recherche d'un communisme de pensée*, 324–30.

11 On the relation between *Le Très-Haut* and the *événements*, see Georges Préli, *La Force du dehors: extériorité, limite et non-pouvoir à partir de Maurice Blanchot* (Paris, Recherches, 1977). In his endeavours to rethink the political Blanchot would seem here to be acting on the warning issued to the rebellious Henri Sorge, in *Le Très-Haut*, by his stepfather – the Egisthus figure in this partial reworking of the Orestes story – to the effect that

the State will know how to use your insubordination, and not only will it take advantage of it, but you, in opposition and revolt, will be its delegate and representative as fully as you might have been in your office, following the law. The only change is that you want change and there won't be any. What you would like to call the destruction of the State will always appear to you really as service to the State. What you will do to escape the law will still have the force of law for you.

(*TH*, 134; 137)

12 [Maurice Blanchot], 'La Clandestinité à ciel ouvert', *Comité*, 1, October 1968, 23.
13 [Maurice Blanchot], 'Le Communisme sans héritage', *Comité*, 1, October 1968, 13 (*BR*, 203).
14 [Maurice Blanchot], 'Les Actions exemplaires', *Comité*, 1, October 1968, 17–18 (18).
15 [Maurice Blanchot], 'Rupture du temps : révolution', *Comité*, 1, October 1968, 18 (*BR*, 205).

Texts by Blanchot

Essays and fiction

Thomas l'Obscur, Paris, Gallimard, 1941.
Comment la littérature est-elle possible?, Paris, José Corti, 1942.
Aminadab, Paris, Gallimard, 1942.
Faux Pas, Paris, Gallimard, 1943.
Le Très-Haut, Paris, Gallimard, 1948.
L'Arrêt de mort, Paris, Gallimard, 1948.
La Part du feu, Paris, Gallimard, 1949.
Lautréamont et Sade, Paris, Minuit, 1949, revised edn 1963.
Thomas l'Obscur (nouvelle version), Paris, Gallimard, 1950.
Au moment voulu, Paris, Gallimard, 1951.
Le Ressassement éternel, Paris, Minuit, 1951.
Celui qui ne m'accompagnait pas, Paris, Gallimard, 1953.
L'Espace littéraire, Paris, Gallimard, 1955.
Le Dernier Homme, Paris, Gallimard, 1957, new version 1977.
Le Livre à venir, Paris, Gallimard, 1959.
L'Attente L'Oubli, Paris, Gallimard, 1962.
L'Entretien infini, Paris, Gallimard, 1969.
L'Amitié, Paris, Gallimard, 1971.
Le Pas au-delà, Paris, Gallimard, 1973.
La Folie du jour, Montpellier, Fata morgana, 1973.
L'Ecriture du désastre, Paris, Gallimard, 1980.
De Kafka à Kafka, Paris, Gallimard: folio, 1981.
La Bête de Lascaux, Montpellier, Fata morgana, 1982.
Après coup, précédé par Le Ressassement éternel, Paris, Minuit, 1983.
La Communauté inavouable, Paris, Minuit, 1983.
Le Dernier à parler, Montpellier, Fata morgana, 1984.

Michel Foucault tel que je l'imagine, Montpellier, Fata morgana, 1986.
Sade et Restif de la Bretonne, Brussels, Éditions Complexe, 1986.
Une voix venue d'ailleurs, Paris, Ulysse-fin de siècle, 1992.
L'Instant de ma mort, Montpellier, Fata morgana, 1994.

Articles, journalism, uncollected texts

This aims to be an exhaustive bibliography, though inevitably there will be some unforeseen gaps. It lists, in chronological order, all Blanchot's signed journalism, literary criticism, and other texts I have been able to trace, together with a number of pieces first published anonymously and subsequently attributed to Blanchot. For the period up to 1976, I am deeply indebted to Peter Hoy and Michael Holland for their work in drawing up the detailed bibliography published in *Gramma*, 3/4, and 5, which I have verified and amended where necessary. Except in the case of texts available in English only in *The Sirens' Song* and *The Blanchot Reader*, to which reference is made separately, page references to collected volumes given here are solely to the standard French editions listed in the preceding section; these are identified by the abbreviations listed at the begining of this volume. These should, however, enable English-speaking readers to find the corresponding English-language volume of any specific text they wish to locate.

'François Mauriac et ceux qui étaient perdus', *La Revue française*, 26e année, 28 June 1931, 610–11.
'Mahatma Ghandi', *Cahiers mensuels*, 3, 7 July 1931, 10–17.
'Comment s'emparer du pouvoir?', *Journal des débats*, 18 August 1931, 1.
'*Deux hommes en moi*, par Daniel-Rops', *La Revue universelle*, XLIV, 21, February 1931, 367–8.
'La Culture française vue par un Allemand', *La Revue française*, 10, 27 March 1932, 363–5.
'Paul Morand : *Flèche d'Orient*', *Réaction*, 10, March 1932, 58–9.
'Nouvelle querelle des anciens et des modernes', *Réaction*, 11, April–May 1932, 11–16.
'*La Guerre à sept ans* [by Jean Maxence]', *La Revue universelle*, XLIX, 7, 1 July 1932, 112–14.
'L'Histoire désarmée', *Journal des débats*, 21 July 1932, 1.
'Les Écrivains et la politique', *Journal des débats*, 27 July 1932, 1.
'Le Monde sans âme', *La Revue française*, 27e année, 3, 25 August 1932, 460–70 (republished in *Gramma*, 5, 1976, 44–52).
'*Ames et visages du XXe siècle* [by André Rousseaux]', *La Revue universelle*, 18, December 1932, 742–5.
'Les Faux-Semblants du savoir', *Journal des débats*, 27 February 1933, 1.
'Les Années tournantes', *Journal des débats*, 21 March 1933, 1.
'Les Communistes gardiens de la culture', *Journal des débats*, 25 March 1933, 1.
'Le Marxisme contre la révolution', *La Revue française*, 28e année, 4, 25 April 1933, 506–17 (republished in *Gramma*, 5, 1976, 53–61).

'Menaces d'inflation', *Le Rempart*, 6, 27 April 1933, 1.

'Le Quai d'Orsay contre la France', *Le Rempart*, 7, 28 April 1933, 3.

'Crise d'autorité', *Journal des débats*, 29 April 1933, 1.

'Quand l'État est révolutionnaire . . .', *Le Rempart*, 8, 29 April 1933, 2.

'La Commission sénatoriale exige du gouvernement un budget en équilibre. Elle repousse le monopole des pétroles', *Le Rempart*, 9, 30 April 1933, 3.

'Des violences antisémites à l'apothéose du travail', *Le Rempart*, 10, 1 May 1933, 3.

'Le Défaitisme à l'école', *Le Rempart*, 13, 4 May 1933, 3.

'Psychose de revendication', *Le Rempart*, 16, 7 May 1933, 2.

'"En vue d'une action." L'Allemagne nouvelle ou le triomphe de la Prusse', *Le Rempart*, 17, 8 May 1933, 2.

'Une apothéose scandaleuse', *Le Rempart*, 19, 10 May 1933, 2.

'Les Illusions dangereuses', *Le Rempart*, 21, 12 May 1933, 2.

'La Levée en masse de l'Allemagne', *Le Rempart*, 22, 13 May 1933, 2.

'M. de Monzie, grand maître en anarchie', *Le Rempart*, 23, 14 May 1933, 2.

'L'Avenir ministériel et le sort du pays', *Le Rempart*, 24, 15 May 1933, 2.

'Crise de l'État', *Le Rempart*, 29, 20 May 1933, 1.

'Politique des chiffres. Le Budget ou l'inutile conscience du mal', *Le Rempart*, 30, 21 May 1933, 1.

'Le Club des conflits. La France à l'aventure', *Le Rempart*, 31, 22 May 1933, 2.

'Les Émeutes de Genève. Bienfaits de la force', *Le Rempart*, 31, 22 May 1933, 6.

'M. de Monzie, émule de Mussolini et de Hitler. Triturons la jeunesse', *Le Rempart*, 32, 23 May 1933, 1–2.

'Le Budget à l'encan. Si les contribuables connaissaient leur force . . .', *Le Rempart*, 33, 24 May 1933, 2.

'Le Gouvernement Daladier au carrefour', *Le Rempart*, 35, 26 May 1933, 2.

'La Révolte des contribuables contre le Parlement', *Le Rempart*, 36, 27 May 1933, 1.

'Les Leçons d'une manifestation', *Le Rempart*, 37, 28 May 1933, 2.

'Le Pacte mortel pour la Paix. L'Europe abandonnée à l'Italie et à l'Allemagne', *Le Rempart*, 38, 29 May 1933, 1.

'La Révolte contre le Pouvoir', *Le Rempart*, 40, 31 May 1933, 1.

'Morale et politique', *La Revue du siècle*, 2, May 1933, 60–5.

'Pour séparer la Petite-Entente de la France, et la Pologne de la Petite-Entente', *Le Rempart*, 41, 1 June 1933, 2.

'Socialisme bourgeois et nationalisme révolutionnaire', *Le Rempart*, 44, 4 June 1933, 1.

'Le Choix entre deux capitulations', *Le Rempart*, 45, 5 June 1933, 1.

'L'Obstination dans la défaite', *Le Rempart*, 46, 6 June 1933, 2.

'La Politique. Les Suprêmes Défaillances', *Le Rempart*, 47, 7 June 1933, 3.

'Les Entretiens de Paris. Les Premiers Effets du Pacte', *Le Rempart*, 48, 8 June 1933, 3.

'Le Pacte. Le Parlement ratifiera-t-il le Pacte?', *Le Rempart*, 49, 9 June 1933, 3.

'La Nouvelle Faillite allemande', *Le Rempart*, 50, 10 June 1933, 1.

'L'Abaissement de la Chambre', *Le Rempart*, 51, 11 June 1933, 2.

'La Conférence de Londres. Il n'y a pas de problèmes des dettes', *Le Rempart*, 52, 12 June 1933, 3.

'Une intervention du Pape. Offrande au paganisme hitlérien des sacrifices de la chrétienté', *Le Rempart*, 54, 14 June 1933, 2.

'Une entrevue Daladier–Hitler. La logique dans l'abaissement', *Le Rempart*, 55, 15 June 1933, 2.

'Les Dettes. La réponse de l'Europe à l'Amérique', *Le Rempart*, 55, 15 June 1933, 3.

'L'Avantage de la résistance. La Leçon des événements autrichiens', *Le Rempart*, 56, 16 June 1933, 3.

'Réponse à *La Croix*', *Le Rempart*, 57, 17 June 1933, 5.

'La Conférence économique. Un centre de manœuvres et de marchandages', *Le Rempart*, 58, 18 June 1933, 3.

'La Conférence dans une impasse', *Le Rempart*, 59, 19 June 1933, 3.

'La Révolte contre le pouvoir', *Le Rempart*, 60, 20 June 1933, 2.

'La Révolte contre le pouvoir. Un projet de loi du Gouvernement menace de prison les contribuables qui veulent se défendre', *Le Rempart*, 61, 21 June 1933, 1.

'Quand l'Europe et l'Amérique collaborent', *Le Rempart*, 61, 21 June 1933, 3.

'La Révolution nécessaire', *Le Rempart*, 62, 22 June 1933, 2.

'Que signifie pour la France l'union de l'Autriche et de la Hongrie. Pouvons-nous accepter que la Hongrie germanophile et révisionniste domine l'Autriche?', *Le Rempart*, 63, 23 June 1933, 1.

'Après les incidents de Bray-sur-Somme. La leçon d'une condamnation', *Le Rempart*, 64, 24 June 1933, 2.

'Le Problème de l'Europe centrale. Le choix entre deux politiques', *Le Rempart*, 65, 25 June 1933, 3.

'De Londres à Genève. La décadence des Assemblées Internationales', *Le Rempart*, 66, 26 June 1933, 3.

'Les Quatre Vérités. La jeunesse française devant le monde', *Le Rempart*, 67, 27 June 1933, 2.

'Le Parlement contre l'économie nationale. La faillite du libéralisme', *Le Rempart*, 68, 28 June 1933, 2.

'La Vraie Menace du Troisième Reich', *Le Rempart*, 69, 29 June 1933, 3.

'Le Quatorzième Anniversaire de la paix', *Le Rempart*, 70, 30 June 1933, 3.

'Le Souvenir et la leçon de Mangin', *Le Rempart*, 81, 11 July 1933, 3.

'La Crise du socialisme', *Le Rempart*, 82, 12 July 1933, 3.

'L'Accord de la France et de l'Italie', *Le Rempart*, 86, 16 July 1933, 3.

'Après la signature du Pacte à Quatre. Le nouveau destin de l'Europe', *Le Rempart*, 87, 17 July 1933, 3.

'Le Socialisme marxiste s'effondre. Un socialisme national se tourne vers de voies nouvelles', *Le Rempart*, 88, 18 July 1933, 3.

'Ce qui menace le socialisme international. Les nouveaux opportunistes', *Le Rempart*, 89, 19 July 1933, 3.

'Tandis que Hitler cherche à se concilier la Reichswehr, les manifestations inconvenantes de M. Henderson', *Le Rempart*, 90, 20 July 1933, 3.

'Le Socialisme national osera-t-il être un mouvement révolutionnaire?', *Le Rempart*, 93, 23 July 1933, 1–2.

'La Révolution est condamnée mais l'État devient révolutionnaire. L'hitlérisme contre Hitler', *Le Rempart*, 94, 24 July 1933, 3.

'Le Bilan de la Conférence de Londres', *Le Rempart*, 95, 25 July 1933, 3.

'Les Chances du néo-socialisme', *Le Rempart*, 130, 29 August 1933, 3.

'M. de Neurath expose les principes de la politique allemande. Un discours logique', *Journal des débats*, 17 September 1933, 1.

'*Positions* [by Jean-Pierre Maxence]', *La Revue du siècle*, 6, October 1933, 75–7.

'Ceux qui ignorent', *Journal des débats*, 12 December 1933, 1.

'La Démocratie et les relations franco–allemandes', *La Revue du XXe siècle*, 4, February 1935, 56–9.

'Le Dérèglement de la diplomatie française', *La Revue du XXe siècle*, 6, May–June 1935, 53–7.

'La Fin du 6 février', *Combat*, 2, February 1936, 26.

'La Guerre pour rien', *Combat*, 3, March 1936, 42–3.

'Après le coup de force germanique', *Combat*, 4, April 1936, 59.

'La Peur des efforts', *Journal des débats*, 29 July 1936, 1.

'Le Terrorisme, méthode de salut public', *Combat*, 7, July 1936, 106 (republished in *Gramma*, 5, 1976, 61–3).

'La Grande Passion des modérés', *Combat*, 9, November 1936, 147.

'Le Caravansérail', *Combat*, 10, December 1936, 171.

'De la révolution à la littérature', *L'Insurgé*, 1, 13 January 1937, 3.

'Réquisitoire contre la France', *L'Insurgé*, 1, 13 January 1937, 4.

'Nous, les complices de Blum . . .', *L'Insurgé*, 2, 20 January 1937, 4.

'*Sangs*, par Louise Hervieu', *L'Insurgé*, 2, 20 January 1937, 5.

'Blum, notre chance de salut . . .', *L'Insurgé*, 3, 27 January 1937, 4.

'*Penser avec les mains*, par Denis de Rougemont', *L'Insurgé*, 3, 27 January 1937, 5.

'Notre première ennemie, la France', *L'Insurgé*, 4, 3 February 1937, 4.

'*L'Été 1914 (Les Thibault, 7e partie)*, par Roger Martin du Gard', *L'Insurgé*, 4, 3 February 1937, 5.

'La Crise qui va s'ouvrir', *L'Insurgé*, 5, 10 February 1937, 4.

'*La Jeunesse d'un clerc*, par Julien Benda', *L'Insurgé*, 5, 10 February 1937, 5.

'L'Impasse', *L'Insurgé*, 6, 17 February 1937, 4.

'*Le Magasin de travestis*, par Georges Reyer, *Zobain*, par Raymond Guérin', *L'Insurgé*, 6, 17 February 1937, 5.

'*La Dentelle du rempart*, par C. Maurras', *L'Insurgé*, 7, 24 February 1937, 5.

'Le Déshonneur français', *L'Insurgé*, 7, 24 February 1937, 6.

'Ce qu'ils appellent patriotisme', *L'Insurgé*, 8, 3 March 1937, 4.

'*Le Saladier*, par Marcel Jouhandeau', *L'Insurgé*, 8, 3 March 1937, 5 (republished in part as 'Chaminadour', *FP*, 260–1).

'Joyeuse Mi-Carême ou l'histoire d'une perquisition', editorial signed by Jean-Pierre Maxence, Thierry Maulnier, Ralph Soupault, Maurice Blanchot, Kléber Haedens, and Guy Richelet, *L'Insurgé*, 9, 10 March 1937, 3.

'M. Delbos paiera', *L'Insurgé*, 9, 10 March 1937, 4.

'*Romanesques*, par Jacques Chardonne', *L'Insurgé*, 9, 10 March 1937, 6.

'Le Temps de la guerre', *L'Insurgé*, 10, 17 March 1937, 4.

'*Réflexions sur la force*, par Alphonse Séché', *L'Insurgé*, 10, 17 March 1937, 5.

'Léon Blum, vous étiez prévenu', editorial signed by Jean-Pierre Maxence, Thierry Maulnier, Ralph Soupault, Maurice Blanchot, Kléber Haedens, and Guy Richelet, *L'Insurgé*, 10 bis, special issue, 17 March 1937, 2 (reprinted in *L'Insurgé*, 11, 24 March 1937, 3).

'*La Rue courte*, par Thyde Monnier, *Bêtafeu*, par Guy Mazeline', *L'Insurgé*, 11, 24 March 1937, 5.

'Préparons la vengeance', *L'Insurgé*, 11, 24 March 1937, 7.

'Blum provoque à la guerre', *L'Insurgé*, 12, 31 March 1937, 4.

'*Ce qui meurt et ce qui naît*, par Daniel-Rops', *L'Insurgé*, 12, 31 March 1937, 5.

'L'Effondrement de la France', *L'Insurgé*, 13, 7 April 1937, 4.

'*Maldagne*, par Hubert Chatelion', *L'Insurgé*, 13, 7 April 1937, 5.

'Les Mystères de Moscou', *L'Insurgé*, 14, 14 April 1937, 4.

'*Joseph et ses frères*, par Thomas Mann', *L'Insurgé*, 14, 14 April 1937, 5.

'M. Delbos a raison', *L'Insurgé*, 15, 21 April 1937, 4.

'*Destin d'une révolution*, par Victor Serge', *L'Insurgé*, 15, 21 April 1937, 5.

'Les Deux Trahisons?', *L'Insurgé*, 16, 28 April 1937, 10, 12.

'Vos vies sont menacées', *L'Insurgé*, 16 bis, special issue, 1 May 1937, 3.

'Demain la guerre', *L'Insurgé*, 17, 5 May 1937, 4.

'*Rêveuse bourgeoisie*, par Drieu La Rochelle', *L'Insurgé*, 17, 5 May 1937, 5.

'La France condamnée à avoir tort', *L'Insurgé*, 18, 12 May 1937, 4.

'*Un homme veut rester vivant*, par Henri Petit', *L'Insurgé*, 18, 12 May 1937, 5.

'Les Français et le couronnement', *L'Insurgé*, 19, 19 May 1937, 4.

'*La Maison au bord du monde*, par Jean Guirec, *La Rue du Chat-qui-pêche*, par Jolan Fœldes*', *L'Insurgé*, 19, 19 May 1937, 5.

'La Guerre de M. Blum et de M. Litvinoff', *L'Insurgé*, 20, 26 May 1937, 4.

'*Journal*, par François Mauriac', *L'Insurgé*, 20, 26 May 1937, 5.

'Le Complot de Genève', *L'Insurgé*, 21, 2 June 1937, 4.

'*Pain de soldat*, par Henry Poulaille, *El Requete*, par Lucien Maulvault', *L'Insurgé*, 21, 2 June 1937, 5.

'Le Chantage à l'antihitlérisme', *L'Insurgé*, 22, 9 June 1937, 4.

'*Les Plus Beaux de nos jours*, par Marcel Arland', *L'Insurgé*, 22, 9 June 1937, 5.

'La Seule Manière d'être français', *L'Insurgé*, 23, 16 June 1937, 4.

'*Nouvelle Histoire de Mouchette*, par Georges Bernanos', *L'Insurgé*, 23, 16 June 1937, 5.

'L'URSS a de plus en plus besoin de la guerre', *L'Insurgé*, 24, 23 June 1937, 4.

'*Souvenirs de guerre*, par Alain', *L'Insurgé*, 24, 23 June 1937, 5.

'Hommage à Claude Séverac', *Aux écoutes*, 26 June 1937, 11.

'Il ne suffit pas de dire : ni Berlin, ni Moscou', *L'Insurgé*, 25, 30 June 1937, 4.

'*Les Aventures de Sophie*, par Paul Claudel', *L'Insurgé*, 25, 30 June 1937, 5.

'Pour combattre l'Allemagne, il faut soutenir Franco', *L'Insurgé*, 26, 7 July 1937, 4.

'*L'Honneur de servir*, par Henri Massis', *L'Insurgé*, 26, 7 July 1937, 5.

'*Faux passeports*, par Charles Plisnier', *L'Insurgé*, 27, 14 July 1937, 5.

'*Le Démon du bien*, par Henry de Montherlant', *L'Insurgé*, 28, 21 July 1937, 5.

'*Les Vergers sur la mer, Mes idées politiques*, par Charles Maurras', *L'Insurgé*, 29, 28 July 1937, 5.

'*L'École du rénégat*, par Jean Fontenoy', *L'Insurgé*, 30, 4 August 1937, 5.

'*La Pêche miraculeuse*, par Guy de Pourtalès, *Camp volant* par André Fraigneau', *L'Insurgé*, 31, 11 August 1937, 5.

'*Journal d'un intellectuel en chômage*, par Denis de Rougemont', *L'Insurgé*, 32, 18 August 1937, 4.

'*Lettres à un jeune poète*, par R. M. Rilke, *Gérard de Nerval*, par Albert Béguin', *L'Insurgé*, 33, 25 August 1937, 4.

'*Les Hommes gris*, par Ettore Settanni [sic]', *L'Insurgé*, 34, 1 September 1937, 4 (republished as 'Le Monologue intérieur', *FP*, 278–81).

'*L'Opéra politique*, par Henri Pollès', *L'Insurgé*, 35, 8 September 1937, 4.

'*La Paix des profondeurs*, par Aldous Huxley', *L'Insurgé*, 36, 15 September 1937, 5.

'*Le Garçon savoyard*, par C.-F. Ramuz', *L'Insurgé*, 37, 22 September 1937, 6.

'*Les Vagues*, par Virginia Woolf', *L'Insurgé*, 38, 29 September 1937, 5 (republished as 'Le Temps et le roman', *FP*, 282–6).

'Pour une diplomatie révolutionnaire', *L'Insurgé*, 42, 27 October 1937, 6.

'La France, nation à venir', *Combat*, 19, November 1937, 131–2.

'On demande des dissidents', *Combat*, 20, December 1937, 154–5 (republished in *Gramma*, 5, 1976, 63–5).

'Procès-verbal de carence' (30.12.37), signed by Henri Israël and Maurice Blanchot, in their role as seconds to Paul Lévy, *Aux écoutes*, 1 January 1938, 17.

'Après une année', from a tribute to Claude Séverac on the anniversary of her death, *Aux écoutes*, 11 June 1938, 25.

'L'Ébauche d'un roman' (on Sartre's *La Nausée*), *Aux écoutes*, 30 July 1938, 31 (*BR*, 33–4).

'Lautréamont', *La Revue française des idées et des œuvres*, 1, April 1940, 67–72 (*FP*, 197–202).

'Chronique de la vie intellectuelle', *Journal des débats*, 16 April 1941, 3.

'Le Silence des écrivains', *Journal des débats*, 19 April 1941, 3 (*BR*, 25–8).

'Le Biographe connaît le "génie" et ignore l'"homme"', *Journal des débats*, 23 April 1941, 3 (republished as 'Le Silence de Mallarmé', *FP*, 117–20).

'Chronique de la vie intellectuelle', *Journal des débats*, 4 May 1941, 3.

'Le Jeune Roman', *Journal des débats*, 14 May 1941, 3 (*FP*, 209–12; *BR*, 35–7).

'*L'Herbe pousse dans la prairie* par Raymond Dumay; *Baragne* par C.-F. Landry', *Journal des débats*, 22 May 1941, 3.

'La France et la civilisation contemporaine', *Journal des débats*, 26–27 May 1941, 3.

'L'Art de Montesquieu', *Journal des débats*, 2–3 June 1941, 3.

'Une œuvre à sauver', *Journal des débats*, 5 June 1941, 1.

'La Naissance d'un mythe', *Journal des débats*, 9–10 June 1941, 3 (*FP*, 219–23).

'Recherche de la tradition', *Journal des débats*, 16–17 June 1941, 3 (*BR*, 29–32).

'La Critique d'Albert Thibaudet', *Journal des débats*, 23–24 June 1941, 3 (*FP*, 323–7).

'La Solitude de Péguy', *Journal des débats*, 30 June–1 July 1941, 3 (*FP*, 318–22).

'Roman et poésie', *Journal des débats*, 7–8 July 1941, 3.

'Roman et morale', *Journal des débats*, 14–15 July 1941, 3 (*FP*, 268–72).

'L'Art du roman chez Balzac', *Journal des débats*, 21–22 July 1941, 3 (*FP*, 203–8).

'Culture et civilisation', *Journal des débats*, 31 July 1941, 3.

'Éloge de la rhétorique', *Journal des débats*, 1 August 1941, 1.

'Chaminadour', *Journal des débats*, 4–5 August 1941, 3 (*FP*, 262–5).

'Une vue de Descartes', *Journal des débats*, 11–12 August 1941, 3.

'Un roman de M. Mauriac', *Journal des débats*, 18–19 August 1941, 3.

'Léon-Paul Fargue et la création poétique', *Journal des débats*, 25–26 August 1941, 3 (*FP*, 170–4).

'Le Secret de Melville', *Journal des débats*, 1–2 September 1941, 3 (*FP*, 273–7).

'La Pensée d'Alain', *Journal des débats*, 11 September 1941, 3 (*FP*, 343–8).

'Jeunes Romanciers', *Journal des débats*, 18 September 1941, 3.

'Le Théâtre et le public', *Journal des débats*, 23 September 1941, 3.

'Inspirations méditerranéennes', *Journal des débats*, 30 September 1941, 3.

'L'Ange du bizarre', *Journal des débats*, 7 October 1941, 3 (*FP*, 256–9).

'Auteurs inconnus ou méconnus', *Journal des débats*, 14 October 1941, 3.

'La Terreur dans les lettres', *Journal des débats*, 21 October 1941, 3 (*CLP*, 9–15; *BR*, 49–53).

'L'Écrivain et le public', *Journal des débats*, 4 November 1941, 3.

'Goethe et Eckermann', *Journal des débats*, 11 November 1941, 3 (*FP*, 306–10).

'Le Secret de J.-K. Huysmans', *Journal des débats*, 18 November 1941, 3.

'Comment la littérature est-elle possible?' (I), *Journal des débats*, 25 November 1941, 3 (*CLP*, 16–20; *FP*, 92–7; *BR*, 53–6).

'Comment la littérature est-elle possible?' (II), *Journal des débats*, 2 December 1941, 3 (*CLP*, 21–7; *FP*, 97–101; *BR*, 56–60).

'L'Homme pressé', *Journal des débats*, 9 December 1941, 3.

'Le Roman de la Sorbonne', *Journal des débats*, 16 December 1941, 3.

'Le *Journal* de Kierkegaard', *Journal des débats*, 23 December 1941, 3 (*FP*, 25–30).

'Paradoxes sur le roman', *Journal des débats*, 30 December 1941, 3.

'De l'insolence considérée comme l'un des Beaux-Arts', *Journal des débats*, 6 January 1942, 3 (*FP*, 349–52).

'Du Moyen Age au Symbolisme', *Journal des débats*, 15 January 1942, 3.

'Littérature', *Journal des débats*, 20 January 1942, 3 (*FP*, 109–14).

'Littérature', *Journal des débats*, 27 January 1942, 3 (republished as 'Romans mythologiques', *FP*, 224–8).

'Un roman de Madame Colette', *Journal des débats*, 3 February 1942, 3.

'Bergson et le symbolisme', *Journal des débats*, 10 February 1942, 3 (republished in part in: *FP*, 132–5).

'Autour de la pensée hindoue', *Journal des débats*, 17 February 1942, 3 (*FP*, 42–6).

'La Poésie de Mallarmé est-elle obscure?', *Journal des débats*, 24 February 1942, 3 (*FP*, 126–31).

'Contes et récits', *Journal des débats*, 3 March 1942, 3.

'La Politique de Sainte-Beuve', *Journal des débats*, 10 March 1942, 1–2.

'Le Mariage du ciel et de l'enfer', *Journal des débats*, 25 March 1942, 3 (*FP*, 37–41).

'Le Silence de Mallarmé', *Journal des débats*, 1 April 1942, 3 (*FP*, 121–5).

'L'Énigme du roman', *Journal des débats*, 8 April 1942, 3 (*FP*, 213–18).

'Récits d'enfance', *Journal des débats*, 15 April 1942, 3.

'Roman et poésie', *Journal des débats*, 22 April 1942, 3 (*FP*, 232–6).

'Une œuvre de M. Paul Claudel', *Journal des débats*, 29 April 1942, 3 (republished as 'Une œuvre de Paul Claudel', *FP*, 328–32, 335–6).

'Le Destin de M. Jean Giono', *Journal des débats*, 6 May 1942, 3.

'La Révélation de Dante', *Journal des débats*, 13 May 1942, 3.

'Les Trois Romans', *Journal des débats*, 20 May 1942, 3.

'Réflexions sur la jeune poésie', *Journal des débats*, 27 May 1942, 3 (*FP*, 149–52).

'Les Poètes baroques du XVIIe siècle', *Journal des débats*, 3 June 1942, 3 (*FP*, 143–8).

'Molière', *Journal des débats*, 10 June 1942, 3 (*FP*, 295–9).

'Après *Les Liaisons dangereuses*', *Journal des débats*, 17 June 1942, 3.

'Les Malheurs de Duranty', *Journal des débats*, 24 June 1942, 3.

'Les Chances du réalisme', *Journal des débats*, 1 July 1942, 3.

'Jupiter, Mars, Quirinus', *Journal des débats*, 8 July 1942, 3.

'Au pays de la magie', *Journal des débats*, 15 July 1942, 3.

'Situation de Lamartine', *Journal des débats*, 22 July 1942, 3 (*FP*, 175–9).

'Histoire de fantôme', *Journal des débats*, 29 July 1942, 3.

'La Poétique', *Journal des débats*, 5 August 1942, 3 (*FP*, 136–42).

'Pour le bon usage de Montherlant', *Journal des débats*, 12 August 1942, 3.

'Le Roman de l'étranger', *Journal des débats*, 19 August 1942, 3 (*FP*, 248–53).

'Stendhal et les âmes sensibles', *Journal des débats*, 26 August 1942, 3 (*FP*, 300–5).

'De l'humour romanesque', *Journal des débats*, 2 September 1942, 3 (republished as 'Romans mythologiques', *FP*, 228–31).

'Considérations sur le héros', *Journal des débats*, 9 September 1942, 3.

"'Le Plus Beau Livre du romantisme'", *Journal des débats*, 16 September 1942, 3.

'Cette affaire infernale', *Journal des débats*, 23 September 1942, 3.

'Roman et souvenirs', *Journal des débats*, 30 September 1942, 3 (republished as 'Poésie et roman', *FP*, 237–41).

'Une édition critique des *Fleurs du mal*', *Journal des débats*, 7 October 1942, 3 (republished as 'Une édition des *Fleurs du mal*', *FP*, 180–6).

'Vigiles de l'esprit', *Journal des débats*, 14 October 1942, 3.

'Le Feu, l'eau et les rêves', *Journal des débats*, 21 October 1942, 3.

'Le Souvenir de Maupassant', *Journal des débats*, 28 October 1942, 3.

'Maître Eckhart', *Journal des débats*, 4 November 1942, 3 (*FP*, 31–6).

'Au sujet des *Nourritures terrestres*', *Journal des débats*, 11 November 1942, 3 (*FP*, 337–42).

'Les Inconnus du romantisme', *Journal des débats*, 18 November 1942, 3.

'Le Mythe de Sisyphe', *Journal des débats*, 25 November 1942, 3 (*FP*, 65–71).

'*Refuges* de Léon-Paul Fargue', *Journal des débats*, 2 December 1942, 3.

'Œuvres poétiques', *Journal des débats*, 9 December 1942, 3 (republished in part as 'Poésie involontaire', *FP*, 154–6).

'Les *Mauvaises Pensées* de Paul Valéry', *Journal des débats*, 16 December 1942, 3.

'Romans nouveaux', *Journal des débats*, 23 December 1942, 3.

'De Taine à M. de Pesquidoux', *Journal des débats*, 30 December 1942, 3.

'Nicolas de Cues', *Journal des débats*, 6 January 1943, 3.

'La Correspondance de Madame de Lafayette', *Journal des débats*, 13 January 1943, 3.

'Le Livre', *Journal des débats*, 20 January 1943, 3.

'Roman et récit de guerre', *Journal des débats*, 17 January 1943, 3.

'André Gide et Goethe', *Journal des débats*, 3 February 1943, 3 (*FP*, 311–17).

'Recherches sur le langage', *Journal des débats*, 10 February 1943, 3 (*FP*, 102–8).

'Charles-Louis Philippe', *Journal des débats*, 17 February 1943, 3.

'Romans de la terre', *Journal des débats*, 24 February 1943, 3.

'Les Souvenirs de Tocqueville', *Journal des débats*, 3 March 1943, 3.

'Rilke', *Journal des débats*, 10 March 1943, 3 (*FP*, 59–64).

'Le Symbolisme et les poètes d'aujourd'hui', *Journal des débats*, 17 March 1943, 3.

'Les Carnets de Léonard de Vinci', *Journal des débats*, 24 March 1943, 3 (*FP*, 86–91).

'Sur la pièce de M. de Montherlant', *Journal des débats*, 31 March 1943, 3.

'Le Roman de Marie Dorval et de Vigny', *Journal des débats*, 8 April 1943, 3.

'Romans', *Journal des débats*, 14 April 1943, 3.

'Machiavel', *Journal des débats*, 21 April 1943, 3.

'L'Éloquence et la littérature', *Journal des débats*, 28 April 1943, 3.

'L'Expérience intérieure', *Journal des débats*, 5 May 1943, 3 (*FP*, 47–52).

'L'Expérience de Proust', *Journal des débats*, 12 May 1943, 3 (*FP*, 52–8).

'De l'œuvre de M. Jouhandeau', *Journal des débats*, 19 May 1943, 3 (republished in part as 'Chaminadour', *FP*, 265–7).

'Les Treize Formes d'un roman', *Journal des débats*, 26 May 1943, 3.

'De la louange à la souveraineté', *Journal des débats*, 2 June 1943, 3.

'La Poésie religieuse', *Journal des débats*, 9 June 1943, 3.

'Romans', *Journal des débats*, 14–15 June 1943, 3.

'Suite française', *Journal des débats*, 23 June 1943, 3.

'Le Fantastique de Hoffmann', *Journal des débats*, 30 June 1943, 3.

'Sur la Chanson de Roland', *Journal des débats*, 7 July 1943, 3.

'Kierkegaard et l'esthétique', *Journal des débats*, 13 July 1943, 3.

'L'Art de la nouvelle', *Journal des débats*, 21 July 1943, 3.

'Le Mythe d'Oreste', *Journal des débats*, 27 July 1943, 3 (*FP*, 72–8).

'La Religion de Rabelais', *Journal des débats*, 4 August 1943, 3.

'Études sur Paul Claudel', *Journal des débats*, 11 August 1943, 3 (republished in part as 'Une œuvre de Paul Claudel', *FP*, 332–5).

'Lecture de Phèdre', *Journal des débats*, 18 August 1943, 3 (republished as 'Le Mythe de Phèdre', *FP*, 79–85).

'Romancières d'aujourd'hui', *Journal des débats*, 25 August 1943, 3.

'Poésie et langage', *Journal des débats*, 1 September 1943, 3 (*FP*, 157–62).

'Voyages de Montesquieu', *Journal des débats*, 8 September 1943, 3.

'Après Rimbaud', *Journal des débats*, 15 September 1943, 2–3 (*FP*, 163–9).

'Une histoire de la littérature française', *Journal des débats*, 22 September 1943, 3.

'L'Influence du roman américain', *Journal des débats*, 29 September 1943, 3.

'La Mystique d'Angelus Silesius', *Journal des débats*, 6 October 1943, 3.

'Récits autobiographiques', *Journal des débats*, 13 October 1943, 3.

'L'Histoire et les chefs-d'œuvre', *Journal des débats*, 20 October 1943, 3.

'Mallarmé et l'art du roman', *Journal des débats*, 27 October 1943, 3 (*FP*, 189–96; *BR*, 43–8).

'Une étude sur l'apocalypse', *Journal des débats*, 3 November 1943, 3.

'La Fontaine sans les Fables', *Journal des débats*, 13–14 November 1943, 2.

'Le Baron d'Holbach', *Journal des débats*, 27–28 November 1943, 3.

'Le Roman pur', *Journal des débats*, 4–5 December 1943, 2 (*BR*, 38–42).

'Les Plaintes de l'ombre', *Journal des débats*, 10 December 1943, 1.

'Le Roman du regard', *Journal des débats*, 18–19 December 1943, 2.

'Tradition et surréalisme', *Journal des débats*, 23 December 1943, 1.

'Sur un monde en ruines', *Journal des débats*, 30 December 1943, 1.

'Le Mystère de la critique', *Journal des débats*, 6 January 1944, 2–3.

'Le Pèlerinage aux sources', *Journal des débats*, 13 January 1944, 2–3.

'D'un roman à l'autre', *Journal des débats*, 20 January 1944, 2–3.

'Les Quatre Évangiles', *Journal des débats*, 27 January 1944, 2–3.

'De Jean-Paul à Giraudoux', *Journal des débats*, 3 February 1944, 2–3.

'Journal sans épisode', *Journal des débats*, 10 February 1944, 2–3.

'Autour du langage', *Journal des débats*, 17 February 1944, 2–3.

'Le Roman d'Aïssé', *Journal des débats*, 24 February 1944, 2–3.

'Le Bonheur de conter', *Journal des débats*, 2 March 1944, 2–3.

'Les Idoles hors la loi', *Journal des débats*, 9 March 1944, 2–3.

'L'Art d'André Dhotel', *Journal des débats*, 16 March 1944, 2–3.

'Le Travail de Balzac', *Journal des débats*, 23 March 1944, 2–3.

'Le Roman noir', *Journal des débats*, 30 March 1944, 2–3.

'Les Secrets du rêve', *Journal des débats*, 6 April 1944, 2–3.

'Un roman de Jarry', *Journal des débats*, 13 April 1944, 2–3.

'Nouvelles et récits', *Journal des débats*, 20 April 1944, 2–3.

'Le Secret de Chateaubriand', *Journal des débats*, 27 April 1944, 2–3.

'Romans fantastiques', *Journal des débats*, 4 May 1944, 2–3.

'L'Air et les songes', *Journal des débats*, 11 May 1944, 2–3.

'Le Premier Roman de Joyce', *Journal des débats*, 18 May 1944, 2–3.

'L'Accent du secret', *Journal des débats*, 25 May 1944, 2–3.

'Le "Je" littéraire', *Journal des débats*, 1 June 1944, 2–3.

'Charles Cros', *Journal des débats*, 8 June 1944, 2–3.

'Naissance de Rome', *Journal des débats*, 15 June 1944, 2–3.

'William Blake', *Journal des débats*, 22 June 1944, 2–3.

'Des diverses façons de mourir', *Journal des débats*, 29 June 1944, 2–3.

'Pages de Paul Claudel', *Journal des débats*, 6 July 1944, 2–3.

'Récits', *Journal des débats*, 13–14 July 1944, 2–3.

'Léon Bloy', *Journal des débats*, 20 July 1944, 2–3.

'Poèmes', *Journal des débats*, 27 July 1944, 2–3.

'Le Souci de sincérité', *Journal des débats*, 3 August 1944, 2–3.

'Fils de personne', *Journal des débats*, 10 August 1944, 2–3.

'L'Expérience magique d'Henri Michaux', *Journal des débats*, 17 August 1944, 2–3.

'Le Tout-Puissant', *La Table Ronde*, 3, July 1945, 189–98 (republished, in a much revised version, in *TH*, 221–4).

'Quelques réflexions sur le surréalisme', *L'Arche*, 8, August 1945, 93–104 (republished as 'Réflexions sur le surréalisme', *PF*, 90–102).

'Autour du roman', *L'Arche*, 9, September 1945, 105–14.

'Les Romans de Sartre', *L'Arche*, 10, October 1945, 120–34 (*PF*, 188–203).

'Le Mythe Giraudoux', *Paysage Dimanche*, 17, 7 October 1945, 5.

'Le Roman de Jean-Paul Sartre', *Paysage Dimanche*, 19, 21 October 1945, 5.

'La Lecture de Kafka', *L'Arche*, 11, November 1945, 107–16 (*PF*, 9–19; *K*, 62–74).

'Les Malheurs de *Peau d'âne*', *Paysage Dimanche*, 21, 4 November 1945, 5.

'A l'ombre du romanesque', *Paysage Dimanche*, 23, 18 November 1945, 3.

'La Critique de Charles du Bos', *Paysage Dimanche*, 25, 2 December 1945, 3.

'L'Enchantement de Melville', *Paysage Dimanche*, 27, 16 December 1945, 3.

'Sur André Malraux', *Paysage Dimanche*, 29, 30 December 1945, 3 (republished as 'Note sur Malraux', *PF*, 204–7).

'Du côté de Nietzsche', *L'Arche*, 12, December 1945–January 1946, 103–12 (*PF*, 278–89).

'*L'Espoir* d'André Malraux', in *L'Espagne libre*, edited by Georges Bataille, Paris, Calmann-Lévy (collection 'Actualité'), 1946, 106–11.

'L'Énigme de la critique', *Carrefour*, 75, 24 January 1946, 6.

'L'Homme noir du XVIIe siècle', *Saisons*, 2, Spring 1946, 69–79.

'Mallarmé et le langage', *L'Arche*, 14, March–April 1946, 134–46 (republished as 'Le Mythe de Mallarmé', *PF*, 35–48).

'En bonne voie', *Cahiers de la Pléiade*, 1, April 1946, 143–51 (republished, in a revised version, in *TH*, 233–8).

'Le Mystère dans les lettres', *L'Arche*, 15, May 1946, 95–111 (*PF*, 49–65).

'Le Paradoxe d'Aytré', *Les Temps modernes*, 9, June 1946, 1576–93 (*PF*, 66–78).

'De Lautréamont à Miller', *L'Arche*, 16, June 1946, 129–39 (*PF*, 160–72).

'Traduit de . . .', *L'Arche*, 17, July 1946, 114–28 (*PF*, 173–87).

'Quelques remarques sur Sade', *Critique*, 3–4, August–September 1946, 239–46.

'L'Honneur des poètes', *L'Arche*, 18–19, August–September 1946, 162–74.

'René Char', *Critique*, 5, October 1946, 387–99 (*PF*, 103–14).

'Adolphe ou le malheur des sentiments vrais', *L'Arche*, 20, October 1946, 82–94 (*PF*, 221–37).

'Valéry et Faust', *L'Arche*, 21, November 1946, 92–102 (*PF*, 263–77).

'La Parole "sacrée" de Hölderlin', *Critique*, 7, December 1946, 579–96 (*PF*, 115–32).

'Gide et la littérature d'expérience', *L'Arche*, 23, January 1947, 87–98 (*PF*, 208–20).

'L'Échec de Baudelaire' (I), *L'Arche*, 24, February 1947, 80–91 (*PF*, 133–42).

'L'Échec de Baudelaire' (II), *L'Arche*, 25, March 1947, 97–107 (*PF*, 142–51).

'Le Sommeil de Rimbaud', *Critique*, 10, March 1947, 195–202 (*PF*, 152–9).

'L'Idylle' (July 1936), *La Licorne*, 1, March 1947, 33–58 (*RE*, 9–97; *AC*, 9–56).

'Note sur Pascal', *L'Arche*, 26, April 1947, 107–21 (republished as 'La Main de Pascal', *PF*, 249–62).

'Grève désolée, obscur malaise', *Cahiers de la Pléiade*, 2, April 1947, 134–7.

'Regards d'outre-tombe', *Critique*, 11, April 1947, 291–301 (*PF*, 238–48).

'Le Roman, œuvre de mauvaise foi', *Les Temps modernes*, 19, April 1947, 1304–17 (*BR*, 61–73).

'Du merveilleux', *L'Arche*, 27, May 1947, 120–33.

Le Dernier Mot (1935), Éditions de la revue Fontaine, Collection 'L'Age d'or' (45), 1947 (*RE*, 99–146; *AC*, 57–81).

'A la rencontre de Sade', *Les Temps modernes*, 25, October 1947, 577–612 (*LS*, 17–49; *BR*, 74–99).

'Le Règne animal de l'esprit', *Critique*, 18, November 1947, 387–405 (republished as the first part of 'La Littérature et le droit à la mort', *PF*, 293–311; *K*, 11–34).

'La Littérature et le droit à la mort', *Critique*, 20, January 1948, 30–47 (*PF*, 312–31; *K*, 35–61).

'"Un livre vivant"', *Critique*, 22, March 1948, 195–205 (republished in Restif de la Bretonne, *Sara*, Paris, Stock, 1949; and in Maurice Blanchot, *Sade et Restif de la Bretonne*, Brussels, Éditions Complexe, 1986, 142–56).

'Lautréamont ou l'espérance d'une tête', *Cahiers d'Art*, 1, 1948, 69–71 (*LS*, 58–9, 84–92).

'Lautréamont et le mirage des sources', *Critique*, 25, June 1948, 483–98 (*LS*, 55–8, 60–70).

'Les Plaisirs de la vertu', *Cahiers de la Pléiade*, 4, June 1948, 71–85 (republished in Restif de la Bretonne, *Sara*, Paris, Stock, 1949; and in Maurice Blanchot, *Sade et Restif de la Bretonne*, Brussels, Éditions Complexe, 1986, 105–42).

'Un récit', *Empédocle*, 2, May 1949, 13–22 (republished as *La Folie du jour*, Montpellier, Fata morgana, 1973).

'Kafka et la littérature', *Cahiers de la Pléiade*, 7, July 1949, 93–105 (*PF*, 20–34; *K*, 75–93).

'Lautréamont ou l'espérance d'une tête', in Lautréamont, *Les Chants de Maldoror*, Paris, Le Club français du livre, 1950, xi–xxvi (*LS*, 58–9, 84–92, 164–5, 166, 185–8; this is an extended version of the text published under the same title in 1948).

'La Condition critique', *L'Observateur*, 6, 15 May 1950, 18.

'Le Docteur Faustus', *L'Observateur*, 8, 1 June 1950, 18.

'Le Compagnon de route', *L'Observateur*, 22 June 1950, 17.

'Au-dessous du volcan', *L'Observateur*, 13, 6 July 1950, 18.

'Les Justes', *L'Observateur*, 15, 20 July 1950, 17.

'Hölderlin', *L'Observateur*, 17, 3 August 1950, 19.

'Le Destin de l'œuvre', *L'Observateur*, 19, 17 August 1950, 19.

'Thomas Mann et le mythe de Faust', *Critique*, 41, October 1950, 3–21.

'Le Musée, l'art et le temps' (I), *Critique*, 43, December 1950, 195–208 (*A*, 21–36).

'Le Musée, l'art et le temps' (II), *Critique*, 44, January 1951, 30–42 (*A*, 36–51).

'La Folie par excellence', *Critique*, 45, February 1951, 99–118 (republished, with a supplementary note in [1970] Karl Jaspers, *Strindberg et Van Gogh, Swedenborg–Hölderlin*, Paris, Minuit, [1953] 1970, 9–32; *BR*, 110–28).

'Les Deux Versions de l'imaginaire', *Cahiers de la Pléiade*, 12, Spring–Summer 1951, 115–25 (*EL*, 266–74).

'Le Retour', *Botteghe Oscure*, VII, 1951, 416–24 (*MV*, 7–25).

'Kafka et l'exigence de l'œuvre', *Critique*, 58, March 1952, 195–221 (*K*, 94–131; republished as 'L'Espace et l'exigence de l'œuvre', *EL*, 45–81).

'L'Art, la littérature et l'expérience originelle' (I), *Les Temps modernes*, 79, May 1952, 1921–51 (republished as 'La Littérature et l'expérience originelle, I: L'Avenir et la question de l'art' and 'La Littérature et l'expérience originelle, II: Les Caractères de l'œuvre d'art', *EL*, 219–44).

'L'Art, la littérature et l'expérience originelle' (II), *Les Temps modernes*, 80, June 1952, 2195–212 (republished as 'La Littérature et l'expérience originelle, III: L'Expérience originelle', *EL*, 245–60).

'Mallarmé et l'expérience littéraire', *Critique*, 62, July 1952, 597–91 (republished as 'L'Expérience de Mallarmé', *EL*, 30–41).

'La Mort possible', *Critique*, 66, November 1952, 915–33 (*EL*, 88–107; and, under the title 'La Mort contente', *K*, 132–9).

'Le Compagnon de route', *Botteghe Oscure*, X, 1952, 39–53 (*CQ*, 7–30, 42–6, 77–8).

'La Solitude essentielle', *La Nouvelle Revue française*, 1, January 1953, 75–90 (*EL*, 11–25).

'Continuez autant qu'il vous plaira', *La Nouvelle Revue française*, 2, February 1953, 308–14 (republished as 'L'Inspiration, le manque d'inspiration', *EL*, 185–91).

'L'Écriture automatique, l'inspiration', *La Nouvelle Revue française*, 3, March 1953, 485–92 (republished as 'L'Inspiration, le manque d'inspiration', *EL*, 191–6).

'La Bête de Lascaux', *La Nouvelle Revue française*, 4, April 1953, 684–93 (republished as a separate volume by GLM in 1958, and again by Fata morgana in 1986; the essay also appears in *L'Herne*, special issue on René Char, 1971, 71–7).

'Rilke et l'exigence de la mort' (I), *Critique*, 71, April 1953, 291–304 (republished as 'Rilke et l'exigence de la mort, 2: L'Espace de la mort', *EL*, 135–50).

'Lire', *La Nouvelle Revue française*, 5, May 1953, 876–83 (*EL*, 199–206).

'Rilke et l'exigence de la mort' (II), *Critique*, 72, May 1953, 387–99 (republished as 'Rilke et l'exigence de la mort, 3: Transmutation de la mort', *EL*, 150–64).

'Le Regard d'Orphée', *Cahiers d'Art*, 28, 1, June 1953, 73–5 (*EL*, 179–84).

'L'Expérience d'Igitur', *La Nouvelle Revue française*, 6, June 1953, 1075–86 (*EL*, 108–20).

'Où va la littérature?' (I), *La Nouvelle Revue française*, 7, July 1953, 98–107 (republished as 'La Disparition de la littérature', *LV*, 237–45; *BR*, 136–42).

'Où va la littérature?' (II), *La Nouvelle Revue française*, 8, August 1953, 291–303.

'Plus loin que le degré zéro', *La Nouvelle Revue française*, 9, September 1953, 485–94 (republished as 'La Recherche du point zéro', *LV*, 246–55; *BR*, 143–50).

'Où maintenant? Qui maintenant?', *La Nouvelle Revue française*, 10, October 1953, 678–86 (*LV*, 256–64; *SS*, 192–8).

'Le Dehors, la nuit', *La Nouvelle Revue française*, 11, November 1953, 877–85 (*EL*, 169–78).

'L'Œuvre et la communication', *La Nouvelle Revue française*, 12, December 1953, 1064–71 (republished as 'La Communication', *EL*, 207–16).

'Dionys Mascolo : *Le Communisme*', *La Nouvelle Revue française*, 12, December 1953, 1096–9 (republished as 'Sur une approche du communisme (besoins, valeurs)', *A*, 109–14).

'Quand la morale se tait', *La Nouvelle Revue française*, 13, January 1954, 96–104 (republished as '"Il ne saurait être question de bien finir"', *LV*, 37–44; *SS*, 45–51).

'Orphée, Don Juan, Tristan', *La Nouvelle Revue française*, 15, March 1954, 492–501 (republished as 'Réflexions sur l'enfer, 4: Orphée, Don Juan, Tristan', *EI*, 280–8).

'Réflexions sur l'enfer' (I), *La Nouvelle Revue française*, 16, April 1954, 677–86 (*EI*, 256–64).

'Réflexions sur le nihilisme' (II), *La Nouvelle Revue française*, 17, May 1954, 850–9 (republished as 'Réflexions sur l'enfer, 2: Victoire logique sur "l'absurde"', *EI*, 264–71).

'Tu peux tuer cet homme' (III), *La Nouvelle Revue française*, 18, June 1954, 1059–69 (republished as 'Réflexions sur l'enfer, 3: Tu peux tuer cet homme', *EI*, 271–80).

'Le Chant des sirènes', *La Nouvelle Revue française*, 19, July 1954, 95–104 (republished as 'La Rencontre de l'imaginaire', *LV*, 9–17; *SS*, 59–65).

'Proust', *La Nouvelle Revue française*, 20, August 1954, 286–94 (republished as 'L'Expérience de Proust, 1: Le Secret de l'écriture', *LV*, 18–26; *SS*, 66–78).

'Jean Santeuil', *La Nouvelle Revue française*, 21, September 1954, 479–87 (republished as: 'L'Expérience de Proust, 2: L'Étonnante Patience', *LV*, 26–34).

'Kafka et Brod', *La Nouvelle Revue française*, 22, October 1954, 695–707 (*A*, 272–84; *K*, 140–54).

'L'Échec de Milena', *La Nouvelle Revue française*, 23, November 1954, 875–88 (*K*, 155–70).

'Le Tour d'écrou', *La Nouvelle Revue française*, 24, December 1954, 1062–72 (*LV*, 155–64; *SS*, 79–86).

'Le Tournant', *La Nouvelle Revue française*, 25, January 1955, 110–20 (republished in part as 'L'Itinéraire de Hölderlin', *EL*, 283–92).

'A toute extrémité', *La Nouvelle Revue française*, 26, February 1955, 285–93 (republished in part as the first section of 'La Mort possible', *EL*, 85–8; and also in part in *LV*, 131–2).

'Mort du dernier écrivain', *La Nouvelle Revue française*, 27, March 1955, 485–91 (*LV*, 265–70; *BR*, 151–6).

'Sur le journal intime', *La Nouvelle Revue française*, 28, April 1955, 683–91 (republished in part as 'Le Journal intime et le récit', *LV*, 224–30).

'Le Secret du Golem', *La Nouvelle Revue française*, 29, May 1955, 870–8 (*LV*, 108–15).

'Notes sur un roman', *La Nouvelle Revue française*, 31, July 1955, 105–12 (republished as 'La Clarté romanesque', *LV*, 195–201; *SS*, 207–12).

'Broch', *La Nouvelle Revue française*, 32, August 1955, 295–303 (republished as 'Broch, 1: Les Somnambules: le vertige logique', *LV*, 136–42).

'L'Autre Claudel', *La Nouvelle Revue française*, 33, September 1955, 404–23 (republished as 'Claudel et l'infini', *LV*, 83–97).

'La Mort de Virgile', *La Nouvelle Revue française*, 34, October 1955, 747–59 (republished as 'Broch, 2: La Mort de Virgile: la recherche de l'unité', *LV*, 143–54).

'Naissance de l'art', *La Nouvelle Revue française*, 35, November 1955, 923–33 (*A*, 9–20).

'Joubert', *La Nouvelle Revue française*, 36, December 1955, 1127–36 (republished as 'Joubert et l'espace, 1: Auteur sans livre, écrivain sans écrit', *LV*, 63–71; *SS*, 52–8).

'Le Calme', *Botteghe Oscure*, XVI, 1955, 28–36 (*DH*, 106–21).

'Joubert et Mallarmé', *La Nouvelle Revue française*, 37, January 1956, 110–21 (republished as 'Joubert et l'espace, 2: Une première version de Mallarmé', *LV*, 71–82).

'Combat avec l'ange', *La Nouvelle Revue française*, 38, February 1956, 288–99 (*A*, 150–61).

'La Douleur du dialogue', *La Nouvelle Revue française*, 39, March 1956, 492–503 (*LV*, 185'–94; *SS*, 199–206).

'L'Homme au point zéro', *La Nouvelle Revue française*, 40, April 1956, 683–94 (*A*, 87–97).

'H.H.', *La Nouvelle Revue française*, 41, May 1956, 872–83 (republished as 'H.H., 1: La Poursuite de soi-même', *LV*, 202–12).

'Le Jeu des jeux', *La Nouvelle Revue française*, 42, June 1956, 1051–62 (republished as 'H.H., 2: Le Jeu des jeux', *LV*, 212–23).

'La Pensée tragique' (I), *La Nouvelle Revue française*, 43, July 1956, 113–22 (*EI*, 137–45).

'Pierre Angélique: *Madame Edwarda*', *La Nouvelle Revue française*, 43, July 1956, 148–50 (republished as 'Le Récit et le scandale', *LV*, 231–3).

'La Pensée tragique' (II), *La Nouvelle Revue française*, 44, August 1956, 299–305 (*EI*, 146–52).

'Freud', *La Nouvelle Revue française*, 45, September 1956, 484–96 (republished as 'La Parole analytique', *EI*, 343–54).

'Le Dernier Homme', *La Nouvelle Revue française*, 46, October 1956, 653–63 (*DH*, 1–23).

'Artaud', *La Nouvelle Revue française*, 47, November 1956, 873–81 (*LV*, 45–52; *BR*, 129–35).

'La Confession dédaigneuse', *La Nouvelle Revue française*, 48, December 1956, 1050–6 (republished as 'La Chute : la fuite', *A*, 228–35).

'Comme un jour de neige', *Botteghe Oscure*, XVIII, 1956, 11–19 (*DH*, 125–7, 134–47).

'La Parole prophétique', *La Nouvelle Revue française*, 49, January 1957, 101–10 (*LV*, 98–107).

'Brecht et le dégoût du théâtre', *La Nouvelle Revue française*, 50, February 1957, 283–92 (republished as 'L'Effet d'étrangeté', *EI*, 529–39).

'D'un art sans avenir', *La Nouvelle Revue française*, 51, March 1957, 488–98 (republished in part under the same title, *LV*, 132–5).

'Le Mal du musée', *La Nouvelle Revue française*, 52, April 1957, 687–96 (*A*, 52–61).

'Le Temps des encyclopédies', *La Nouvelle Revue française*, 53, May 1957, 863–74 (*A*, 62–8).

'La Grande Tromperie', *La Nouvelle Revue française*, 54, June 1957, 1061–73 (*BR*, 157–66).

'Simone Weil et la certitude', *La Nouvelle Revue française*, 55, July 1957, 103–14 (republished as 'L'Affirmation (le désir, le malheur)' I, *EI*, 153–65).

'L'Expérience de Simone Weil', *La Nouvelle Revue française*, 56, August 1957, 297–310 (republished as 'L'Affirmation (le désir, le malheur)' II, *EI*, 165–79).

'Ecce liber', *La Nouvelle Revue française*, 58, October 1957, 726–40 (republished as 'Le Livre à venir, 1: Ecce liber', *LV*, 271–83; *SS*, 227–35).

'Le Livre à venir', *La Nouvelle Revue française*, 59, November 1957, 917–31 (republished as

'Le Livre à venir, 2: Une entente nouvelle de l'espace littéraire', *LV,* 283–97; *SS,* 235–48).

'L'Infini et l'infini', *La Nouvelle Revue française,* 61, January 1958, 98–110 (republished in part as 'L'Infini littéraire: L'Aleph', *LV,* 116–19, SS, 222–5, and in its entirety, together with a letter to Raymond Bellour, in *L'Herne,* 1966, special issue on Henri Michaux, 80–8).

'Musil', *La Nouvelle Revue française,* 62, February 1958, 301–9 (republished as 'Musil, 1: La Passion de l'indifférence', *LV,* 165–173).

'Musil' (II), *La Nouvelle Revue française,* 63, March 1958, 479–90 (republished as 'Musil, 2: L'Expérience de "l'autre état"', *LV,* 173–84).

'La Puissance et la gloire', *La Nouvelle Revue française,* 64, April 1958, 683–90 (*LV,* 298–304).

'La Cruelle Raison poétique', *Cahiers de la compagnie Madeleine Renaud–Jean-Louis Barrault,* 22–3, May 1958, 66–73 (republished as 'La Cruelle raison poétique: rapace besoin d'envol', *EI,* 432–8).

'L'Attrait, l'horreur du jeu', *La Nouvelle Revue française,* 65, May 1958, 856–65.

'Jean-Jacques et la littérature', *La Nouvelle Revue française,* 66, June 1958, 1057–66 (republished as 'Rousseau', *LV,* 53–62).

'La Passion de l'indifférence', *La Nouvelle Revue française,* 67, July 1958, 93–101 (republished as 'La Terreur de l'identification', *A,* 236–45).

'Nietzsche, aujourd'hui', *La Nouvelle Revue française,* 68, August 1958, 284–95 (republished as 'Réflexions sur le nihilisme, 1: Nietzsche, aujourd'hui', *EI,* 201–15).

'Passage de la ligne', *La Nouvelle Revue française,* 69, September 1958, 468–79 (republished as 'Réflexions sur le nihilisme, 2: Passage de la ligne', *EI,* 215–27).

'Le Refus', together with an extract from a letter by Blanchot, *Le 14 Juillet,* 2, 25 October 1958, 3 (*A,* 130–1).

'L'Étrange et l'étranger', *La Nouvelle Revue française,* 70, October 1958, 673–83.

'La Vocation de Virginia Woolf', *La Nouvelle Revue française,* 71, November 1958, 865–73 (republished as 'L'Échec du démon: la vocation', *LV,* 120–8; *SS,* 87–96).

'L'Attente', *Botteghe Oscure,* XXII, 1958, 22–33 (*AO,* 7–13, 16–18, 19–21, 26–7, 31–4, 38, 44–5, 47–8, 49, 50–1, 52–3).

'Le Bon Usage de la science-fiction', *La Nouvelle Revue française,* 73, January 1959, 91–100.

'Qu'en est-il de la critique?', *Arguments,* 12–13, January–February–March 1959, 34–7 (*LS,* 9–14).

'Le Dernier Mot de Kafka' (I), *La Nouvelle Revue française,* 74, February 1959, 294–300 (republished as 'Le Dernier Mot', *A,* 285–91; *K,* 202–9).

'Le Dernier Mot de Kafka' (II), *La Nouvelle Revue française,* March 1959, 481–88 (republished as 'Le Dernier Mot', *A,* 291–9; *K,* 209–18).

'"Vaste comme la nuit"', *La Nouvelle Revue française,* 76, April 1959, 684–95 (*EI,* 465–77).

'Enquête auprès d'intellectuels français', signed by Maurice Blanchot, André Breton, Dionys Mascolo, and Jean Schuster, *Le 14 Juillet,* 10 April 1959 (reprinted in *Le 14 Juillet,* 3, 18 June 1959, 1).

'La Perversion essentielle', *Le 14 Juillet,* 3, 18 June 1959, 18–20 (*BR,* 167–73).

'Gog et Magog' (I), *La Nouvelle Revue française*, 78, June 1959, 1068–74 (*A*, 259–65).

'Enquête sur la méthode critique d'Henri Guillemin, réponse de Maurice Blanchot', *Les Lettres nouvelles*, 24 June 1959, 9–10.

'Gog et Magog' (II), *La Nouvelle Revue française*, 79, July 1959, 101–7 (*A*, 265–71).

'La Fin de la philosophie', *La Nouvelle Revue française*, 80, August 1959, 286–98 (republished as 'Lentes Funérailles', *A*, 98–108).

'Le Grand Refus', *La Nouvelle Revue française*, 82, October 1959, 678–89 (republished as 'Le Grand Refus, I', *EI*, 46–57).

'Comment découvrir l'obscur?', *La Nouvelle Revue française*, 83, November 1959, 867–79 (republished as 'Le Grand Refus, 2: Comment découvrir l'obscur?', *EI*, 57–69).

'L'Attente', *Martin Heidegger zum siebzigsten Geburtstag*, Pfullingen, Verlag Günter Neske, 1959, 217–24 (*AO*, passim; *BR*, 272–8).

'Héraclite', *La Nouvelle Revue française*, 85, January 1960, 93–106 (*EI*, 119–31).

'Albert Camus', *La Nouvelle Revue française*, 87, March 1960, 403–4 (republished as the opening section of 'Le Détour vers la simplicité', *A*, 214–15).

'Entretien sur un changement d'époque', *La Nouvelle Revue française*, 88, April 1960, 724–34 (*EI*, 394–404).

'Le Détour vers la simplicité', *La Nouvelle Revue française*, 89, May 1960, 925–37 (*A*, 215–27).

'La Marche de l'écrevisse', *La Nouvelle Revue française*, 91, July 1960, 90–9 (republished as 'Parler, ce n'est pas voir', *EI*, 35–45).

'Reprises', *La Nouvelle Revue française*, 93, September 1960, 475–83 (reproduced in part as the opening sections of 'L'Effet d'étrangeté', *EI*, 528–9; the remainder reproduced in part as 'Traduire', *A*, 69–73).

'Déclaration sur le droit à l'insoumission dans la guerre d'Algérie', signed by Maurice Blanchot and 120 others, *Vérité-liberté*, 4, September–October 1960 (reprinted in *Gramma*, 3/4, 1976, 27–31).

'Oublieuse mémoire', *La Nouvelle Revue française*, 94, October 1960, 746–52 (*EI*, 459–64).

'La Question la plus profonde' (I), *La Nouvelle Revue française*, 96, December 1960, 1082–6 (*EI*, 12–16).

'La Question la plus profonde' (II), *La Nouvelle Revue française*, 97, January 1961, 85–9 (*EI*, 16–21).

'Interview de certains signataires', interviews by Madeleine Chapsal with Maurice Blanchot, Nathalie Sarraute, Simone Signoret, and Jean Baby, *Le Droit à l'insoumission: 'le dossier des 121'*, Paris, François Maspero: Cahiers libres (14), 1961, 89–99 (the interview with Blanchot is on 90–3; *BR*, 196–9).

'La Question la plus profonde' (III), *La Nouvelle Revue française*, 98, February 1961, 282–91 (*EI*, 21–32).

'Notre épopée', *La Nouvelle Revue française*, 100, April 1961, 690–8 (republished as 'Les Paroles doivent cheminer longtemps', *EI*, 478–86).

'Rêver, écrire', *La Nouvelle Revue française*, 102, June 1961, 1087–96 (*A*, 162–70).

'Rimbaud et l'œuvre finale', *La Nouvelle Revue française*, 104, August 1961, 293–303 (republished as 'L'Œuvre finale', *EI*, 421–31).

'L'Oubli, la déraison', *La Nouvelle Revue française*, 106, October 1961, 676–86 (*EI*, 289–99; compare *AO*, 87).

'Connaissance de l'inconnu', *La Nouvelle Revue française*, 108, December 1961, 1081–94 (*EI*, 70–83).

'Tenir parole', *La Nouvelle Revue française*, 110, February 1962, 290–8 (*EI*, 84–93).

'L'Indestructible', *La Nouvelle Revue française*, 112, April 1962, 671–80 (republished in part, with extensive additions, as 'Le Rapport du troisième genre: Homme sans horizon', *EI*, 99–100, 102–3; the remainder republished as 'L'Indestructible, 2: L'Espèce humaine', *EI*, 191–200).

'Edmond Beaujon: *Le Dieu des Suppliants*', *La Nouvelle Revue française*, 113, May 1962, 910–13 (republished as 'La Mesure, le suppliant', *EI*, 132–6).

'L'Homme de la rue', *La Nouvelle Revue française*, 114, June 1962, 1070–81 (republished as 'La Parole quotidienne', *EI*, 355–65).

'Etre juif' (I), *La Nouvelle Revue française*, 116, August 1962, 279–85 (republished as 'L'Indestructible, 1: Etre juif', *EI*, 180–6).

'Etre juif' (II), *La Nouvelle Revue française*, 117, September 1962, 471–6 (republished as 'L'Indestructible, 1: Etre juif', *EI*, 187–90).

'L'Expérience-limite', *La Nouvelle Revue française*, 118, October 1962, 577–92 (republished as L'Expérience-limite, 1: L'Affirmation et la passion de la pensée négative', *EI*, 300–13).

'L'Amitié', *Les Lettres nouvelles*, 29, 1962, 7–12 (*A*, 326–30).

'La Littérature encore une fois' (I), *La Nouvelle Revue française*, 120, December 1962, 1055–61 (*EI*, 583–90).

'La Littérature encore une fois' (II), *La Nouvelle Revue française*, 121, January 1963, 102–7 (*EI*, 590–5).

'La Pensée et sa forme' (I), *La Nouvelle Revue française*, 123, March 1963, 492–6 (republished as 'La Pensée et l'exigence de discontinuité', *EI*, 1–6).

'La Pensée et sa forme' (II), *La Nouvelle Revue française*, 124, April 1963, 684–8 (republished as 'La Pensée et l'exigence de discontinuité', *EI*, 6–11).

'Ars Nova', *La Nouvelle Revue française*, 125, May 1963, 879–87 (*EI*, 506–14).

'A Rose is a rose . . .', *La Nouvelle Revue française*, 127, July 1963, 86–93 (*EI*, 498–505).

'René Char et la pensée du neutre', *L'Arc*, 22, Summer 1963, 9–14 (*EI*, 439–46).

'Le Jeu de la pensée', *Critique*, 195–6, August–September 1963, 734–41 (republished as 'L'Expérience-limite, 2: Le Jeu de la pensée', *EI*, 313–22).

'Traces', *La Nouvelle Revue française*, 129, September 1963, 472–80 (republished in part in *A*, 246–52).

'Le Problème de Wittgenstein', *La Nouvelle Revue française*, 131, November 1963, 866–75 (*EI*, 487–97).

'La Parole vaine', in Louis-René Des Forêts, *Le Bavard*, Paris, Union générale d'éditions, 1963, 163–84 (*A*, 137–49).

'Le Pont de bois', *La Nouvelle Revue française*, 133, January 1964, 90–103 (republished as 'Le Pont de bois (la répétition, le neutre)', *EI*, 568–82; *K*, 185–201).

'L'Apocalypse déçoit', *La Nouvelle Revue française*, 135, March 1964, 488–96 (*A*, 118–27).

'La Conquista dello spazio', translated into Italian by Guido Neri, *Il Menabò*, 7, 1964, 10–13 (*BR*, 269–71).

'Il nome Berlino', translated into Italian by Guido Neri, *Il Menabò*, 7, 1964, 121–5 (republished, in an English translation by James Cascaito, as 'The Word Berlin', in *Semiotext(e)*, IV, 2, 1982, 60–5; then, as 'Le Nom de Berlin', in a French version reconstructed by Hélène Jelen and Jean-Luc Nancy, in *Der Name Berlin/Le Nom de Berlin*, Berlin, Merve Verlag, 1983 and in *Café librairie*, 3, Autumn 1983, 42–6; finally, this last version, under the title 'Berlin', together with parallel English, German, and Russian translations by Aris Fioretos, Werner Hamacher, and Mikhail Yampolsky, is republished in: *MLN*, 109, 1994, 345–55; *BR*, 266–8).

'La Parola in arcipelago', translated into Italian by Guido Neri, *Il Menabò*, 7, 1964, 156–9 (republished in the original French as 'Parole de fragment', in *L'Endurance de la pensée*, essays in honour of Jean Beaufret, Paris, Plon, 1968, 103–8; and in *EI*, 451–5).

'Il "Quotidiano"', translated into Italian by Gabriella Zanobetti, *Il Menabò*, 7, 1964, 260–1 (republished in the original French, in dialogue form, as the closing page of 'La Parole quotidienne', *EI*, 366).

'L'Interruption', *La Nouvelle Revue française*, 137, May 1964, 869–81 (republished in part as 'L'Interruption (comme sur une surface de Riemann)', *EI*, 106–12; the remainder republished as part of the essay 'Traces', *A*, 252–8).

'L'Athenaeum', *La Nouvelle Revue française*, 140, August 1964, 301–13 (*EI*, 515–27).

'La Voix narrative', *La Nouvelle Revue française*, 142, October 1964, 675–85 (republished as 'La Voix narrative (le "il", le neutre)', *EI*, 556–67; *K*, 171–84).

'Le Héros', *La Nouvelle Revue française*, 145, January 1965, 90–104 (republished as 'La Fin du héros', *EI*, 540–55).

'Les Grands Réducteurs', *La Nouvelle Revue française*, 148, April 1965, 676–86 (*A*, 74–86).

'Le Rire des dieux', *La Nouvelle Revue française*, 151, July 1965, 91–105 (*A*, 192–207).

'Français, encore un effort...', *La Nouvelle Revue française*, 154, October 1965, 600–18 (republished as 'L'Expérience-limite, 3: L'Insurrection, la folie d'écrire', *EI*, 323–42).

'L'Entretien infini', *La Nouvelle Revue française*, 159, March 1966, 385–401 (republished, without its title, in *EI*, ix–xxvi).

'Nietzsche et l'écriture fragmentaire' (I), *La Nouvelle Revue française*, 168, December 1966, 967–83 (republished as 'Réflexions sur le nihilisme, 3: Nietzsche et l'écriture fragmentaire', *EI*, 227–42).

'Nietzsche et l'écriture fragmentaire' (II), *La Nouvelle Revue française*, 169, January 1967, 19–32 (republished as 'Réflexions sur le nihilisme, 3: Nietzsche et l'écriture fragmentaire', *EI*, 242–55).

'Le Demain joueur', *La Nouvelle Revue française*, 172, April 1967, 863–88 (*EI*, 597–619).

'L'Athéisme et l'écriture. L'Humanisme et le cri' (I), *La Nouvelle Revue française*, 178, October 1967, 586–604 (*EI*, 367–84).

'L'Athéisme et l'écriture. L'Humanisme et le cri' (II), *La Nouvelle Revue française*, 179, November 1967, 812–21 (*EI*, 384–93).

'Le Tout Dernier Mot', *La Nouvelle Revue française*, 185, May 1968, 780–808 (*A*, 300–25; *K*, 219–48).

'Il est capital que le mouvement des étudiants oppose et maintienne une puissance de refus', statement signed by Maurice Blanchot and 34 others, including Robert Antelme, Maurice Nadeau, Louis-René Des Forêts, Marguerite Duras, Jean Schuster, Michel Leiris, Dionys Mascolo, Jérôme Peignot, Pierre Klossowski, Nathalie Sarraute, Monique Wittig, Jean Ricardou, André Gorz, Jean-Paul Sartre, Jacques Lacan, Henri Lefebvre and François Châtelet, *Le Monde*, 10 May 1968, 9.

'La Rue', leaflet distributed 17 July 1968, subsequently published in *Comité*, 1, October 1968, 11, attributed to Blanchot by Dionys Mascolo.

'Lettre ouverte au Parti Communiste de Cuba', signed by Maurice Blanchot, with Robert Antelme, Marguerite Duras, and Dionys Mascolo, *L'Archibras*, 5, hors série, 30 September 1968, 9.

'En état de guerre', *Comité*, 1, October 1968, 3–4 (published anonymously, attributed to Blanchot by Dionys Mascolo).

'Affirmer la rupture', *Comité*, 1, October 1968, 4–5 (first published anonymously, republished in part and attributed to Blanchot by Dionys Mascolo in 'Mots de désordre', *Libération*, 28–9 January 1984, 23; *BR*, 200–1).

'Aujourd'hui . . .', *Comité*, 1, October 1968, 7 (published anonymously, attributed to Blanchot by Dionys Mascolo).

'La Mort politique', *Comité*, 1, October 1968, 8 (first published anonymously, republished in part and attributed to Blanchot by Dionys Mascolo in 'Mots de désordre', *Libération*, 28–9 January 1984, 23; *BR*, 201–2).

'Le Communisme sans héritage', *Comité*, 1, October 1968, 13 (first published anonymously, republished and attributed to Blanchot in *Gramma*, 3/4, 1976, 31–3; *BR*, 202–4).

'Depuis longtemps, la brutalité . . .', *Comité*, 1, October 1968, 14 (published anonymously, attributed to Blanchot by Dionys Mascolo).

'Tracts, affiches, bulletin', *Comité*, 1, October 1968, 16 (first published anonymously, republished and attributed to Blanchot in *Gramma*, 3/4, 1976, 33–4; *BR*, 204–5).

'Que l'immense contrainte . . .', *Comité*, 1, October 1968, 17 (published anonymously, attributed to Blanchot by Dionys Mascolo).

'Les Actions exemplaires', *Comité*, 1, October 1968, 17–18 (published anonymously, attributed to Blanchot by Dionys Mascolo).

'Deux innovations caractéristiques', *Comité*, 1, October 1968, 18 (published anonymously, attributed to Blanchot by Dionys Mascolo).

'Rupture du temps : révolution', *Comité*, 1, October 1968, 18 (first published anonymously, republished in part and attributed to Blanchot by Dionys Mascolo in 'Mots de désordre', *Libération*, 28–9 January 1984, 23; *BR*, 205).

'Pour le camarade Castro', *Comité*, 1, October 1968, 22–3 (published anonymously, attributed to Blanchot by Dionys Mascolo).

'La Reddition idéologique', *Comité*, 1, October 1968, 23 (published anonymously, attributed to Blanchot by Dionys Mascolo).

'La Clandestinité à ciel ouvert', *Comité*, 1, October 1968, 23 (published anonymously, attributed to Blanchot by Dionys Mascolo).

'Conseils aux gens de la rue', *Comité*, 1, October 1968, 27 (published anonymously, attributed to Blanchot by Dionys Mascolo).

'Lire Marx', *Comité*, 1, October 1968, 31 (first published anonymously, republished as 'Les Trois Paroles de Marx', *A*, 115–17).

'L'Absence de livre', *L'Éphémère*, 10, April 1969, 201–18 (*EI*, 620–36).

'La Facilité de mourir', *La Nouvelle Revue française*, special issue devoted to Jean Paulhan, May 1969, 743–64 (*A*, 172–91; *BR*, 301–16).

'Sur les Comités d'action', *Les Lettres nouvelles*, June–July 1969, 184–5 (letter first published anonymously, subsequently attributed to Blanchot by Dionys Mascolo in Dionys Mascolo, *A la recherche d'un communisme de pensée, entêtements*, Paris, Éditions fourbis, 1993, 359–60).

'Détruire', *L'Éphémère*, 13, June 1970, 22–6 (*A*, 132–6).

'L'Exigence du retour', *L'Arc*, 43, 1970, 48–53 (*PA*, 7, 10–15, 21–7, 33–6, 73).

'En guise d'introduction', letter to Piera Aulagnier, *Topique*, 4–5, October 1970, 7–10.

'Fragmentaires', *L'Ephémère*, 16, January 1971, 376–99 (*PA*, 121–36, 156, 137–9, 140–52).

'Une nouvelle raison?', *La Nouvelle Revue française*, 223, July 1971, 94–101.

'Le "Discours philosophique"', *L'Arc*, 46, 1971, 1–4.

'Le Dernier à parler', *La Revue de Belles-Lettres*, 96, 2–3, 1972, 171–83 (republished as *Le Dernier à parler*, Montpellier, Fata morgana, 1984; *ACTS: A Journal of New Writing*, 8/9, 1988, special issue on 'Translating Tradition: Paul Celan in France', Benjamin Hollander (ed.), 228–39).

'Sur Edmond Jabès', *Les Nouveaux Cahiers*, 31, Winter 1972–73, 51–2 (*PA*, 156, 56–7, 49).

'La Comédie d'avoir de l'ordre', *La Quinzaine littéraire*, 171, 16–30 September 1973, 3–4.

'Discours sur la patience', *Le Nouveau Commerce*, 30–1, 1975, 19–44 (*ED*, 7–10, 28–49, 52–5, 220, 15, 16, 17).

'Fragment', *Change*, 22, February 1975, 223 (*ED*, 64).

'Fragmentaire', in Pierre Alechinsky *et al.*, *Celui qui ne peut se servir des mots*, Montpellier, Fata morgana, 1975, 19–31 (*ED*, 23–5, 27, 24, 14, 27, 23, 72, 49, 17, 18, 61, 18–19, 22, 26, 49, 53, 56, 57–8, 65–7, 67–8, 71, 72, 72–4, 78–9, 76–80).

'On tue un enfant', *Le Nouveau Commerce*, 33–4, Spring 1976, 19–29 (*ED*, 108–17).

'Trois lettres à Christian Limousin', *Gramma*, 3/4, 1976, 5–7 (republished in part in *ED*, 64).

'Une scène primitive', *Première livraison*, 4, 1976, 1.

'La Poésie, mesdames, messieurs', *Givre*, special issue devoted to Bernard Noël, 2–3, 1977, 176–7 (*ED*, 143–4).

'Une lettre', fragment of a letter to Emmanuel Levinas (1969), in Emmanuel Levinas, *Du sacré au saint*, Paris, Minuit, 1977, 48–9.

'Il n'est d'explosion', in Maurice Blanchot *et al.*, *Misère de la littérature*, Paris, Christian Bourgois, 1978, 11–12 (republished in part in *ED*, 190–1).

'Une scène primitive', *Le Nouveau Commerce*, 39–40, Spring 1978, 43–51 (*ED*, 191–6, 202–6).

'Ne te retourne pas', *Digraphe* 18/19, 1979, 160–3.

'Lettre à Jeffrey Mehlman [26 November 1979]', fragment of a letter reproduced in Jeffrey Mehlman, 'Blanchot at *Combat*: Of Literature and Terror', *MLN*, 95, 1980, 819.

'Notre compagne clandestine', in François Laruelle (ed.), *Textes pour Emmanuel Lévinas*, Paris, Jean-Michel Place, 1980, 79–87 (*Face to Face with Levinas*, Ralph A. Cohen (ed.), Albany, NY, State University of New York Press, 1986, 41–50).

'L'Ecriture du désastre', *La Nouvelle Revue française*, 330–1, July–August 1980, 1–33 (*ED*, 60–107, 120–1).

'Une lettre [11 février 1980]', *Exercices de la patience*, 1, 1980, 67.

'Refuser l'ordre établi', response to a questionnaire on literary commitment, *Le Nouvel Observateur*, special issue, May 1981, 45–6.

'Prière d'insérer', *Exercices de la patience*, 2, Winter 1981, 104–7.

'La Maladie de la mort (éthique et amour)', *Le Nouveau Commerce*, 55, Spring 1983, 31–46 (*CI*, 58–77).

'Nous travaillons dans les ténèbres', *Le Monde*, 22 July 1983, 9.

'Les Intellectuels en question', *Le Débat*, 29, March 1984, 3–24 (*BR*, 206–27).

'La Parole ascendante, ou: Sommes-nous encore dignes de la poésie? (notes éparses)', in Vadim Kozovoï, *Hors de la colline*, translated by the author with Michel Deguy and Jacques Dupin, Paris, Hermann, 1984, 19–27.

'Les Rencontres', response to a questionnaire on the occasion of the magazine's twentieth anniversary, *Le Nouvel Observateur*, 1045, special issue, November 1984, 84.

'Pourquoi écrivez-vous?', response to a questionnaire, *Libération*, hors-série, March 1985, 64 (reproduced in *Pourquoi écrivez-vous? 400 écrivains répondent*, Jean-François Fogel and Daniel Rondeau (eds), Paris, Le Livre de poche, 1988, 188).

'Le Bienfait le plus lourd', *Le Nouvel Observateur*, 31 May–6 June 1985, 79.

'Blanchot ouvre Laporte', *Libération*, 6 March 1986, 35.

'N'oubliez pas!', *La Quinzaine littéraire*, 459, 16–31 March 1986, 11–12.

'Notre responsabilité', in *Pour Nelson Mandela*, Preface by Dominique Lecoq, Paris, Gallimard, 1986, 215–17.

'*L'Excès-l'usine* ou l'infini morcelé' (on *L'Excès-l'usine* by Leslie Kaplan), *Libération*, 24 February 1987, 35.

'Penser l'apocalypse', *Le Nouvel Observateur*, 22–28 January 1988, 77–9.

'"N'oubliez pas"', letter to Salomon Malka, *L'Arche*, May 1988, 68–71 (*BR*, 244–9).

'Ce qui m'est le plus proche . . .', *Globe*, 30, July–August 1988, 56.

Author's blurb, *Le Très-Haut*, Paris, Gallimard: L'Imaginaire, 1988.

'La Poursuite tempérée-éperdue', in Roger Laporte, *Lettre à personne*, Paris, Plon, 1989, 91–5.

'L'Écriture consacrée au silence', *Instants*, 1, 1989, 239–41.

'Une voix venue d'ailleurs', *La Quinzaine littéraire*, 1–15 July 1989, 5–6 (*UV*, 13–17).

'Qui?', *Cahiers Confrontation*, 20, Winter 1989, 49–51 (*Who Comes After the Subject?*, Eduardo Cadava, Peter Connor and Jean-Luc Nancy (eds), New York, Routledge, 1991, 58–60).

'André Delmas: L'Arrière-Monde', *La Nouvelle Revue française*, 440, September 1989, 58–60.

'Oui, le silence est nécessaire à l'écriture . . .', *Le Monde*, 26 January 1990, 27 (also in *Globe*, 44, February 1990, 72).

'Grâce (soit rendue) à Jacques Derrida', *Revue philosophique*, 2, April–June 1990, 167–73 (*BR*, 317–23).

'Oh tout finir', *Critique*, 519–20, August–September 1990, 635–7 (*BR*, 298–300).

'Textes préparatoires de "La Revue internationale"', *Lignes*, 11, September 1990, 179–91.

'Correspondances', exchange of letters between Blanchot, Hans-Magnus Enzensberger, Louis-René Des Forêts, Uwe Johnson, Francesco Leonetti, Dionys Mascolo, Iris Murdoch, Richard Seaver, and Elio Vittorini (1960–5), *Lignes*, 11, September 1990, 218–301.

'Lettre à Diane Rubenstein [20 August 1983]', fragment of a letter reproduced in Diane Rubenstein, *What's Left: the École Normale Supérieure and the Right*, Madison, University of Wisconsin Press, 1990, 187.

'Sur le nationalisme', response to a questionnaire, *La Règle du jeu*, 3, January 1991, 221–2.

'Lettre à Bernard-Henri Lévy [15 September 1989]', fragment of a letter reproduced in Bernard-Henri Lévy, *Les Aventures de la liberté*, Paris, Grasset, 1991, 311.

'Le Blanc Le Noir', *Le Temps qu'il fait*, Cahier 6/7, special issue on Louis-René Des Forêts, edited by Jean-Benoît Puech and Dominique Rabaté, 1991, 231–2 (*UV*, 21–4).

'Énigme', *Yale French Studies*, 79, 1991, 5–7.

'L'Existence posthume', response to a questionnaire, *La Règle du jeu*, 6, January 1992, 181.

Author's blurb, *Thomas l'Obscur*, nouvelle version, Paris, Gallimard: L'Imaginaire, 1992, 5–6.

'Adresses', response to a questionnaire on Salman Rushdie, *La Règle du jeu*, 10, May 1993, 206.

'Appel à la fondation d'un Parlement international des écrivains', signed by Maurice Blanchot and more than 300 others, Strasbourg, 31 July 1993.

'Pour l'amitié', in Dionys Mascolo, *A la recherche d'un communisme de pensée, entêtements*, Paris, Éditions fourbis, 1993, 5–16.

'"Dans la nuit surveillée"', with two extracts from *L'Espèce humaine* by Robert Antelme, *Lignes*, 21, January 1994, 127–31.

'Appel à la vigilance', petition against the rise of the far right in Europe, signed by Maurice Blanchot and some 2,000 others, *Le Monde*, 13 July 1945, 15 (originally published, without Blanchot's signature, in *Le Monde*, 13 July 1993, 8).

'Pour une reconnaissance légale du couple homosexuel', petition in favour of legal recognition of lesbian and gay couples, signed by Maurice Blanchot and 232 others, *Le Nouvel Observateur*, 9–15 May 1996, 44–5.

'Extracts from a letter to Roger Laporte (9 December 1984)', in Leslie Hill, 'Introduction', *Blanchot and the Demand of Writing*, Carolyn Bailey Gill (ed.) (London, Routledge, 1996), 9–10.

'A letter [to Roger Laporte, 24 December 1992]', *Blanchot and the Demand of Writing*, 209–11.

'Une lettre de Maurice Blanchot [2 September 1996]', letter to Bruno Roy, *La Quinzaine littéraire*, 1–15 November 1996, 5.

'Appel à la désobéissance civile contre les lois sur l' immigration', petition signed by sixty-six film-makers and theatre directors and fifty-five writers, including Maurice Blanchot, *Le Monde*, 14 February 1997, 8.

Works in English translation

The Blanchot Reader, edited with an Introduction by Michael Holland, with translations by Susan Hanson, Leslie Hill, Michael Holland, Roland-François Lack, Ian Maclachlan, Ann Smock, Chris Stevens, and Michael Syrotinski, Oxford, Blackwell, 1995.

Death Sentence, translated by Lydia Davis, New York, Station Hill Press, 1978.

The Gaze of Orpheus and Other Literary Essays, translated by Lydia Davis, edited with an Afterword by P. Adams Sitney, New York, Station Hill Press, 1981.

The Infinite Conversation, translated by Susan Hanson, Minneapolis, University of Minnesota Press, 1993.

The Last Man, translated by Lydia Davis, New York, Columbia University Press, 1987.

'The Last One to Speak', translated by Joseph Simas, *ACTS: A Journal of New Writing*, 8/9, 1988, special issue on 'Translating Tradition: Paul Celan in France', edited by Benjamin Hollander, 228–39.

The Madness of the Day, translated by Lydia Davis, New York, Station Hill Press, 1981.

Michel Foucault as I Imagine Him, translated by Jeffrey Mehlman, in *Foucault/Blanchot*, New York, Zone Books, 1987.

The Most High, translated by Allan Stoekl, Lincoln, Neb., University of Nebraska Press, 1995.

The One Who Was Standing Apart From Me, translated by Lydia Davis, New York, Station Hill Press, 1993.

'Our Clandestine Companion', translated by David B. Allison, in *Face to Face with Levinas*, Ralph A. Cohen (ed.), Albany, NY, State University of New York Press, 1986, 41–50.

'Our Responsibility', in *Texts for Nelson Mandela*, New York, Seaver, 1987.

The Sirens' Song, translated by Sacha Rabinovitch, Gabriel Josipovici (ed.), Brighton, Harvester, 1982.

The Space of Literature, translated by Ann Smock, Lincoln, Neb. and London, University of Nebraska Press, 1982.

The Step Not Beyond, translated by Lycette Nelson, Albany, NY, State University of New York Press, 1992.

Thomas the Obscure, translated by Robert Lamberton, New York, Station Hill Press, [1973] 1988.

The Unavowable Community, translated by Pierre Joris, New York, Station Hill Press, 1988.

Vicious Circles, followed by 'After the Fact', translated by Paul Auster, New York, Station Hill Press, 1985.

When the Time Comes, translated by Lydia Davis, New York, Station Hill Press, 1985.

'Who?', in *Who Comes After the Subject?*, Eduardo Cadava, Peter Connor and Jean-Luc Nancy (eds), New York, Routledge, 1991, 58–60.

The Work of Fire, translated by Charlotte Mandell, Stanford, Stanford University Press, 1995.

The Writing of the Disaster, translated by Ann Smock, Lincoln, Neb. and London, University of Nebraska Press, 1986.

Index